## DATE DUE

| | | | |
|---|---|---|---|
| | | | |
| | | | |
| | | | |
| | | | |
| | | | |
| | | | |
| | | | |
| | | | |
| | | | |
| | | | |
| | | | |
| | | | |
| | | | |
| | | | |
| | | | |
| | | | |
| | | | |

DEMCO 38-296

# CONTEMPORARY MUSICIANS

ISSN 1044-2197

# CONTEMPORARY MUSICIANS

## PROFILES OF THE PEOPLE IN MUSIC

**MICHAEL L. LaBLANC,**
**Editor**

VOLUME 7

Includes Cumulated Indexes

*Gale Research Inc.* · DETROIT · LONDON

## STAFF

Michael L. LaBlanc, *Editor*

Suzanne M. Bourgoin, Julia M. Rubiner, *Associate Editors*

David Bianco, Barbara Carlisle Bigelow, Marjorie Burgess, David Collins, Tim Connor, Simon Glickman,
Joan Goldsworthy, Lloyd Hemingway, Anne Janette Johnson, Jeanne M. Lesinski, Meg Mac Donald,
Louise Mooney, Michael E. Mueller, Rob Nagel, Nancy Pear, Nancy Rampson, Megan Rubiner, Iva Sipal,
Calen D. Stone, B. Kimberly Taylor, Elizabeth Wenning, *Contributing Editors*

Peter M. Gareffa, *Senior Editor, Contemporary Biographies*

Jeanne Gough, *Permissions Manager*
Margaret A. Chamberlain, *Permissions Supervisor (Pictures)*
Pamela A. Hayes, *Permissions Associate*
Amy Lynn Emrich, Karla L. Kulkis, Nancy M. Rattenbury, Keith Reed, *Permissions Assistants*

Mary Beth Trimper, *Production Director*
Shanna Philpott Heilveil, *Production Assistant*
Arthur Chartow, *Art Director*
Cynthia Baldwin, *Graphic Designer*
C.J. Jonik, Yolanda Y. Latham, *Keyliners*

Special thanks to the Biography Division Research staff

Cover Illustration by John Kleber

∞™ This book is printed on acid-free paper that meets the minimum requirements of American National Standard for Information Sciences— Permanence Paper for Printed Library Materials, ANSI Z39.48-1984.

ISBN 0-8103-5402-0
ISSN 1044-2197

# Contents

Introduction   ix

Photo Credits   xi

Cumulative Subject Index   273

Cumulative Musicians Index   283

# Introduction

## Fills the Information Gap on Today's Musicians

Contemporary Musicians profiles the colorful personalities in the music industry who create or influence the music we hear today. Prior to *Contemporary Musicians,* no quality reference series provided comprehensive information on such a wide range of artists despite keen and ongoing public interest. To find biographical and critical coverage, an information seeker had little choice but to wade through the offerings of the popular press, scan television "infotainment" programs, and search for the occasional published biography or expose. *Contemporary Musicians* is designed to serve that information seeker, providing in one ongoing source in-depth coverage of the important figures on the modern music scene in a format that is both informative and entertaining. Students, researchers, and casual browsers alike can use *Contemporary Musicians* to fill their needs for personal information about the artists, find a selected discography of the musician's recordings, and read an insightful essay offering biographical and critical information.

## Provides Broad Coverage

Single-volume biographical sources on musicians are limited in scope, focusing on a handful of performers from a specific musical genre or era. In contrast, *Contemporary Musicians* offers researchers and music devotees a comprehensive, informative, and entertaining alternative. *Contemporary Musicians* is published twice yearly, with each volume providing information on 80 to 100 musical artists from all the genres that form the broad spectrum of contemporary music—pop, rock, jazz, blues, country, new wave, New Age, folk, rhythm and blues, gospel, bluegrass, rap, and reggae, to name a few, as well as selected classical artists who have achieved "crossover" success with the general public. *Contemporary Musicians* will occasionally include profiles of influential nonperforming members of the music industry, including producers, promoters, and record company executives.

## Includes Popular Features

### In *Contemporary Musicians* you'll find popular features that users value:

- **Easy-to-locate data sections**—Vital personal statistics, chronological career summaries, listings of major awards, and mailing addresses, when available, are prominently displayed in a clearly marked box on the second page of each entry.

- **Biographical/critical essays**—Colorful and informative essays trace each personality's personal and professional life, offer representative examples of critical response to each artist's work, and provide entertaining personal sidelights.

- **Selected discographies**—Each entry provides a comprehensive listing of the artist's major recorded works.

- **Photographs**—Most entries include portraits of the artists.

- **Sources for additional information**—This invaluable feature directs the user to selected books, magazines, and newspapers where more information on listees can be obtained.

## Helpful Indexes Make It Easy to Find the Information You Need

*Contemporary Musicians* features a Musicians Index, listing names of individual performers and musical groups, and a Subject Index that provides the user with a breakdown by primary musical instruments played and by musical genre.

## We Welcome Your Suggestions

The editors welcome your comments and suggestions for enhancing and improving *Contemporary Musicians*. If you would like to suggest musicians or composers to be covered in the future, please submit these names to the editors. Mail comments or suggestions to:

The Editor
*Contemporary Musicians*
Gale Research Inc.
835 Penobscot Bldg.
Detroit MI 48226-4094
Phone : (800) 347-4253
Fax: (313) 961-6241

# Photo Credits

**PHOTOGRAPHS APPEARING IN *CONTEMPORARY MUSICIANS*, VOLUME 7, WERE RECEIVED FROM THE FOLLOWING SOURCES:**

**Photograph by Phoebe Ferguson, courtesy of Gramavision:** p. 1; **MICHAEL OCHS ARCHIVES/Venice, CA:** pp. 4, 39, 192, 269; © **Mark Seliger/Outline:** p. 6; **Courtesy of Columbia Records:** p. 10; **Reuters/Bettmann:** pp. 13, 34, 114; **AP/Wide World Photos:** pp. 15, 19, 24, 45, 52, 61, 67, 77, 80, 83, 86, 89, 100, 111, 118, 124, 143, 146, 149, 158, 162, 179, 183, 186, 197, 207, 217, 236, 239, 242, 251, 257; **Courtesy of The Philadelphia Orchestra:** p. 22; **Courtesy of Shanachie Records:** p. 26; **UPI Bettmann:** pp. 31, 74, 107, 266; **Photograph by Sunny Bak,** © **1990 Def American Recordings, Inc.:** p. 42; **Photograph by Douglas Brothers, courtesy of Tommy Boy Records:** p. 49; **Courtesy of Atco Records:** p. 55; **Photograph by Peter Nash,** © **1991 Warner Bros. Records:** p. 58; **Photograph by Glen LaFerman,** © **1989 Reprise Records:** p. 64; **Photograph by Sikay Tang,** © **1991 Sony Music:** p. 70; **Photograph by Susan Wilson, courtesy of Round River Productions:** p. 94; **Photograph by Carol Freidman, courtesy of Verve Records:** p. 97; **Photograph by Harrison Funk,** © **1991 Sire Records Company:** p. 103; **Photograph by Aaron Rapoport,** © **1991 Reprise Records:** p. 121; © **Ron Akiyama, courtesy of Atlantic Records:** p. 126; **Photograph by Femi Bankole Osunla, courtesy of Shanachie Records:** p. 130; **Courtesy of Tom Lehrer:** p. 133; **AP/Wide World Photos:** p. 136.

**Photograph by Richard Holt, courtesy of IMG Artists:** p. 139; **Photograph by Ross Halfin** © **May 1991, courtesy of Elektra Entertainment:** p. 152; **Photograph by Don Hunstein, courtesy of ICM Artists Ltd.:** p. 155; **Ray Avery/MICHAEL OCHS ARCHIVES/Venice, CA:** p. 165; **Photograph by Christian Steiner, courtesy of Shaw Concerts, Inc.:** p. 170; **Courtesy of Kathy Gangwisch & Associates, Inc.:** p. 175; **Photograph by William Claxton, courtesy of Verve Records:** p. 189; **Courtesy of The Helvering Agency:** p. 195; **Photograph by McGuire, courtesy of Oh Boy Records:** p. 200; **Chris Cuffaro/Visages,** © **1991 Warner Bros. Records:** p. 203; **Photograph by Daniel Corrigan,** © **1990 Reprise Records:** p. 211; **Photograph by O'Brian and Schridde,** © **1991 Warner Bros. Records:** p. 214; **Varrick/Rounder Records:** p. 220; **Photograph by Patti Perret, courtesy of Blue Note Records:** p. 223; **Courtesy of The Terrie Williams Agency:** p. 226; **Photograph by Henry Grossman, courtesy of ICM Artists Ltd.:** p. 229; **Courtesy of Williams Artists Management:** p. 233; **Photograph by Dean Dixon,** © **1991 Warner Bros. Records:** p. 245; **Photograph by Marc Norberg, courtesy of Blue Note Records:** p. 248; **The Bettmann Archive:** p. 260; **Courtesy of RCA Records:** p. 263.

# CONTEMPORARY MUSICIANS

# Ray Anderson

**Trombonist**

"**A**nderson mashes the [jazz] eras together, as his trombone skitters out on its own, chasing often sophisticated ideas with a giddy joy," wrote John Leland in *Newsweek* about jazz trombonist Ray Anderson. "He's an approachable face of the avant-garde, as rich in humor as in musical adventure." Named premier trombonist in several *Down Beat* magazine critics polls, Anderson has earned praise for his performances with the group Slickaphonics, Anthony Braxton's quartet, and as a leader. "Anderson, it appears," remarked Bill Shoemaker in *Down Beat,* "can do it all." Tutelage under Keshavan Maslak, Charles Moffett, Stanley Crouch, Braxton, and Barry Altschul cultivated his technical command without sacrificing his quirky style. "Equal parts experimentalist, vaudevillian, and virtuoso," proclaimed Josef Woodard in *Entertainment Weekly,* "Anderson is more than the class clown of the trombone world. He gets to the heart of the music by way of the funnybone."

A versatile performer comfortable in duo, trio, quartet, and orchestra settings, Anderson consummated a musical tenure that included the traditional, neo-bop, Latin, and hard funk idioms. Though schooled in cornet, tuba, alto trombone, and slide trumpet, he first embraced the less-esteemed trombone as a fourth grader. "One of the far-out things about trombone," Anderson explained to Fred Bouchard in *Down Beat,* "is this duality between the ridiculous and the majestic. It has the role of being the ultimate clown instrument, and yet it can be the saddest instrument. [German composer Felix] Mendelssohn called it 'the voice of God.'"

### Preferred Flea Markets and Nightclubs

Born in Chicago, Illinois, in 1952, Ray Anderson received plenty of exposure to jazz, listening to his father's Dixieland albums. A professor at the Chicago Theological Union, the elder Anderson sent Ray to the University of Chicago's experimental, musically strong elementary school. As an eight-year-old, Anderson met fellow student George Lewis, the future trombone virtuoso. Both boys studied under the renowned Frank Tirro, who later taught at Yale University. As an adolescent, Anderson took classical lessons with Dean Hay but stayed away from his teacher's middle-class neighborhood, instead frequenting the flea markets on Maxwell Street where he listened to the bands play Chicagoland blues.

Though he received a scholarship to the University of Illinois's summer jazz workshop after his senior year in high school, Anderson was expelled when he preferred jamming in restricted neighborhood clubs. He sojourned

## For the Record. . .

Born in 1952 in Chicago, IL; father was a professor at the Chicago Theological Union. *Education:* Studied trombone under Frank Tirro and Dean Hay; attended University of Illinois, Macalester College, and California Institute of the Arts.

Jazz, funk, and jazz-rock fusion trombonist. Gigged in funk bands in Minnesota and California; moved to New York City; sat in with Charles Mingus, 1972; played in Tommy Dorsey's band and Hidden Strength; played in Surrealistic Ensemble, mid-1970s; replaced George Lewis and played in Anthony Braxton Quartet, beginning in 1977; performed with Roscoe Mitchell-Leo Smith Orchestra at Moers Festival, 1979; free-lance trombonist, 1977—; toured Europe, 1980; led funk band the Slickaphonics with Mark Helias, c. 1980—. Debuted as a leader on album *Harrisburg Half Life,* Moers Music, 1980; recorded with major jazz performers, including John Scofield, Henry Threadgill, Bennie Wallace, Gerry Hemingway, Mark Helias, Anthony Braxton, George Russell, Tim Berne, Bobby Previte, and Barbara Dennerlein.

**Awards:** Named premier trombonist most deserving of wider recognition, 1981, and top trombonist, several years, in *Down Beat* magazine's critics polls.

**Addresses:** *Record company*—Gramavision, 260 West Broadway, Suite 2D, New York, NY 10013.

in California and Europe with only a sax and a knapsack the next year, but returned to attend Macalester College in Minneapolis, Minnesota. After a year at Macalester, where he played funk and fusion, Anderson went back to California to educate himself at the California Institute of the Arts with such jazz masters as saxophonist Keshavan Maslak, drummer Charles Moffett, and percussionist Stanley Crouch.

In 1972 Anderson moved to New York City, where he sat in on trombone with Charles Mingus. His first paycheck was meager in the Tommy Dorsey band, but he gained experience in the funk band Hidden Strength and Maslak's Surrealistic Ensemble. He also encountered the Yale contingent of jazz musicians, including Gerry Hemingway, Mark Helias, Anthony Davis, Allan Jaffe and Lewis, with whom he would later record. But the turning point in Anderson's career came in 1977 when he was called to replace George Lewis in the Anthony Braxton quartet, only a month after he began rehearsals with Barry Altschul.

## Helped Bring Trombone to the Foreground

Performing with Altschul and Braxton led to appearances at prestigious events, including the 1979 Moers Festival with the Roscoe Mitchell-Leo Smith orchestra, but Anderson still had to free-lance to support himself and purchase treatment for his diabetes. Around 1980 he toured Europe as a leader and formed the Slickaphonics with Mark Helias. Anderson has racked up an impressive oeuvre as a sideman working with such jazz impresarios as John Scofield and Bennie Wallace, but his career as a leader is tantamount.

Named premier trombonist deserving of wider recognition by *Down Beat* magazine's 1981 critics poll, Anderson followed the innovative wave of improvisation and funk that had begun in the 1960s. The trombone was no longer a prop of bebop background music; Shoemaker cited Anderson as being at "the vanguard of the baby-boom generation of American improvising musicians." His first album as a leader, *Harrisburg Half Life,* merited four stars in *Down Beat,* and as his recording increased through the 1980s, so did his favor with reviewers. Critics in *Down Beat* voted him top trombonist for several years straight, beginning in 1987.

"Blessed with astounding technical skills," wrote Frank-John Hadley in *Down Beat* in 1989, describing Anderson's performance on his album *Blues Bred in the Bone,* "he works the slide and manages the embouchure with keenness and authority, giving sonic shape to music ideas that most often carry the element of eccentric surprise. . . . [Anderson and the album] bring to mind an apposite, timeless proverb by [British writer] John Ruskin: 'Fine art is that in which the hand, the head, and the heart of man go together.'" A year later, *Down Beat* contributor Stephanie Stein faulted Anderson for having "too many ideas," which resulted in "overly long solos" on his fifth album as a leader, *What Because.* But the reviewer noted that "on the whole, the album's tremendous vitality keeps drawing the listener in Anderson's steady flow of surprises irresistible."

## Spiritual Insight Through Humor

Also in 1989, Francis Davis pointed out in *Connoisseur* that Anderson's versatility may have hurt him in terms of audience recognition, but rendered him a critic's delight. The album *What Because,* for example, demonstrated the extent of overtones and chords that Anderson's circular breathing technique, plungers, and mutes produced on an instrument thought to be incapable of attaining such a range. Critics have found that with each new release, Anderson only gets better. Labeling *Wishbone* "his best album to date" in 1991, Woodard wrote that Anderson "has crafted music bristling with humor, respect for the mainstream jazz tradition, and effortless technical command."

"Specifically, I know that humor comes out in my music," conjectured Anderson, as quoted by Jeff Levenson in *Down Beat*. The musician also pointed out that the significance of humor in his work goes beyond the obvious farcical powers of the trombone. "I think humor is divine. I think human beings really learn something and are most true to a spiritual thing when they laugh, as opposed to when they get serious." An extraordinary trombonist, Anderson continues to ascribe to the window theory of jazz, which states that through play comes self-revelation. To imitate the great clowns, whose humor went beyond slapstick to uncover various aspects of the human condition, is his goal. "Ultimately," Anderson disclosed to Levenson, "in order to play music successfully you have to learn to be alive successfully. That's the key to the whole thing."

## Selected discography

*Harrisburg Half Life,* Moers Music, 1980.

*Right Down Your Alley,* Soul Note, 1984.
*Old Bottles-New Wine,* Enja, 1985.
*It Just So Happens,* Enja.
*Blues Bred in the Bone,* Gramavision, 1990.
*What Because,* Gramavision, 1990.
*Wishbone,* Gramavision, 1991.
(With the Slickaphonics) *Slickaphonics Live,* Teldec.
(With Anthony Braxton) *Performance,* Hat Art.
(With Anthony Braxton) *Composition,* Hat Art.
(With Barbara Dennerlein) *Straight Ahead!,* Enja.

## Sources

*Connoisseur,* August 1990.
*Down Beat,* July 1982; October 1986; April 1989; August 1989; May 1990; June 1990; November 1990.
*Entertainment Weekly,* June 7, 1991.
*Newsweek,* April 29, 1991.

—Marjorie Burgess

# Brook Benton

**Singer, songwriter**

Singer-songwriter Brook Benton was one of the top performers of the early 1960s. In addition to writing hits for other famous vocalists, he gave music fans the gift of his own smooth baritone voice on popular ballads such as "It's Just a Matter of Time," "Endlessly," and "A Rainy Night in Georgia." Benton also garnered applause singing duets with famed jazz artist Dinah Washington and staged a brief comeback during the 1970s.

Benton was born Benjamin Franklin Peay in Camden, South Carolina, on September 19, 1931. His father was a Methodist minister, and Benton sang in his church as a child. His interest in gospel music continued into his teens, and he performed with local gospel groups for a time. But when he was seventeen, Benton left for New York City to try and make it in more secular music. At first he had to make his living driving trucks and washing dishes, but eventually he found work singing on demo tapes for songwriters who were trying to sell their compositions to established stars.

## Formed Successful Songwriting Team

Benton began writing songs of his own and in 1955 formed a writing partnership with Clyde Otis. The pair made demo tapes of their compositions, with Benton providing the vocals. Benton and Otis's big break came when the legendary Nat King Cole heard their "Looking Back" and decided to record it; when it became a huge success, more business was drawn to the duo. They sold other songs to Cole as well, and wrote the smash "A Lover's Question" for rhythm-and-blues artist Clyde McPhatter. Benton and Otis also provided hits for the likes of Patti Page and Roy Hamilton.

By 1959 Benton realized that what *Rolling Stone* critic Anthony DeCurtis labeled his "elegant" baritone was being wasted on demo tapes. After he and Otis composed the sad but hopeful "It's Just a Matter of Time," Benton won the attention of Mercury Records, and the company signed the young vocalist. As a reporter for *Ebony* magazine noted, "'It's Just a Matter of Time' skyrocketed up the charts." A series of solo hits followed, including "Endlessly," "Thank You, Pretty Baby," and "So Close." Benton added to his fame when he recorded the album *The Two of Us* with acclaimed jazz singer Dinah Washington. Together they climbed the charts with the upbeat "Baby, You've Got What It Takes" and "A Rockin' Good Way."

Benton began to have career troubles in 1961, right after his humorous story tune "The Boll Weevil Song" gained popularity. The single was the last success he would share with Otis during that decade; the two dissolved their partnership due to what *Ebony* cited as "personal differences and industry pressures." Another of Benton's partnerships, that with Washington, ended with her death in 1963. That same year he suffered a severe physical beating, which *Ebony* linked to his refusal to perform a second show at a St. Louis club because he claimed that the orchestra there did not play his music correctly. He continued to sing in nightclubs and also tried acting for a time, but little came of it. In 1970 he managed a brief return to the spotlight with his plaintive rendition of "A Rainy Night in Georgia."

### Comeback Attempt

But Benton was unable to follow up on the song's success. For a period of three years Benton was not allowed to record because of contract disputes and he dropped from public attention except for club appearances and some beer commercials he did to help support himself. During the late 1970s, he contemplated a comeback, and when record companies told

Benton he was too old for them to take a chance on him, he reasoned, according to *Ebony,* that "Bing Crosby wasn't too old, and Elvis Presley wasn't too old." He finally landed a recording contract with Olde World Records in 1978. For this company, Benton recorded *Making Love Is Good for You;* to his satisfaction, the single of the same title became a modest hit. He also, like many artists of his heyday, received a boost in popularity when music fans became nostalgic for the tunes of the 1950s and 1960s.

Though in 1978 *Ebony* predicted that Benton's comeback would be a long one, they were apparently wrong. Little else was heard from Benton, and he died of pneumonia in New York City on April 9, 1988.

## Selected discography

### Singles

"It's Just a Matter of Time," Mercury, 1959.
"Endlessly," Mercury, 1959.
"So Close," Mercury, 1959.
"Thank You, Pretty Baby," Mercury, 1959.
"Kiddio," Mercury, 1960.
"Fools Rush In," Mercury, 1960.
"The Boll Weevil Song," Mercury, 1961.
"Frankie and Johnny," Mercury, 1961.
"Lie to Me," Mercury, 1962.
"A Rainy Night in Georgia," Mercury, 1970.
"Making Love Is Good for You," Olde World, 1978.

### LPs

(With Dinah Washington) *The Two of Us* (includes "Baby, You've got What It Takes" and "A Rockin' Good Way"), Mercury, 1960.
*Making Love Is Good for You,* Olde World, 1978.

## Sources

*Ebony,* May 1978.
*New York Times,* April 10, 1988; April 11, 1988.
*Rolling Stone,* May 19, 1988.
*Time,* April 25, 1988.

—*Elizabeth Wenning*

# The Black Crowes

**Rock band**

The 1990s have been good to the Black Crowes. As the decade dawned the rhythm-and-blues rock group catapulted their first record, *Shake Your Money Maker*—which *Rolling Stone's* David Fricke aptly dubbed "a guitar-party cracker that marries white Southern R&B crunch and Anglo cock-strutting attitude in the beloved early-Seventies manner of the Faces and the Rolling Stones"—to double platinum sales by playing no frills, old-line rock and roll. Throughout 1990 and 1991 they entranced audiences across the U.S. and Europe opening for Heart, Aerosmith, Robert Plant, and ZZ Top.

The masterminds of one of the few rock debut albums to go platinum in 1990—indeed, it had been a year since a rock band had hit Number One on the *Billboard* album chart—the Atlanta quintet went from relative obscurity to pop celebrity in a matter of months. They topped both *Rolling Stone's* 1991 readers and critics polls as best new American band, won an Elvis Award for artist of the year and album of the year at the 1991 International Rock Awards, and earned a Grammy

Award nomination for best new artist, also in 1991. According to *People* magazine, after late night television host David Letterman heard the Crowes perform the single "Jealous Again," led by the Robinson brothers—Chris, a captivating singer and the band's lyricist, and reserved, guitar-playing Rich—he summed up their improbably wanton success by asking "Isn't that rock and roll the way God wanted it to be?"

Sensitive to claims that their sound and style is unduly derived from early 1970s-era British rhythm-and-blues rock bands, the cheeky and effusive Chris retorted to Kim Neely in *Rolling Stone,* "There's no new music ever, period. It's all an interpretation of music that's come before." Nicknamed the "Rotten Twins" by bassist Johnny Colt, Chris and Rich—a basically loving, though occasionally squabbling twosome—nonetheless depart from their influences in avoiding the drug binges and groupie orgies that purportedly characterized the heyday of the Stones' Keith Richards and Faces-era Rod Stewart.

## Exotic Stage Trappings

The boys insist that though they are a Southern group, they are not a rebel band. The Tibetan human-bone jewelry, "gris-gris" charm pouches, voodoo paraphernalia and candle-burning featured in their stage shows, they assure their public, signify nothing more than an interest in the exotic. Stressing that they don't rely on some "black magic" image to promote themselves, Chris—who also eschews the scantily-clad women customary in rock videos—passionately assured *Rolling Stone's* Neely that he can sell his band on performance alone. "You know, there *are* people out there who really care and who don't call records *product.* A Poptart is a product. I make music. I don't want to be a f—king *product,* I want to be a piece of your *life.*"

Born three years apart in the late 1960s, in Atlanta, Georgia, Chris and Rich Robinson are the only children of Stan and Nancy Robinson. Former singer Stan briefly landed a pop single, "Boom-a-Dip Dip," in the Top 40 charts in 1958, but after four lean years of touring his performing career dwindled to a close. The elder Robinson happily introduced his sons to a sundry collection of blues, rhythm and blues, gospel, and rock. Neither parent was pleased when Chris and Rich decided to pursue music. By the early eighties, however, their mother relented and purchased the boys guitars. A few months later, dispensing punk rockish numbers—the only tunes they could play—the brothers named their first band Mr. Crowe's Garden after a childhood fairy tale.

## Developed Bluesy Barroom Sound

In 1984 18-year-old Chris and 15-year-old Rich made their professional stage debut in Chattanooga, Tennessee. Though the check covering their $50 performance bounced, the boys persisted. School was decidedly secondary as the brothers honed their skills, performing at area gigs. Rich attended five different prep and public schools before high school graduation; Chris made an abrupt exit from Georgia State University. "Look, Jack Kerouac, you want to be a rock star," Chris's father told him, according to *People's* Steve Dougherty, "you can sleep in the backyard." Chris left home to room with drummer Steve Gorman. The two began developing a demo tape of original numbers with Rich in 1987. The makeshift group's bluesy barroom sound took shape over the next two years, featuring Rich's experiments with Muddy Waters-style open-G tuning and what *Rolling Stone's* Fricke termed "six-string slash and slippery country-funk grease," and was bolstered in 1988 by the addition of second guitarist Jeff Cease and bassist Johnny Colt. After some advantageous exposure and a name change, the Black Crowes signed a contract with Def American Records in January of 1989 and released their first album roughly a year later.

"There's a flip side to the bottled razzle-dazzle of Milli Vanilli: bottled authenticity," remarked John Leland in *Newsweek* after the Crowes' debut recording went Top Ten and had sold a million copies—within a year of its release. "It's the neatly packaged return of the real thing. And no one hawks it with as much spunk as the Black Crowes." Hawking the album was of paramount importance to the Crowes, whose 14 months of opening sets, along with heavy radio airplay of the mega-hit single "She Talks to Angels"—written by Rich Robinson back when he was 17—and enthusiastic MTV rotation of their videos deftly marketed their classic rock and roll. *Rolling Stone* reported that *Shake Your Money Maker* "sold 108,000 copies in a single day." The group largely considered a contemporary oddity— "a youthful American band that shuns the alternative and metal scenes," according to *Rolling Stone*—had made a record *Audio* called "one terrific rock 'n' roll album. Nothing real progressive or strange. Just some damn fine, down-the-line, bluesy rock."

### Bounced From ZZ Top Tour

In March of 1991 the Black Crowes found themselves dismissed from the ZZ Top tour, over the course of which they had received almost as much attention as the headlining Top. Chris Robinson's routine reminder to audiences—this time in front of a hometown crowd of 16,000—that the Crowes play live rock and roll, as opposed to just doing "commercials" for their "product," finally rankled corporate tour sponsors Miller Lite beer. By *Rolling Stone*'s account, Robinson had been cautioned against "saying 'anything about commercialization, commercials, sponsorship or endorsements.'" Unwilling to bow to what he saw as censorship, Robinson recalled, "I said, 'Don't tell me what to say. Kick us off.' And they did."

On May 29, 1991, Chris Robinson's formidable verbal facility again brought the Crowes controversy. After a Denver, Colorado, concert appearance— according to an early June report on MTV News—Robinson was arrested and charged with assault and disturbing the peace, the result of an altercation with a Twinkie-buying 7-Eleven convenience store customer. The brouhaha, as represented by the *Rocky Mountain News*'s coverage of the customer's story, was sparked when she remarked to a star-struck friend that she didn't know who the Black Crowes were and did not recognize Robinson, thus apparently raising Robinson's ire.

The scene developed as Robinson, perhaps already irritated that he and his entourage could not—by Colorado law—purchase beer as it was after midnight, allegedly insulted the woman and spit on her.

### 7-Eleven Incident Resolved in Court

For his part, Robinson told MTV News that in fact, he had spit on the floor *at* the customer—not *on* her—after the customer had verbally abused *him*. Before his court date, the Crowes' downright skinny frontman collapsed while traveling in the U.K. Exhaustion and malnutrition were deemed the culprits. Finally, MTV News revealed in early August that Robinson had pleaded "no contest" to the charge of disturbing the peace. The charge would be dropped from Robinson's record if he were able to clear six months' probation. The singer was fined $53 in court costs.

Fall of that year saw the Crowes perform for 500,000 Soviet heavy metal fans at the Moscow stop of the

---

*"There's no new music ever, period. It's all an interpretation of music that's come before."*
—Chris Robinson

---

mammoth Monsters of Rock tour. Though maybe a bit light for many of the attendant "headbangers" and not yet "mature" enough to shine in such a setting, *Rolling Stone* correspondent Artemy Troitsky nonetheless enjoyed their set. Early in 1992, Black Crowes guitarist Jeff Cease was replaced by Marc Ford, formerly of the group Burning Tree. Though the band's lineup had seemed solid to many of their fans, this shakeup was actually one of a long line of early personnel changes.

"Rap and computer-driven dance music have pushed orthodox rock into the margins," summed *Newsweek*'s Leland, explaining the appeal of the Black Crowes' "loving rehashes" of early 1970s British rock. "The success of the Black Crowes is a response to this. These guys are orthodox with a vengeance: they wear the red velvet pants and the scarves, and purse their lips just right, even when there isn't a mirror in sight." One review, in *Rolling Stone,* began "Imitations of imitations . . .," but went on to qualify this initial pronouncement: "The Black Crowes aren't merely trying to 'reinvent' the Faces' gin-soaked rock; instead, they manage to reinvest it with innocent fervor and a swaggering grace. . . . *This* is how the Stones might sound today if Keith [Richards] had spent his salad days banging steroids instead of smack." To retain the spirit of rock forged in the epoch of their elders, the Black Crowes conform to a personal tenet Chris Robinson related to *Billboard* contributor Chris Morris. "I want to stir the soul," he confessed, "or at least mine."

# Selected discography

*Shake Your Money Maker* (includes "Jealous Again" and "She Talks to Angels"), Def American, 1990.
*The Southern Harmony and Musical Companion,* Def American, 1992.

# Sources

*Audio,* August 1990.
*Billboard,* January 19, 1991.
*Newsweek,* February 11, 1991.
*People,* March 11, 1991.
*Rocky Mountain News* (Denver, CO), May 31, 1991.
*Rolling Stone,* May 31, 1990; June 14, 1990; December 13, 1990; January 24, 1991; May 30, 1991; November 14, 1991.
*Spin,* May 1991.
*Variety,* January 7, 1991.

Information for this profile was obtained from MTV News reports broadcast June 4-5, 7-10, 12-13, and August 1-2, 1991.

—*Marjorie Burgess*

# Blood, Sweat and Tears

**Jazz rock band**

In 1967 veteran musician Al Kooper began to assemble Blood, Sweat and Tears, the large blues/jazz rock band that had occupied his imagination for many years. A former member of the 1950s pop group the Royal Teens ("Short Shorts"), session musician for Bob Dylan, and member of New York City's Blues Project, Kooper wanted to expand the scope of rock to include the more polite forms of jazz and, simultaneously, to bring jazz to a larger and more general audience.

Envisioning a jazz-rock fusion, Kooper recruited musicians with strong jazz and rock backgrounds for his eight-ten member band: guitarist Steve Katz, for instance, was another Blues Project member; drummer Bobby Colomby played for folk-blues singer Odetta; bass player Jim Fielder worked with the Mothers of Invention and Buffalo Springfield; and the group's unusually large horn section (two trumpeters, two trombonists, and a saxophonist) hailed from New York jazz and studio bands.

Blood, Sweat and Tears launched its innovative sound with the album *Child Is Father to the Man*, reinventing

Band founded in 1968 by **Bobby Colomby** (drums; born December 20, 1944, in New York, NY), **Steve Katz** (guitar, vocals; born May 9, 1945, in Brooklyn, NY), and **Al Kooper** (keyboards, vocals; born February 5, 1943, in New York); **David Clayton-Thomas** (lead vocals; born September 13, 1941, in Surrey, England) replaced Kooper in 1969; other early members included **Jim Fielder** (bass; born October 4, 1947, in Denton, TX), **Jerry Hyman** (trombone; born May 19, 1947, in Brooklyn), **Dick Kalligan** (keyboards, trombone, flute; born August 29, 1943, in Troy, NY), **Fred Lipsius** (alto sax, piano; born November 19, 1943, in New York), **Lew Soloff** (trumpet, flugelhorn; born February 20, 1944, in Brooklyn), and **Chuck Winfield** (trumpet, flugelhorn; born February 5, 1943, in Monessen, PA).

Band subject to frequent personnel changes; later members included **Dave Bargeron** (trombone, tuba, trumpet; born September 6, 1942, in Massachusetts), **Jerry Fisher** (vocals; born c. 1943 in Dekalb, TX), **Tom Malone** (trumpet, flugelhorn, trombone, saxes), **Lou Marini, Jr.** (saxes, flute; born in Charleston, SC), **George Wadenius** (guitar; born in Sweden), and **Larry Willis** (keyboards; born c. 1942 in New York). During major reorganization in 1972 lead singer Clayton-Thomas left; he returned in 1974, became co-owner of band's name and catalog, and group has been billed as Blood, Sweat and Tears featuring David Clayton-Thomas since 1975.

**Awards:** Three Grammy Awards, including one for album of the year, 1969, for *Blood, Sweat and Tears.*

the songs of Harry Nilsson, Randy Newman, Carole King, and others through the heavy use of brass and jazz. Recognized as a milestone in rock music, the album nonetheless fell short of commensurate commercial success. Kooper decided to leave the band in favor of record producing (two other members left as well), and many feared the group would fold before it had a chance to get off the ground. Leadership fell to Katz and Colomby; new musicians joined the ranks, and this time the public proved ready for the new ensemble.

### Gained Commercial Success

When Kooper left Blood, Sweat and Tears Canadian rock star David Clayton-Thomas became the band's lead singer—his powerful rasping vocals soon became identified with the group and its subsequent commer-

cial success. With Clayton-Thomas, the 1969 album *Blood, Sweat and Tears* became a blockbuster hit, the number one LP for seven straight weeks. Introducing three gold singles, the Grammy-winning album remained on the charts for more than two years. The album featured big band jazz-rock arrangements of old and new songs by such artists as Brenda Holloway, Billie Holiday, Laura Nyro, and Steve Winwood; the three cuts "Spinning Wheel," "And When I Die," and "You've Made Me So Very Happy" climbed to the top of the charts.

*Blood, Sweat and Tears 3,* appearing a year later, was nearly as successful, introducing the hit singles "Hi-De-Ho" and "Lucretia MacEvil." At the height of its popularity, the band was enlisted by the U.S. State Department for a 1969 goodwill tour of Yugoslavia, Romania, and Poland. The band's acclaim was short-lived, however; the 1971 single "Go Down Gamblin'" proved to be the group's last big hit. Other horn rock bands had sprung up by then: Chase, the Ides of March, and the highly regarded and commercially successful Chicago Transit Authority (later renamed Chicago).

### Popularity Faded

Beset by internal dissent and frequent personnel changes, Blood, Sweat and Tears was dealt a serious blow when Clayton-Thomas left in 1972 to pursue a solo career; engaging a succession of lead singers, the band enjoyed a brief return of popularity when Clayton-Thomas rejoined in 1974. Others pointed to Blood, Sweat and Tears's commercialism as a reason for its steady decline: the group rarely engaged in the improvisation so integral to jazz (duplicating recordings note for note in concert), and many questioned the earnestness of its jazz-rock experiment.

Becoming a regular act in Las Vegas, the band was charged with being hollow and pretentious, swapping its original rock audience for older, cabaret-oriented listeners, abandoning—according to *The Illustrated Encyclopedia of Rock*—"the very road of rock it set out to re-surface." Still, fans of the group defended its right to evolve, deeming its brassy commercial style worthwhile. Yet others acknowledged that before Blood, Sweat and Tears fell away from Kooper's original vision it was the best of the jazz-rock bands and that it was owed a debt of gratitude for the musical possibilities it opened to those who came after.

## Selected discography

### LPs

*Child Is Father to the Man,* Columbia, 1968.
*Blood, Sweat and Tears,* Columbia, 1969.
*Blood, Sweat and Tears 3,* Columbia, 1970.
*Blood, Sweat and Tears 4,* Columbia, 1971.
*Blood, Sweat and Tears Greatest Hits,* Columbia, 1972.
*New Blood,* Columbia, 1972.
*No Sweat,* Columbia, 1973.
*Mirror Image,* Columbia, 1974.
*New City,* Columbia, 1975.
*More Than Ever,* Columbia, 1976.
*Brand New Day,* ABC, 1977.
*Classic Blood, Sweat and Tears,* Columbia, 1980.
*Nuclear Blues,* LAX, 1980.

## Sources

### Books

*The Illustrated Encyclopedia of Rock,* Harmony Books, 1976.
*The Rolling Stone Encyclopedia of Rock and Roll,* edited by Jon Pareles and Patricia Romanowski, Summit Books, 1983.
Stambler, Irwin, *Encyclopedia of Pop, Rock and Soul,* revised edition, St. Martin's, 1989.

### Periodicals

*Down Beat,* September 1987.
*People,* June 2, 1980.
*Stereo Review,* November 1980.

—Meg Mac Donald

# Liona Boyd

---

**Classical guitarist, composer**

---

"Liona Boyd has been stretching the boundaries of the classical guitar almost since she first established herself on the classical circuit more than a dozen years ago," Jon Sievert wrote in *Guitar Player.* In that time, Boyd has toured the globe, playing as a featured soloist with orchestras in Europe, China, Japan, and the Americas. She has performed privately for such political dignitaries as Ronald Reagan, Margaret Thatcher, Fidel Castro, Pierre Trudeau, Queen Elizabeth II of England, and the King and Queen of Spain. Boyd has also recorded 15 albums and won numerous honors, including four Juno awards—the Canadian equivalent of the American Grammy Award. In her homeland of Canada and in areas around the world, Boyd receives both popular and critical acclaim. But in some circles, purists question her for having a repertoire more popular than that of other serious classical guitarists and for recording albums that do not adhere to traditional musical genres.

Although she is hailed as Canada's "first lady of the guitar" (coincidentally, a title from one of her albums), Boyd was born in England and lived her first seven years there before moving with her family to Toronto. Boyd's unaffected childhood—she danced, wrote poetry, painted—gave little indication of her future course in music. But when she was fourteen years old and heard a concert by classical guitarist Julian Bream, she found direction. "I probably would have been a writer if I hadn't gone to that concert," she told Gail Buchalter in *People,* "but I fell in love with the guitar." She then began guitar studies with Eli Kassner at the Royal Conservatory of Music in Toronto and eventually graduated from the University of Toronto with a bachelor's degree in music. That same year, Boyd won a national competition and began a two-year study program in Paris as classical guitar master Alexandre Lagoya's private pupil. When she returned to Canada, she signed her first recording contract.

Boyd approached her first recordings with customary classical offerings: transcriptions of standard works. She did, however, debut pieces written by modern Canadian composers and even performed one of her own compositions, albeit an elaboration on a previous composer's theme. But as she told *Canadian Composer* contributor Michael Schulman at the time, "I really don't think of myself as a composer. . . . I would do more composing if I had more time to experiment with it, but I know my talents lie in performing."

It was her trademark performance on these recordings—clean, soft, melodic, without the usual guitar string squeaks and buzzes—that caught the attention of folk superstar Gordon Lightfoot, who asked Boyd to appear as the opening act on his 1976 tour of North

approach, writing in a hybrid style of rock and classical
that is indicative of her unwillingness to conform to a
single genre. She conceded to Ferguson that "there is
something very magical about how the classical guitar
can create an entire piece of music, but a whole new
world has opened up for me that involves playing with
other musicians and using synthesizers and drum ma-
chines. I enjoy playing concerts with a band; I'm more
relaxed."

Boyd's desire to extend musical boundaries has not
only helped her reach a broader audience but has also
brought a wide range of critical reaction to her recordings and concerts through the years. A *Variety* reviewer
who saw Boyd perform early in her career noted that
her soft approach to the guitar "leaves her somewhat
short in the pyrotechnical area," but allowed, "She is a
master technician who plays with a great deal of both
understanding and feeling for her material." While
Buchalter noted that at least one critic lamented Boyd's
transition to the "very, very popsy," the guitarist's consistently rich orchestration and skillful execution seem
to have earned her an unparalleled following among
classical and pop fans alike.

## Selected discography

*The Guitar,* Boot, 1975.
*The Guitar Artistry of Liona Boyd,* London, 1976.
*The First Lady of the Guitar,* CBS, 1978.
*Works for Guitar and Strings,* CBS, 1979.
*Spanish Fantasy,* CBS, 1980.
*A Guitar for Christmas,* CBS, 1981.
*Best of Liona Boyd,* CBS, 1982.
*Virtuoso,* CBS, 1983.
*Liona Live in Tokyo,* CBS, 1984.
*First Nashville Guitar Quartet,* CBS, 1986.
*Romantic Guitar of Liona Boyd,* CBS, 1986.
*Persona,* CBS, 1986.
*Encore!,* A&M, 1988.
*Highlights,* A&M, 1989.
*Christmas Dreams,* A&M, 1989.

America. This subsequent exposure brought her a
wider listening audience and a gradual artistic change
of heart. Shortly after the Lightfoot tour, Boyd explained
to Carolyn Nott in *Gramophone* that she wouldn't become a pop artist because she loves "the subtle shad-
ings and colours of [the guitar] too much for that." But
she did admit to Schulman that the applause of a pop
crowd far outweighs the criticism of a few traditionalists
who question her commercial leanings: "I got a standing ovation . . . from nearly 10,000 people. So if one or
two voices are horrified, I don't care."

In time, Boyd shifted her position from using "the
entertainment world to promote the classical guitar," as
she told Nott, to using more popular pieces in her
classical concerts and recordings, including collaborations
with country king Chet Atkins and rock demigod Eric
Clapton. Jim Ferguson quoted Boyd in *Guitar Player* on
her later stance: "A lot of classical purists have given up
on me anyway. . . . But what the narrow-minded classical public feels is not really of concern to me. Recently
I've made quite a career change, and I'm very happy
with my new way of expression and working with other
instrumentalists." Boyd composed more under her new

## Sources

*Canadian Composer,* May, 1977.
*Gramophone,* January, 1980.
*Guitar Player,* December, 1984; April, 1987; July, 1987; Decem-
ber, 1989.
*People,* May 18, 1981.
*Stereo Review,* October, 1978.
*Variety,* March 26, 1980.

*—Rob Nagel*

# Billy Bragg

**Singer, songwriter, activist**

**B**riton Billy Bragg began his career as a self-described "hard-core folksinger." His marriage of the angry, "in-your-face" sensibility of punk rock with the humanitarian, activist ideals of traditional folk music made Bragg a particularly strange hybrid in the music business. Influenced by the seminal punk group the Clash and grim social conditions under conservative former British prime minister Margaret Thatcher, Bragg set his unapologetic socialist politics to spare electric guitar melodies in service to both his music career and the higher purpose of inspiring his listeners to rethink their social and political complacency. Yet throughout his career, Bragg has managed to avoid the preachy posturing of many a pop star by mixing his messages with arch wit and self-mocking warmth.

Born Steven William Bragg on December 20, 1957, Bragg was raised in the East London neighborhood of Barking—a working-class locale of row houses that produced his characteristic Cockney accent. He left school at 16, bought a cheap guitar, and embarked on a series of day jobs that included stints as a bank messenger and goatherd. By most accounts he actually learned how to play his guitar from his boyhood chum and current guitarist-confidante, Wiggy. Bragg's music career began in earnest in 1977 when he and Wiggy formed the punk band Riff Raff. Bragg played rhythm guitar and contributed vocals. After releasing several independent singles, Riff Raff unveiled an EP titled *I Wanna Be a Cosmonaut* in July of 1978. Their musicianship of dubious quality—a *Melody Maker* reviewer remarked of the record, as reprinted in the *Billy Bragg Songbook:* "Riff Raff, 'I Want to be a Cosmonaut,' I wish he would and take his record with him"—Riff Raff drew little acclaim and folded early in 1981. "'Failure to come to terms with abject poverty,' was the official reason for the split," the *Songbook* explained.

Suddenly unemployed and frustrated by the dissolution of his band, Bragg joined Her Majesty's Forces at Catterick Camp, where he hoped to learn tank-driving skills. He realized immediately, though, that he had no business in the military, served out his 90-day term, and retired from the service. Bragg returned to Barking, where he concentrated on both his songwriting and facility with the guitar.

### Galvanized by Margaret Thatcher

While paying his dues as a musician, according to a 1991 *Monthly Review* interview with author David Batstone, Bragg became galvanized politically by the 1983 reelection of Margaret Thatcher, whose Tory government had ruthlessly cut the social programs Bragg had taken for granted. He told Batstone: "Then in '84, of

## For the Record. . .

Born Steven (one source says Stephen) William Bragg, December 20, 1957, in Barking, London, England; father was a building-supplies salesman.

Singer, songwriter, activist, 1977—. Worked variously as a shipping clerk, bank messenger, dog groomer, gas station employee, record shop assistant, and goatherd. Member of band Riff Raff, 1977-1981; began solo career, performing in pubs, billed as Spy vs. Spy, 1982; released *Life's a Riot With Spy vs. Spy* on GO! Discs, 1983; toured U.K., Europe, and U.S., 1984; performed at Feed the Miners benefits in British coalfields, 1984. *Military service:* British Army, 1981.

**Addresses:** *Manager*—Peter Jenner; c/o Sincere Management, 6B, Bravington Rd., London W9 3AH, England. *Record company*—Elektra Entertainment, 75 Rockefeller Plaza, New York, NY 10019.

course, was the miners' strike, which was the big political catalyst for my generation. . . . A lot of us who had started to write political songs had the opportunity to find out whether those songs actually meant anything in a real political context."

After a series of subway performances and club gigs, at which Bragg—billed as Spy vs. Spy—showcased his increasingly political songs, a lucky break arrived when a prescient soul gave him an opportunity to make demo recordings; several of these stripped-down "live" recordings would eventually find their way onto Bragg's first album, *Life's a Riot With Spy vs. Spy.* Recorded in three days in February of 1983, the seven-song, roughly 17-minute EP contained what Bragg called during a 1984 appearance in Boston "high-speed punk-folk numbers." The record, featuring both sweet-clever love songs—"The Milkman of Human Kindness"—and fierce indictments of British class structure and diminishing economic opportunity—"To Have and to Have Not"—did not immediately find its niche with any record company.

However, visionary Peter Jenner, at the time creative director of Charisma Records, spotted in Bragg's unusual talent advantages where other record-company recruiters saw only liabilities. Bragg's first effort was finally released in July of 1983 on Charisma's Utility label. Although *Life's a Riot* was not an immediate hit, *The Billy Bragg Songbook* reports that *Melody Maker* contributor Adam Sweeting was in the vanguard when he called Bragg a "hit and run attraction" spinning "deceptively robust melodies and razor-sharp earthy

wit." London disc jockeys John Peel and Kid Jensen gave Bragg's career a further boost by playing cuts from the record on their popular radio shows.

That September, Charisma was swallowed by Virgin Records, and Bragg and Utility were transferred to the GO! Discs label; there, the record began to take off. Buoyed by public enthusiasm for the track "A New England," which featured the refrain "I don't want to change the world/I'm not looking for a new England/I'm just looking for another girl," *Life's a Riot* reached the top spot on the British independent charts in January of 1984—remaining there for three months—and eventually sold over 500,000 copies to earn a gold record. Putting his friend-of-the-workingman philosophy to practical use, Bragg caused a brouhaha when he insisted that copies of the record be labeled with a maximum-price sticker, thereby guaranteeing that retailers would not charge more than a low, preset price; as the record had been made on a shoestring budget, Bragg reasoned, the savings should be passed on to the consumer. Triumphant in the ensuing struggle with infuriated distributors of his record, Bragg was soon on tour in Europe and the U.S. warming up for better-known acts. September of that year saw him performing in British coalfields for a Feed the Miners benefit.

*Brewing Up With Billy Bragg,* the singer's second solo release, appeared in October of 1984. It reached Number 16 on the British LP chart—without a single or video—before dropping from sight. The 11-song release added organ and trumpet to Bragg's trademark lacerating rhythm guitar. *Brewing Up* mixed outrage at the careless acceptance of undisguised sexist and right-wing propaganda in England's newspapers, in "It Says Here," with bitter contemplation of betrayed emotional commitment, in "The Myth of Trust."

The next record, 1985's four-track *Between the Wars EP*—released in conjunction with a Jobs for Youth tour sponsored by Britain's Labour Party—featured the song "Between the Wars," which radiated Bragg's ripening songwriting gift and vocal nuances; a tender, pacifist ballad, sung from a workingman's point of view, the song captures Bragg's suspicion of the military's role in economic recovery and his belief that it is the fundamental responsibility of government to provide its citizens with "a living wage." Arguably one of his most moving compositions, "Between the Wars" has an anthem-like quality that surfaces frequently in Bragg's work.

### Made News on College Charts

The American music press began to take notice of

Bragg in 1985. *People* contributor Susan Schindehette summed up initial U.S. response: "In concert he just stands there in a spotlight wearing blue jeans and a polo shirt, bashing on an old electric guitar. Then he stops and talks about miners' strikes and the welfare state. What's *wrong* with this guy?" American students, nonetheless, seemed to feel there was nothing wrong with Bragg; his records regularly held their own at the top of the college charts.

The previous year Bragg had articulated his politics and motivation for his growing American audience. He stated in *Rolling Stone,* "Some things have to be defended: the welfare state, free education, free health care, the right for old people to retain their dignity. My government just doesn't care anymore, and if that doesn't inspire you to write songs. . ." With typical understatement, he added, "I'm not a revolutionary. Just someone who managed to overcome the shyness of my generation to sing political songs."

1987 marked the release of Bragg's third LP, *Talking With the Taxman About Poetry. Taxman* further enlarged Bragg's sound—this time with a variety of instrumental, and some vocal, accompaniment; the raw style so evident on the early records had been enriched by a distinct flavor of pop and rhythm and blues. "While purists might bitch," allowed *Rolling Stone* reviewer David Handelman, "the result is a winning mesh, by turns as political as the Clash, as clever as [acerbic wit] Elvis Costello, as melodic as [Kinks front man] Ray Davies and as rocking as [rock and roll pioneer] Chuck Berry." The inclusion of songs like "There Is Power in a Union" and "Levi Stubbs' Tears" indicates that Bragg was equally concerned with the ideas of communist theory and the comforting power of Motown tunes.

When not in the studio, Bragg continued to tour, joined by local grassroots activists who gathered petition signatures for human rights organizations, encouraged voter registration, and distributed free condoms in the lobbies of concert halls. In 1988 he made news by cofounding Red Wedge—described by *The Progressive* as "a coalition of artists and musicians supporting the Labour Party and various progressive causes in Great Britain"—and by releasing a live EP called *Help Save the Youth of America,* culled from performances in Moscow, London, and Washington, D.C.

Also in 1988 Bragg unveiled *Workers Playtime,* its title borrowed from a post-World War II radio show. Fans and critics again found Bragg flexing his musical muscles; *Workers Playtime* includes a haunting a cappella examination of the special bond between soldiers called "Tender Comrade," a bouncy sing-along titled "Waiting for the Great Leap Forwards," full of clever, self-

referential couplets that address Bragg's mix of "pop and politics," and perhaps the record's strongest cut, "Must I Paint You a Picture," which exposes a guilty lover claiming that "Virtue never tested is no virtue at all."

### *Workers Playtime* a Breakthrough

With *Workers Playtime* American critics woke up to Billy Bragg. Said Michael Small in *People,* "Bragg defiantly bucks the trends by writing sweet melodies that are easy to sing and adding lyrics that are clear, clever, and meaningful." *Stereo Review* contributor Steve Simels, on the other hand, averred, "Like anybody else who's got strong opinions, Bragg can be a bloody bore as often as he can be compelling," concluding, "He doesn't have a good beat, and you can't dance to him." But most reviewers echoed David Fricke's *Rolling Stone* comment on *Workers Playtime:* "Bragg's pithy, poignant wordplay, combining . . . tragicomic ingenuity . . . with the directness of a political tract, is a treat in itself."

---

*"Because we can't get Utopia tomorrow doesn't mean we should stop trying."*

---

Bragg moved a giant step closer toward his goal of media access for his causes with the 1991 release of *Don't Try This at Home.* On it Bragg effortlessly mixes flawed romance, weighty social issues, ingenious puns, and a head-spinning variety of musical genres, all in an impressively broadened, though still heavily accented, voice. In England the single "Sexuality"—from which a very un-Bragg-like dance mix was made—became a runaway hit. The song's dynamic and responsible attitude toward the title subject, its catchy melody, and lines like "Just because you're gay/I won't turn you away" seemed positively revolutionary and attracted attention on both sides of the Atlantic. Teaming with Michael Stipe and Peter Buck, members of the rock band REM, Bragg also recorded the rollicking, country-tinged "You Woke Up My Neighborhood." Another standout on the record was "Cindy of a Thousand Lives," its lush, surging production almost obscuring the cut's dark lyrics of envisioned ruin and paranoia.

*Don't Try This at Home,* which presented Bragg for the first time with a full band, received raves from almost every critical corner. One dissenter, *Rolling Stone* contributor Rob Tannenbaum, groused that "[Bragg's] songs are so full of Britannia . . . that his albums should come with footnotes." Calling the record "morose" and "sometimes listless," Tannenbaum nevertheless mustered some praise: "With his consistently fresh rhymes and winning sense of self-parody, Bragg sings about racism, jingoism and other liberal themes without succumbing to a stiff political correctness." Sally Margaret Joy was less ambivalent in *Melody Maker,* enthusing, "'Don't Try This at Home' is Bragg's most complete and accessible album to date. He has waded into the waters of pop and his principles haven't dragged him down."

The further spread of Bragg's message is difficult to predict; what is certain, however, is that he will continue to use his personal experiences to explore the human condition and urge his listeners to social action—whether or not he succeeds critically and commercially. As he stated to David Fricke in *Rolling Stone* of his aspirations for society, "Because we can't get Utopia tomorrow doesn't mean we should stop trying."

# Selected discography

(With Riff Raff) *I Wanna Be a Cosmonaut* (EP), Chiswick Records, 1978.

*Life's a Riot With Spy vs. Spy* (mini-LP; includes "The Milkman of Human Kindness," "To Have and to Have Not," and "A New England"), GO! Discs/Utility Records, 1983.

*Brewing Up With Billy Bragg* (includes "It Says Here" and "The Myth of Trust"), GO! Discs, 1984.

*Between the Wars EP* (includes "Between the Wars"), GO! Discs, 1985.

*Back to Basics* (contains *Life's a Riot With Spy vs. Spy, Brewing Up With Billy Bragg,* and *Between the Wars EP*), Elektra, 1987.

*Talking With the Taxman About Poetry* (includes "There is Power in a Union" and "Levi Stubbs' Tears"), Elektra, 1987.

*Help Save the Youth of America,* Elektra, 1988.

*Workers Playtime* (includes "Tender Comrade," "Waiting for the Great Leap Forwards," and "Must I Paint You a Picture"), Elektra, 1988.

*The Internationale* (EP), Elektra, 1990.

*Don't Try This at Home* (includes "Sexuality," "You Woke Up My Neighborhood," and "Cindy of a Thousand Lives"), Elektra, 1991.

*The Peel Sessions: 1983-88,* Strange Fruit, 1992.

Also recorded several independent singles with Riff Raff.

# Sources

### Books

*The Billy Bragg Songbook,* International Music Publications, 1985.

### Periodicals

*Audio,* January 1989.

*In These Times,* November 13, 1991.

*Melody Maker,* September 14, 1991.

*Metro Times* (Detroit), November 20, 1991.

*Monthly Review,* February 1991.

*Mother Jones,* November/December 1990.

*Musician,* December 1991.

*New Musical Express,* September 14, 1991.

*New Statesman & Society,* June 22, 1990.

*People,* July 29, 1985; December 5, 1988; August 13, 1990; February 3, 1992.

*The Progressive,* July 1988.

*Pulse!,* November 1991.

*Rolling Stone,* September 12, 1985; March 26, 1987; June 2, 1988; November 17, 1988; January 12, 1989; October 18, 1990; November 15, 1990; January 24, 1991; June 27, 1991; October 13, 1991; January 23, 1992.

*Select,* September 1991.

*Spin,* April 1991; November 1991.

*Stereo Review,* February 2, 1989.

—*Julia M. Rubiner*

# Nell Carter

**Singer, actress**

In 1978 singer Nell Carter drew national attention for her role in *Ain't Misbehavin'*, the Broadway show celebrating the 1930s black composer, musician, and comic entertainer Fats Waller, who was responsible for such classic songs as "Honeysuckle Rose," "I'm Gonna Sit Right Down and Write Myself a Letter," "Your Feet's Too Big," and "Black and Blue." A New York singer and stage actress for nearly a decade, Carter had always been cast as a belting soprano, but in *Ain't Misbahavin'* she found a vehicle for her substantial range and versatility, emerging as the star of the production. Her highly acclaimed performance earned her Tony, OBIE, and Drama Desk awards; a subsequent contract with NBC to star in the hit television comedy *Gimme a Break* further demonstrated her scope as an entertainer.

Profiling the *Ain't Misbehavin'* star in a 1978 article for the *New York Times,* John S. Wilson wrote that her "singing voice . . . has the raw, penetrating quality of a steel-tipped drill," and noted that "Miss Carter adjusts her vocal style to bring out shades of wistfulness that other singers miss, wistfulness with an undercore of gutty determination." The writer further pointed out that when Carter "can cut loose . . . or get into a raucous vaudeville exchange . . . her voice cuts laser flashes through the auditorium." Deeming the actress "the Joshua of the [*Ain't Misbehavin'*] cast," a *Time* reviewer found that "her remarkable voice can be as powerful as a trumpet and as plaintive as a flute, and when she sings 'Mean to Me' and 'It's a Sin to Tell a Lie,' she is like a whole orchestra."

Born in Alabama on September 13, 1948, Carter grew up with racial bigotry and was determined to escape it as soon as she could. While her family encouraged her to become a teacher, she felt that show business was the way out; a local celebrity with the singing group Y-Teens, she left for New York City at age 19 with $300 in her pocket. At first finding work as a folk singer and guitarist at coffeehouses, Carter advanced to performing pop and blues in Manhattan nightclubs after a successful appearance on television's *Today* show. Stage roles soon came her way, including parts in *Hair, Jesus Christ Superstar,* and *Miss Moffat.* While never unemployed, Carter admitted to Wilson that she "made a lot of wrong decisions" in her career, choosing lesser projects over such Broadway hits as *Bubblin' Brown Sugar* and *The Wiz.* Even *Ain't Misbehavin'* began in a little downstairs barroom at the Manhattan Theater Club; its enormous popularity eventually warranted a Broadway run.

Buoyed by her New York success, Carter headed for Hollywood, turning to television and motion pictures in the early 1980s. She became the star of the hit television series *Gimme a Break* in 1981, playing a feisty maid in a white middle-class household. While some critics felt that her considerable talents were wasted in the situation comedy, the performer countered that a black woman in Hollywood has few options: "The public knows what it wants," she informed Suzanne Adelson in *People,* blaming audiences more than the industry for black actors' limited roles.

The 1980s were also a time of major change in Carter's personal life. In 1983, she separated from her second husband, Georg Krynicki, whom she wed in May of 1982, and also began a strict diet in order to slim her rotund 4'11" frame. "I was very sick," she told Malcolm Boye in *People.* "I had diabetes, ulcers, an enlarged heart and an irregular heartbeat. Everything that could go wrong with me was wrong with me. And I was incredibly unhappy. Doctors told me I was obese, and I told them it was their imagination."

Tension was felt on the set of *Gimme a Break* when irritability and fatigue began affecting Carter's work. By November of 1983, though, after having dined mostly on roast chicken and pineapple since May, Carter had lost 81 pounds and noted to Boye, "I've managed to completely reeducate myself into making eating secondary. I used to eat all the time because the food was there. Now I feel like a kid in school who is gaining points for behaving. And I love myself for it."

Aside from her role on *Gimme a Break,* which ran until 1987, Carter has continued performing in musicals, starring in such stage productions as *Blues Is a Woman;* she also reprised her *Ain't Misbehavin'* role on television and in her concert tours. Favoring theater songs over standard nightclub fare, the vocalist has made just a handful of recordings, guest starring on Ben Bagley's revival albums, which feature the forgotten works of various Broadway composers. Describing the 1981 release *Ben Bagley's Everyone Else Revisited* in *Stereo Review,* Paul Kresh related that "the menu includes such mouth-watering desserts as Nell Carter's terrific treatment of 'Black Diamond' . . . and the lovely lullaby 'Sleep, Baby, Don't Cry.'" "And when the material gets thin," continued the reviewer, "Carter . . . keeps it going anyway."

In 1988, Carter made a concert appearance with an 11-piece band at New York City's Village Gate, winning praise from Stephen Holden in the *New York Times,* who labeled her "a solid, heartfelt southern soul singer." Continuing her work on television, she made a guest appearance on the show *227* in 1989 and went on to star in the 1990 CBS sitcom *You Take the Kids* and the 1992 television film *Maid for Each Other.* "I never say no to nothin'," the versatile Carter declared in *Jet* in 1989. "If you close the door on something, it'll only swing back and hit you later."

## Selected discography

### With others

*Ben Bagley's Everyone Else Revisited,* Painted Smiles, 1981.
*Kurt Weill Revisited,* Painted Smiles, 1982.
*Kurt Weill, Volume 2,* Painted Smiles, 1982.
*Leonard Bernstein Revisited,* Painted Smiles, 1983.

## Sources

*Ebony,* September 1980.

*Jet,* January 20, 1992.

*Newsweek,* May 22, 1978.

*New York,* January 13, 1992.

*New Yorker,* September 5, 1988.

*New York Times,* February 24, 1978; April 18, 1988.

*People,* June 21, 1982; November 14, 1983; December 17, 1990; January 23, 1992.

*Stereo Review,* May 1981.

*Time,* June 5, 1978.

*Variety,* December 24, 1990.

—*Nancy Pear*

# Sarah Chang

**Violinist**

At the ripe age of ten, Sarah Chang is already rated one of the world's most promising young concert musicians. Chang is a violin prodigy, a riveting soloist who performs with a three-eighths-size instrument. In her 1990 debut with the New York Philharmonic Orchestra, the youngster drew six standing ovations for her interpretations of several technically demanding classical works. Her teachers and fellow musicians alike are astonished by her poise and natural ability. As Daniel Webster put it in the *Philadelphia Inquirer,* "When the violin is under [Chang's] chin, she is a commanding speaker."

*Associated Press* writer Kelly Smith Tunney has contended that Chang is an outstanding example of a larger phenomenon—a fascination among Koreans and Korean-Americans with Western fine arts. Tunney explained: "Encouraged by liberalization of the new democracy, by money from its economic successes, Koreans are in a maniacal rush to become the best musicians, the best dancers, the best performers. Better than the Japanese, the Chinese, the Italians and everyone else." And although Chang's parents—both born in Korea—are musicians, her success stems less from their prodding than from a love of performing and an abiding fascination with music that began when she was a toddler.

Chang was born in Philadelphia. Her family had moved to the United States in 1979 so that Chang's father could study for an advanced music degree at Temple University. Her mother too was pursuing musical studies, taking composition classes at the University of Pennsylvania. Chang's father told the *Philadelphia Inquirer* that as a very young child she liked to play one-finger melodies on the piano. "She wanted to play my violin," he added, "but I couldn't let her put her sticky fingers on my violin. When she was four, we rented a one-sixteenth-size violin, and she seemed naturally able to play." Chang learned the basics from her father, and in 1986 was accepted into classes at Temple University's Center for Gifted Children. Her teacher there, Julian Meyer, told the *Philadelphia Inquirer* that Chang was "the most phenomenal talent I have seen in 19 years of teaching."

Word of the child prodigy's ability spread throughout Philadelphia. In 1988 Philadelphia Orchestra concertmaster Norman Carol heard her play at a private dinner party. Carol asked the orchestra's concertmaster, Riccardo Muti, to listen to the girl. Several weeks later, Chang stepped onto an empty stage at the city's Academy of Music and stunned a small audience—including Muti—with her finesse. Her repertoire, which she had written on a sheet of paper shaped like an ice cream cone and decorated with glitter, included works

## For the Record. . .

**B**orn Sarah Yong-chu Chang, 1980, in Philadelphia, PA; daughter of a music teacher, and a composer; career managed by her father. *Education:* Studies music at Juilliard School, New York City, and attends private school in Germantown, PA.

Concert violinist, 1989—. Has made solo appearances with the New York Philharmonic Orchestra, the Montreal Symphony, the Philadelphia Orchestra, and the La Scala Orchestra, Milan, Italy.

by foremost classical composers Niccolo Paganini and Pyotr Ilich Tchaikovsky, among others.

By 1990 Chang was no longer a local phenomenon. She made her debut with the prestigious New York Philharmonic Orchestra and the Montreal Symphony, earning praise from critics and fellow musicians for both performances. In 1991 she soloed with the Philadelphia Orchestra and with Muti's other symphony, the La Scala Orchestra in Milan, Italy. So far, however, only a lucky few—those who have been able to catch her live performances—have heard Chang's magic. She has, nonetheless, made some recordings with a London-based company, EMI Records. Tony Caronia, president of EMI, told the *Philadelphia Inquirer:* "We are recording Sarah, perhaps not for release now, but as a means of keeping in contact with her."

Chang has handled the publicity heralding her triumphs—and the pressure—with a grace far exceeding her years. Her parents have said that they are trying to keep her formative years as normal as possible. They have also encouraged the youngster to keep her options open and to explore other possible careers as well as music. With that in mind, Chang attends grade school in the Philadelphia area and studies music on the weekends at New York City's famed Juilliard School. "I come home and do my homework, practice some and play with my little brother," she told the *Philadelphia Inquirer.*

It seems unlikely that Chang will opt for a career outside music. She is gifted with a natural talent that is the envy of many an adult musician, and she can handle solo work with poise and flair. In his story on Chang, the *Inquirer's* Webster concluded that "performing is a kind of exhibitionism. The player has to be convinced that her message is too important to be kept in private." He added that Sarah Chang "has the natural performer's exhilaration at standing up and playing."

## Selected discography

Chang has recorded unreleased material for EMI Records, London.

## Sources

*Associated Press* (wire report), April 7, 1991.
*Philadelphia Inquirer,* January 16, 1991.

—Anne Janette Johnson

# Chubby Checker

## Singer

**D**eemed "one of the pop-cultural symbols of the early '60s" by Hugh Boulware in the *Chicago Tribune,* Chubby Checker is practically synonymous in the minds of most music buffs with the 1960s dance craze, the Twist. Though rhythm and blues singer Hank Ballard had recorded "The Twist" earlier, it was Checker's version of the song that became the most popular and spread the dance throughout the world. "What we started in the '60s set the stage for what is still going on," Checker told Boulware. "We invented dancing apart." Checker continued to capitalize on the twist— which he described to Jon Bowermaster in *Newsday* as a movement akin to "drying your butt with a towel while grinding out a cigarette"—and other dances during the early 1960s with such follow-up hits as "Limbo Rock," "Pony Time," and "Let's Twist Again."

Checker was born Ernest Evans on October 3, 1941, in South Carolina. Moving with his family to Philadelphia, Pennsylvania, when he was eight years old, the youngster became a shoe shiner and was earning $60 a day at the age of nine. He then turned to the chicken-plucking business for a time while amassing fame in his neighborhood for his accurate impressions of singers Fats Domino, Jerry Lee Lewis, and Elvis Presley. Performing at work, in church, and on the streets by night with his harmonizing group, the Quantrells, Chubby— as he was nicknamed because of his portly build—was eventually offered a recording contract by Cameo Records.

Checker's first two singles for Cameo, "The Class" and "Dancing Dinosaur," failed to attract much in the way of public notice. As Ballard's version of "The Twist" began to gain favor with dancers, Cameo decided to have Checker make a cover recording of it. Fortunately, Philadelphia, Cameo's locale, was also home to Dick Clark's nationally televised dance show *American Bandstand.* Chubby landed an appearance on the popular program, earning the surname "Checker" from Clark's wife, who likened the singer to Fats Domino, and ensuring a wide audience for his catchy song and dance routine. As Ed Ward put it in his book *Rock of Ages: The Rolling Stone History of Rock and Roll,* it wasn't long before the performer "claimed the top slot on the pop charts," despite the fact that "it was a nearly identical copy" of the other artist's version, "right down to Ballard's signature cry of *eee-yah.*"

And the twist dance craze didn't let up as fast as others. When teenagers' interest in the song abated, adults began to request it in clubs, perhaps because the dance itself "was so simple," in Ward's words. As Checker's popularity grew among adults, he was invited to sing "The Twist" on *The Ed Sullivan Show;* this induced Cameo to re-release the single, and at the beginning of 1962, it once again climbed to the top of the charts. Between its two release dates, "The Twist" was Number One for a total of 40 weeks.

Banking on the huge popularity of the twist, Checker followed his hit tune with a succession of similar songs, including "Twistin' USA," "Let's Twist Again," "Twist It Up," and "Slow Twistin'," and had six Top Ten hits between 1961 and 1963. Though the singer tried to inspire such dance crazes as the hucklebuck, the pony, the fly, the slop, and the limbo, like many other U.S. musical acts of the 1960s, he suffered from the impact of British groups on the music industry. Nevertheless, Checker enjoyed continued success as a club performer. "I got a trailer, four musicians, and hit the road," he recalled to Boulware. "I realized that if I was going to continue to make bucks in this business, I had to forget about the stardom and start at the bottom."

Checker made a recording comeback in 1982, releasing the album *The Change Has Come* under the MCA label, but fans seemed more interested in hearing him perform his older songs at nostalgia concerts than having him put out new material. Like other musical acts of his heyday, Checker has profited from a revival of interest in early rock and roll, tirelessly touring over 300 days a year with his band the Wildcats. But the singer still finds time for recording; he saw a re-release of "The Twist"—performed with the rap group Fat Boys—break into the Top 20 in 1988.

Checker has also earned visibility among television audiences with his 1990 appearances in commercials for Oreo cookies, in which he links his famous twist dance with the idea of twisting apart the two-layered treat. In an effort to secure his rights to the use of "The Twist" for commercial purposes, he held a press conference in January of 1992 and announced a $17 million lawsuit against McDonald's Restaurants of Canada for using the song in a television advertisement without his consent. The singer still holds ambitions for

another Number One hit and reflected to Boulware,"If you look at the twist as the top of my life . . . forget about it. There's so much more Chubby Checker that I'm just dying to tell the world about."

## Selected discography

### Singles; on Cameo Records

"The Class," c. 1959.
"Dancing Dinosaur," c. 1959.
"The Twist," 1960.
"Pony Time," 1961.
"Let's Twist Again," c. 1962.
(With Dee Dee Sharp) "Slow Twistin'," c. 1962.
"Limbo Rock," 1963.

### Albums; on Cameo Records except where noted

*Twist,* 1960.
*Twistin' Round the World,* 1961.
*Your Twist Party,* 1961.
*Let's Twist Again,* c. 1962.
*For Twisters Only,* c. 1962.
*For Teen Twisters,* 1962.
*Don't Knock,* 1962.
*Limbo Party,* 1963.
*Let's Limbo More,* 1963.
*Chubby Checker's Biggest Hits,* 1963.
*Beach Party,* 1963.
*Chubby Checker in Person,* 1963.
*Folk Album,* 1964.
*Chubby's Dance Party,* Dominion.
*The Change Has Come,* MCA, 1982.

## Sources

### Books

Stambler, Irwin, *The Encyclopedia of Pop, Rock, and Soul,* St. Martin's, 1989.
Ward, Ed, Geoffrey Stokes, and Ken Tucker, *Rock of Ages: The Rolling Stone History of Rock and Roll,* Summit Books, 1986.

### Periodicals

*Atlanta Constitution,* May 28, 1985.
*Chicago Tribune,* March 16, 1989.
*Maclean's,* December 30, 1991.
*Newsday,* December 15, 1985.
*People,* April 5, 1982.
*Rolling Stone,* January 23, 1992.

—*Elizabeth Wenning*

# The Chieftains

---

**Irish folk ensemble**

---

In the early 1950s Irish music wasn't even popular in Ireland. When a young Paddy Moloney began learning traditional music, his Dublin neighbors found it quite odd. At the time, according to *St. Paul Pioneer Press Dispatch* contributor Jay Walljasper, Irish kids were learning American and British pop music and trying to play guitars and saxophones; it seemed that only old people cared about the national music. Back then a big festival of traditional music would attract only a few hundred participants. Fortunately for Moloney, however, what seemed to be the end of Irish folk music was actually the beginning of a revival and he was in the middle of it. Decades later, as the leader of the Chieftains, he still is. More precisely, Moloney and the Chieftains are at the top of Irish folk music—unquestionably its leading artists.

"As ambassadors for traditional Irish music, the Chieftains are without peer," stated Rick Mason in the *Pioneer Press.* "And although their rabid following is still considered cultish compared to, say, [rock band] Bon Jovi, it is devoted and widespread. Folk music isn't

supposed to be this popular." Performing together since the early 1960s, the Chieftains have built a following that spans the musical spectrum; pop, rock, folk, and classical music critics alike rave about their albums and performances and their collaborators have ranged from traditional Chinese ensembles to classical flutist James Galway and rocker Elvis Costello. They are praised for both their musical skills, which Mason called "technically superb," and their live performances. "Sheer, unabashed virtuosity is the Chieftains' strongest selling point, whether they are piping hot or cool. When they take off together on a madcap reel or jig, the effect is electrifying," wrote *Time.* Mason echoed this sentiment: "Paddy Moloney and the boys are the quintessential Irish band: poignant, exuberant, playful, occasionally raucous and never taking themselves too seriously."

The Chieftains' virtuosity is enhanced by the individual talents of its members. According to Stephen Holden of the *New York Times,* Paddy Moloney is "the master of

the bellows-blown instrument know as the uilleann pipes." These are Irish pipes, similar to the Scottish bag pipes, but pumped by bellows under the arm rather than breath-blown. Moloney is also an accomplished composer and the Chieftains' primary producer. Both harpist Derek Bell and fiddler Martin Fay are classically trained, and Sean Keane was an all-Ireland fiddle champion. All of the members of the band share in the musical arrangements. In *Rolling Stone* Scott Isler noted that it is the band's credentials, as well as their arrangements, that "distinguish the Chieftains from [other] tradition-bound Irish groups."

## Performed Together in Ceoltoiri Chualann

Before 1960 ensemble performances of Irish music were rare. Musicians played solo or in groups of two or three. Sean O Riada, a classically trained composer and performer, envisioned something different and formed Ceoltoiri Chualann—a sort of Irish folk orchestra. He was joined by several future Chieftains: Moloney, Fay, Sean Potts, Michael Tubridy, and Peadar Mercier. O Riada's experiment eventually became the norm and before long ensembles were common.

In 1963 Moloney, Tubridy, Potts, Fay, and David Fallon formed the Chieftains. Their name came from poet John Montague's work "Death of a Chieftain." According to *Irish Folk Music's* Deborah Schaeffer, their first album— recorded on Dublin's Claddagh label in 1964—was an experiment; after it was completed the members of the band continued with their regular jobs, occasionally performing on evenings and weekends.

The ensemble hoped to do something new with Irish music. Although their pieces were classically arranged, the Chieftains played them only on traditional instruments: Tubridy on flute and concertina, Potts on tin whistle, Fay on fiddle, Fallon on bodhran (a goat-skin drum), and Moloney on tin whistle and uilleann pipes. "It was their goal to restore a music downgraded in the cities of Ireland, and to do so with only such instruments as would have been traditionally available," noted James Tarbox of the *Pioneer Press.* Another unusual aspect of the Chieftains' music was its blending of traditions: "The music of the Chieftains is an amalgam of two distinct Irish traditions: the single-voiced, unaccompanied pipe tunes of the folk people, and the richer, harmonized rustle of the Irish harp. It is the careful blending of the two that give the Chieftains their special sound," explained *Time.*

The success of the Chieftains' first album led Moloney to a job with Claddagh Records, where he produced dozens of albums. The Chieftains did not record a second album for five years. They did, however, continue to play together—with Ceoltoiri Chualann and as the Chieftains—and their audience grew. In 1970 Ceoltoiri Chualann disbanded, leaving Moloney and company more time to devote to the Chieftains. They had recorded their second album, *The Chieftains 2,* the previous year. This time Mercier joined them on bodhran and bones (animal bones played like castanets), and Keane joined as well. But even with a second album and the dissolution of their other ensemble, the Chieftains still held onto their day jobs.

The ensemble continued to record intermittently throughout the early 1970s and their roster grew; with *The Chieftains 3* harpist Derek Bell became a permanent member. According to the *Penguin Encyclopedia of Popular Music,* Bell became a "leading light in the band, with extrovert stage antics, patter as well as virtuosity." By this time traditional Irish music was becoming increasingly popular throughout the world and by mid-decade the Chieftains were in high demand.

### Became Full-Time Chieftains

1975 proved to be a big year in the Chieftains' career. In January they signed a managing contract with Jo Lustig, finally gave up their other jobs, added Ronnie McShane on bones, and generally began devoting more time to musical pursuits. The next album, *The Chieftains 5,* was their first released in the United States; its debut was followed by the ensemble's first U.S. tour. The Chieftains were no less popular on their own side of the Atlantic. *Time* reported that Britain's *Melody Maker* named them top group of the year—"for making unfashionable music fashionable"—and they sold out London's 8,000-seat Albert Hall twice. As if this weren't enough, the Chieftains capped the year by winning an Oscar for their soundtrack for Stanley Kubrick's *Barry Lyndon.*

During the late seventies the Chieftains' following grew and their lineup changed. They continued to record for film and television and in 1979 performed in front of the largest audience ever assembled—1.2 million people plus 800 million watching on television—when Pope John Paul II visited Dublin. *The Chieftains 9: Boil the Breakfast Early,* released in 1980 and nominated for a Grammy, marked substantial changes in the ensemble. For the first time a Chieftains album included vocals, provided by Kevin Conneff, who had earlier replaced Mercier on bodhran. By this time Tubridy and Potts had left the group and their space was taken up by Matt Molloy on flute and tin whistle.

By 1980 the Chieftains were firmly established as the best and best-known performers of traditional Irish music. "In importance and fame, the Chieftains are the Rolling Stones of their field," *Rolling Stone's* Isler wrote that year. Despite these lofty heights, however, the Chieftains began to expand their range, taking side trips into related fields. This direction was apparent in their 1981 release, *The Chieftains 10: Cotton-Eyed Joe;* Schaeffer described the title track in *Irish Folk Music* as "Texas meets the Chieftains."

### Brought Irish Music to China

As if Texas weren't far enough from Irish tradition, the Chieftains next jaunt took them to China; in 1983 they became one of the first Western groups to perform in China and the first to play with a traditional Chinese folk orchestra. Rather than going to China to simply play Irish music, the Chieftains wanted to blend the Irish and Chinese musical traditions. At first Moloney was anx-

> *"We would never come down the ladder. True, traditional playing in our way is what we want to do."*
> —*Paddy Moloney*

ious about their ability to do this. "Before we left Ireland, I sent over some music for [the Chinese] to have a go at," he told *Pioneer Press* contributor Tarbox. "But I didn't know what would be going on until we got there. The Chinese have more than 200 traditional instruments, and any combination might be waiting for us." Much to his delight, Moloney discovered that the Chinese used the same musical system he used and that their instruments blended beautifully. During the tour the Chieftains used their Irish instruments to create traditional Chinese sounds. Schaeffer noted that the Irish and Chinese instruments are similar in harmonies and that the "Chinese flavor gives a baroque mood to these selections."

The Chieftains' next production took them out of the Irish tradition again, but this time they remained within their musical family, exploring the music of their Celtic relatives in Brittany, a historical peninsular region of northwest France. The pieces performed on this album—*Celtic Wedding*—were taken from a collection assembled by Polig Monjarret and published in his

*Toniou Breizh-Izell (Traditional Tunes From Brittany). Consumers' Research* magazine described the album as "fascinating . . . spirited, [and] charming, though occasionally tinged with sadness."

As the Chieftains experimented with different musical traditions, they also began working with an eclectic group of performers. Their fans and collaborators had long included many musical luminaries: Paul McCartney, Eric Clapton, Jerry Garcia, Jackson Browne, the Rolling Stones, and Don Henley. In 1987 the group recorded and toured with Irish classical flutist James Galway, who set aside his usual fare of classical music and joined the Chieftains in their characteristic jigs, reels, and airs. A year later they joined another famous Irish performer, pop singer Van Morrison, to record *Irish Heartbeat*. The album, which was nominated for a Grammy Award for best folk recording, included both traditional Irish songs and original Morrison compositions. As David Browne wrote in *Rolling Stone, Irish Heartbeat* was a very natural, and even expected, merger of two of Ireland's most widely loved musical entities. "Yet even those expectations don't prepare one for the splendor and intense beauty of *Irish Heartbeat,* a collection of ballads that finds both acts at the top of their form."

### More Collaboration With Pop Performers

1991 found the Chieftains collaborating with pop musicians again, this time on a Christmas album entitled *The Bells of Dublin.* Joining the group in this effort were Elvis Costello, Jackson Browne, Marianne Faithfull, Nanci Griffith, Rickie Lee Jones, Kate and Anna McGarrigle, and Northumbrian pipes player Kathryn Ticknell. The album mixed traditional Irish hymns and dances with new compositions; *Rolling Stone's* assessment of the work was succinct, stating that the music was "of course, exactly what you might expect from the Chieftains—magnificent."

No matter the direction they take, the Chieftains most likely will not stray from their roots and traditions. According to *Pioneer Press* contributor Mason, they are "staunch purists" when it comes to traditional music. "We would never come down the ladder," Moloney told him. "True, traditional playing in our way is what we want to do. We want to pursue that line all the time. But now and again we sidetrack a little bit. . . . And all these little sidetracks are always something that suits the instruments and the style of how we play traditional Irish music. If it's a good, well-constructed tune, then we respond." And the Chieftains' strict adherence to the traditions of Irish music have indeed served them well. "There is something in this venerable music—handed down from generation to generation, often in defiance of British Law—that kindles a good feeling in almost everyone who hears it," Jay Walljasper wrote in the *St. Paul Pioneer Press.* "The rollicking jigs, reels and slow melodic airs will be played . . . as they might have been at a wedding dance 300 years ago. This historical continuity—oblivious to the fads and fetishes of fashion—is one of the things making Irish music so powerful."

## Selected discography

### Albums

*The Chieftains 1,* Shanachie, 1964.
*The Chieftains 2,* Shanachie, 1969.
*The Chieftains 3,* Shanachie, 1971.
*The Chieftains 4,* Shanachie, 1973.
*The Chieftains 5,* Shanachie, 1975.
*The Chieftains 6: Bonaparte's Retreat,* Shanachie, 1976.
*The Chieftains 7,* Columbia, 1977.
*The Chieftains Live,* Shanachie, 1977.
*The Chieftains 8,* CBS, 1978.
*The Chieftains 9: Boil the Breakfast Early,* Columbia, 1980.
*The Chieftains 10: Cotton-Eyed Joe,* Shanachie, 1981.
*The Chieftains in China,* Shanachie, 1985.
*Celtic Wedding: Music of Brittany Played by Irish Musicians,* RCA, 1987.
(With James Galway) *James Galway and the Chieftains in Ireland,* RCA Red Seal, 1987.
(With Van Morrison) *Irish Heartbeat,* Mercury, 1988.
*A Chieftains Celebration,* RCA, 1989.
*The Chieftains: "Reel Music,"* RCA, 1991.
(With Rickie Lee Jones, Marianne Faithfull, Elvis Costello, Nanci Griffith, Kate and Anna McGarrigle, Jackson Browne, Kathryn Ticknell, the Renaissance Singers, and Burgess Meredith) *The Bells of Dublin,* RCA, 1991.
*The Best of the Chieftains,* Legacy, 1992.
(With Roger Daltry and Nanci Griffith) *The Chieftains: An Irish Evening—Live at the Grand Opera House, Belfast,* RCA, 1992.

### Film and television soundtracks

*Barry Lyndon/Music From the Soundtrack,* Warner Bros., 1976.
*Year of the French,* Shanachie, 1982.
*Ballad of the Irish Horse,* Shanachie, 1985.
*The Grey Fox,* DRG, 1983.

### Other

(Paddy Moloney and Sean Potts) *Tin Whistles,* Claddagh.
(Michael Tubridy) *The Eagle's Whistle,* Claddagh.
(Sean Keane), *Gusty Frolicks,* Claddagh.
(Keane) *Sean Keane,* Shanachie.
(Keane and Matt Molloy) *Contentment is Wealth,* Green Linnet.
(Molloy) *Matt Molloy,* Green Linnet.

(Molloy) *Heathery Breeze,* Shanachie.
(Molloy) *Stony Steps,* Green Linnet.
(Molloy, with Paul Brady and Tommy Peoples) *Matt Molloy, Paul Brady, Tommy Peoples,* Green Linnet.
(Kevin Conneff, with James Galway) *Annie's Song and Other Galway Favorites,* RCA.
(Conneff, with Christy Moore) *Prosperous,* Tara.

# Sources

## Books

Baggelaar, Kristin and Donald Milton, *Folk Music: More Than a Song,* Thomas Y. Crowell, 1976.
*The Penguin Encyclopedia of Popular Music,* edited by Donald Clarke, Viking, 1989.
Sandberg, Larry and Dick Weissman, *The Folk Music Sourcebook,* Knopf, 1976.

Schaeffer, Deborah L., *Irish Folk Music: A Selected Discography,* Greenwood, 1989.

## Periodicals

*Billboard,* April 7, 1990.
*Consumers' Research,* February 1988.
*Frets,* January 1988; October 1988.
*New York Times,* March 19, 1988.
*Pulse!,* December 1991.
*Rolling Stone,* June 12, 1980; August 11, 1988; December 12, 1991.
*St. Paul Pioneer Press Dispatch,* March 12, 1981; February 21, 1985; February 28, 1985; July 19, 1987; March 3, 1988; December 21, 1989.
*Time,* January 12, 1976.

*—Megan Rubiner*

# Clarence Clemons

---

**Saxophonist, singer, songwriter**

---

For almost two decades Clarence Clemons was the source of the driving tenor saxophone riffs in Bruce Springsteen's E Street Band. Known as the King of the World, the Master of Disaster, and especially the Big Man, Clemons provided energetic backup vocals and music on many of Springsteen's best-selling albums. Onstage, the towering Clemons proved the perfect counterpart to the wiry Springsteen throughout years of hectic touring. *Down Beat* contributor Don Palmer noted in 1984 that the Big Man was "the troubleshooter, the enforcer, a bloodline to the [rhythm and blues] ancestors" and offered "legitimacy and a sense of cohesion for what might otherwise be just another band trying to cover an attitude."

Clemons's long dedication to the E Street Band has not hampered his solo career, however. Since 1981 he has been cutting albums on his own, and he has worked with other rock and roll and rhythm and blues entertainers as well. Freed from his commitment to the E Street Band in 1989, Clemons was even more excited about forging his own signature style. He noted in the *Phoenix Gazette* at the time that working with Springsteen had a number of drawbacks. "I was constantly in a shadow," he recalled. "I wasn't playing what I wanted to hear; it was always what [Springsteen] wanted to hear. . . . That's not what I want to do in my life; I didn't want to be a dwindling sideman. So I'm pretty happy . . . now. [Leaving the E Street Band] gives me the opportunity to go out and become Clarence Clemons."

The oldest of three children, Clemons was born in Norfolk, Virginia, in 1942. His parents were hardworking and deeply religious, and the youngster sang in the church choir and with a family gospel group. "I grew up fast because I had to," Clemons remarked in *Down Beat.* "My father owned a fish market, and I helped him in the shop. We lived 15 miles from school, so I'd get up in the morning, go to school, and work at the market or deliver fish after school. It was late, and I was tired by the time I got home at night. This went on every day. I also had a lot of responsibilities for the family because my mother was going to school. She graduated from college at the same time I finished high school. I tell you, I didn't have much time for childhood innocence."

### Jammed on the Jersey Shore

One Christmas, Clemons asked for an electric train and got a Pan American alto saxophone instead. "I'd never even seen a saxophone before, and didn't really know why [my father] gave it to me," he told *Down Beat.* Clemons's father also enrolled him in private music lessons at a nearby state college. "My dad made me practice in the backroom of the store, while the other kids were out playing baseball, and I hated it," Clemons said. "He had the noisiest fish market in Norfolk."

In high school Clemons had two loves—saxophone and football. He switched to baritone sax and played in the Crestwood High School jazz band. His religious background shielded him somewhat from exposure to the early development of rock and roll, but he eventually heard the vibrant tenor saxophone work of R & B artist King Curtis. "In my senior year of high school, I heard King Curtis," Clemons remembered in *Down Beat*. "He turned me on, and it was then that I decided I wanted to play tenor. His sound and tone were so big on those sessions he did, and his feeling was right from the heart. Here was a guy who gave me something."

Clemons attended Maryland State College on a music and football scholarship. He majored in sociology, but his ambition was to become a professional football player. He continued playing the saxophone, and during summer breaks he often signed on to play with combos or larger ensembles, working with such outfits as the Vibratones, the Newark Bears, and the Jersey Generals. He quit college just before graduating and moved north to Newark, New Jersey, where he became a counselor for emotionally disturbed children. While holding the day job he spent many nights jamming in various bands along the Jersey Shore.

Clemons was working with a group called Joyful Noise— performing principally R & B covers—when his path crossed Bruce Springsteen's. Both artists were playing in Asbury Park, New Jersey, at bars about a city block apart. One rainy night, Clemons strolled down to take in Springsteen's show. The Big Man recounted the event in *People* magazine: "I had my saxophone with me, and when I walked in this club—no lie—a gust of wind just blew the door down the street. Boof! I say, 'I want to play. Can I sit in?' Bruce says, 'Hey, you can do anything you want. Take a couple of background singers, anything.' I sat in with him that night. It was phenomenal. We'd never even laid eyes on each other, but after that first song, he looked at me, I looked at him, and we said, 'This is it.' After that I was stoked."

Though his decision contributed to the demise of his first marriage, Clemons quit his job and joined the E Street Band. "I was making like $15 a week with Bruce then," he told *People*. "Had no place to stay. But I had faith. It was like following Jesus."

### Productive Partnership With Springsteen

Clemons's faith was well-founded. After a few exploratory albums, Springsteen and the E Street Band's hit LP *Born to Run* went platinum and the group became—in the eyes of critics and fans alike—the premier American rock band of the 1970s. "Since 1973 the Springsteen/Clemons partnership has reaped great rewards and created insightful, high energy rock & roll," declared Don Palmer in *Down Beat* in 1984. "Their music, functioning like the blues from which it originated, chronicled the fears, aspirations, and limitations of suburban youth. Unlike many musicians today, Springsteen and Clèmons were more interested in the heart and substance rather than the glamour of music."

From the recording booth to the stage, the Clemons-Springsteen partnership fairly seethed with vitality. Analyzing his place in the band in 1984, Clemons told Palmer: "The sax adds color to situations, and it has that urgency. Bruce allows me a certain space within which I'm free to do whatever I want, and we interact so well together that it's no problem backing him. On stage, we can dance around and play off each other, which gives the crowd a show and generates energy."

In what little free time he could find while working with Springsteen, Clemons formed his own band, the Red Bank Rockers, and signed a recording contract with Columbia Records. When his schedule allowed, he cut tracks for a debut album, *Rescue,* and performed at his own night club, Big Man's West, in Red Bank, New Jersey. He occasionally offered saxophone backup on the recordings of other noted artists, including Aretha Franklin's well-received *Freeway of Love* album. Always somewhat in the shadow of Springsteen's superstardom, the Big Man nonetheless began to assert his independence and to search for a sound that would validate his rock and roll calling.

As the 1980s wore on, Clemons made some changes in his personal lifestyle while still maintaining his professional pace. Once a perpetual party animal, he swore off alcohol and took an interest in Eastern religion and meditation. The saxophonist continued to record and tour with the E Street Band, but he also cut his own albums, took occasional television roles, and jammed with other groups. He even made it to the Top Twenty in 1988, with a Jackson Browne duet, "You're a Friend of Mine."

### Most at Home With His Saxophone

In 1989 Clemons joined an impromptu group led by ex-Beatle Ringo Starr. Billed as Ringo Starr and His All-Starr Band, the group also included Dr. John, Billy Preston, Rick Danko, Joe Walsh, Nils Lofgren, Levon Helm, and Jim Keltner. The troupe enjoyed a successful American tour in the fall of 1989; Clemons pointed out in the *Phoenix Gazette* that the association was "one of the most joyous times of my life." While touring in Japan with Starr, Clemons received a telephone call from Springsteen, informing him that he would no longer be needed in the E Street Band.

"[Springsteen] said he wanted to try something new, do something different," Clemons explained in the *Phoenix Gazette*. "It was quite a shock; you go through all the emotions of a divorce, all the emotions, instantly. I didn't say much to him. I just said, 'Good luck.' But before long I started to see the good side."

The "good side" for Clemons meant expanded opportunities to jam with other groups—including Starr's ensemble and the Grateful Dead—and the freedom to pursue his solo career without interruption. His albums have drawn reviewers' praise and have explored rock, old rhythm and blues standards, and high-tech dance music. Although he has become more comfortable as a singer, Clemons is still most at home with his saxophone. "I know that the tenor can affect people because it is an emotive instrument," he told *Down Beat*.

"It's so strong the way you can come in on tenor. Because of my size, the tenor is a lot easier for me to play. It's just a natural extension of me, of my personality, and I'm a positive person." He concluded: "The thing about it is that the tenor can be played in two totally different ways. I play it with a positive energy because I want to give something to the audience, and it should be something good."

## Selected discography

**With Bruce Springsteen and the E Street Band; on Columbia Records**

*Greetings From Asbury Park*, 1973.
*The Wild, the Innocent & the E Street Shuffle*, 1973.
*Born to Run*, 1975.
*Darkness on the Edge of Town*, 1978.
*The River*, 1980.
*Born in the U.S.A.*, 1984.
*Tunnel of Love*, 1987.

**Other; on Columbia Records**

(With the Red Bank Rockers) *Rescue*.
(With Ian Hunter) *All of the Good Ones Are Taken*.
*Hero*, 1985.
*A Night With Mr. C*, 1989.

## Sources

**Books**

Marsh, Dave, *Born To Run: The Bruce Springsteen Story*, Doubleday, 1979.

**Periodicals**

*Akron Beacon Journal*, December 18, 1989.
*Daily News* (Los Angeles), September 1, 1989.
*Down Beat*, April 1984.
*People*, November 4, 1985; October 16, 1989.
*Phoenix Gazette*, February 6, 1990.

—Anne Janette Johnson

# George Clinton

## Singer, songwriter, producer

G eorge Edward Clinton was born in an outhouse in poverty-ridden Kannapolis, North Carolina, on July 22, 1941, ensuring that, eventually, the music world would be jarred for over three decades by monstrous funk and rhinestone rap n' rock. Moving from Kannapolis to Washington D.C. to Virginia, the Clinton family finally settled in Newark, New Jersey. Clinton's first job was at the Wham-O hula-hoop factory, where he worked as a foreman during junior high school. At the tender age of 14 Clinton founded a doo-wop group called the Parliaments with Charles Davis, Gene Boykins, and Herbie Jenkins. The group played at local hops, school dances, and on street corners. By day, when not in school, group members styled hair at a Plainfield, New Jersey, barbershop called the Tonsorial Parlor.

In 1956 the Parliaments—then comprised of Clinton, Davis, Robert "Walkin' Pneumonia" Lambert, Grady Thomas, and Calvin Simon—recorded for the first time in a record booth in Newark; they sang "The Wind" and "Sunday Kind Of Love." Two years later they recorded a pair of songs for Hull Records—"Poor Willie" and "Party Boys," and the following year, "Lonely Island" and "Cry." In June of 1959 the Hull recordings were released on ABC records, a Paramount Films subsidiary label, but sales were not heartening. In 1962 Clinton started working for Jobete, the New York branch of Motown Records's publishing company. A year later a somewhat altered Parliaments lineup went to Detroit for an audition in the Motown offices, but met with little success. Looking for other avenues for his burgeoning musical entrepreneurship, Clinton began producing records on a free-lance basis.

In 1964 the Parliaments cut various demo tapes for Jobete, including "I'm Into Something, I Can't Shake It Loose," later recorded by the Supremes, "I'll Bet You," later recorded by the Jackson Five, and the original version of "I Misjudged You," which would later appear on the platinum-selling *Chocolate City* album that Clinton produced with his group, Parliament, in 1975. Although copies of "I Misjudged You" were eventually pressed by VIP Records, a subsidiary of Motown, Motown chose not to release any of the Parliaments' original recordings.

### Fled Music Biz for Hairdressing

Also in 1964, Ed Wingate opened the Golden World recording studio in Detroit and founded two labels: Golden World and Ric-Tic. Clinton sensed opportunity there and joined forces with ex-Jobete coworker Sydney Barnes and Motown saxophonist Mike Terry to create a production team called Geo-Si-Mik. For two years Clinton flew to Detroit each Monday and returned

## For the Record. . .

**B**orn George Edward Clinton, July 22, 1941, in Kannapolis, NC; the first of nine children born to Julia Keaton; children: Tracey Lewis (son).

Singer, songwriter, producer, and funk institution, c. 1968—. Worked as a hairdresser at the Uptown Tonsorial Parlor, Plainfield, NJ, c. 1955-67. Formed doo-wop group the Parliaments, Newark, NJ, 1955; masterminded groups Funkadelic, 1968, and Parliament, 1970, Uncle Jam record label, 1980, and mega-group the P-Funk All-Stars, 1983; also helped spawn the Parliament/Funkadelic satellite bands Zapp, Parlet, Bootsy's Rubber Band, the Horny Horns, and the Brides of Funkenstein.

Has collaborated with guitarists Eddie Hazel, Lucius Tunia "Tawl" Ross, Phelps "Catfish" Collins, Garry Shider, DeWayne "Blackbyrd" McKnight, Michael Hampton, and Cordell "Boogie" Mosson, bassists William Billy Bass Nelson, Jr., and William "Bootsy" Collins, drummers Ramon "Tiki" Fulwood, Frankie "Rash" Waddy, and Tyrone Lampkin, and keyboard player Bernard "Bernie DaVinci" Worrell. Began solo career, 1982. Produced Red Hot Chili Peppers record *Freaky Styley*, EMI, 1985; worked with Ladysmith Black Mambazo. Appeared in film *House Party*, 1989, and began work on Parliament/Funkadelic-based science fiction/comedy film, 1991.

**Awards:** Platinum records for Parliament's *Chocolate City* and *Mothership Connection*, and for Funkadelic's *One Nation Under a Groove*.

**Addresses:** *Record company*—Paisley Park Records, Warner Bros., 75 Rockefeller Plaza, New York, NY 10022. *Other*—Peter Jebsen, *New Funk Times*, c/o Funkateers International, Dept. WB-UK, Ehrenstrasse 19, 5000 Koln 1, Germany.

to New Jersey each Friday to work at the barbershop over the busy weekends. In 1965 and 1966 Geo-Si-Mik produced Pat Lewis's "Can't Shake It Loose," Theresa Lindsey's "I'll Bet You," and J. J. Barnes's "Day Tripper." Clinton alone produced the Fantastic Four's single "Girl Have Pity" in 1966 as well as Lewis's "Look at What I Almost Missed." Around this time Wingate's business partner, LeBaron Taylor, founded his own labels called Revilot and Solid Hit. In late 1966 the Parliaments recorded two songs for Revilot, "I Want To Testify," and "I Can Feel the Ice Melting," but the many difficulties of making inroads into the music business finally frustrated Clinton, who decided to move back to New Jersey and work full-time in the barbershop.

Clinton wasn't discouraged for long, however; on February 9, 1967 "(I Just Wanna) Testify" rose to Number 20 on the pop charts and to Number Five on the rhythm and blues charts—more than half a year after it was recorded. The Parliaments' next single, "All Your Goodies Are Gone (The Loser's Seat)"—cut in a single session with "A New Day Begins," "I'll Wait," "Little Man," "The Goose (That Laid the Golden Egg)," "Time," and a cover of The Beatles' "Sergeant Pepper's Lonely Hearts Club Band"—also did well on the charts. By then the Parliaments were backed by Eddie Hazel on lead guitar, Lucius Tunia "Tawl" Ross on rhythm guitar, William Billy Bass Nelson, Jr., on bass, and Ramon "Tiki" Fulwood on drums. Clinton and his cohorts moved to Detroit in 1967. Despite the growing success of the Parliaments, however, Clinton continued his outside projects, cowriting and coproducing the Flaming Embers' "Hey Mamma (Whatcha Got Good for Daddy)" and Pat Lewis's "I'll Wait", and cowriting J. J. Barnes's "So Called Friends" and the Debonaires "Loving You Takes All My Time" and "Headache in My Heart."

In 1968 Golden World recording and publishing was bought out by Motown's Berry Gordy, and its cofounder, LeBaron Taylor, leased the Parliaments single "A New Day Begins" to Atlantic subsidiary Atco. Soon after, Taylor's Revilot label folded without paying any money to the Parliaments; they survived primarily by touring. Just prior to Motown's purchase of Golden World and the demise of Revilot, however, Clinton had recruited his Parliaments support musicians to form a new group called Funkadelic. The concept behind the name stemmed from the funk of "Godfather of Soul" James Brown and the psychedelics of the MC5 and the Stooges, two Detroit bands Clinton came to know and appreciate. In late 1968 Bernard "Bernie DaVinci" Worrell, a classically trained keyboard wizard, joined Funkadelic. Backing Rose Williams, Clinton and posse recorded "Whatever Makes My Baby Feel Good" and released it on their own Funkadelic label.

## Birth of Parliament/Funkadelic

Around this time Clinton temporarily lost the right to use the name the *Parliaments* due to legal differences among various record labels. He won it back shortly thereafter, but decided nonetheless to drop the *s* and use the name Parliament. When former Motown songwriting team Holland-Dozier-Holland formed their Invictus label in 1967, they signed Parliament. At this point Clinton found himself in the rare position of leading two on-the-rise bands—Parliament *and* Funkadelic—simultaneously.

There is, however, some contention over Clinton's role

in the formation of Funkadelic, now widely held to be the first black rock band—defined most notably by the group's screaming guitar sound (Parliament's reputation eventually evolved more toward funk and dance grooves). Bassist for Funkadelic from 1966 to 1972, Billy Bass Nelson, Jr., in a 1992 issue of *Guitar Player* magazine, refocused the origins of the band. Nelson gave ample credit for the inauguration of Funkadelic to guitarist Eddie Hazel, but claimed, "The truth of the matter is that if I hadn't gone out on the road with the Parliaments in 1967, there wouldn't be any such group as Funkadelic. I brought all of the original members to the group, with the exception of the original rhythm guitarist, Tawl Ross."

Despite the varied accounts of Funkadelic's conception, it is certain that it's birth coincided with that of Detroit entrepreneur Armen Boladian's Westbound Records; Westbound released the Funkadelic single "Music for My Mother" and the band's debut album, *Funkadelic,* which was recorded in 1968 and 1969 and featured *three* musicians—Mickey Atkins, Motown's Ivy Hunter, and Bernie Worrell—on keyboards.

In 1970 Parliament released its debut album, *Osmium,* on the Invictus label. Funkadelic followed closely behind, releasing *Free Your Mind and Your Ass Will Follow* on Westbound. In March of 1970 the first Parliament LP rose to Number 126 on the pop charts and Number Fight on the rhythm and blues charts. Funkadelic's *Free Your Mind* hit Number 92 on the pop charts and Number 11 on the rhythm and blues charts. Despite its Number Eight position on the R & B charts, Parliament's *Osmium* was considered a flop and Billy Bass Nelson and Tawl Ross left the band. In 1971 Funkadelic released *Maggot Brain,* which was largely a comment on the Vietnam War. Almost from the start, a core group of musicians participated in the production of both Parliament and Funkadelic records. By 1972 the lineup included singer-guitarist Garry Shider and guitarist Cordell "Boogie" Mosson, both from the band United Soul, and drummer Tyrone Lampkin, of Gutbucket.

In 1972 bass player Bootsy Collins, his guitarist brother Catfish, and drummer Frankie "Rash" Waddy—all former sideman for James Brown—joined the group of more than 25 musicians then working with Clinton in Parliament and Funkadelic. Bootsy Collins was soon cowriting and coproducing much of the groups' music; he added a distinctive new groove to their sound. Funkadelic's 1972 album, *America Eats Its Young,* was an example of the fresh, creative boost Collins delivered. The album was recorded partly in London with Rolling Stones producer Jimmy Miller.

1973 saw Funkadelic record *Cosmic Slop,* which Clinton considered the closest thing to his original concept for the group. Later that year the Collins brothers and Waddy took a respite from Parliament/Funkadelic's constant touring to form their own band, Complete Strangers, which failed to produce a hit. In 1974 Funkadelic released *Standing on the Verge of Getting It On* and Parliament unveiled *Up for the Down Stroke,* both on Casablanca Records. Bootsy Collins returned as a session player then, and songwriter and ex-Madhouse singer-drummer Gary "Mudbone" Cooper joined Parliament/Funkadelic.

### Blacks in Space

In 1975 Funkadelic's *Let's Take It to the Stage* was released, introducing William Collins's electronically enhanced "Bootsy" vocals on "Be My Beach." Funkadelic put out a greatest hits package that year. Also in 1975, Parliament released *Chocolate City* and *Mothership Connection,* and singer-guitarist Glenn Goins, guitarist Michael "Kidd Funkadelic" Hampton, and drummer Jerome Brailey were added to the fast-growing funk mob. The expression *P-Funk* was coined for Parlia-

---

> *"I'm glad the rappers and all those have kept the funk alive."*

---

ment—P as in pure—and Clinton introduced the notion of blacks in space, creating a thriving world of fictional musical characters like Dr. Funkenstein, Sir Nose D'Voidoffunk, and Star Child. Both *Chocolate City* and *Mothership Connection* were million-sellers.

1976 was a fertile year for Clinton and company; four new albums were released by the prolific, popular, funk machine: Funkadelic's *Tales of Kidd Funkadelic,* the last album on Westbound, and *Hardcore Jollies,* their first on Warner Bros., Parliament's *The Clones of Dr. Funkenstein,* and Bootsy's Rubber Band's debut, *Stretchin' out in Bootsy's Rubber Band.* Bootsy's Rubber Band was one of Parliament/Funkadelic's most successful spinoffs; *Stretchin' out* went platinum. By then Collins had begun to embody various characters on his recordings and onstage, including Bootsy, the diamond-cool rhinestone rock star, Bootzilla, Bootsy's mischief-making evil twin, and Casper the Friendly Ghost, the latter inspired by the cartoon character. Other satellite Parliament/Funkadelic groups were Zapp, the Brides of Funkenstein, Fred Wesley and The Horny Horns, Parlet, Sweat Band, and Godmoma.

Not slowing down in 1977, Funkadelic released *The Best of the Early Years,* Vol. I, a Westbound compilation, and Parliament rustled up *Funkentelechy vs. the Placebo Syndrome* and *Live, P-Funk Earth Tour.* Bootsy's Rubber Band came out with the cash-register-ringing *Ahh . . . The Name Is Bootsy, Baby!* Parliament/Funkadelic spawned several solo albums that year as well, including Fuzzy Haskins's *A Whole Nother Thang,* Eddie Hazel's *Games, Dames, and Guitar Things,* and Fred Wesley and the Horny Horns' *A Blow for Me, A Toot to You.* But it was in 1978 that funk music reached its peak. Funkadelic's platinum *One Nation Under A Groove* took music charts by storm, landing at Number One on the rhythm and blues charts, Number 28 on the pop charts and even Number Nine on the British pop charts. That year also saw the release of Parliament's *Motor Booty Affair,* Bootsy's Rubber Band's *Player of the Year,* Fuzzy Haskins's *Radio Active* and Bernie Worrell's *All the Woo in the World.* Parliament/Funkadelic singers Dawn Silva and Lynn Mabry teamed up to form the Brides of Funkenstein, while their colleagues Mallia Franklin, Jeanette Washington, and Shirley Hayden created the group Parlet. All these culminated in the monstrous 1978-1979 Parliafunkadelicment Mothership Connection tour—"complete with space craft descending onstage to reveal a spaced-out Clinton," recounted *Guitar Player*—which presented a hefty sampling of Parliament/Funkadelic personnel, filled large auditoriums all over the country, and consistently kept audiences dancing well into the wee hours.

### Went Solo

After the 1979 release of Funkadelic's *Uncle Jam Wants You,* which boasted the popular tune "(Not Just) Knee Deep," Parliament's *Gloryhallastoopid,* and a host of adjunct offerings, Clinton moved to a country retreat west of Detroit and announced that he wished to retire from the grind of live performance to concentrate on production and start his own record label, Uncle Jam Records. In 1980 Uncle Jam produced records for the Sweat Band and Philippe Wynne. Clinton was also busy with Parliament and Parlet in the studio that year. Then, in a glimpse of troubles to come, former Funkadelic members Fuzzy Haskins, Calvin Simon, and Grady Thomas erroneously claimed that they owned 42.9 percent of the name *Funkadelic* and released an album titled *42.9 Percent,* the name of which was eventually changed to *Connections & Disconnections.*

After having sold over ten million funk albums in the U.S. alone, Clinton began to encounter legal disputes: numerous lawsuits involving his organization, several record companies, and disgruntled musicians brought his musical activities to a standstill in 1980. Clinton was able to produce Funkadelic's 1981 LP, *the Electric Spanking of War Babies,* which featured rhythm and blues star Sly Stone, however, before his break from Parliament/Funkadelic became officially mandated.

The following year, in spite of his legal battles, Clinton managed to obtain a recording contract for a solo deal with Capitol Records. His first solo album, *Computer Games,* produced the infectious, bark-laden hit "Atomic Dog." Clinton followed up *Dog* with a second release on Capitol, *You Shouldn't-Nuf Bit Fish.* His next move was to create the P-Funk All-Stars. The All-Stars continued the Parliament/Funkadelic groove with *Urban Dance Floor Guerilla,* released by Uncle Jam/CBS, which featured revered rhythm and blues songsmith Bobby Womack, Sly Stone, and Philippe Wynne. 1985 saw the release of Clinton's third solo effort, *Some of My Best Jokes Are Friends.* Not content to rest on his laurels, Clinton in 1985 also produced *Freaky Styley* for the popular funk/metal outfit the Red Hot Chili Peppers, and an album for his brother, Jimmy Giles, called *Federation of Tackheads.*

The last Clinton albums on Capitol Records, in 1986, were *R & B Skeletons in the Closet*—featuring the single "Do Fries Go With That Shake"—*The Best of George Clinton,* and *The Mothership Connection Live From Houston.* 1988 witnessed the reunion of Clinton and Bootsy Collins on the production of the Incorporated Thang Band's *Lifestyles of the Roach and Famous.* The enormous influence of Clinton's work on subsequent generations of musicians became apparent in 1989 when the New York rap duo De La Soul scored a major hit with "Me Myself and I," which sampled lengthy sections of Funkadelic's "(Not Just) Knee Deep." Further testimony to Clinton's authority was mega-star Prince's request that he cut a record on Prince's Paisley Park label. The result was 1989's *The Cinderella Theory,* which marked Clinton's formal signing on at Paisley Park. Clinton wrapped up the eighties with a P-Funk All-Star tour of the U.S. and Japan, work on African a cappella group Ladysmith Black Mambazo's *Scatter the Fire,* and a cameo appearance in the sleeper-hit feature film *House Party.*

### Made Significant Mark on Rap Music

A tireless performer, Clinton and the All-Stars toured Europe *twice* in 1990. In fact, the early nineties were exceptionally kind to the father of funk. Aside from the homage paid him by fellow artists—the Beastie Boys, Jungle Brothers, Public Enemy, Stetsasonic, Ice Cube, Grace Jones, L.L. Cool J, Hammer, Queen Latifah, Young M.C., and Herbie Hancock—a general resurgence of interest in black dance music of the 1970s ushered in extensive reissues of classic Parliament and Funkadelic albums, which paved the way, after thirty-five years, for more original funk bombs from Clinton and his far-flung cohorts. Clinton was onstage again in the fall of 1991 at New York City's Palladium with P-Funk All-Star guitarists Blackbyrd McKnight, Garry Shider, Boogie Mosson, and Eddie Hazel, drummer DeAnthony "Tony T" Thomas, and bass player Rodney "Skeets" Curtis. "Shider stalked the stage in his signature diaper while Clinton, sporting multi-colored hair and a graffiti-sprayed toga, led the crowd in chants. . . . It was probably the largest, rowdiest, funkiest pep rally the city has ever seen," reported *Guitar Player*.

Although it's rarely clear where Clinton will turn up next—a movie, a new album, behind the scenes, or on stage—the result is sure to be stupefyingly funny and funky. He told *Uncut Funk* magazine's David Mills in 1990, "Prince keeps telling me that he wants everyone to know who I am, know the history. Once you get to the top, you ain't got nowhere to go. I enjoy chasing it. As long as I know I'm right behind it, or almost there, I'm happy. When I get a hit record, then I can groove for a minute. . . . I'm glad the rappers and all those [have] kept the funk alive."

# Selected discography

### Funkadelic LPs

*Funkadelic,* Westbound, 1969.
*Free Your Mind and Your Ass Will Follow,* Westbound, 1970.
*Maggot Brain,* Westbound, 1971.
*America Eats Its Young,* Westbound, 1972.
*Cosmic Slop,* Westbound, 1973.
*Standing on the Verge of Getting It On,* Casablanca, 1974.
*Let's Take It to the Stage,* Westbound, 1975.
*Greatest Hits,* Westbound, 1975.
*Tales of Kidd Funkadelic,* Westbound, 1976.
*Hardcore Jollies,* Warner Bros., 1976.
*The Best of the Early Years,* Volume I, Westbound, 1977.
*One Nation Under a Groove,* Warner Bros., 1978.
*Uncle Jam Wants You,* Warner Bros., 1979.
*The Electric Spanking of War Babies,* Warner Bros., 1981.

*By Way of the Drum,* MCA, 1992.

### Parliament LPs

*Osmium,* Invictus, 1970.
*Up for the Down Stroke,* Casablanca, 1974.
*Chocolate City,* Casablanca, 1975.
*Mothership Connection,* Casablanca, 1975.
*The Clones of Dr. Funkenstein,* Casablanca, 1976.
*Funkentelechy vs. the Placebo Syndrome,* Casablanca, 1977.
*Live, P-Funk Earth Tour,* Casablanca, 1977.
*Motor Booty Affair,* Casablanca, 1978.
*Gloryhallastoopid,* Casablanca, 1979.
*Trombipulation,* Casablanca, 1980.

### Other

(Sweat Band) *Sweat Band,* Uncle Jam, 1980.
(Philippe Wynne) *Wynne Jammin',* Uncle Jam, 1980.
(P-Funk All-Stars) *Urban Dance Floor Guerilla,* Uncle Jam/CBS, 1983.

### Solo LPs

*Computer Games,* Capitol, 1982.
*You Shouldn't Nuf-Bit Fish,* Capitol, 1983.
*Some of My Best Jokes Are Friends,* Capitol, 1985.
*The Mothership Connection Live From Houston,* Capitol, 1985.
*R & B Skeletons in the Closet,* Capitol, 1986.
*The Best of George Clinton,* Capitol, 1986.
*The Cinderella Theory,* Paisley Park, 1989.
*George Clinton Presents Our Gang Funky,* MCA, 1989.
*Hey Man, Smell My Finger,* Paisley Park, 1992.

# Sources

*Guitar Player,* November 1991; February 1992.
*New Funk Times,* Number 3, March 1990; Number 4/5, Summer 1990.
*New York Times,* June 27, 1991.
*People,* February 7, 1977.
*Rolling Stone,* June 23, 1983; September 20, 1990.
*Uncut Funk,* Number I, Winter 1990; Number 3, Summer 1991.

—B. Kimberly Taylor

# The
# Country
# Gentlemen

**Bluegrass band**

The Country Gentlemen, in the eyes of many critics, have done more to popularize bluegrass music than almost any other modern band. At a time when bluegrass was all but disappearing from radio and stage, the members of the band infused the genre with an innovative energy and gave it a whole new direction, prompting its new label, "newgrass." In his book *Bluegrass,* Bob Artis wrote, "Except, possibly, for [Lester] Flatt and [Earl] Scruggs, the Country Gentlemen made more bluegrass converts than anyone. In terms of bringing in new fans who had always been disdainful of the raw hillbilly aspects of bluegrass, they undoubtedly did as much as Flatt and Scruggs. In 1969 they were the only name act at the festivals who could consistently bring the audience to its feet."

One might say the Country Gentlemen were part of the second generation of bluegrass music—men who grew up imitating such pioneers as Bill Monroe and Earl Scruggs, but who also responded to the folk music revival and the rock and roll scene. Artis noted that the Gentlemen "were one of the first bands to have two

## For the Record. . .

Group formed July 4, 1957, in Washington, DC. Original members include **John Duffey** (madolin), **Bill Emerson** (banjo), **Earl Taylor** (bass), and **Charlie Waller** (guitar); **Eddie Adcock** replaced Emerson on banjo, and band was named the Country Gentlemen. Group has had numerous personnel changes over the years and has included **Mike Auldridge, Jimmy Bowen, Kevin Church, Jerry Douglas, Jimmy Gaudreau, Tom Gray, Doyle Lawson, Keith Little, Ricky Skaggs, Norman Wright,** and **Bill Yates.** Band has toured the United States, Canada, and the Far East.

**Selected awards:** Named contemporary bluegrass band of the year at the Bluegrass Music Award Convention, 1986.

**Addresses:** *Record company*—Rebel Records, Box 3057, Roanoke, VA 24015.

sources of ideas. One, of course, was the world of straight bluegrass. The other was the then-hip world of folk music. They were transition-oriented enough to seek out some of the best and least-known songs of traditional bands like the Stanley Brothers and give that material a sophisticated rearranging. But they also had an ear for the trends of popular music, much of it thoroughly adaptable to bluegrass."

### Group Formed "by Accident"

The Washington, D.C., area has always been an important hub for bluegrass music. Its urban and suburban population includes large numbers of former Appalachian dwellers who moved north and east to find jobs. Bluegrass flourished in the bars of Washington and Baltimore, Maryland, when it seemed to be all but dying out elsewhere, and the Country Gentlemen's members learned their craft in the region's rowdier night spots.

Ironically, an automobile accident led to the formation of the Country Gentlemen. The collision injured Buzz Busby, a well-known bluegrass musician who was a regular entertainer at Washington's Admiral Grill. Busby's banjoist, Bill Emerson, tried to keep the Admiral gig by phoning some of his musician friends, notably a Louisiana-born guitarist named Charlie Waller and a young local mandolin player named John Duffey. Together with some of Busby's other sidemen, the trio managed to hold down the job, and after a few weeks they realized that they were clicking as a group.

The official date for the beginning of the Country Gen-

tlemen is cited as the fourth of July, 1957. From its beginning the band underwent numerous personnel changes, but its fledgling membership included Duffey on mandolin, Waller on guitar, and Eddie Adcock on banjo. All three were talented instrumentalists, but they brought more than just their musical proficiency to the group. Both Duffey and Adcock enjoyed clowning around and improvising onstage; the performers were creative, spontaneous, and even silly at times.

Artis observed, however, that the outstanding characteristic of the Country Gentlemen was the vocal harmonies the trio of Duffey, Adcock, and Waller achieved. "The Country Gentlemen has been a uniformly superb band since the first," commented the critic. "[The] trio was sterling, and it was not the bluegrass trio almost everyone had been accustomed to. Theirs were three thoroughly unique voices that happened to mesh into one of the two or three best bluegrass trios ever assembled. Waller had a voice that was technically better than the average bluegrass singer. . . . Duffey, possibly the loudest tenor in bluegrass, had little of that high, nasal quality to his voice. It wasn't operatic, but it was full and rich, not the flat, twangy sound so many associate with the tenor singing of bluegrass. Adcock's warbling baritone was hushed and breathy, complimenting Duffey's unique voice and making their trio truly one of a kind."

### Clowned Around Onstage

The Gentlemen picked up a following in the Washington, D.C., area and soon began playing the college and festival circuit as well. Theirs was a bluegrass band with a difference—all of them, especially Waller, had been influenced by early rock and roll. As a result, they began to adapt rock and folk songs to the bluegrass style. The group was among the first to play and sing bluegrass renditions of songs by such varied artists as Harry Belafonte, Simon and Garfunkle, the Kingston Trio, and Crosby, Stills, Nash, and Young. This tactic earned the disdain of many bluegrass purists, but it attracted a whole new generation of bluegrass fans—young listeners who eventually gained an appreciation for the musical style as a whole.

In addition to their rather daring playlist, the Country Gentlemen became renowned for their boisterous performances. Artis noted that "in a field where the musicians were almost universally depicted as sullen and soulful, the effect [of the Gentlemen] was more than funny. It was irreverent, and the irreverence was part of what the Country Gentlemen were." The group sang riotous takeoff songs and launched into long, dueling riffs that generally ended with everyone—even the string bass player—picking his instrument behind his back. Joking onstage had also been frowned upon in bluegrass circles, but most considered this aspect of the Gentlemen's work a refreshing change from more formal bluegrass performances.

By 1969 the Country Gentlemen had ascended to the first ranks in bluegrass. That same year, Duffey left the group. Adcock followed soon after, but Waller persevered, filling the vacant positions with other talented artists. Since then the band has counted among its members some of the finest bluegrass musicians, including Ricky Skaggs, Doyle Lawson, Jerry Douglas, and Jimmy Gaudreau. When it entered its third decade in the late 1980s, the group had only one original member—Charlie Waller—but it persisted. *Chicago Tribune* contributor Jack Hurst called the Country Gentlemen "a veritable incubator for the development of bluegrass and country stars."

### "Fathers of Modern Bluegrass"

The group has also recorded some of the biggest hits in modern bluegrass music. One of the most frequently requested bluegrass tunes is a Country Gentlemen number, "The Rebel Soldier," a tear-jerker about the dying moments of an American Civil War infantryman. Another is the equally touching "Bringin' Mary Home," in which a ghostly little girl visits her home. The Gentlemen have also made hits of two semi-religious numbers, "God's Coloring Book" and "The In Crowd."

Critics have remarked that the Country Gentlemen have always been able to perform both traditional and progressive bluegrass numbers with equal finesse, so their style has never become dated or obsolete. Waller told the *Chicago Tribune* in 1989 that the band—and bluegrass in general—endure because the sound is "as American as apple pie." The artist added, "I've always thought of bluegrass as being the real country music. I don't go for what Nashville's doing right now, the cry-in-your-beer kind of stuff. Bluegrass deals with a lot of sad songs, too, but they're real tragedy songs, not just 'Let's get a six-pack and split up.'"

Over the years various incarnations of the Country Gentlemen have reunited for special concerts or recording sessions. While they were once considered bluegrass mavericks, Waller, Adcock, and Duffey continue to be venerated for their contributions to a stag-

nating genre. Artis declared in 1975 that the Country Gentlemen may well be the "fathers of modern bluegrass"—musicians who "were a big push behind the progressive bluegrass movement, which in turn will have an effect on the directions bluegrass might take tomorrow."

## Selected discography

*New Look, New Sound: The Country Gentlemen,* Rebel.
*Play It Like It Is,* Rebel.
*The Award-Winning Country Gentlemen,* Rebel.
*Bringin' Mary Home,* Rebel.
*Sound Off,* Rebel.
*Traveler,* Rebel.
*Yesterday & Today,* Rebel.
*Young Fisher Woman,* Rebel.
*The Country Gentlemen,* four volumes, Folkways.
*The Country Gentlemen Featuring Ricky Skaggs on Fiddle* (reissue), Vanguard, 1985.
*Good As Gold!,* Sugar Hill, 1984.
*Gospel Album,* Rebel.
*River Bottom,* Sugar Hill.
*Sit Down Young Stranger,* Sugar Hill.
*Classic Country Gents Reunion,* Sugar Hill.
*Return Engagement,* Rebel, 1988.
*Live in Japan,* Rebel, 1989.
*25 Years,* Rebel, 1989.
*Country Songs Old and New* (reissue), Smithsonian/Folkways, 1990.
*Folksongs and Bluegrass,* Smithsonian/Folkways.

## Sources

### Books

Artis, Bob, *Bluegrass,* Hawthorn, 1975.

### Periodicals

*Chicago Tribune,* March 30, 1989.
*Country Music,* November/December 1991.
*Los Angeles Magazine,* December 1984.
*Stereo Review,* June 1984; June 1986.

—Anne Janette Johnson

# Danzig

**Heavy metal band**

Tattooed men with hair flowing down their shirtless backs who jammed high-volume, guitar-and-drum rock and roll with blues underpinnings demarcated the heavy metal music genre, until the advent of American bands like Danzig. Glenn Danzig, lead singer and songwriter for the group that bears his name, pens lyrics that traverse disturbing domains. More sophisticated in his handling of the wordplay in the netherworld than his most often-cited precursor, Black Sabbath, Danzig belongs to a surge of innovative groups whose music is diverse enough to render the term heavy metal too restrictive. The band's delvings into the demonic dimension of the genre often unnerve its critics. "When I see films and videos of us I laugh, because I guess I am kind of scary," Glenn Danzig related to Legs McNeil in *Spin*. "It's weird. I don't try to analyze it, but when I sit down and think about it, I think, yeah, very dangerous, very violent."

Danzig was conceived, in part, as a result of the lessons Glenn Danzig learned as lead singer and songwriter in two previous groups. In the early 1980s,

when he wrote and sang for the Misfits, his campy lyrics, which dealt with such B-level horror movie mainstays as chopping heads and digesting brains, elated fans. One of the first groups to embody hardcore rock, the Misfits took on almost fabled proportions. Though their musical influence was still active after their demise, Danzig did not consider the Misfits the apex of his career. "The funny thing is that the Misfits weren't really popular when they were around," he commented to McNeil. "Also, they weren't very good live. I was good, as good as you can be at eighty-million miles an hour." Disappointed by the lack of professionalism in the group, Danzig felt a commitment to fans the other band members did not share. "I don't think a lot of people got what I was doing in the Misfits," Danzig revealed in *Spin*. "The guys in the band didn't even get it."

## Glenn Danzig Reminiscent of Jim Morrison

After the Misfits disbanded, Danzig formed another group, the experimental and short-lived Samhain, which included his friend, bassist Eerie Von. When all the band members left Samhain, except Eerie Von, Danzig contemplated forming a new group under the same name. With the additions of drummer Chuck Biscuits and lead guitarist John Christ, Danzig reconsidered. It was a brand new band, and Danzig wanted it to have its own identity; he decided to drop Samhain and give the group his surname.

In 1986 Rick Rubin, the cofounder of Def Jam Records and head of Def American Records, heard Danzig perform at the New Music Seminar. He invited Glenn Danzig to New York City and subsequently signed him to the Def American label. Glenn Danzig's physical resemblance to Jim Morrison, the deceased lead singer of the Doors, coupled with the intonations of his baritone voice—which were also reminiscent of Morrison—brought the group immediate attention. And, though the singer also exhibited an eroticism similar to Morrison's, his bold ventures into the netherworld became the mark of his originality.

## A "Soothing and Savage" Debut Album

Producer Rick Rubin spent two years with Danzig working on their self-titled debut album, a carefully instrumented record that wedded elusively eerie minutia to basic guitar-and-drum tunes. The sounds of backwards-masked Latin hauntingly pervade one introduction, while bells mix lightly with guitar in another number. "Rubin's keen understanding of dynamics permeates nearly every track," observed Kim Neely in *Rolling Stone*. "The songs, at once soothing and savage, provide a perfect foil for Danzig, who makes a habit of vocally lulling you into a peaceful state and then scaring the pants off you with a guttural, tormented wail." Though she pointed out that Danzig took credit on the album for "The Hunter," a song by bluesman Albert King, Neely was more surprised by the "creepy realism" of the songwriter. "Whether this album is the heartfelt product of Danzig's personal beliefs or just an exercise in maudlin role playing, the fact that one even wonders is a tribute to his abilities as a lyricist; it's easy to come away from Danzig convinced that its author is consumed by some very nasty business indeed."

## Departure Into the Netherworld

While Toby Goldstein, writing in the *Wilson Library Bulletin*, noted Glenn's debt to Jim Morrison on Danzig's second album, *Danzig II-Lucifuge*, he argued that Danzig's departure into the underworld might have been the natural outcome of Morrison, had he lived. "The erotic component of Danzig's music isn't that far afield from another sexually obsessed composer—The Doors' Jim Morrison—and that's not really surprising, considering that Danzig's vocal style owes more than a small debt to Morrison. . . . But where Danzig gets into its own forbidden territory is with its leader's fascination with spirituality's dark side. . . . Set to a throbbing, guitar-based hard rock beat, *Lucifuge* contains the kind of disturbing images that taunts its detractors. Then again, if Jim Morrison were a brash young rocker today, he'd likely be writing and sending out a very similar message."

*Rolling Stone* summed up the reaction of many critics when it termed *Lucifuge* "bizarre realism," but *Spin* took a different slant and declared Danzig symbolic. "No, this isn't about satanism or a struggle between church and state. Nor is it about censorship. This goes way beyond that. . . . Glenn Danzig is a new hero to America's post-apocalyptic youth—a comic book cover come to life, proving that they can flourish and endure in the wasteland." Danzig makes its own bid at durability by maximizing terror and the lawlessness in human hearts and producing music that is difficult for the most astute reviewer to categorize. "You know if you're gonna fantasize go all the way," Glenn Danzig told McNeil. "That's my problem with people. They fantasize half-way. I always believed fantasy was, How far can your mind go? Don't settle for nothin' when you can have everything. That's how my life is. Why set your sights on ten when you can set your sights on a million, a billion, a trillion?"

## Selected discography

*Danzig,* Def American, 1988.
*Danzig II-Lucifuge,* Def American, 1990.

## Sources

*Rolling Stone,* November 17, 1988; October 4, 1990.
*Spin,* January, 1991.
*Wilson Library Bulletin,* September, 1990.

—*Marjorie Burgess*

# Jack DeJohnette

---

**Pianist, percussionist**

---

**P**ointing out the far-reaching talents of Jack DeJohnette, *Down Beat*'s Bill Milkowski labeled the jazz musician "swinging and brilliant no matter what context he's in." The versatile artist has been a drummer, keyboardist, pianist, composer, and producer involved in numerous jazz projects. His work with John Coltrane, Charles Lloyd, Miles Davis, John Abercrombie, Keith Jarrett, New Directions, and Special Edition underscores the fact that he is one of the most coveted drummers of the modern jazz era.

Jack DeJohnette was born August 9, 1942, in Chicago to Jack and Eva Jeanette DeJohnette. Although his parents enjoyed music, DeJohnette was influenced at an early age by his uncle, Roy Woods, to take a particular interest in jazz. A jazz disc jockey who later became vice-president of the Black Network of Broadcasters, Woods owned a collection of 78s that included recordings by Louis Armstrong and Billie Holiday; he encouraged DeJohnette to play the albums on an old Victrola. "I couldn't even read—I was about three or four at the time," DeJohnette recalled to Chip Stern in *Down Beat,* "but I could tell what record I wanted to hear by the label, and the distance from the end of the record to the label."

DeJohnette was four when his mother and grandmother decided he should study piano with Antoinette Rich, the leader of an all-female symphony orchestra in Chicago. Rich was struck by the youngster's perfect pitch, which she discovered when DeJohnette performed on the kazoo. Becoming proficient on the instrument at an early age, DeJohnette was only five years old when he played the kazoo on stage with T-Bone Walker at a Chicago jazz club called the Persian. The kazoo, however, remained secondary to his classical training, which was continued under his next teacher, Viola Burns. Though he studied the piano for ten years, DeJohnette lost interest in early adolescence.

### Great Moments in Chicago

DeJohnette returned to the piano as a high schooler, when he heard Fats Domino play his classic song, "Blueberry Hill." Though he began taking drum lessons at the age of 13 in order to join the high school band, he continued to pound out 1950s hits on the piano at home. From 1957 to 1965, he exhibited his talents as a pianist in various jazz bands around Chicago. "At that time you didn't have to come to New York City because there was so much music in Chicago," DeJohnette recalled to Stern. "There used to be jams going on all the time. . . . There were so many great musicians in Chicago—the scene was really happening."

Also during this time, the musician began taking drums seriously, and in studying other percussionists, he found his greatest inspiration in Max Roach, whom DeJohnette felt was a complete musician. He also took courses at the American Conservatory of Music, played avant-garde gigs, performed with the Association for the Advancement of Creative Musicians (AACM) Big Band, and discovered his social consciousness when he was prohibited from fraternizing with the white people in the piano bars where he played on the North Side.

But DeJohnette also had some stellar moments in Chicago. "The biggest thrill I got when I was playing in Chicago was the time Coltrane came to town," he told Stern. "There were many beacons, but in jazz none shone so brightly as John Coltrane. . . . His music was a projection of love and peace; it was medicinal; it was a healing force." DeJohnette became Coltrane's drummer in 1962, but he felt he had exhausted all of his opportunities in Chicago; he left for New York City in April of 1956 upon the encouragement of his first wife, Deatra.

That same year, DeJohnette joined Charles Lloyd, whose group was the first jazz band to play the Fillmore. A member of one of the most popular jazz groups of the late 1960s, DeJohnette stayed with Lloyd until 1969, when he recorded *Bitches Brew* with Miles Davis. He joined Davis in 1970, and DeJohnette's reputation burgeoned as one of the most highly respected of world-class drummers with the recording *Live-Evil.*

## Jazz With a Pop Appeal

After his stint with Davis, which ended in 1971, DeJohnette began a series of groups made up of like-minded musicians. "I call what I do 'multidirectional music,'" he explained to Jeff Levenson in *Down Beat,* noting the eclectic approach that he evolved, which had a pop appeal but still qualified as good jazz. Although the group Compost was formed in 1972 with some friends, DeJohnette confessed to Howard Mandel in *Down Beat* that the music was too cerebral and experimental to be commercially successful.

The musician's next efforts fared better. During the late 1970s to the early 1980s, he formed Directions with Alex Foster, Mike Richards, and John Abercrombie, and the New Directions, featuring Lester Bowie, Eddie Gomez, and Abercrombie. In addition, he made recordings under the ECM label as a leader, beginning in 1976. With the formation of the ensemble Special Edition and the subsequent release of *Album Album* in 1985, DeJohnette found his greatest response. "Of course," he told Mandel, "[Saxophonist] Arthur Blythe was hitting then, and David Murray was hitting—they were both in the band—and the World Saxophone Quartet was hitting, and there was a play called *Zoot Suit* on Broadway, and my tune "Zoot Suite" on the record—which is also on *Album Album. . . .* The timing of that first record was just right."

Over the years, the make-up of Special Edition varied, but the prestige of the group, led by the man chosen top drummer in seven consecutive *Down Beat* readers polls, was fixed with the albums *Irresistible Forces, Audio Visualscapes,* and 1992's *Earth Walk.* "Special Edition hones the venerable dialectic of group over individual, sounding grand and expansive, but still lean and mean," declared critic Fred Bouchard in *Down Beat. People* contributor Eric Levin stated that DeJohnette and Special Edition deliver "thrilling virtuosity and freshness, a tempestuous ride across the frontiers of jazz-rock fusion, where the terrain is by turns slippery and sinister, eerily beautiful, sparkling and convoluted."

## Penned *The Art of Inspiration*

The success of the Special Edition albums prompted DeJohnette to keep the format of assembling highly talented musicians, and in 1990 he recorded *Parallel Realities,* a decision that was not without some risk.

Josef Woodard expounded in a *Down Beat* review that "all-star outings can be thrilling blowing sessions. They can also be stillborn by virtue of crossed signals, battling humility (or hubris), or a confused sense of direction. The mating of DeJohnette, [Pat] Metheny, and [Herbie] Hancock turns out to be something altogether different, a highly original project in which the elements come together in a marvel of empathy."

In spite of his many musical projects, DeJohnette found time to author *The Art of Improvisation* in 1981. The multifaceted, award-winning musician has made a home near Woodstock, New York, with his second wife Lydia Ann Herman—whom he married August 4, 1968—and his daughters, Farah, Minya, and Erica. He has found additional creative inspiration in this wooded setting to make his music both aesthetically pleasing and consciousness-raising.

"That's what's so fascinating about jazz," he remarked to Levenson. "It's that you have individualism within the collective context, but it works democratically. We've got to get to the point where money is not the issue, but substance is. Everything now is based on dollars, not on compassion and caring. That's what we really need. We've got to get decent housing for people, get homeless people off the streets. . . . The demise of certain things always opens the doors to other things. There are alternatives coming. It's not as bleak as it seems. People want to hold onto things, to musical things, to bebop, to the mainstream, to whatever. We have to be able to be renewed. We have to keep renewing ourselves. When stuff gets too safe and comfortable, that's when it falls apart. We ought to come up with alternative ways of thinking."

# Selected discography

*The Jack DeJohnette Complex*, Milestone, 1968.
*Complex*, Milestone.
*Have You Heard?*, Milestone, 1970.
*Cosmic Chicken*, Prestige, 1974.
*Sorcery*, Prestige, 1974.
*Untitled*, ECM, 1976.
*Pictures*, ECM, 1976.
*New Rags*, ECM, 1977.
*New Directions*, ECM, 1978.
*New Directions in Europe*, ECM, 1979.
*Special Edition*, ECM, 1980.
*Tin Can Alley*, ECM, 1980.
*Inflation Blues*, ECM, 1982.
*The Jack DeJohnette Piano Album*, 1985.
*Album Album*, ECM, 1985.
*Irresistible Forces*, MCA/Impulse, 1987.
*Audio Visualscapes*, MCA/Impulse.
*Parallel Realities*, MCA, 1990.

## With Keith Jarrett

*Changes*, ECM.
*Standards Vol. 2*, ECM.
*Standards Vol. 1*, ECM.
*Rita and Daitya*, ECM.

## With Charles Lloyd

*Soundtrack*, Atlantic.
*Journey Within*, Atlantic.
*In the Soviet Union*, Atlantic.
*In Europe*, Atlantic.
*Flowering of the Original Quartet*, Atlantic.
*Love In*, Atlantic.
*Dream Weaver*, Atlantic.
*Best Of*, Atlantic.
*Forest Flower*, Atlantic.

## With John Abercrombie

*Timeless*, ECM.
*Gateway One*, ECM.
*Gateway Two*, ECM.
*Night*, ECM.

## With Miles Davis

*Live-Evil*, Columbia, 1970.
*Live at the Fillmore*, Columbia, 1970.
*Bitches Brew*, Columbia, 1970.
*In a Silent Way*, Columbia.

## Other

(With Pat Metheny/Ornette Coleman) *Song X*, Geffen.
(With Metheny) *80/81*, ECM.
(With Dave Holland) *Triplicate*, ECM.
(With Lester Bowie) *Zebra*, MCA, 1989.
(With Eliane Elias) *Cross Currents*, Denon.
(With Tommy Smith) *Step by Step*, Blue Note.
(With Ralph Towner) *Batik*, ECM.
(With Collin Walcott) *Cloud Dance*, ECM.
(With George Adams) *Sound Suggestions*, ECM.
(With JoAnne Brackeen) *Keyed In*, Columbia.
(With Brackeen) *Ancient Dynasty*, Columbia.
(With McCoy Tyner) *Supertrios*, Milestone.
(With Miroslav Vitous) *Mountain in the Clouds*, Atlantic.
(With Terje Rypdal and Vitous) *To Be Continued*, ECM.
(With Rypdal and Vitous) *Trio*, ECM.
(With Jan Garbarek) *Places*, ECM.
(With Kenny Wheeler) *GNU High*, ECM.
(With Wheeler) *Deer Wan*, ECM.
(With Gary Peacock) *Tales of Another*, ECM.
(With Richie Beirach) *ELM*, ECM.
(With Bill Evans) *At the Montreux Jazz Festival*, Verve.
(With Sonny Rollins) *Reel Life*, Milestone.
(With Special Edition), *Earth Walk*, Blue Note, 1992.

# Sources

*Audio,* December 1989; May 1990.

*Down Beat,* November 2, 1978; May 1981; August 1987; September 1987; February 1988; March 1988; November 1988; January 1989; December 1989; May 1990; March 1992.

*High Fidelity,* March 1988.

*People,* October 31, 1988.

*Rolling Stone,* September 18, 1980.

*Stereo Review,* August 1987; February 1989; September 1989; December 1989.

*Variety,* June 17, 1987.

*—Marjorie Burgess*

# De La Soul

---

**Rap trio**

---

De La Soul's pioneering sound, incorporating sampled children's records and TV themes, humorous sketches, and thoughtful lyrics, challenged the rap status quo, which until De La Soul's appearance had been dominated by machismo, serious social commentary, and heavy beats. This new trio's approach, tagged by critics as psychedelic, represented one of the first forays into rap and hip-hop by middle-class black artists.

Formed in 1985 in Amityville, Long Island, New York, De La Soul consists of Posdnuos (Kelvin Mercer), Trugoy the Dove (David Jolicoeur), and Baby Huey Maseo, also known as Pasemaster Mase (Vincent Mason, Jr.). The three chose their stage names from "in" jokes and references; "Trugoy" is "yogurt," Jolicoeur's favorite food, spelled backwards, and "Posdnuos" is a reversal of Mercer's former nickname as a DJ.

The three met in high school and after playing in various groups began putting together a rap act distinguished by an offbeat selection of beats and samples and the three friends' personal slang. De La Soul

presented their first demo, "Plug Tunin'," to local rap star Prince Paul (Paul Houston) of the band Stetsasonic. Houston was impressed enough to play the tape for a number of DJ's and other music figures, and De La Soul became the unsigned sensation of the New York rap scene. The band decided to sign with Tommy Boy Records in 1988.

## Debut Album a Hit

The trio's debut album, *Three Feet High and Rising,* produced by Prince Paul and featuring guest turns by rappers the Jungle Brothers and Q-Tip from A Tribe Called Quest, hit the stores in 1989. It was a smash, and introduced a new look to the rap world: the psychedelic style of The D.A.I.S.Y. Age, which stands for "Da Inner Sound, Y'all." The flowers that adorned the album's cover led many listeners to pigeonhole De La Soul as hippies. But, as Trugoy told *New York*'s Matthew Weingarden, the band refused the label from the start: "We don't mind if people say, 'You *remind* us of the hippie days, of sixties things,' because there is some of that in our music. But we're not trying for that look— we're just being us."

Compared with many other late-1980s pop artists under the sway of 1960s and 1970s culture, De La Soul used their influences creatively and often subversively. Their samples frequently came from obscure sources like cartoons, game shows, and non-rock pop records—some of which came from their parents' collections—as well as familiar rhythm-and-blues, funk, and rock tunes. "The Magic Number," one of several popular tracks from *Three Feet High,* sampled a 1970s educational cartoon about the number three, turning the refrain into an anthem for De La Soul's three members.

Indeed, anyone who accused De La Soul of trendiness and image obsession only had to listen to "Take it Off," nearly two minutes of the group listing various trendy articles that their listeners should cast aside. "We don't wish to offend people with our suggestions of taking off these certain items we've named (which are capitalizing on fads)," declared the album's liner notes, "BUT if you're offended then take it off." Despite this celebration of individuality, the group's flowerpower look became one of the fashion markers of the late eighties.

## Loved by Reviewers

Reviewers of the album were almost as enthusiastic as the group's fans. *Cosmopolitan*'s Michael Segell called *Three Feet High* not only funny but "funky, sexy, literate, romantic, and eminently groovable. . . . Whereas rap's more muscular shock troops preach a kind of urban guerilla warfare, De La Soul is psychedelic sugar and spice, with some safe sex thrown in. . . . Psychedelic may be too thin a word for a prankster trio with the bold idea of tacking sixties flower power onto late-eighties angst. Whatever it is, however they do it, it works." According to Alan Light of *Rolling Stone, Three Feet High* "represented the triumphant coming of age of middle-class, black suburban children of the Seventies."

On a less triumphant note, the first album brought about a $ 1.7 million lawsuit by former members of the pop band the Turtles, who wrote some of the music sampled on *Three Feet High* and hadn't been approached for permission to use it. Though the issue was settled out of court in 1990 for an undisclosed sum, De La Soul had to be much more careful about getting permission for everything they sampled. For a time, the band members admitted, it seemed that everyone was listening to their records carefully for signs of unacknowledged sampling.

## Changed Thematic Direction

De La Soul's popularity extended to many audiences rap didn't usually reach, particularly white college students, who, some speculated, found the D.A.I.S.Y. sound less threatening than the violent intensity of N.W.A. or the political force of Public Enemy. The "sugar and spice" and "suburban" qualities noted by Segell and Light may well have translated into accusations of softness to De La Soul, who decided to ditch the D.A.I.S.Y. image in favor of a tougher stance. Their second album made no bones about the change; released in 1991, it was titled *De La Soul is Dead.*

The cover showed an overturned pot of daisies, and the

contents of the album, while still making liberal use of off-the-wall humor and unusual samples, showed an increased seriousness. While the first album used a game-show format, the second was arranged like a read-along recording with tones signaling the turn of a page. Among the more disconcerting lessons in this new storybook were drug addiction, addressed in "My Brother's a Basehead," a bonus track on the CD based on Posdnuos's personal experience, and incest, illustrated by "Millie Pulled a Pistol on Santa," the tale of a young girl sexually abused by her social-worker father, who also works as a department store Santa Claus. The unusual style and language of De La Soul create a different effect here from the upbeat humor of their debut.

Though the second record featured plenty of jokes and sketches, critics noticed and, for the most part, approved of the band's new attitude. *Billboard* commented that *De La Soul is Dead* "finds the rap group in a darker, albeit still experimental mood. . . . [The] trio swings its way through its menu of children's-record samples and off-kilter beats with brio. . . . [The] Outfit may not be quite at [the] top of its game, but major sales are still a natural." According to *Musician,* the album "isn't simply about the Soulsters' aversion to image; it's about learning to deal with reality—whether that's things not being the way they seem . . . or not being seen for who you are. . . . On that front, De La Soul is all the way live." *People*'s David Hiltbrand called the record "a boisterous package of playful, clever, suburban rap."

*Village Voice* critic Nelson George, however, saw the trio's new direction as a surrender to rap-world "ghettocentricity," the tendency to make the ghetto the center of one's thinking. "In order to prove their manhood to challengers who thought them soft (in all ghettocentric meanings of the word) and maybe even to themselves," George wrote, "De La Soul have opted for a semimacho stance at odds with their landmark introduction." Posdnuos suggested to *Rolling Stone* that the group was struggling with just these issues. "I feel like we're showing something else to the people we

introduced to a whole new sound on the first album. Like a lot of the white kids—we're bringing them to more of a street level this time." Mase's explanation emphasized the band's attempt to find a middle passage between hard rap and unthreatening pop: "We wanted to show the one side that, yo, it ain't gotta be a rough beat all the time. And let the other side know there is a rough side." De La Soul seemed committed, in any case, to following its own path. After a critically acclaimed and enormously popular debut, the three young rap artists faced the task of staying vital and original in a business that encourages pigeonholing and duplication of successful formulas. As Posdnuos remarked to Weingarden, "Everything is coming from within—our own thoughts, not the guidance of others."

## Selected discography

*Three Feet High and Rising* (includes "The Magic Number," "Take it Off," and "Plug Tunin'"), Tommy Boy, 1989.
*De La Soul is Dead* (includes "My Brother's a Basehead" and "Millie Pulled a Pistol on Santa"), Tommy Boy, 1991.

## Sources

### Periodicals

*Billboard,* June 1, 1991.
*Cosmopolitan,* June 1989.
*Musician,* July 1991.
*New York,* March 27, 1989.
*People,* May 13, 1991.
*Rolling Stone,* April 18, 1991.
*Village Voice,* May 21, 1991.

### Other

*Three Feet High and Rising* CD liner notes, Tommy Boy, 1989.

—Simon Glickman

# Little Jimmy Dickens

---

**Singer, guitarist**

---

**S**tanding just under five feet tall and performing with an outsized guitar, Little Jimmy Dickens has been a Grand Ole Opry regular since 1948. Well past the age when most people retire, Dickens was still going strong in the early 1990s as a host and featured performer on the Opry and is a special favorite of the many senior citizens peppering a typical Opry audience. Although his long career includes a string of country hits released throughout the 1940s and 1950s—and even a major crossover pop hit—Dickens contents himself with serving as a jovial, genial reminder of the Opry's colorful past.

Born in rural Bolt, West Virginia, on December 19, 1920, Dickens was the youngest of 13 children; he has often joked about being the "runt of the litter," especially since he grew no taller than 4'11". He was raised on a farm and, like many rural folk, taught himself to play the guitar for entertainment. "As a child I wanted to be a professional entertainer, so I worked at it. I picked up what I could from my mother and my uncle—when they'd let me have the guitar," he recalled to Kyle Cantrell in the album liner notes to *Straight . . . From the Heart, 1949-55*. Dickens learned to play and sing what he heard on the radio—the country, western, and string band music of the Appalachian Mountain region.

### The Famous WJLS Rooster

The young Dickens earned good grades in high school, where he became interested in acting and was even afforded the opportunity to audition for a role in a Broadway play. "In high school, I was very active in dramatics and public speaking, and did a lot of high school plays and so forth," he related to Cantrell. After graduating, Dickens enrolled at the University of West Virginia. He stayed there only briefly, however, because the prospects looked promising for a career in music. Some years shy of 20, he won his first professional singing job with station WJLS in Beckley, West Virginia. There, calling himself "Jimmy the Kid," he worked with Johnny Bailes and His Happy Valley Boys, opening the morning show with his famous rooster crow. The group moved to the slightly larger WMNN in Fairmont before disbanding during World War II.

The mid-1940s found Dickens working as a solo act for large stations in the Midwest. He moved from WING in Dayton, Ohio, to WLW in Cincinnati, and until 1948 he worked for WKNX in Saginaw, Michigan. At the latter station he met country giant Roy Acuff, who invited him to make a guest appearance on the Grand Ole Opry.

Dickens hit Nashville, Tennessee, in 1948 without a recording contract, a virtual unknown outside the Mid-

Born James Cecil Dickens, December 19, 1920, in Bolt, WV; son of a farmer; wife, Ernestine, is deceased; children: Pamela Jean. *Education:* Attended University of West Virginia.

Country singer, guitarist, and songwriter, 1943—. As Jimmy the Kid, sang on several radio shows in West Virginia, including WJLS in Beckley and WMNN in Fairmont. Moved to the Midwest in the mid-1940s; appeared on WKNX, Saginaw, MI; WING, Dayton, OH; and WLW, Cincinnati, OH. Host and performer on the Grand Ole Opry, 1948—. Signed with Columbia Records, c. 1947; released first hit, "Take an Old Cold Tater," in 1949. Has made numerous guest appearances on television programs, including *The Tonight Show, Hee Haw,* and *The Jimmy Dean Show.*

**Selected awards:** Inducted into the Country Music Hall of Fame, 1983.

**Addresses:** *Record company*—Rounder Records, One Camp St., Cambridge, MA 02140.

western cities where he had been working during the war. Nevertheless, he was an instant hit with the Opry audience and brought down the house. Two weeks later, the Opry management invited him back as a regular. Columbia Records signed him shortly thereafter, and he began releasing what would become a long string of hits.

### More Than Just a Novelty Singer

While not a prolific songwriter himself, Dickens chose material that reflected his hillbilly upbringing and diminutive stature. In 1949 he had his first Top Ten country hit with "Take an Old Cold Tater." He followed this success with other, similar numbers: "Country Boy," "A-Sleeping at the Foot of the Bed," "Hillbilly Fever," "Out Behind the Barn," and "I Got a Hole in My Pocket." His repertoire of charted hits also included the usual love and heartbreak songs, including two he wrote himself, "Sea of Broken Dreams" and "I Sure Would Like to Sit a Spell With You."

Dickens made his biggest mark as a singer of loud and sometimes silly novelty songs. These became a staple of his Opry performance and the cornerstone of the show he took on tour around the world. He also made guest appearances on a number of television pro-

grams, including the *Tonight Show, Hee Haw,* and *The Jimmy Dean Show.*

According to Bill C. Malone in *Country Music U.S.A.,* however, Dickens was more than a mere novelty singer. "Dickens' voice conveyed great emotional strength (a trait displayed by many West Virginia singers) and he possessed probably the most pronounced vibrato in country music," Malone noted. "No one has ever been a better performer of 'heart' songs or of honky-tonk weepers. Dickens' soulful intensity—displayed on such songs as 'Take Me As I Am,' 'We Could,' 'Just When I Needed You,' and 'What About You'—made him a much-admired entertainer among his singing contemporaries and contributed to his success of jukeboxes all over the nation."

### Inducted Into Country Music Hall of Fame

Few country singers survived the advent of rock and roll without somehow modifying their acts. Just as Dickens seemed about to fade into obscurity in 1965, he released a raucous novelty tune, "May the Bird of Paradise Fly up Your Nose." The song—a string of humorous curses similar to the title—became an enormous hit, topping both the country and pop charts. After 13 years as a country headliner, and approaching age 40, Dickens found himself in greater demand than ever. He even quit the Opry for a time in order to stay on the road for longer periods.

By 1979 Dickens was back with the Opry and in 1983 he was inducted into the Country Music Hall of Fame. With his flashy attire and down-home patter, he harkens back to the Opry's glory years of the 1940s, when radio reigned supreme and each performer had a distinct personality. As Melvin Shestack put it in *The Country Music Encyclopedia,* "Everybody who is interested in country music has heard of Little Jimmy Dickens." Shestack concluded: "His name undoubtedly draws old-timey fans in rural areas who still play his happy novelty numbers. He is, as they say, a credit to country music."

## Selected discography

*Little Jimmy Dickens,* Columbia.
*Big Songs,* Columbia.
*Behind the Barn,* Columbia.
*Best of Little Jimmy Dickens,* Harmony.
*Old Country Church,* Harmony.
*Ain't It Fun?,* Harmony.
*Little Jimmy Dickens Sings,* Decca.
*Big Man in Music,* Columbia.

*May the Bird of Paradise,* Columbia.

*Little Jimmy Dickens* (anthology, 1949-60), Columbia Historic
    Editions.

*Straight . . . From the Heart, 1949-55,* Rounder Records, 1990.

## Sources

### Books

*The Illustrated Encyclopedia of Country Music,* Harmony, 1977.

Malone, Bill C., *Country Music U.S.A.,* revised edition, University
    of Texas Press, 1985.

Shestack, Melvin, *The Country Music Encyclopedia,* Crowell,
    1974.

Stambler, Irwin and Grelun Landon, *The Encyclopedia of Folk,
    Country, and Western Music,* St. Martin's, 1969.

### Periodicals

*Country Music,* March/April 1990.

Other sources include album liner notes to *Straight . . . From the
Heart,* Rounder Records, 1990.

*—Anne Janette Johnson*

# Dr. John

Pianist, singer

**Pianist, singer**

A prolific session recorder dating back to his mid-teens, Dr. John has also become a headliner in his own right. Exposed to musicians by working in his father's appliance and music store and later performing in sessions with such New Orleans musical greats as Professor Longhair, Frankie Ford, and Joe Tex, Dr. John is considered one of the forerunners of a distinctly New Orleans brand of rhythm and blues, which he described to Jay Cocks in *Time* as "Afro-Caribbean, Afro-Cuban and Mardi Gras Indian" combined with "natural street rhythms." In fact, some point to him as one of the reasons for the late twentieth-century resurgence of interest in this musical style.

Born Malcolm Rebennack, Jr., in the middle-class third ward of New Orleans, Dr. John soon entered the world of show business when his fashion model mother got his face on Ivory Soap boxes. As a youngster he was fond of hanging around in his father's appliance/music store. "Pop's store catered to a lot of youngsters from Dillard University, which was a very hip black school," the musician recalled in *Melody Maker*. "The kids were listening to bebop and other modern jazz, also very much to gut-bucket blues; stuff by Memphis Minnie, Champion Jack Dupree, Big Bill and people like that." The young John also followed his father around to local clubs where the older Rebennack repaired sound systems. It was on one of these trips that John met Professor Longhair, whose boogie-woogie, blues, jazz, and New Orleans-style music would have a profound effect on the musician. The two artists, in fact, would eventually develop a close relationship; in later years, Dr. John referred to Longhair as a father figure.

## Recorded First Album

Dr. John also frequented the studio of Cosimo Matassa of J&M Music, which, in the early 1950s, was the only recording studio in New Orleans. At first he would wait there until the studio had closed and then sneak into shows where his idols, including Charles Brown, Amos Milburn and Ray Charles, were playing. At the age of 14, the musician landed a regular job playing guitar with Leonard James' band. Dr. John remembered in *Down Beat,* "We used to work a lot of clubs and backed up about five or six local singers, like Jerry Byrne and Frankie Ford. At that time we had the only band in town that could read [music], and we picked up a lot of work backing up touring acts. The rhythm section couldn't read, but all the horn players could read good, so we could cut the shows."

Soon hired by Ace Records where he worked illegally in studio sessions, Dr. John made an album of instrumental numbers, but only one single was released, "Storm

## For the Record. . .

Born Malcolm Rebennack, Jr., in 1941, in New Orleans, LA; son of Malcolm (an appliance salesman) and Dorothy (a fashion model) Rebennack.

Model for Ivory Soap boxes as a child; session work with Professor Longhair, Frankie Ford, and Joe Tex, c. 1955; joined black artists' cooperative AFO (All For One) Records; played with the Zu Zu Band, Drits and Dravy, and Morgus and the Three Ghouls; producer and session arranger for Lee Allen, Red Tyler, and Earl Palmer, c. 1960; moved to Los Angeles, CA, and became a session regular, c. 1965; played under name Dr. John Creaux the Night Tripper, 1968; regular performer at the New Orleans Jazz Heritage Festival; worked in band Triumvirate, 1973; appeared in motion pictures, including *The Last Waltz*, 1978, and in television shows, including *Second City*; has written commercials for Popeye's Chicken, Tic Tacs, and Wendy's Hamburgers; toured with funk group the Louisiana Luminoids.

**Addresses:** *Record company*—Warner Bros. Records, 3300 Warner Blvd., Burbank, CA 91510.

---

Warning." The song became a sort of cult hit in 1958, and soon after, Dr. John got together with Frankie Ford and Jerry Byrne, forming the group Morgus and the Three Ghouls for a novelty recording titled *Morgus the Magnificent.* In 1959, the musician began working with several labels, including Ric and Ronn Records, Spinnet Records, and Instant Records. He also recorded, with Professor Longhair, the classic song "Go to Mardi Gras."

Though still in his teens, Dr. John had already been accepted by the established New Orleans musical clique. "Music was the only thing I was interested in," he noted in *Melody Maker.* "I left school very early to travel with road bands, and I guess I'd already made up my mind to make my living from music. To tell you the truth, it was one of those unusual incidents that decided me quite suddenly: I saw snow one day in New Orleans and resolved to quit school and go on the road and see the world, 'cos I never saw snow before."

### Joined AFO Records

At home in New Orleans, Dr. John also started mixing with such musicians as Papoose, Jesse Hill, and Alvin Robinson, learning creole rituals and voodoo. When saxophonist Harold Battiste and trumpeter Melvin Lastie founded All For One (AFO) Records, a musician's

collective, Dr. John joined. He continued to do prolific studio work until 1962, when under-the-table dates began being policed by the musician's union. "They had a union stoppage of all the sessions in [1963]," John remarked in *Down Beat,* "and when that happened, AFO Records pulled out of New Orleans and went to [Los Angeles].

"That's when we really got in a lot of trouble, because we kept on doing sessions, and the union had already told me I couldn't do any recordings for the people I worked for. I kept getting caught, then I'd lie to them and get in more trouble because I lied. One good thing came of it, though—a lot of new studios opened. But the union would find out the addresses and they'd come in and bust them all. You'd think it was a police bust the way they would operate."

After he was kicked out of the union, Dr. John continued to pick up small jobs at strip shows and with local bands in New Orleans, eventually moving to Los Angeles, where he would work with musicians like the Allman Brothers and Frank Zappa. He soon found a niche there in a partnership with Battiste, who was working with Sonny Bono. In 1968, Dr. John took a risk that brought him out of the anonymity of session work and backup bands. He and Ronnie Barron planned to come out with elaborate creole personas for a one-shot performance and album, but Barron dropped out, leaving Dr. John to introduce Dr. John Creaux the Night Tripper—a name soon reduced to Dr. John—on his own. In *Down Beat* Larry Birnbaum described the stage act as "a heavy-lidded, gravel-throated chanter. . . . Costumed in sequined robe, strings of beads, and a plumed snakeskin hat, the hulking, bearded Dr. John, also known as the Night Tripper, was the self-styled voodoo shaman of the psychedelic generation, a spell-casting, snakedancing, patois-sprouting mystery man whose cajun conceptualism was concocted, seemingly, of two parts Creole gumbo, one part medicinal herbs, and one part Hollywood snake oil."

The album that resulted, *Gris-Gris,* featured some of the finest New Orleans musicians of the time. "All these cats were really fluent, creative players, and we had a lot of vocalists too," Dr. John recalled to Birnbaum. "I think we had as many people from New Orleans in the [Los Angeles] area at that time as you could have picked up in the studio in New Orleans." The record, nonetheless, was kept off the shelves for a few years until a reluctant Atco—a subsidiary of Atlantic Records—finally released it. *Gris-Gris* soon picked up a cult following, and the musician toured under his Dr. John persona for a few years. He also won a following among rock and roll fans with such LPs as his most famous, a 1973 collaboration with Allen Toussaint titled

*In the Right Place.* Other albums featured rock heavy-weights Mick Jagger and Eric Clapton.

### Won Increased Media Exposure

In the 1980s, John enjoyed television, radio, and movie exposure. He recorded several albums while living in New York City and also wrote some commercial jingles for Popeye's Chicken, TicTacs candy, and Wendy's Hamburgers. He has continued to perform at jazz festivals around the country, spreading his distinctly New Orleans style of music. A long proponent of the genre, Dr. John commented in *Melody Maker* that Louisiana rhythm and blues "will survive as long as there are guys that take some real interest in preserving not only the form and structure but this special quality. It's like if there's one guy that's doing it right, that is better than a hundred of them doing it wrong."

In 1989 John departed from his regular mode of recording by releasing *In a Sentimental Mood,* a compilation of ballads that won critical and popular success. Jeff Hannusch noted in *Rolling Stone* that "while tunes like 'My Buddy,' 'In a Sentimental Mood' and 'Candy' might seem to have come off a set list at a piano bar, Dr. John manages to keep from dragging, and the swirling string section makes things sound especially sweet." Another album, entitled *Bluesiana Triangle* and recorded in 1990 with fellow New Orleans bluesmen Art Blakey and David "Fathead" Newman, won Dr. John further acclaim. *Down Beat*'s Larry Birnbaum declared the LP "an extraordinary meeting of musical minds—a loose, spontaneous interaction among three mature masters . . . that showcases each of their strengths in an unaccustomed context."

Branching out into other media, Dr. John also released a video in 1990 entitled *Dr. John Teaches New Orleans Piano, Vols. I and II.* The tapes are aimed at intermediate-level piano players and explain the techniques of famous New Orleans musicians, including Longhair, Toussaint, Fats Domino, and James Booker. A reviewer in *People* found that "Dr. John cuts a colorful figure at the baby grand, singing, playing and dispensing musical wisdom" and concluded that the video "offers a rollicking two hours of fun."

At the end of 1991 Dr. John was scheduled to release yet another album. Never aspiring to superstar status in the music world, he continues to perform his unique type of music. "Do what is true to yourself," the musician commented in *Melody Maker.* About his long career, Dr. John declared: "If you're sincere about music I think it's worth all the hassles to stick to it."

## Selected discography

(With others) *Gris-Gris,* Atco, 1968.
*Babylon,* Atco, 1969.
*Remedies,* Atco, 1970.
*The Sun, Moon & Herbs,* Atco, 1971.
*Dr. John's Gumbo,* Atco, 1972.
(With Allen Toussaint) *In the Right Place,* Atco, 1973.
*Desitively Bonnaroo,* Atco, 1974.
*Cut Me While I'm Hot,* DJM, 1975.
*Hollywood Be Thy Name,* United Artists, 1976.
*City Lights,* Horizon, 1978.
*Tango Palace,* Horizon, 1979.
*Dr. John Plays Mac Rebennack,* Clean Cuts, 1981.
*In a Sentimental Mood,* Warner Bros., 1989.
(With Art Blakey and David "Fathead" Newman) *Bluesiana Triangle,* Windham Hill Jazz, 1990.
*Goin' Back to New Orleans,* 1992.
*One Night Late,* Karate Records.
*Dr. John,* Springboard.
*Love Potion,* Accord Records.

Contributor to the Dirty Dozen Brass Band album *Voodoo,* Columbia, 1989; contributed "Deal" to the Grateful Dead tribute album *Deadicated,* Arista Records, 1991.

### Other

*Dr. John Teaches New Orleans Piano, Vols. I and II* (video), Homespun, 1990.

## Sources

Down Beat, September 1982; December 1985; August 1990; October 1991.
*Melody Maker,* July 5, 1980.
*People,* May 29, 1989; October 15, 1990.
*Rolling Stone,* April 20, 1989; June 29, 1989; November 1, 1990.
*Time,* July 26, 1982.

—Nancy Rampson

# Holly Dunn

**Singer, songwriter**

Holly Dunn has combined versatility and hard work to become a popular country singer. A musician who writes or co-writes her hit songs, she also oversees production of her records and videos and performs some two hundred live shows each year. It is no wonder, then, that the trim, long-haired beauty has won several of country music's most prestigious awards and in 1989 was named a regular cast member of the Grand Ole Opry.

Dunn's music is considered typical of "country-fried feminism," a tougher approach to lyrics that removes women from traditional victim roles. Her songs—most notably "You Really Had Me Going" and "Maybe I Mean Yes"—fairly shine with self-respect and self-determination. This theme is hardly surprising for a woman who has engineered a top-level career for herself and has written songs for others as well. Dunn commented to the *Associated Press,* "I'm the only one, as far as I know on the female side, who writes, produces and sings the material. I think this gives me a real legitimacy, a genuineness. I'm not just up there standing where they tell me to stand, singing what they tell me to sing. I 'feel' what I do."

Holly Dunn was born and raised in San Antonio, Texas, the daughter of a minister. She had a happy childhood in a large family and was particularly close to her father. While growing up, she enjoyed many different types of music. Her father was a friend of country singer Sonny James, so as a child, Dunn was often allowed backstage at country concerts to meet the stars. On the other hand, she also loved pop music, especially the Beatles, James Taylor, Carole King, and Barbra Streisand.

### Headed for Nashville

"I've always been a writer of some kind," Dunn remarked in the *Arizona Republic.* "Even back when I was just a little kid, like 7 years old, I was writing, little journal kinds of things. By the time I was in high school, my proficiency on guitar was good, and I started writing songs." Dunn also enjoyed singing, and as a teenager she won a spot with the Freedom Folk Singers, a group that represented Texas at the White House bicentennial celebrations in 1976. During her college years at a small Christian university in Texas, she continued to perform folk and country music, and after graduating, she headed straight for Nashville, Tennessee.

During her first year in Nashville, Dunn worked as a clerk in a bookstore and then as a travel agent while trying to land a job in the music industry. Before long she earned a songwriting contract with CBS Records, and she spent nearly four years writing hits for such entertainers as Louise Mandrell, Terri Gibbs, Marie Osmond, and the Whites. Though she was successful as a writer, Dunn longed to perform her own songs. In 1985 she was offered a contract with MTM Records and released her first album, *Holly Dunn*.

## Frugal on the Road

Even before the album was finished, MTM released a Dunn single, "Daddy's Hands." A touching memoir of a child's loving relationship with her father, "Daddy's Hands" became a Number One country hit and has since become a country classic. Dunn earned her first Grammy Award nomination for the work, and she was also named top new female vocalist by the Academy of Country Music. The following year she earned the prestigious Horizon Award—given to a newcomer showing the most promise of a stellar career—from the Country Music Association.

Though Dunn is often referred to as an overnight success, her accomplishments were won with hard work and sacrifice. Since she was recording with a small label—which has since folded—Dunn traveled and performed without many of the perks big country stars receive, including deluxe touring buses and expensive costumes. For more than a year Dunn and her band traveled to gigs in a Toyota van pulling a U-Haul trailer. A string of country hits later, she was still touring in a 27-

foot recreation vehicle with the trailer attached. She sewed sequins on her costumes and hand painted them to enhance her appearance onstage, and she did her share of late-night driving.

"It's pretty embarrassing to pull into a place where you're opening for [singer] George Strait or somebody down in Texas and have his four buses and all his crew and high-dollar production there, and you roll in looking like the Beverly Hillbillies in your RV," Dunn recalled in the *Chicago Tribune*. "All we needed was Granny in a rocker on top." Dunn added, however, that she made the decision to tour in this manner herself. "I actually made money that year, and I talked to other artists at that level who weren't making anything," she said.

Dunn's frugality on the road and her intelligence in the studio helped her to sustain a career that might well have faltered. The artist told the *Chicago Tribune* that her momentum sagged after her initial success with "Daddy's Hands" and "Only When I Love." "I felt there was a whole pack of us [young country vocalists] starting out more or less together," Dunn explained, "and I kind of pulled ahead there for awhile. But after the Horizon Award, those people who had been kind of behind me passed me up, and that was frustrating."

## A Regular on the Grand Ole Opry

Dunn struggled along with MTM Records until 1989. Just before MTM folded, she moved to Warner Bros., a larger label that was able to market her wares more effectively; she has consistently produced hits ever since. Also in 1989, she was named to the regular cast of the Grand Ole Opry, a significant honor for any country performer.

Dunn continues to write many of her own songs. She has a collaborator, her brother Chris Waters, who also helps oversee the production of her albums. With her strong voice, wholesome beauty, and catchy lyrics, Dunn seems destined for a fruitful career in Nashville. She knows what country fans want—basic, traditional tunes with perhaps a little kick to them—and she is glad to oblige. The singer remarked in the *Orlando Sentinel,* "The day-to-day lifestyles and emotions and values of American life are what country music is all about. Growing up in the heart of Americana, I learned from my parents about those lifestyles and emotions and values. And true country music is the best outlet for me to talk about what I know."

## Selected discography

*Holly Dunn,* MTM, 1985.
*Cornerstone,* MTM, 1986.
*Across the Rio Grande,* MTM, 1988.
*The Blue Rose of Texas,* Warner Bros., 1989.
*Heart Full of Love,* Warner Bros., 1990.
*Milestones,* Warner Bros., 1991.

## Sources

### Books

Vaughan, Andrew, *Who's Who in New Country Music,* St. Martin's, 1989.

### Periodicals

*Akron Beacon Journal,* October 2, 1989.
*Arizona Republic,* June 7, 1991.
*Associated Press* (wire report), September 14, 1990.
*Chicago Tribune,* August 20, 1989; October 26, 1989.
*Country America,* February 1991.
*Orlando Sentinel,* June 18, 1989.

*—Anne Janette Johnson*

# Electric Light Orchestra

**Rock band**

The Electric Light Orchestra, whose fusion of rock and classical sounds made it one of the most innovative groups to come out of the 1970s, had its origins in the mod-dadaist group the Move, one of England's more enigmatic and controversial bands of the late 1960s. It is difficult to imagine that such an unusual ensemble as the Move, infamous in Britain for wild stage antics that included smashing television sets and pianos, would give rise to the Electric Light Orchestra (also commonly known by the abbreviation ELO), a seemingly cultured pop orchestra that exerted a significant influence on contemporary music, with the use of strings, synthesizers, and exquisitely layered vocals.

The Move was a band in constant turmoil with personnel changes; some of their personality conflicts led to fistfights. The lack of cohesion showed in the group's music, the bulk of which has been hailed as imaginative by critics. Onstage violence and manic behavior were a creation of the group's manager, though leader Roy Hood was known for his own stage antics, a trait that

## For the Record. . .

Group formed in 1970 (some sources say 1971), in Birmingham, England, by active members of the English rock group the Move: **Bev Bevan** (drums; born November 25, 1946), **Jeff Lynne** (guitar, synthesizer, and lead vocals; born December 30, 1947, in Birmingham, England), **Rick Price** (bass), and **Roy Wood** (guitar and vocals); Price and Wood left band in 1972, were replaced by **Michael de Albuquerque** (bass), **Mike Edwards** (cello), **Wilf Gibson** (violin), **Richard Tandy** (guitar and keyboards; born March 26, 1948, in Birmingham, England), and **Colin Walker** (cello); Gibson and Walker left band in 1973, were replaced by **Mik Kaminski** (violin; born September 2, 1951, in Harrogate, England) and **Hugh McDowell** (cello; born July 31, 1953, in London, England); de Albuquerque left band in 1974, replaced by **Kelly Groucutt** (bass and vocals; born September 8, 1945, in Coseley, England); Edwards left band in 1974, replaced by **Melvyn Gale** (cello; born January 15, 1952, in London); Gale, Kaminski, and McDowell left band in 1977; band formally dissolved, 1986.

accompanied him into other projects. During the band's first four years of existence, the Move managed to record only two albums and were the focus of an ongoing legal dispute with the then-prime minister of England, Harold Wilson. Charged with character defamation, the band eventually lost the suit.

Though popular with the underground London music scene as a singles band, the Move went unrecognized in the United States until after they had disbanded. Before the group dissolved, however, after a long string of personnel changes had whittled the group down to Hood, drummer Bev Bevan, and newcomer Jeff Lynne, the Move issued their last (and possibly finest) album of new material, *Message from the Country,* in 1971. Contractual disputes eventually led to the Move's demise, but before the band was finished, the remaining trio recorded what would become ELO's first album, *No Answer.* A well-received disc, it yielded the English hit single "10538 Overture" and started the band members on a new path.

## Formed from Survivors of The Move

The Electric Light Orchestra was the brainchild of remaining Move members Lynne, Bevan, and Hood, who is credited with conceiving the idea of a fully electric rock band augmented by a classical string section. Where the Move had been a wild ensemble of clashing talents, ELO was formed as a more traditional pop orchestra. *No Answer,* released in 1972 and featuring soloists from the London Symphony Orchestra, failed to please members of the band. To complicate matters, their early tours were depressing, tense events affected by Hood's bizarre stage antics. Following a tour of England, leader Hood parted company with ELO to form the rock and roll band Wizzard. He also recorded, produced, and engineered a solo album as well as a 1950s tribute album, *Eddy and the Falcons* (with the members of Wizzard). His subsequent solo albums never matched the success of ELO, which was taken over by Lynne.

As main songwriter and lead vocalist, Lynne became central to the group's sound and eventual success. He had been critical of music from a young age, rebelling against his father's love of classical music and participating in school choir only to get out of lessons. He changed his mind when he borrowed a plastic guitar with only one string from a friend. Knowing nothing about chords, he was quite pleased with the instrument. When his father later bought him a Spanish guitar, he was delighted.

A school dropout, Lynne soon found himself fired from his first job and bounced from one job to another almost as frequently as he changed musical groups—for it seemed everyone in the 1960s was involved with a band, and he was no different. In 1970 he left the Idle Race (with whom he had recorded one album, *The Birthday Party*), joined the Move, and as the Move disintegrated and ELO prospered, the stage was set for Lynne's unique talents as a composer, lyricist, producer, and musician.

Following another round of personnel changes ELO debuted at the Reading Festival. Later additions to the group included Melvyn Gale (cello), Hugh MacDowell (cello), Bev Bevan (percussion), Rich Tandy (keyboards), Kelly Groucutt (bass and vocals), Mik Kaminski (violin), and Steve Woolam (violin and vocals).

Early success for ELO came as they opened for artists including Edgar Winter and B. B. King. In the United States they found a far more receptive audience than in Britain; Americans, it seemed, were ready for the new sound ELO was developing. *ELO II,* released in 1973, put the group in the spotlight as one of the new progressive classical-rock bands of the decade. The single "Roll over Beethoven," which featured a surprising contrapuntal slice of Beethoven's *Fifth Symphony,* placed at the top of English charts for several weeks, going on to become the band's first American hit. During the same year the group completed its first American tour and released a second album, *On the Third Day.*

### Major Success in 1974

In 1974 "Can't Get It out of My Head," from *Eldorado*, provided the group with their first major American hit, and the album was certified gold in 1975. Throughout the decade and in the 1980s ELO had a number of top-selling singles, including Lynne's side-long "Concerto for a Rainy Day" on *Eldorado* and such pop hits as "Strange Magic" and "Evil Woman" from *Face the Music;* "Telephone Line" from their first platinum album, *A New World Record;* "Don't Bring Me Down" from *Discovery;* "Xanadu" with Olivia Newton-John from the soundtrack of the same name; and "Hold on Tight" and "Twilight" from *Time.* Despite such successful singles, they remain best known for their albums and live performances.

The 1978 ELO stage show featured laser beams ricocheting off a mirrored ball hung from an ascending hot-air balloon and incorporated a five-ton, sixty-foot-wide fiberglass structure resembling a spaceship—the perfect prop to accompany the *Out of the Blue* album. During this time period the band's worst critic, perhaps, was its own leader. According to a 1978 *People* article, Lynne was "uncommonly modest for a rock star" and brutally honest in his critique of ELO's work. He called their first album "a self-indulgent nonevent," the second "pretentious," and even the eighth, *Out of the Blue,* merely "artistically honest pop music."

### Perfected the Genre

Moving to Columbia Records in 1979, ELO recorded *Discovery,* a landmark album featuring a forty-two-piece orchestra and thirty-voice male choir. It was soon hailed as an attempt to expand the marriage of rock and classical music and yielded two hits in "Shine a Little Love" and "Don't Bring Me Down." In the face of growing success, the band's reputation remained surprisingly good. Nevertheless, some critics viewed the band as being too pompous—particularly for the spectacle they put on during half of their 1978 concerts with the rising spaceship stage. That and other grandiose props gave ELO a certain anonymity as individuals that did not seem to overly concern them.

Following the recording of *Discovery* the group participated in the 1980 film soundtrack *Xanadu,* which produced major hits with "I'm Alive," "All Over the World," and a smash hit with the title song sung by Olivia Newton-John. In 1981 the concept album *Time* received vastly mixed reviews. At once an impressive and creative look back on history in pop-music form, it was faulted for sounding *too* contemporary by some critics. Other reviewers felt the album had an impres-

sive overall consistency, engaging in its futuristic impersonation.

The band's last album of new material, 1986's *Balance of Power,* was well received, compliments going to Lynne for tinkering with songs to enhance them and for his layering of vocals into a chorus. After the band dissolved Lynne scored success as a songwriter and record producer for others, including former Beatle George Harrison, and as a performer with the Traveling Wilburys, which also featured rock greats Harrison, Bob Dylan, Tom Petty, and the late Roy Orbison.

## Selected discography

*No Answer,* United Artists, 1972.
*ELO 2,* Harvest, 1973.
*On the Third Day,* Warner Bros., 1973.
*Eldorado,* Warner Bros., 1975.
*Face the Music,* Jet, 1975.
*Ole ELO,* Jet, 1976.
*A New World Record,* Jet, 1976.
*Out of the Blue,* Jet, 1977.
*The Light Shines On,* Harvest, 1977.
*3 Light Years,* Jet, 1978.
*ELO,* Jet 1978.
*The Light Shines On, Volume 2,* Harvest, 1979.
*Discovery,* Jet, 1979.
*Greatest Hits,* Jet, 1979.
*Xanadu* (soundtrack), Jet, 1980.
*Box of Their Best,* Jet, 1980.
*Time,* Jet, 1981.
*Secret Messages,* CBS, 1983.
*Balance of Power,* CBS, 1986.
*Afterglow* (greatest hits compilation), Epic, 1990.
*ELO Part II* (greatest hits compilation), Scotti Bros., 1991.

## Sources

### Books

Nite, Norm N., *Rock On,* Volume 2, updated edition, Harper, 1984.

### Periodicals

*New York Times,* June 25, 1973; November 10, 1974; February 13, 1977; October 11, 1981.
*People,* February 13, 1978; April 21, 1986.
*Rolling Stone,* August 24, 1978; October 4, 1979; December 10, 1981.

—*Meg Mac Donald*

# Faith No More

**Rock band**

The year 1990 left the members of the San Francisco rock band Faith No More a little dazed. Early in the year they were playing small clubs in support of an LP that wasn't selling impressively; by the fall they were a Grammy-winning sensation, appearing on the covers of major music magazines and opening for some of the biggest names in rock. Thanks to an elaborate and bizarre video for their single "Epic," Faith No More— self-described "dirtheads" more interested in upsetting fans' expectations than in currying their favor— moved to the top of the alternative rock scene.

However meteoric their rise to fame had been, the band's founding members—drummer Mike Bordin, bassist Billy Gould, and keyboardist Roddy Bottum— worked tirelessly for seven years to find the sound that they ultimately achieved on their 1989 album *The Real Thing.* The trio began collaborating in 1982, becoming part of a California scene that receives far less publicity than the slick world of Los Angeles rock. Gould and Bottum, in fact, had been veterans of the L.A. punk scene and had moved to San Francisco to attend

school. Gould answered Bordin's ad soliciting musicians to help create what the drummer—a fan of African percussion—called "atmospheres."

### Struggled in San Francisco Clubs

Soon Gould brought Bottum into the project, and Bordin recruited guitarist Jim Martin, a hard rock musician who had played in a band with Cliff Burton, the late bassist for metal superstars Metallica. Soon the "atmospheres" began fitting together as songs, and Faith No More played the Bay Area club scene; true to its anarchic musical instincts, the band let audience members become vocalists-for-the-night. A frequent volunteer was an eccentric character named Chuck Mosely, who screamed and thrashed his way through performances, frequently wearing a dress.

Despite Mosely's erratic temperament, the band played West Coast venues—mostly tiny avant-garde nightspots like L.A.'s Anticlub—and in 1986 released an album on the independent Mordam label. This LP, titled *We Care a Lot,* garnered the band a college radio cult following, due in part to the title song's disco-style parody of the Live Aid anthem "We Are the World." Warner Bros. affiliate Slash Records signed the band on the strength of their debut, and in 1987 they released *Introduce Yourself.*

Faith No More toured in Europe to support *Introduce Yourself,* and though their unpredictable live shows and genre-busting sound appealed to underground fans on the continent, the British press picked up on

tensions within the band. Mosely was an unreliable front man, to say the least: in the words of a Warner press release, "his unpredictable behavior on stage and off took its toll on the band's collective sanity." After the group's second European tour in the spring of 1988, he was kicked out of the band.

### New Singer Led to New Image

Upon their return to San Francisco, the band held auditions for a new singer. They quickly found twenty-one-year-old Mike Patton, a native of Eureka, California, and lead vocalist for Mr. Bungle, which Patton described to *Spin*'s Frank Owen as "a Laurel and Hardy death-metal band." Patton's combination of silliness and sarcasm suited Faith No More's attitude, and he added two things Mosely hadn't: rock star looks and strong, versatile singing. The band had an album's worth of musical ideas when they hired Patton; in a week he wrote an album's worth of lyrics. The result was 1989's *The Real Thing. Rolling Stone's* Kim Neely called Patton's lyrics "a marvel of musical role playing," and Robert Hilburn of the *Los Angeles Times* deemed the LP "a championship album."

*The Real Thing* appeared in June of 1989, and within a few months it dropped from view commercially. Faith No More continued to impress fans with its unpredictable shows, gaining a certain notoriety from its selection of cover songs alone. Their already famous version of "War Pigs," by metal pioneers Black Sabbath, was often performed side-by-side with such selections as the smooth soul tune "Easy" by the Commodores, "Vogue" by dance-music goddess Madonna, and even the jingle for a Nestle's chocolate bar. Patton added an often perverse theatricality to the musical stew, sometimes sporting leisure slacks and monster masks on stage. Though they appreciated their core audience, the band members wanted to reach out. "There's always been this misconception that 'commercial' means 'stupid,'" Gould told Neely. "Just because something is accepted by a lot of people, it doesn't mean there isn't some interesting thought behind it, you know? You can actually do a lot of damage on a mass scale."

### Grammy Nomination and Commercial Success

The damage Faith No More would be able to do seemed limited until February, 1990, some eight months after the album's release. Though they had toured with metal giants Metallica in the fall of 1989, they hadn't made a particularly favorable impression on that group's fans. Their Monsters of Rock festival performance turned a lot of heads, particularly since they were virtual unknowns compared to the megastars on the bill. Then Faith No More was nominated for a Grammy Award for best heavy metal performance, spurring increased sales and substantial MTV airtime for their video of "Epic," the first single from *The Real Thing.*

"Epic" mixes funk-rap verses with polished hard-rock choruses, and ends with an unexpectedly lovely piano coda; in the video, the piano blows up. The video features not only Patton's manically fascinating presence but a variety of slick special effects; its images introduced a whole new audience to Faith No More's music. By July the album went gold, entering the Top 20. The single eventually cracked the Top 10, and *The Real Thing* went platinum.

Faith No More was suddenly the band of the moment, heralded by critics like Jonathan Gold of the *Los Angeles Times* as the leaders of the neo-metal movement. *Spin, Rip,* and *Music Express* named them artists of the year for 1990, and *Rolling Stone* readers voted them runners-up for best new American band as well as for best video (for "Epic"). *Kerrang!* readers rated them highly in most categories, including runner-up for best retail video for their concert video release *Faith No More Live At Brixton Academy: You Fat B\*\*tards.*

### Year of Praise, Side Projects

In 1991 Faith No More took five of the seven statuettes for which they were nominated by the Bay Area Music Awards. They received "Bammies" for "outstanding" male vocalist, keyboardist, drummer, group, and song ("Epic"). The band scored again on MTV with the surrealistic video for the next single, "Indecision," another catchy mixture of rap and commercial hard rock thrown slightly off balance by Bottum's eerie keyboard textures. The video reinforced Faith No More's "edge" by dressing Patton as a blood-covered surgeon.

Though the accolades continued to pour in, the group seized the opportunity after a grueling fourteen months of touring—during which they opened for rock superstar Billy Idol, among others—to work on some side projects. Patton was able to release a Mr. Bungle album, Gould traveled to Samoa to record tribal music,

Bordin played on an album by the thrash-funk band Primus, and Bottum added some keyboards to a new release by the band Field Trip. Gould was the most active, having produced several others bands before and after his Samoa trip and directing and editing the video for Faith No More's "Surprise! You're Dead." The band contributed the song "The Perfect Crime" to the soundtrack album for *Bill and Ted's Bogus Journey,* a film in which Martin played a small role.

Faith No More saw 1991 out by working on a new album, which they hoped to release in 1992. Whether the record would yield a single as massively successful as "Epic" or not, the band members remained committed to a path of their own. "We were never anybody's marketing fantasy," Bordin remarked to Owen. Martin, a man of few words, summed up the closest thing to Faith No More's recipe for success: "I mean, nobody really knows what they're doing, so you just think you know what you're doing and do it."

## Selected discography

*We Care a Lot* (includes "We Care a Lot"), Mordam, 1986.
*Introduce Yourself,* Slash/Reprise, 1987.
*The Real Thing* (includes "Epic," "Indecision," "War Pigs," and "Surprise! You're Dead"), Slash/Reprise, 1989.
*Bill and Ted's Bogus Journey* (motion picture soundtrack; includes "The Perfect Crime"), Warner Bros., 1991.

## Sources

*BAM,* October 5, 1990.
*Details,* September 1989.
*Los Angeles Times,* October 14, 1990; December 2, 1990.
*Musician,* October 1989.
*New York Times,* July 9, 1990.
*Rolling Stone,* September 6, 1990.
*Spin,* December 1990.

Information for this profile was obtained from a Faith No More press kit, Slash/Reprise, 1991.

—*Simon Glickman*

# Maynard Ferguson

## Trumpet player, bandleader

Jazz legend Maynard Ferguson far surpasses the title "trumpet player"; he is an internationally famous big-band leader, one of the world's great brass players, an instrument designer, record producer, composer, arranger, producer of film soundtracks, and dedicated teacher. He is also a three-time Grammy Award nominee and *Down Beat* magazine award winner. The prolific bandleader has recorded over 60 albums in his lifetime. The alumni list of his band members over four decades reads like a Who's Who of the jazz world: Chick Corea, Chuck Mangione, Bill Chase, Bob James, Slide Hampton, Wayne Shorter, Greg Bissonette, Peter Erskine, Joe Zawinul, Willie Maiden, and Don Ellis are just some of the greats Ferguson's bands have bred. Ferguson emerged from big-band swing and worked his way through jazz, bebop, rock, funk, disco, and fusion. When he wasn't actually playing his horn, he conducted, cueing his men, or just snapped his fingers and enjoyed the music. He has been a hustler, a tireless worker, and remarkably generous with his musical abilities. Few careers have spanned so many different forms of music, tribute indeed to Ferguson's flexibility and staying power.

Ferguson was a child prodigy who first soloed with the Canadian Broadcasting Company Orchestra at the age of 11. He was born in the Montreal suburb of Verdun on May 4, 1928. His mother was a violinist with the Ottawa Symphony Orchestra and later, a teacher who helped introduce music into the curriculum of the Montreal public school system. His father was a high-school principal. By the time Ferguson was four, he too was playing the violin as well as the piano. At the age of nine he was enrolled in the French Conservatory of Music to receive formal training. He has cited his main influences as his mother and Louis Armstrong.

### American Debut in 1948

Ferguson attended Montreal High School, but quit at age 15 to pursue music as a vocation. Around that time he played in a dance band, led by his brother Percy, with another budding musician, jazz pianist Oscar Peterson. By the age of sixteen Ferguson was leading his own jazz and dance band. All of the musicians in his band were twice his age, except Percy, with whom he had effectively reversed roles. In 1948 the 20-year-old Ferguson moved to the U.S. and made his debut in Boyd Raeburn's progressive band. He also played with Jimmy Dorsey and Charlie Barnet, and performed on woodwind and brass as a one-man act in New York's cafe society.

From 1950 to 1953 Ferguson's lashing, high-register

## For the Record. . .

**B**orn May 4, 1928, in Montreal, Quebec, Canada; son of Perry (a public school administrator) and Olive (a schoolteacher and former symphony violinist) Ferguson; married wife, Florence, 1952; children: Kim, Corby, Lisa, Bentley, Wilder.

Trumpet player and bandleader. Began playing trumpet in Montreal clubs, c. 1943; made American debut with Boyd Raeburn band and played with Jimmy Dorsey orchestra, 1948; became headline trumpet player for Stan Kenton orchestra, 1949; formed, and performed with Birdland Dreamband, 1955-66; first-call studio trumpet player for Paramount Pictures, mid-1950s; formed 13-piece touring orchestra and performed with various jazz soloists, 1957-65; formed sextet, 1965; toured Europe with a succession of bands, including Top Brass, and engaged in genre experimentation; founded Maynard Ferguson Music Inc.; formed 7-piece electric fusion band High Voltage, 1986; formed Big Bop Nouveau Band, 1990.

**Awards:** Three Grammy Award nominations, one in 1977, for "Gonna Fly Now" theme to the film *Rocky,* from the album *Conquistador;* first place in *Down Beat* magazine's best trumpeter award, 1950, 1951, and 1952; first place in *Billboard* magazine's pop instrumental category, 1977.

**Addresses:** *Office*—Maynard Ferguson Music, P.O. Box 716, Ojai, CA 93023.

trumpet was the cornerstone of Stan Kenton's enormous brass section. During his years with Kenton, Ferguson built a reputation that relied more on his dazzling technique—screech trumpeting in the dizzying upper register of his instrument—than his creativity as a soloist. The fire-breathing trumpeter took first place in *Down Beat* magazine's best trumpeter poll for three successive years beginning in 1950. After his stint with Kenton, Ferguson spent three years as first-call studio trumpeter for Paramount Pictures and recorded film soundtracks for Paramount, including that of the Biblical epic *The Ten Commandments*. In 1955 Ferguson joined Leonard Bernstein for a performance of the "Titans," by William Russo, with the New York Philharmonic Orchestra.

The following year, after a period of free-lancing, Ferguson formed the first of several thirteen-piece orchestras, which were noted for the biting precision of their brass sections. On the striking "Frame for the Blues," off the *Message From Newport* album, Ferguson's dramatic solo style sears, and Don Sebesky, Don Menza, and Slide Hampton offer some of their best

arrangements. Other noteworthy soloists featured on that applauded recording were Jaki Byard, Don Ellis, Joe Farrell, and Chuck Mangione. In 1959 an International Critic's Poll, conducted by *Down Beat,* voted the Maynard Ferguson Orchestra first place in the "new star" big-band division. But, as the popularity of big bands waned in the mid-1960s, Ferguson was forced to economize; he toured less frequently with the big band, favoring a smaller sextet instead. Finally, in 1967, he disbanded and his group began to follow a new path.

### Spiritual Renewal in India

In 1968 and 1969 Ferguson taught at the Krishnamurtl-based Rhishi Valley School near Madras, India, which widened both his spiritual and musical horizons. He took his family with him to India, and they eventually moved to England. There Ferguson toured as the leader of a band called Top Brass. He also manufactured personally designed trumpets and mouthpieces from his home in Manchester. Being situated in England made touring Europe easier for Ferguson, and he took advantage of this proximity by embarking on forays across the continent with a variety of ensembles.

In 1969 Ferguson signed with CBS Records in England and created a repertoire for his new British band in which pop and rock songs were rearranged into a big-band format, with electronic amplification. This was Ferguson's response to the psychedelic sixties. He produced contemporary arrangements of late 1960s and early 1970s hits like "MacArthur Park" and the Beatles' "Hey Jude." Ferguson's recording of "Gonna Fly Now"—the theme from the hit film *Rocky*—catapulted Maynard into mainstream popularity with a Top-10 single, a gold album, and a Grammy nomination in 1978. His album *Conquistador,* from which "Gonna Fly Now" sprang, earned Ferguson an unusual place in the history of music; with *Conquistador,* he alone was able to crack the pop charts, where countless jazz musician had failed before him. The album reached Number 22 on *Billboard's* pop albums charts in 1977. Ferguson's efforts helped rekindle the public's interest in big bands; his fanfare solos, along with his expertise on several brass instruments—often demonstrated in a single performance—set a dazzling example of sheer technical virtuosity.

### Big Bop Nouveau

In addition to the trumpet, Ferguson plays the trombone, saxophone, clarinet, violin and piano. He stands five feet, nine inches tall, and attributes his horn-power to yogic concentration, which he claims enables him to control his central nervous system and make his lungs generators of energy. He is a family man, married since 1952 to his wife, Flo, and quick to speak proudly of his son and four daughters. One of his daughters, Kim, manages his current outfit, the Big Bop Nouveau Band. Started in the late 1980s, the band leans heavily toward more traditional jazz, reflecting both Ferguson's roots and major strengths. In the spring of 1990 Ferguson released the *Big Bop Nouveau* album, a combination of studio recordings and live takes from his 60th Birthday Band Tour. With the Big Bop Nouveau Band there is a new stress on instrumentation, marking Ferguson's return to where critics have so often preferred him: in front of a jazz-flavored big band. The Nouveau Band avoids overly-synthesized sounds, and focuses on hard-edged, straight-ahead be-bop jazz music—the sound that established Ferguson in the late 1950s and early 1960s.

As a young man in the 1950s Ferguson set the jazz world aflame with his innovative Birdland Dreamband. Four decades later—after much broadening and ex-perimentation—he has come full-circle back to his role as legendary, premier big-band leader. Over his life-time career in music, Ferguson has displayed many peaks and valleys, often straying far from his roots; as a result, his sound is much richer, as are his devoted followers. Although it's never clear where Ferguson may roam next, it's certain that it will be a lively journey.

## Selected discography

*Si Si!*, Roulette Birdland Series, 1952, reissued, 1991.

(With Chris Connor and Jaki Byard), *Two's Company,* Roulette Birdland, 1953.
*A Message From Birdland,* Roulette Birdland, 1959.
*Maynard '61,* Roulette Birdland, 1961, reissued, Blue Note, 1990.
*Maynard '64,* 1964.
*Ridin' High,* Enterprise Records, 1968.
*Maynard Ferguson,* Columbia, 1973.
*Chameleon,* Columbia, 1974, reissued, 1990.
*Primal Scream,* Columbia, 1976.
*Conquistador,* Columbia, 1977.
*Carnival,* Columbia, 1978.
*Maynard Ferguson,* Columbia, 1979.
*Best of Maynard Ferguson,* Columbia, 1980.
*Body & Soul,* Blackhawk Records, 1986.
*High Voltage,* Intima Records, 1987.
*The Birdland Dreamband,* Bluebird Records, 1987.
*Big Bop Nouveau,* Intima Records, 1990.
*The Blues Roar,* Mobile Fidelity.
*M. F. Horn 1 & 2,* Columbia.

## Sources

*Christian Science Monitor,* December 20, 1976.
*Los Angeles Times,* January 9, 1986; March 18, 1990.
*New York Daily News,* November 14, 1978.
*New York Post,* February 14, 1977.
*New York Times,* February 6, 1978; June 28, 1979; June 30, 1984.
*Ojai Valley Voice* (CA), October 1991.
*Variety,* March 15, 1978.

—*B. Kimberly Taylor*

# Fishbone

**Funk-rock fusion band**

"Who says a rock band can't play funky?" sang George Clinton's groundbreaking band Funkadelic in the 1970s. "Who says a funk band can't play rock?" That these questions needed to be asked underlined a major division in popular music. Among the listeners to Funkadelic's innovative fusion of hard rock and heavy funk were seven kids who would one day be the members of Fishbone. This ambitious crew blended the structural complexity of progressive rock and fusion, the crazed intensity of punk, the rhythmic ecstasy of ska and funk's relentless groove, producing a mixture that other groups would successfully exploit before Fishbone itself broke through in 1991.

The group's wild palette of musical styles encountered mostly indifference when they signed with Columbia Records in 1985. Audiences and executives threw in the band's face precisely the myths it wished to dispel: that rock was "white" music and funk "black" music, and that radical mixtures of reggae, punk, progressive rock and dance music would never find a mass audience. While the band fought its way to mass-market

## For the Record. . .

B and formed in 1979 in Los Angeles; founding members include **John "Norwood" Fisher** (bass and vocals), **Phillip "Fish" Fisher** (drums), **Kendall Jones** (guitar and vocals), **Angelo Moore** (vocals and saxophone), **Christopher Dowd** (keyboards and vocals), and **Walter Kibby** (trumpet, trombone, and vocals); **John Bigham** (guitar) joined band c. 1990; prior to signing with Columbia, band was known by a variety of names, including Hot Ice, Counterattack, Diamonds & Thangs, Megatron, and Melodia; released first record, *Fishbone* (six-song EP), for Columbia Records, 1985.

**Addresses:** *Record company*—Columbia Records, 666 Fifth Ave., P.O. Box 4455, New York, NY 10101-4455.

success to disprove the latter idea, it has dedicated itself to addressing the former in interviews.

## Defied Easy Categorization

In an interview with *Guitar Player,* guitarist Kendall Jones referred to the classification of music by color as "brainwashing." Jones, like the rest of the band, insists that rock and roll was pioneered by black artists—he poured scorn on white rock idol Elvis Presley in an interview with *Spin*—and that black radio's reluctance to play records outside its format has limited the receptivity of black audiences. "You could be making millions, millions, millions," Jones complained to *Guitar Player,* "but if they haven't heard your stuff on [black] radio, you ain't shit. You need to get another job."

The band's earliest incarnations—which sported such names as Hot Ice, Counterattack, Diamonds & Thangs, Megatron, and Melodia—began searching for their ideal musical fusion in 1979. Its founding members—Jones, brothers John "Norwood" Fisher, bassist, and drummer Phillip "Fish" Fisher, singer-saxman Angelo Moore, keyboardist Christopher Dowd, and brass wizard Walter Kibby—got together in high school in California's San Fernando Valley. They liked funk, reggae, punk, hard rock, progressive rock and ska.

Although early publicity suggested that the white kids at the school to which all but Moore were bused from South Central Los Angeles introduced Fishbone to hard rock, Norwood says otherwise. "[Canadian progressive-rock power trio] Rush was about the coolest thing we found out," he told *Rolling Stone's* David Fricke; he noted in the *Guitar Player* interview that "as

soon as I heard punk, all that progressive rock and fusion started not to mean a damn thing to me." Somewhere between the energy and rebellion of punk, the musical integrity of fusion, Funkadelic's groove-oriented eccentricity, and what Norwood Fisher called the "kicking flavor" of his favorite reggae bassist lay the territory Fishbone would claim.

## Early Records Reached Cult Following

The band's stage shows earned them a reputation for wild humor that would be a blessing and a curse. Although the manic energy in their songs assisted them in getting a record deal with Columbia, Dowd recalled to *Spin*'s Bill Holdship, the label wanted them to be "those crazy new wave negroes from South Central Los Angeles!" Despite its wildness in performance and its often bizarre song concepts, Fishbone had a lot to say, and it felt that the record company was uninterested. In 1985 the band released *Fishbone,* a six-song EP; it included "Party at Ground Zero," an irresistible stew of ska, pop, and a guitar motif plucked from the Bizet opera *Carmen*.

"Party at Ground Zero" fared well on alternative radio stations like Los Angeles's KROQ, which gave it substantial rotation, but the record—produced by David Kahne, a veteran producer of "new wave" rock bands—didn't lead to any big breaks for Fishbone. It did, however, catch the attention of some discriminating listeners. As Havelock Nelson wrote in his review of the record in *High Fidelity,* the band's "style adds a potent, hard-driving edge to what has always been—and will always be—a good time." Nelson admired Columbia's "taking a chance" on an adventurous band, though he doubted Fishbone's bold eclecticism would find its way into the Top Forty.

Nelson's prediction held true for some time. The group's next effort, 1986's *In Your Face,* expanded the musical range explored on the debut record but once again was not promoted by the label. *In Your Face* included trademark ska workouts like "A Selection," the reggae ballad "Turn the Other Way," and the gospel-tinged rocker "Give it Up." The lyrics touched on the band's central preoccupations: sex, social independence, and the incompetence of America's political leaders. The latter subject is illuminated without words on the album's final track, a minute-long instrumental clown theme—led by Kibby's trombone—called "Post Cold War Politics." Although they continued to wow the faithful with their stage shows, the members of Fishbone were caught in the limbo of record company indifference. The message was not getting through.

## Swam Toward Success

It wasn't until 1988 that the band completed *Truth and Soul,* an album that demonstrated a further leap in Fishbone's musical ambition and thematic scope. The album opens with a cover version of Curtis Mayfield's moody 1970s classic, "Freddie's Dead," which made the biggest wave of the band's early career as a single and video; it proceeds through an array of genres and arrangements that are impressive even when compared to the band's earlier work. Though the sexual swagger and funny voices associated with Fishbone's "zany" image are integral to the record, there is a seriousness of purpose here: "Question of Life" and "Change" are somber pleas for social justice, and "One Day" and "Ghetto Soundwave" address the situation of urban blacks with greater maturity than anything the band had done previously.

Instrumentally, *Truth and Soul* allowed the band to branch out radically. "Change," with its acoustic guitar and evocative melody, recalls the fine textures of the best progressive rock. "Bonin' in the Boneyard," one of Fishbone's many anthems to sexual freedom, has the funky abandon of Clinton's feel-good classics. "Ma and Pa" retooled the group's well-known ska approach for a serious subject: a family torn apart by divorce. The band's calls for independence were matched by its own: Kahne, who had been an important musical and technical contributor to the first two records, hung back. "By the time of *Truth and Soul,* I was doing much less," he told *Musician*'s Roy Trakin. "And that's the way I wanted it." Even so, the band didn't have a hit single, and Columbia didn't push the record. They were still in limbo.

Meanwhile, as the 1980s came to an end, rock and roll saw an explosion of bands who challenged the rigid formats of commercial radio. Groups like Living Colour, The Red Hot Chili Peppers—whose founding members jammed with Fishbone in Los Angeles—and Faith No More played volatile mixtures of funk and hard rock. Living Colour's Vernon Reid was a black guitar hero who mixed metal licks with rhythm-and-blues riffs; Faith No More's Mike Patton was a white rapper-singer; the Chili Peppers' Flea was a white bassist who played funk with a punk accent. These groups amassed huge audiences, reorienting alternative radio and throwing the smug assumptions of programmers and record executives out the window. Columbia, the members of Fishbone believe, finally realized it had been sitting on a gold mine.

Of course, there had been some changes at the label. Many of the executives who had ignored Fishbone had moved on, and Kahne became head of the company's A&R division. By the time the band finished its third full-length album, *The Reality of My Surroundings,* in 1991, they found an unprecedented enthusiasm in their label's response. Columbia booked Fishbone to appear on NBC's *Saturday Night Live* before *Reality* came out, and the first single, a sleek rocker called "Sunless Saturday," made an impressive display on MTV, with a video directed by filmmaker Spike Lee. With the second single, however, Fishbone finally broke through the clouds. "Everyday Sunshine," a gospel-soul workout that many critics compared with the sound of funk pioneer Sly Stone, became a hit, partly thanks to an exuberant video that MTV played liberally.

Jones told Trakin he considered *The Reality of My Surroundings* "the first fully functional Fishbone record." It is certainly the most relentless. New guitarist

---

*Fishbone's wild palette of musical styles encountered mostly indifference when they signed with Columbia Records in 1985.*

---

John Bigham now shared six-string duties with Jones, giving the band an even heavier sound. In addition to the party-ska raveups—such as the frantic skanking of the three-part "If I Were A . . . I'd . . ." and the frenetic "Housework"—*Reality* features the metallic riffing of "Fight the Youth," the slamming funk beat of "Naz-tee May'en," and the psychotic fusion of "Behavior Control Technician." The lyrics further focused Fishbone's concern for black survival, even as they argued for fun. Both "Sunless Saturday" and "Everyday Sunshine" use weather as metaphors for inner-city life. The reggae/soul tune "Pray to the Junkiemaker" addresses all kinds of addiction.

### Reaped Critical Praise

*Down Beat* labelled *The Reality of My Surroundings* "One of this year's most exciting albums," calling the music "adventurous and teeming with life." Reviewer Dan Ouellette awarded the record four and one-half stars. "What makes this album so remarkable," he wrote, "is how effortlessly Fishbone has stitched together such a wide variety of black-music traditions." *Creem*'s Sean O'Neill dubbed the band's new effort "the best record of this nascent decade." *Musician* agreed: "This band isn't as good as they say: It's better." *People* called the record "the group's most impressive." And according to *Billboard,* the "Rich, dense new album is a thrill for the ears, and may remind many of Funkadelic's best."

Fishbone finally got the attention it had been striving for and was vindicated by both commercial and critical success. In 1991 it went on tour with fellow funk-and-rollers Primus and vowed to continue on its mission to promote awareness and fun. "When we first started, our whole thing was to get everybody to unify in the house," Dowd told Fricke. "Black, white, whatever. Feel like brothers. Because even then we realized the system works to keep people separated." As drummer Fish reminded Trakin, this issue of unity was central to the band's commercial accessibility as well as its social message: "Basically you have to play for those who are in your congregation, and ours is still growing. We're doing what we can to reach our people, too."

## Selected discography

### On Columbia Records

*Fishbone* (six-song EP; includes "Party at Ground Zero"), 1985.

*In Your Face* (includes "Turn the Other Way," "Give it Up," and "Post Cold War Politics"), 1986.
*Truth and Soul* (includes "Freddie's Dead," "Question of Life," "Change," "One Day," "Ghetto Soundwave," "Bonin' in the Boneyard," and "Ma and Pa"), 1988.
*The Reality of My Surroundings* (includes "Sunless Saturday," "Everyday Sunshine," "If I Were A . . . I'd . . .," "Housework," "Fight the Youth," "Naz-tee May'en," "Behavior Control Technician," and "Pray to the Junkiemaker"), 1991.

Also backed Little Richard on "Rock Island Line," from *Folkways: A Vision Shared (A Tribute to Woody Guthrie and Leadbelly),* Columbia, 1988.

## Sources

*Billboard,* April 27, 1991.
*Creem,* June-July 1991.
*Down Beat,* July 1991.
*Guitar Player,* August 1991.
*High Fidelity,* September 1985.
*Musician,* May 1991; July 1991.
*Rolling Stone,* October 3, 1991.
*Spin,* July 1991.

—*Simon Glickman*

# Pete Fountain

---

**Clarinetist**

---

For the past four decades, Pete Fountain has been among the more recognizable jazz artists in the United States, and one of the most commercially successful, with nearly 50 albums to his credit. The energetic and affable New Orleans clarinetist first rose to prominence in the 1950s as a featured performer on *The Lawrence Welk Show,* and in the following decades became well known through frequent appearances on television. In a 1985 *Down Beat* profile, Howard Mandel described Fountain's lively performances on *The Tonight Show:* "There's Pete Fountain, the smooth-skulled clarinetist, blowing fiercely amidst select musicians from Doc Severinsen's *Tonight Show* band. I watched once recently as he concentrated all the air in his thick body through his tight embouchure, squealing and piping quite oblivious to anything else."

Fountain's career and sound are invariably connected to his musical hometown, New Orleans. Gunther Schuller, in *The Swing Era: The Development of Jazz, 1930-1945,* called him representative of "true New Orleans-style clarinet-playing." Many consider Fountain the personification, together with trumpeter Al Hirt, of the city's famed jazz venue, Bourbon Street. In the foreword to Fountain's autobiography, *A Closer Walk: The Pete Fountain Story,* Bob Harrington depicted how Fountain echoes the gusto of early New Orleans jazz pioneers, with musical roots in the "heartfelt expression" of gospel songs: "Pete is a prime example of this great musical legacy, handed down carefully and lovingly from the stellar performers of yesterday to our own generation. In his music you can hear the notes and the tones that have permeated Bourbon Street for more than 75 years."

## Therapeutic Use of the Clarinet

As a young boy, Fountain listened to jazz at the Top Hat Dance Club, an establishment in his neighborhood that featured prominent New Orleans jazz musicians. Another early influence was his father, who could play a number of instruments by ear and first introduced Fountain to improvisation. Sickly as a child, Fountain received his first clarinet when a physician recommended playing it to improve his lung strength. He took formal lessons, but preferred studying the recordings of his idols, Benny Goodman and Irving Fazola, while trying to imitate their sound and style. "It was tough putting the whole thing together," Fountain remembered in his autobiography. "I wanted to play jazz, and I was ready to swing even if my fingers weren't."

Growing up in New Orleans, however, the jazz enthusiast progressed quickly as a musician. He played in his high-school jazz band, and became an avid follower of jazz recordings and radio programs. In his free time, Fountain frequented Bourbon Street music clubs, where he would sneak in back doors to catch performances. "It was from these nights, when I hid behind bandstands or trash containers, that I began to feel the soul and the heartbeat of jazz," Fountain revealed in *A Closer Walk*. "Things were starting to fall into place for me." At 16 he formed his first band, the Basin Street Four, and was afforded the opportunity to play sets at the Parisian Room, a famous jazz spot in New Orleans. Occasionally Fountain's band members would be allowed to sit in with the headlining bands. "Playing shoulder to shoulder with the jazz giants of the city taught us this timing, and it also taught us a tremendous amount of stage presence," Fountain related. Eventually those sessions were broadcast nationally on a radio program, "The Dixieland Jamboree," and by the time he was a high-school senior, Fountain was earning union scale as a musician—$125 a week.

## New Orleans Called Him Home

Fountain continued to work with a number of New Orleans bands and artists, and soon began appearing on recordings. In 1950 he co-founded the Basin Street Six, a Dixieland comic band that landed a television contract with a local station. But Bebop, not Dixieland, was becoming the rage at this time and the Basin Street Six found it difficult booking work. They eventually disbanded and Fountain headed to Memphis and Chicago with a new group, the Three Coins. The move from New Orleans—and his family—however, took its toll. The clarinetist recounted in his autobiography that he began drinking heavily at this time, and contemplated giving up music altogether. He returned to New Orleans in the mid-1950s, not sure whether he would resume his music career.

Fountain's plans changed dramatically in 1956; bandleader Lawrence Welk, impressed with recordings of Fountain that he'd heard and wanting to "jazz up" his band, asked Fountain to join his national television show, which was produced in California. Fountain accepted, and his performances on the popular show generated hundreds of fan letters each week. Fountain headlined with Welk's band, and was featured in advertisements for its national concert tours, one of which took the group to Carnegie Hall, a thrill for Fountain. Exposure from the Welk show made Fountain a household name, and he soon became a frequent performer on television specials. Despite his success in California, however, Fountain and his family were continually homesick for New Orleans.

## Opened Jazz Hot Spots

In 1959, at the height of his television popularity, Fountain returned to his hometown. Before leaving, though, he had signed a lucrative contract with Coral Records; his first two albums, *Pete Fountain's New Orleans* and *The Blues,* were particularly big sellers. Fountain enjoyed his newly acquired autonomy and soon formed a band in New Orleans; his name had made him one of the city's biggest attractions. In 1960 he established his own jazz club, "The French Quarter Inn," which became one of the hottest spots in New Orleans. Nine years later Fountain opened "Pete's Place" at 231 Bourbon Street, and later relocated to a posh 500-seat room in the New Orleans Hilton. Today, Fountain and his band still play at the Hilton; he has truly become one of New Orleans's local legends.

The title of Fountain's 1972 autobiography, in which he recalls his life and career, is taken from one of his trademark songs, "Just a Closer Walk With Thee." New Orleans remains home to Fountain and he continues his love affair with jazz and the clarinet. Musically, he adheres to the older-style jazz that made him famous: "My solos change—from reed to reed," he told *Down Beat's* Mandel. "They change personality from what I eat, from my day. I try to keep the improvisation alive, and not get stale that way, or into a rut. But the licks in the background stay the same." Content with his life in the city that has been his inspiration, and with his stature in American music, Fountain nonetheless spoke with some nostalgia of his younger days: "I've had my good times; I feel good now, and don't want to burn myself out. I only drink wine now; I used to like bourbon, then vodka, then it got time to cool it. But I'm still enjoyin'. I enjoy everything I have. But if I had that youth again—whew!"

## Selected discography

*Pete Fountain's New Orleans,* Coral.
*The Blues,* Coral.
*Pete Fountain at the Bateau Lounge,* Coral.
*New Orleans at Midnight,* Coral.
*Licorice Stick,* Coral.
*Plenty of Pete,* Coral.
*French Quarter New Orleans,* Coral.
*Pete's Place,* Coral.
*Standing Room Only,* Coral.
*Swing Low, Sweet Clarinet,* Coral.
*Pete Fountain's Music From Dixie,* Coral.
*The Best of Pete Fountain* (two volumes), MCA.
*Dr. Fountain's Magical Licorice Stick,* Coral.
*New Orleans, Tennessee,* Coral.

*Mr. New Orleans,* MCA.
*Candy Clarinet,* Coral.
(With the Basin Street Six) *Strictly Dixie,* Mercury.
(With Al Hirt) *Jazz Band Ball,* Verve.
(With Lawrence Welk) *Lawrence Welk Presents Pete Fountain,* Coral.
*Swingin' Blues,* Ranwood, 1991.

## Sources

### Books

Fountain, Pete, with Bill Neely, *A Closer Walk: The Pete Fountain Story,* Regnery, 1972.
Rose, Al, and Edmond Souchon, *New Orleans Jazz: A Family Album,* Louisiana State University Press, 1984.
Schuller, Gunther, *The Swing Era: The Development of Jazz, 1930-1945,* Oxford University Press, 1989.

### Periodicals

*Down Beat,* January 1985.

—*Michael E. Mueller*

# Vince Gill

**Singer, songwriter, guitarist**

Vince Gill worked at the very edges of success for more than a decade before breaking through to country music superstardom in 1990. For many years Gill's vocal and instrumental talents were put to use in the studio by a wide spectrum of country artists. Finally, after struggling to launch his solo career for years, he found his way to fame with a haunting neo-traditional country single, "When I Call Your Name." *Chicago Tribune* music critic Jack Hurst wrote of Gill: "After six years in Nashville, a man who has sung backup on the records of more than 100 other artists finally has a megahit of his own to his credit."

Many country-music enthusiasts have long felt that the talented Gill was a candidate for top success in the industry from his earliest professional efforts. In *Who's Who in New Country Music,* for instance, Andrew Vaughan noted that Gill "has for years been touted as the man most likely to become a star." With many friends in Nashville and a long string of credits for session work, songwriting, and vocals, Gill needed only to find the style that would best showcase his assets. He succeeded—after years of lackluster work for RCA Records—with his first MCA Nashville release, a project he has called "the right record at the right time."

Vince Gill was born in 1957 in Norman, Oklahoma, where he was also raised. Fascinated by country, western, and bluegrass music from childhood, he was playing guitar and singing with a local bluegrass band while still in his teens. Gill's high, expressive tenor was ideally suited for bluegrass and in his early years he worked with such groups as the Bluegrass Alliance and a West Coast band, Sundance. Like many of the other musicians he knew, Gill was strongly influenced by rock as well as country and bluegrass. Playing with such avant-garde artists as the Bluegrass Alliances's Sam Bush and Sundance's Byron Berline, he developed a rock-flavored picking style that proved quite popular in California. He also learned to play banjo, dobro, and mandolin—ideal preparation for the studio work that would sustain him down the road.

### Joined Pure Prairie League

In the mid-1970s Gill joined Pure Prairie League, a soft-rock band based in California; he was featured on three late-seventies Pure Prairie League albums, though the group's heyday preceded Gill's arrival. In 1979, during his stay in California, Gill married Janis Oliver, herself a would-be singer-songwriter. For several years Gill and his wife were content to live and work on the West Coast. Then Gill made a controversial career deci-

### Tried to Bridge the Pop-Country Gap

The sailing was not smooth thereafter, however; Gill had grand ambitions for his music, ambitions that ran counter to the prevailing winds in Nashville. "I felt I was going to be the one who could really bridge the gap between pop and country and get rock fans interested in country music," he told the *Chicago Tribune*. Through three RCA releases Gill explored his personal vision, bringing all his acoustic and vocal talents to bear. He achieved modest success and even cracked the country Top Ten with a duet—"If It Weren't for Him"—recorded with Rosanne Cash. Still, as Vaughan pointed out in *Who's Who in New Country Music,* Gill "wasn't the star the pundits had predicted."

In 1990 Gill severed his relationship with RCA and moved down the street to MCA Nashville, where his friend Tony Brown was working as a producer. Gill's first MCA recording, *When I Call Your Name,* was far more traditional than his previous work; it featured an Oklahoma swing number and several compelling country ballads. The album became Gill's biggest—selling four or five times more units than any of his previous releases. "It's the first real country record I've ever made, and I'm extremely proud of it," he told the *Chicago Tribune*.

sion—one that absolutely confounded his California friends.

Gill had known singer Rodney Crowell since the days when the latter sang backup for country star Emmylou Harris. When Crowell decided to go solo and form his own band, he asked Gill to back him up. It was a demotion, in effect, as Gill had been singing lead with Pure Prairie League. "People were telling me, 'Man, how could you make that step backward?,'" Gill recalled in the *Lexington Herald-Leader*. "Musically, that was a giant step [forward] for me." As the 1980s began Gill moved with more focus into purely country music, forging lasting relationships with Crowell, Harris, and the man who would become his producer, Tony Brown.

Nashville proved a congenial environment for both Gill and his wife, Janis. The up-and-coming singer found as much work as he could handle as a session vocalist and musician; he worked with Crowell, Harris, Bonnie Raitt, Rosanne Cash, and Patty Loveless, to name a few. About that time Janis persuaded her sister to move east as well and the two began recording as Sweethearts of the Rodeo. In 1984 Gill signed a contract for solo work with RCA Records. His first RCA release, a mini-album called *Turn Me Loose,* yielded a Top Twenty hit and earned Gill the Academy of Country Music's top new male vocalist award.

### Broke Through With *When I Call Your Name*

Gill's pride was justifiable in light of the awards he garnered for the album's title song. "When I Call Your Name" was judged the best single of the year by the Country Music Association and was awarded a Grammy as best country song of 1990. The album yielded other hits as well, including the Reba McEntire duet "Oklahoma Swing" and the bluegrass-styled "Never Knew Lonely." At long last Gill had stepped out of the shadows of the Nashville recording studios and into the spotlight many felt he richly deserved. His tenor vocals and chilling harmonies may not have closed the gap between country and pop, but they had enriched and enlarged the scope of bluegrass in a country format.

Gill followed up *When I Call Your Name* with *Pocket Full of Gold,* an effort replete with no-nonsense shuffles, love ballads, and a rocking version of an old traditional song. *Country Music* reviewer Rich Kienzle opened his critique of *Pocket* by stating unequivocally that the record deserved the acclaim it had garnered and allowing that it "nearly" equalled the "special" nature of *When I Call Your Name*. Citing what he felt were a few clunkers—but mostly praising the album's stand-outs—the writer applauded "Gill's talent for uncanny twists in his songs," and in one instance, his "anguished delivery." Kienzle finished his appraisal by declaring: "Gill deserves credit for maintaining his original direction. With tight production ... combined with his clear, beautifully focused voice, he's moving in a direction that is right for him. Others should be so lucky."

Considering his wide instrumental experience and proficiency in many styles, Gill is likely to continue to offer a variety of work on each album. He told the *Chicago Tribune* that he consciously tries to put "different things" on his releases so that he does not become associated with one particular sound. His biggest challenge, he said, is to find "something to home in on, something folks [are] going to react to."

## Selected discography

*Turn Me Loose*, RCA, 1984.
*The Things That Matter*, RCA, 1985.
*The Way Back Home*, RCA, 1987.
*The Best of Vince Gill*, RCA, 1989.
*When I Call Your Name*, MCA Nashville, 1989.
*Pocket Full of Gold*, MCA Nashville, 1991.

## Sources

### Books

Vaughan, Andrew, *Who's Who in New Country Music*, St. Martin's, 1989.

### Periodicals

*Chicago Tribune*, September 13, 1990.
*Country Music*, March/April, 1991; November/December, 1991.
*Lexington Herald-Leader* (KY), July 29, 1990.
*People*, June 10, 1991.
*Stereo Review*, April 1991.
*Variety*, December 23, 1991.

—*Anne Janette Johnson*

# Mickey Gilley

---

**Singer, songwriter**

---

**C**ountry performer Mickey Gilley was able to transcend comparisons to his cousin, rock and roll superstar Jerry Lee Lewis, to become a successful musician in his own right. Beginning on small record labels and building a huge local following at his nightclub—Gilley's in Pasadena, Texas—he scored his first hit in 1974 with "Roomful of Roses." Gilley became even more famous when his club served as the setting for the 1980 film *Urban Cowboy,* and he recorded a single, the hit "Stand By Me," for the soundtrack album.

Gilley was born in the late 1930s in Natchez, Louisiana, but while he was still very young, his family moved to nearby Ferriday. There he grew up in close contact with Lewis and another cousin who would later become famous—evangelist Jimmy Swaggart. All three boys were musically inclined and spent their time sneaking off to black boogie-woogie and blues joints and begging their parents to buy them pianos. Despite Mrs. Gilley's low $18-a-week waitress salary, she managed to accumulate a savings and buy the instrument for her son when he was ten years old. He became quite proficient on it by the time he reached adolescence.

### Became a Local Success

Unlike Lewis, though, Gilley did not count on his musical abilities to provide him with a career. He married and relocated to Houston, Texas, finding work in the parts department of an engineering firm. But in 1956, after hearing one of Lewis's recordings, Gilley decided to follow a music career himself. He released a few singles on the Houston label Gold Star, but these efforts were dismissed as too similar in style to Jerry Lee's hits. Gilley did, however, manage to obtain session work as a piano player at several Houston-area recording studios, and he began to perform in local clubs as well. Eventually the musician became popular enough to land gigs in clubs throughout the southern United States. Meanwhile, Gilley worked his way through several small labels before landing a contract with Dot Records; he subsequently released the single "Call Me Shorty," which enjoyed moderate success.

But by 1959, Gilley returned to Houston discouraged. Despite scoring a local hit soon afterwards with "Is It Wrong?," he moved his focus from the recording studio to club work. He made a successful living performing in the Houston area and continued to do so throughout the 1960s, particularly at the Nesadel Club. He also achieved another local chart-climber with "Lonely Wine" in 1964.

## Opened Gilley's

In the early 1970s, Gilley teamed up with longtime friend Sherwood Cryer to open his own club in Pasadena called Gilley's. Gilley himself, of course, sang and played piano for the house band, and the club quickly became an area favorite. Meanwhile, Gilley attempted to record again, this time cutting an album with GRT Records. In order to avoid duplicating the sound of his cousin Jerry Lee, he changed his style and even refused to play the piano at these recording sessions. The GRT album, however, did not gain Gilley the more widespread attention he sought.

Instead, the prolific segment of the musician's recording career started by accident. A Gilley's employee requested that the performer record one of her favorite songs, "She Calls Me Baby," on a local label so that it could be stocked in the club's jukebox. He agreed, recording a remake of a George Morgan song, "Room Full of Roses," on the B side. Gilley was dissatisfied with the way the latter tune was recorded; he felt the engineer had mixed in the steel guitar too loudly. Nevertheless, "Room Full of Roses" became a huge hit in the Houston area, and with his hope renewed, Gilley traveled to Nashville to see if he could land a major record deal. He won a contract with Playboy Records, which released the single nationwide, and "Room Full of Roses" quickly became Gilley's first Top Ten hit.

## Appeared in *Urban Cowboy*

Once Gilley broke this barrier, he continued to release country smashes. He recorded a Number One hit in 1975, "City Lights," and followed with other successful singles, including 1976's "Don't the Girls All Get Prettier at Closing Time" and 1977's "Honky Tonk Memories." Though his newfound recording stardom sent him on concert tours throughout the United States, he still found time to perform at Gilley's on a regular basis. The club remained a popular country hangout, and was selected as the setting for the 1980 film about the country nightclub scene, *Urban Cowboy*. Gilley and his band appeared in the film, and a country-flavored remake of Ben E. King's "Stand By Me" that the singer recorded was featured on the film's soundtrack. Gilley's version of "Stand By Me" became one of his biggest hits, and he began touring more and appearing at larger concert venues.

Once Gilley began spending more time away from his beloved club—which, after the release of *Urban Cowboy,* became an increasingly popular tourist attraction—he began to hear a growing number of complaints about the bar's quality. He asked Cryer to implement some improvements, and when Cryer refused, Gilley filed a lawsuit that was not settled until 1989. Gilley won damages, and the club kept his name while Cryer appealed the judgment.

In addition to releasing an album entitled *Chasing Rainbows* in 1989, Gilley hoped to start over again with a new club; the singer stated to John Morthland in *Country Music,* "I'm thinking already about doing another Gilley's and this time doing it right. Only this time I'd get people who know how to do it. I don't want to run a club myself, but I am interested in there still being a Gilley's club."

# Selected discography

### Singles

*"Call Me Shorty,"* Dot, c. 1958.
*"Room Full of Roses,"* Playboy, 1974.
*"City Lights,"* Playboy, 1975.
*"Bouquet of Roses,"* Playboy, 1975.
(With Barbi Benton) *"Roll You Like a Wheel,"* Playboy, 1975.
*"Don't the Girls All Get Prettier at Closing Time,"* Playboy, 1976.
*"Bring It on Home to Me,"* Playboy, 1976.
*"Honky Tonk Memories,"* Playboy, 1977.
*"Chains of Love,"* Playboy, 1977.
*"Here Comes the Hurt Again,"* Playboy, 1978.
*"The Song We Made Love To,"* Playboy, 1978.
*"Just Long Enough to Say Goodbye,"* Epic, 1979.
*"My Silver Lining,"* Epic, 1979.
*"A Little Getting Used To,"* Epic, 1979.
*"True Love Ways,"* Epic, 1980.
*"Stand By Me,"* Asylum, 1980.
*"That's All That Matters To Me,"* Epic, 1980.

"A Headache Tomorrow," Epic, 1981.
"Lonely Nights," Epic, 1981.
"You Don't Know Me," Epic, 1981.

## Albums

City Lights, Playboy, 1975.
Overnight Sensation, Playboy, 1976.
First Class, Playboy, 1977, reissue, Epic, 1987.
Encore, Epic, c. 1980.
(With others) Urban Cowboy, Asylum, 1980.
That's All That Matters to Me, Epic, 1980.
You Don't Know Me, Epic, 1981.
Greatest Hits, Vol. 1, Epic, 1987.
Chasing Rainbows, Airborne, 1989.
Biggest Hits, Columbia.
Christmas at Gilley's, Columbia.
Live at Gilley's, Epic.
Ten Years of Hits, Epic.
With Love From Pasadena, Texas, Intermedia.

Greatest Hits, Vol. 2, Playboy.

# Sources

### Books

Stambler, Irwin, and Grelun Landon, The Encyclopedia of Folk, Country, and Western Music, St. Martin's, 1984.

### Periodicals

Country Music, May/June 1985; May/June 1989.
High Fidelity, March 1982.
People, December 21, 1981; May 28, 1984; October 27, 1986.
Stereo Review, November 1980; May 1982; December 1982.
Variety, November 7, 1984.

—Elizabeth Wenning

# Amy Grant

**Singer, songwriter**

Amy Grant is one of the first Christian singers to attract the attention of mainstream pop music fans. After gaining prominence in the early 1980s for her gospel songs, her 1985 album *Unguarded* propelled her into the realm of pop stardom. Grant and her back-up band have appeared in concert throughout the United States, garnering a steady following. Her award-winning albums have sold in the millions and engendered hit singles and videos. Grant has appeared often on talk shows and has been featured on a televised Christmas special.

The youngest of four daughters of a prominent radiologist, Grant was born in Augusta, Georgia, and raised in Nashville, where she and her family attended the local Church of Christ. She did not become particularly interested in music until her teenage years, when she taught herself to play the guitar and began to write songs. She never had a formal music teacher. While attending Harpeth Hall, an exclusive girl's prep school, Grant worked part-time at a recording studio, demagnetizing tapes and doing janitorial chores. She used the facilities at hand to make a tape for her parents of her own songs, which she accompanied on guitar. Unknown to Grant, someone at the Texas-based Word Records heard the tape, and she was later approached about recording an album.

## Established a Musical Following

Released in 1976 on Word Records' Myrrh label, Grant's self-named debut album became an immediate best-seller in the field of Christian music. During the following years, the teenage singer tried to balance a recording career with her education. After graduating from Harpeth Hall, she attended Furman University in South Carolina before transferring to Vanderbilt University, where she majored in English. At this stage in her budding career, Grant performed solo in churches to her own guitar accompaniment. Two of her albums culled from concert performances became bestsellers in their field.

The late 1970s and early 1980s marked a period of striking change in both the personal and professional aspects of Grant's life. In 1979, she met her future husband, guitarist and songwriter Gary Chapman, who would later become a member of Grant's ten-piece touring band. While at Vanderbilt University in 1983, she recorded *Age to Age*, the first of her albums to see sales figures rise dramatically. With such promising indications of a successful performance career, Grant dropped out of college to become a professional singer.

### Chartered New Territory

In 1985 Word Records signed a distribution deal with A&M Records to launch various gospel artists. Grant was one of them. With its synthesized sound and upbeat songs expressing subtle Christian lyrics, her album *Unguarded* received much airplay and sold more than a million copies. When the single "Find a Way" hit the pop charts, and a duet with Peter Cetera, "The Next Time I Fall," topped *Billboard*'s pop chart in 1987, Grant garnered criticism from some Christians who thought that in her quest for success, she had lost sight of her spiritual roots. Grant countered by suggesting that her songs need not mention Jesus by name in order to portray the message of love that he taught. Critics generally maintain that in concert, Grant aims to entertain her audience; she does not overtly attempt to convert listeners to Christianity.

At the end of the tour to promote *Unguarded,* Grant and her entourage needed a rest. Following a three-year recording hiatus, she released the 1988 album *Lead Me On,* which represents an even further departure from Grant's previous efforts. Unlike the upbeat synthesized sound of *Unguarded, Lead Me On* primarily utilizes acoustic instrumentation, and the songs revolve around somber themes. The album reflects many of Grant's concerns during her absence from the concert stage: accusations that she had sold out her faith, the trauma of a miscarriage, a difficult period in her marriage that was overcome through counseling, and the birth of her son, Matthew. Because none of its songs lent themselves readily to radio airplay, the album was largely ignored by radio stations. Nonetheless, Grant's following remained loyal.

### Topped the Pop Charts

Grant made a distinct attempt to find a place in the pop market with her 1991 release *Heart in Motion,* which contains songs that contemplate the earthly side of human love. "I did that for a few different reasons," she told Chris Willman of the *Los Angeles Times*. "I have invested so much of my time and creative energy [in] writing contemporary Christian songs, and I was really wanting to try something new." To answer her critics in the Christian community she added, "It had nothing to do with a loss of faith or change of lifestyle. . . . I think that Christians, no matter where they are, should be the same person whether they're singing Gospel music or writing and performing a pop album. . . . We just ought to get out there and live life and be true to what we believe, and for those of us that write, just let what we do reflect that."

Fans have had a chance to see Grant's latest efforts portrayed on the small screen as well. When her video "Baby, Baby" aired on MTV, it caused considerable controversy and sparked both positive and negative criticism. While the song was inspired by Millie, the singer's daughter, in the video Grant is seen singing romantically to a handsome actor—not her husband, with whom Grant has often performed in concert. In spite of the uproar surrounding the release, *Heart in Motion* brought Grant several 1992 Grammy nominations and a legion of new listeners.

## Selected discography

*Amy Grant,* Word Records, 1976.
*My Father's Eyes,* Word Records, 1977.
*Never Alone,* Word Records, 1978.
*Amy Grant in Concert,* Word Records, 1979.
*Amy Grant in Concert II,* Word Records, 1980.
*Age to Age,* Word Records, 1983.
*A Christmas Album,* Word Records, 1983.
*Straight Ahead,* A&M, 1984.
*Unguarded,* A&M, 1985.
*Amy Grant: The Collection,* A&M, 1986.
*Lead Me On,* A&M, 1988.
*Heart in Motion,* A&M, 1991.
*Contemporary Christmas Classics,* Word Records.
*Animals' Christmas,* Columbia Records.

# Sources

## Books

Millard, Robert, *Amy Grant,* Doubleday, 1986.

## Periodicals

*Atlanta Journal,* March 1, 1986; November 25, 1988.
*Austin American Statesman,* November 5, 1988.
*Birmingham News,* November 25, 1988.
*Christian Herald,* September/October 1991.
*Commercial Appeal* (Memphis), June 26, 1985.
*Focus on the Family Parental Guidance,* June 1991.
*Grand Rapids Press,* October 14, 1984.
*Indianapolis Star,* October 22, 1988.
*Los Angeles Herald Examiner,* May 2, 1986.

*Los Angeles Times,* April 16, 1991.
*Morning Advocate* (Baton Rouge, LA), June 14, 1985.
*Nashville Banner,* July 28, 1989.
*News and Observer* (Raleigh, NC), March 16, 1986.
*New York Daily News,* October 7, 1984.
*New York Tribune,* July 25, 1989.
*People,* July 15, 1991.
*Plain Dealer* (Cleveland), August 9, 1985.
*Providence Journal,* October 5, 1984.
*Saturday Evening Post,* November/December 1991.
*St. Paul Pioneer Press-Dispatch,* October 27, 1988.
*Tennessean* (Nashville), August 3, 1985; December 14, 1986; October 15, 1988.
*Today's Christian Woman,* May/June 1991.
*Tulsa World,* March 16, 1986.

—Jeanne M. Lesinski

# Dave Grusin

---

**Composer, pianist, record producer**

---

**D**ave Grusin is a pianist, keyboardist, arranger, record producer, and cofounder of GRP Records who likes the title "solo artist" least. Winner of a Grammy Award for best instrumental arrangement on the album *Harlequin* in 1985 and an Oscar for the motion picture score *The Milagro Beanfield War* in 1989, he told Scott Yanow in *Down Beat,* "I still don't think of myself as a performer. I don't have a burning desire to go out and play before people. I do it occasionally to try to spread the word about my records, but basically I've never felt like a performer. I much prefer the creative process in the studio, the writing and the recording."

Grusin was born on June 26, 1934, in Littleton, Colorado, to parents who were both classical musicians. "My father was a very good violinist and a perfect teacher," Grusin explained to Yanow. "He didn't push music on us, but it was such an inherent part of our lives that it became a natural part of my childhood. My mother played piano and I started it when I was four, having the usual lessons." At home, Grusin's musical training was in the classical genre, but the youngster was also exposed to jazz. Although he remembers no jazz records being played at home, his parents took him to concerts in Denver, Colorado, where he saw such performers as Ray Brown, Ella Fitzgerald, Hank Jones, Gene Krupa, Illinois Jacquet, and Flip Phillips. "It was very exciting," Grusin recalled to Yanow, "and set the stage for me gaining an interest in jazz."

## Became Andy Williams's Piano Player

Growing up in an agricultural community, where he worked on a ranch through high school, Grusin originally planned to be a veterinarian. "Three weeks before entering college," he told Yanow, "I switched to music out of guilt for the immense effort and expense that my father had spent on my musical education. He did not force me to study music but I knew that he'd approve of the switch. Grusin majored in piano and minored in clarinet at the University of Colorado, where he also backed performers like Anita O'Day at local clubs when he was not in class.

In 1959 Grusin went to New York City to begin graduate work at the Manhattan School of Music. Discovering that he had to wait six months before his union membership transferred locally, Dave was forced to find a job outside the city to support his young family. He related to Yanow, "An ex-roommate of mine found out that [singer] Andy Williams needed a piano player. Andy had had a couple of hit records but he was still a new guy." The work for the singer involved extensive travel, so Grusin eventually left graduate school.

The musician soon found himself in Los Angeles, where he was appointed Williams's musical director and arranger when the vocalist began a weekly television variety show. Grusin noted in *Down Beat,* "It was a nice music show in the early '60s and we didn't perform any music that we would be ashamed of, even though it was on commercial television. It was a grind, a very hard job; but for me it turned out to be an amazing workshop." Also at this time Grusin made some recordings, including *Subways Are for Sleeping, Piano, Strings and Moonlight,* and *Kaleidoscope,* which reflected the influence of Art Tatum and other jazz artists.

## Cofounded GRP Records

In 1964 Grusin left *The Andy Williams Show* to write music for motion pictures. He stated in *Down Beat,* "Getting the first assignment is always the hardest because if you haven't written before, no one wants to talk about it. I'll always be grateful to [writer] Norman Lear and [director] Bud [Yorkin] for taking a chance on me and hiring me for [the 1967 film] *Divorce American Style.*" Throughout his career, Grusin has written and arranged scores for more than 50 movies, including *The Graduate, Heaven Can Wait, The Goodbye Girl, Reds, On Golden Pond, Tootsie,* and *Tequila Sunrise,* and for such television shows as *Baretta* and *St. Elsewhere.* Nominated four times previously, he won an Academy Award in 1989 for the musical score he composed for the film *The Milagro Beanfield War.*

His main occupation—writing and arranging musical

scores for films—did not deter Grusin from taking on additional work in the music field. In 1976 he began producing records with partner Larry Rosen, whom he had met earlier when he hired Rosen as a drummer for Andy Williams's band. The musicians started as independent producers, but eventually formed their own record company, GRP Records, in 1983. Many best-selling albums by various jazz-influenced artists followed, and the producers have received critical acclaim and numerous awards.

## Producer of "Fusion Jazz" Artists

In 1985 Grusin won a Grammy Award for best instrumental arrangement of a cut on the album *Harlequin,* and over the years GRP has received numerous Grammy Awards and nominations; the company boasts a roster of artists that includes Lee Ritenour, Diane Schuur, Chick Corea, Eddie Daniels, Dave Valentin, and Kevin Eubanks. "We're not an avant garde or a mainstream label," Grusin explained to Yanow in *Down Beat,* "but we're also not interested in making a sort of formula new age product either. We're comfortable in a type of fusion jazz that feels like it's going somewhere and will continue to develop."

Critical reaction to GRP's interpretations of contemporary jazz varies. A reviewer in *High Fidelity* described GRP recordings as "mostly lightweight," concentrating on a "sweeter, often electrified product." Though Robin Tolleson labeled one Grusin number "nice ear candy" in a review in *Down Beat, Stereo Review* noted GRP Records's "penchant for polished production."

In 1986 Grusin moved to Santa Fe, New Mexico, fulfilling a desire to live near the Rocky Mountains. He decided to make an album in 1988 with his brother, keyboardist Don Grusin, and the two recorded the electronic duet *Sticks and Stones.* Though his time is severely limited, the multitalented musician and businessman yearns to fulfill an additional career goal: "Someday I'd like to write a serious piece of classical music," Grusin expressed to Yanow in *Down Beat.* "I find it difficult to do in a life full of assignments, but eventually I want to compose some non-jazz music in a contemporary vein."

# Selected discography

*Subways Are for Sleeping,* Epic.
*Piano, Strings, and Moonlight,* Epic.
*Kaleidoscope,* Columbia.
*Dave Grusin and the N.Y./L.A. Dream Band,* GRD.
*Night-Lines,* GRD.

*Mountain Dance,* GRD, 1979.
*Out of the Shadows,* GRD.
*One of a Kind,* GRD.
*Cinemagic,* GRD.
*The Dave Grusin Collection,* GRD.
*The Gershwin Collection,* GRP Records, 1991.

**With Lee Ritenour**

*Harlequin,* GRP Records, 1985
*Festival,* GRP Records, 1989.
*Rio,* Elektra/Musician.
*On the Line,* Elektra/Musician.
*Earth Run,* GRP Records.

**With Quincy Jones**

*Body Heat,* A & M.
*I Heard That!,* A & M.

**With Earl Klugh**

*Earl Klugh,* Blue Note.
*Living Inside Your Love,* Blue Note.

**Other**

(With Don Grusin) *Sticks and Stones,* GRD, 1988.
(With GRP All-Stars) *GRP Super Live in Concert,* GRD, 1988.
(With Eddie Daniels) *Blackwood,* GRD.
(With Kevin Eubanks) *Face to Face,* GRP Records.
(With Ray Brown) *Brown's Bag,* GTI.
(With Art Farmer) *Crawl Space,* CTI.
(With John Klemmer) *Barefoot Ballet,* ABC.
(With Harvey Mason) *Marching in the Street,* Arista.
(With Sergio Mendes) *My Favorite Things,* Atlantic.
(With Gerry Mulligan) *Little Big Horn,* GRP Records.
(With Grover Washington, Jr.) *A Secret Place,* Kudu.

## Sources

*Audio,* March 1988.
*Down Beat,* June 1987; July 1989; January 1990; February 1990.
*High Fidelity,* October 1988.
*Stereo Review,* August 1988; February 1989; March 1989.

—*Marjorie Burgess*

# W. C. Handy

**Singer, composer, cornet player**

**W**. C. Handy's remarkable life started eight years after the conclusion of the American Civil War. Born in a log cabin in Florence, Alabama, on November 16, 1873, William Christopher Handy entered into a new era for black people—an era that he himself would help define by introducing his people's music to the world. He thereby became the "Father of the Blues."

The predecessors of the blues were around long before Handy ever picked up a cornet, but they had no name. They were the "folk music" songs of black-American slaves, sung as a deeply emotional and personal response to the brutality and desperation of their lives. It was an undefined sound that was derived from the varied African cultures touched by the slave trade, a sound rooted in firm African traditions carried halfway across the world. It was the song of the poorest of the poor, even among slaves, and it belonged to the most illiterate and forgotten, the so-called "cornfield niggers."

As a trained musician Handy would come to recognize

what he once regarded "primitive" as a viable form of music. He sought a way to translate the blues into compositional form. He set about codifying it: a three-line, 12-bar pattern, with flat third or "blue" note. Though there is a recipe for the blues, its quality is elusive. The fine points of timing and the subtle vocal and pitch variations are essential. It is generally regarded as a music that is deceivingly simple and too easily unappreciated by the untrained ear.

## Music Was His Destiny

Handy's parents and grandparents were among the four million slaves freed by President Abraham Lincoln's Emancipation Proclamation of 1863. One in a sea of liberated souls, his paternal grandfather, William Wise Handy, became a well-respected citizen of Florence and the Methodist minister of his own church. Handy's father followed in those footsteps, and the same future was planned for the young Handy. It was the boy's maternal grandmother who hit upon his destiny by suggesting that her grandson's big ears symbolized a talent for music.

The words thrilled him. At the age of 12, he fell in love with a guitar in a shop window, and one day, after counting out the salvaged earnings from his string of odd jobs, he was finally able to take his prize home. According to Handy's autobiography, *Father of the Blues,* his parents were shocked and dismayed by his interest in the guitar. His outraged father apparently demanded that he return the "devil's plaything" and exchange it for "something that'll do you some good." The bewildered boy traded it in for a new *Webster's Unabridged Dictionary*—and his father paid for organ lessons.

Handy received his education in the rudiments of music during his 11 years at the Florence District School for Negroes. His teacher was a lover of vocal music and took time to give his students voice and music instructions that would enable them to sing religious material—without the accompaniment of instruments. The students were introduced to works by classical composers such as Wilhelm Richard Wagner, Georges Bizet, and Giuseppe Verdi. They learned to sing in all keys, measures, and movements. But Handy longed to play instruments, so on the sly he bought an old cornet and took lessons from its former owner.

## Down-and-Out in St. Louis

At age 15, Handy joined a minstrel show and began his musical career. But after touring only a few towns, the troupe fell apart, and the teenager found himself walking the railroad tracks back to Florence. In 1892, after graduating from the Huntsville Teachers Agricultural and Mechanical College and squeezing in a summer of teaching experience, he arrived in Birmingham to take the teachers' examination. But when he heard that he could expect a salary of $25 or less per month, it didn't take him long to opt for a job at a pipeworks company in the city of Bessemer instead. When wages there were cut, Handy returned to Birmingham, where he organized the Lauzette Quartet. At the announcement of the

Chicago World's Fair, the quartet boarded a tank car and, with only 20 cents between them, headed for fame. But once in Chicago they learned that the fair had been postponed for a year. The dejected band traveled south to St. Louis, Missouri, where they were soon forced to break up. The country was experiencing an economy in panic.

The St. Louis days would imprint themselves on W. C. Handy's mind and music. They would bring the educated son of a minister closer to the experience of the downtrodden negro. Surrounded by misery and opulence alike, the young black man suffered from hunger and lice, slept in a vacant lot, slumped in a poolroom chair, in a horse's stall, and on the cobblestones of the levee of the Mississippi. As he related in his autobiography, his inner voice said repeatedly, "Your father was right, your proper place is in the ministry," and his old schoolteacher's words rang through his head, "What can music do but bring you to the gutter?," but he never gave in. The musician continued to eke out a living playing his cornet and later noted that these down-and-out days would lead to the birth of his "St. Louis Blues."

It was in Evansville, Kentucky, that Handy first gained popular attention. While playing with several local brass bands, word about his talent spread to Henderson, Kentucky, and he was soon hired by its Southern aristocracy. "I had my change that day in Henderson," Handy wrote in his autobiography. "My change was from a hobo and a member of a road gang to a professional musician." In Henderson, Handy also found another opportunity to expand his music education. He angled a job as a janitor in a German singing society only to get close to its director, a professor who was an accomplished teacher, music director, and author of several successful operas. Handy pounced on his every word: "I obtained a post-graduate course in vocal music—and got paid for it," he proclaimed. It was also in that town that Handy met and married his first wife, Elizabeth Virginia Price.

In 1896, Handy was invited to Chicago to join W. A. Mahara's Minstrels, a move he would look back at as "the big moment that was to shape my course in life." As bandleader and soloist he toured with the Minstrels from 1896 to 1900 and again from 1902 to 1904. In the years between he was music teacher and bandmaster at his old college in Huntsville. The Minstrels had an adventurous on-the-road history together, crisscrossing the South and traveling as far as Cuba. When the band had an engagement in Alabama, Handy Sr. took in the show. The minister evidently had a change of heart: "Sonny," he said, as recounted in *Father of the Blues,* "I haven't been in a show since I professed religion. I

enjoyed it. I am very proud of you and forgive you for becoming a musician." Welcome words from the man who once told his young son that he'd rather follow his hearse than see him follow music.

## Vote Crump for Mayor

The year was 1909 and Edward H. "Boss" Crump was running for mayor of Memphis. He needed a campaign band. Handy's group was hired, and "Mr. Crump," the campaign song, came to be. Handy had written it without words but soon—without the reformist candidate's knowledge—the song included lyrics based upon spontaneous comments from the disgruntled crowd: "Mr. Crump won't 'low no easy riders here/Mr. Crump won't 'low no easy riders here/We don't care what Mr. Crump don't 'low/We gon'to bar'l-house anyhow—/Mr. Crump can go and catch hisself some air!"

Crump was elected—perhaps in spite of the song—and the campaign tune was to meet its end, but by that

---

*W. C. Handy did more to carry the blues into the mainstream of music than any other man.*

---

time it had gained such popularity that Handy decided to have it published. He changed the embarrassing lyrics, and "Mr. Crump" turned into "Memphis Blues." Handy entered into an agreement with two white men. One was to arrange the printing and the other, who owned a music publishing company and a record store, would take care of the distribution.

After repeated rejections from stores, the defeated Handy agreed to cover his costs and sell the copyright of "Memphis Blues" to the second man for $50. What Handy did not know then was that the "exploiter," as the musician referred to him in his autobiography, had printed twice the agreed-upon number of records and was successfully distributing them in the North. Despite the injustice, the copyright of "Memphis Blues" marked the first time that the blues had ever been set in print.

### "Heart Like a Rock"

Melancholy about the growing popularity of a song that was no longer his, Handy started searching for a second hit. He holed himself up in a rented room and set to work. Snatches of street life drifted in through the window. "Ma man's got a heart like a rock cast in the sea," is said to have come from the lips of a drunken black woman stumbling down the dimly lit street. The mournful words worked their way into his soul and triggered the flood of memories of his own lost and hungry St. Louis days. He wrote, "I hate to see de evenin sun go down," and between midnight and dawn, a classic—"St. Louis Blues"—was born.

"St. Louis Blues" was followed by a flurry of other compositions, including "Jogo Blues," "Yellow Dog Blues," "Joe Turner Blues," and "Beale Street Blues." In 1908, Handy and Harry H. Pace, a singer and songwriter, created the Pace & Handy Music Company. The company soon thrived. Handy and the blues were on their way.

Handy found that he could no longer endure the rising racial tensions in the South. In 1918, the year that saw the end of World War I, the Pace & Handy Music Company moved to Manhattan. After two years of popular if not monetary success, Pace decided to pull out and go in his own direction. Pace & Handy was renamed Handy Brothers Music Company and can still be found at the same Broadway address today. Throughout his life Handy was troubled with failing eyesight, and it was at this fiscally shaky time that he went totally blind. But it was a temporary condition. He regained his sight and composed "Aunt Hagar's Children Blues," which turned out to be the hit that put him on a solid financial ground. In 1926, Handy edited *Blues: An Anthology*. His public continued to grow, and the blues gathered speed.

### "Father of the Blues"

In 1928, Carnegie Hall witnessed its first evening of black music. By entering this bastion of white classical music, W. C. Handy and the blues stepped arm-in-arm into the limelight, and half a century later, his daughter, Katherine Handy Lewis, would be back at the Hall to sing at the 1981 recreation of that historic milestone. The World War II years continued to be productive and brought increased fame to Handy. He even managed to heal an old disappointment by being honored at the 1940 New York World's Fair. A year later the composer told his story in his autobiography, *Father of the Blues,* and then in 1958, he was portrayed by Nat King Cole in Paramount's *St. Louis Blues,* a film based on his life.

Streets and parks from Alabama to Memphis to New York were named after him. The "Father of the Blues" has remained a beloved public figure decades after his death in 1958.

Handy's life was a rich one, but it was not untouched by sorrow. In 1937, his beloved wife, Elizabeth, died of a cerebral hemorrhage. Years earlier the couple had lost one of their six children, and in 1943 Handy himself came perilously close to death after falling off a New York City subway platform and fracturing his skull. The accident left him blind and bound to a wheelchair for the remainder of his life.

The composer of more than 80 hymns, marches, and blues tunes, W. C. Handy did more to carry the blues into the mainstream of music than any other man. His contribution is a legacy that has exerted a profound and lasting influence on twentieth-century music—a legacy that includes rock 'n roll, which was an offshoot of Chicago's electrified blues. It was Handy's background of solid education and training in classical music that set him apart from his fellow black musicians. It seems to have taken someone with a foot in each world to open the door between them and let the blues come in.

## Selected discography

"Memphis Blues" (originally "Mr. Crump," 1909), Handy Brothers Music Co., 1912.
"Jogo Blues," Handy Brothers Music Co., 1913.
"Yellow Dog Blues," Handy Brothers Music Co., 1914.
"St. Louis Blues," Varsity, 1914.
"Hesitating Blues," Handy Brothers Music Co., 1915.
"Joe Turner Blues," Robbins Music Corp., 1915.
"Beale Street Blues," Handy Brothers Music Co., 1917.
"Aunt Hagar's Children Blues," Handy Brothers Music Co., 1921.
"Loveless Love" (better known as "Careless Love"), Varsity, 1921.

## Selected writings

*Father of the Blues,* Collier Books, 1941.

Editor of studies of black musicians and anthologies of black spirituals and blues.

## Sources

### Books

Handy, W. C., *Father of the Blues,* Collier Books, 1941.
Palmer, Robert, *Deep Blues,* Penguin Books, 1982.

**Periodicals**

*Boston Globe*, November 1949.
*Ebony*, December 1957; February 1959.
*Newsweek*, April 1958.
*United Press*, August 1944.

*—Iva Sipal*

# Bill Harley

**Family entertainer**

Family entertainer Bill Harley has won acclaim across the United States for his blend of song and story that entertains adults and children alike. Described as the Mark Twain of contemporary children's music, Harley has performed as a soloist or with his band the Troublemakers at schools, coffee houses, festivals, and on the theater stage since 1980, logging over two hundred shows per year. To quote *Child Magazine,* "There are a lot of performing artists out there singing, stomping, and storytelling their way into kids' audio cassette players. But few do it with as much spirit and success as Bill Harley."

Born William Harley, the entertainer is the middle of three sons of Max Harley, a lawyer, and Ruth Harley, a children's literature writer. During his childhood, Bill took piano lessons and wrote stories. After moving to the East Coast during his high school years, Harley became interested in folk music and began playing the guitar and banjo. He later attended Hamilton College in Clinton, New York, where he majored in religious studies. Following his graduation, Harley worked as a waiter, directed programs in inner city and rural schools to help children, parents, and teachers to deal effectively with conflict and violence in their lives, and played in coffee houses and small clubs.

In 1980 Harley and his wife, Deborah Block, moved to Providence, Rhode Island, where Block had a job at Brown University. Harley and a friend started the Learning Connection, a community-based learning program that grew to include hundreds of courses. About that time, Harley also founded a storytelling group called the Spellbinders. Within a short time Harley—a man of medium height, bushy mustache, thinning hair, and large eyes—found himself performing more and more at elementary schools.

He incorporated a wide variety of musical forms and traditions (reggae, doo-wop, jazz) into his programs, made up of songs and stories embellished with silly voices, tone inflections, body language, sound effects, and gestures. Harley makes up his own stories and draws on folk literature, Indian legend, books, and the works of other storytellers. He engages the youngsters in sing-alongs, fill-in-the-blanks, and question-and-answers, thus making his entertainment into a two-way event. Before adding stories to his repertoire, Harley often tries them out on his sons Noah and Dylan.

## Formed Record Company

In 1984 Harley and Block took out a second mortgage on their house in Seekonk, Massachusetts, to found Round River Records and cut Harley's first album—

*Monsters in the Bathroom.* The album's success encouraged him to try evening family concerts, which proved popular because Harley's music speaks to both children and adults. Harley told *Contemporary Musicians:* "I perform to remind everyone, including myself, that regardless of where we come from or how old we are or what we think, we have a great deal in common—and the things we don't have in common, the things that make each one of us unique, are things worth celebrating. I like family audiences, and I've found that material that works, really works, for kids, also works for adults—for the obvious reasons: we're all people and adults remember growing up. And if they don't remember, I remind them."

Many of Harley's nine albums, which are geared to children of grade school age, have been award-winners because he strives to understand children's points of view. Harley borrows Fred Roger's (celebrated host of TV's *Mr. Roger's Neighborhood*) term "emotional archaeology" when referring to what he attempts to do in getting in touch with his own childhood experiences. "A lot of my writing is trying to go back and touch the kid within me, always hoping that the kid is still there," Harley told Danny McCue of the *Long Island Parenting News.*

The title song from *Fifty Ways to Fool Your Mother* lists in rap fashion fifty excuses to get out of going to school. In

*You're in Trouble*'s "Dad Threw the TV Out the Window" Harley tells kids that they can live without the television; in "No School Today" he sings the praises of a snow day; and in the title song he recounts what happens when a young boy comes home from school to find a plate of cookies with the note "Don't touch! These are for dessert."

### Approach to Songwriting

Harley described his songwriting approach to Howard Scott in the *Providence Sunday Journal Magazine:* "Sometimes I come up with an emotion, and hunt for a way to express the feeling. Other times, I have an idea or image in mind. Often, I'll carry the thought in my head for a while. Then I'll sit down and begin writing. I don't always get it the first time. The ending to 'Dad Threw the TV Out the Window,' where the kid joyously throws his father's television out the window took me a year to come up with."

Harley has expressed his creativity in a number of different ways. He recorded a collection of folk songs for adults (*Coyote*), and with songwriter/storyteller Peter Alsop he created a collection of songs about serious illness and hospitals (*Peter and Bill in the Hospital*). In 1991, in conjunction with WGBH-Radio in Boston, he produced *I'm Gonna Let It Shine: A Gathering of Voices for Freedom,* a collection of freedom songs featuring original voices of the Civil Rights Movement and nationally recognized singer/activists, among others. Harley has also written and narrated a series of filmstrips for Learning Tree Films and has written a theater piece.

## Selected discography

### On Round River Records

*Monsters in the Bathroom,* 1984.
*Fifty Ways to Fool Your Mother,* 1986.
*Dinosaurs Never Say Please and Other Stories,* 1987.
*Cool in School: Tales from 6th Grade,* 1987.
*Coyote,* 1988.
*Peter and Bill in the Hospital* (with Peter Alsop), 1988.
*You're in Trouble,* 1988.
*Grownups Are Strange,* 1990.
*Come on Out and Play,* 1990.

## Sources

*American Bookseller,* August 1990.

*Booklist,* January 15, 1990.

*Child Magazine,* April 1991.

*Christian Science Monitor,* February 7, 1986.

*Entertainment Weekly,* July 6, 1990; October 19, 1990.

*Heartsong Review,* Fall 1990/Winter 1991.

*Long Island Parenting News,* March 1991.

*Los Angeles Times,* January 3, 1991.

*MetroKids* (Philadelphia), March 1991.

*The National Storytelling Journal,* Summer 1986.

*Providence Journal,* April 20, 1989; November 13, 1990; December 27, 1990; April 14, 1991.

*Providence Sunday Journal Magazine,* March 11, 1990.

*St. Louis Post-Dispatch,* May 4, 1989.

*Sun Chronicle* (North Attleboro, MA), April 20, 1989.

*—Jeanne M. Lesinski*

# Shirley Horn

---

**Singer, pianist**

---

T rained to play time-honored classical master-pieces, jazz vocalist and pianist Shirley Horn switched to jazz at the age of 17. When a patron of the Washington, D.C., restaurant where she performed classical music handed her a four-foot turquoise bear after she sang his request, "Melancholy Baby," Horn disclosed to John S. Wilson in a *New York Times* profile, "Oscar Peterson became my Rachmaninoff and Ahmad Jamal became my Debussy." In 1991 "the enthralling Shirley Horn," as she has been called in *Down Beat* magazine, released her 14th record, *Billboard*'s Number One jazz album, *You Won't Forget Me.* The record, which features jazz greats Wynton and Branford Marsalis, Toots Thielemans, and Miles Davis, caused a sensation.

A singer who kept her career on a slow but sure path, Horn has long made her home life her highest priority. As the nineties dawned, however, Horn—nearing sixty—was "front and center," reported Jay Cocks in *Time,* with a sold-out debut in Paris and a premiere at New York City's prestigious Carnegie Hall. Cocks observed that "her jazz essence—is still intact. It's what draws you first when you hear the smoky timber of her voice, the leisured elegance of her phrasing. And it's what holds you, wondering about the magic she brings to tunes as varied as 'Don't Let the Sun Catch You Crying' and 'You Won't Forget Me.'"

Born on May 1, 1934, in Washington, D.C., Horn was a child prodigy who started piano lessons at four. At 12 she began studying classical composition at the Howard University Junior School of Music; when Horn did not have adequate funds to accept the scholarship she had won to the famed Juilliard School—which would have necessitated her living in New York City—her doctor uncle paid for four years of lessons at Howard. The owner of the Washington restaurant where she played classical music routinely in late adolescence requested that she sing jazz after he heard her vocal rendition of "Melancholy Baby." Horn effectively studied jazz by watching dinner shows at Washington's Olivia's Patio Lounge. Comfortable with the intimate style of a small group, she formed the first of her trademark trios in 1954.

### Early Association With Miles Davis

In 1959 Horn's ensemble released *Embers and Ashes* on the Stereo-Craft label, an event that prompted legendary jazz trumpet player Miles Davis to take note. He phoned Horn, reaching her at her mother-in-law's Virginia residence, to invite her to New York to perform with him at the revered Village Vanguard. "Opening night was like something out of a dream," she told *New York Times* contributor Wilson. "Lena Horne was there and Claudia McNeill. And Sidney Poitier offered me a drink. After the set, I sat in the kitchen of the club with Miles and the guys in his band—Wynton Kelly, Paul Chambers, and Jimmy Cobb. I was in heaven!"

Though a five-year recording contract with Mercury Records followed her Vanguard debut, Horn made only three albums before becoming disenchanted with the music industry. Accustomed to accompanying herself on piano, she was uneasy as a stand-up singer backed by an orchestra. Touring and drug use—the latter almost as inescapable in the music scene as the former—were particularly distasteful to Horn, especially after she lost three friends to drugs. Crowds she disliked might watch her disappear in the middle of a set, never to return; her heart was elsewhere—with her husband, Shep Deering, a mechanic for the Washington, D.C. Metropolitan Transit Authority, and her daughter, Rainey, born in 1962. Horn chose to sing close to home in the Bohemian Caverns until civil disturbances, which erupted in Washington in 1967, closed that venue. During the 1960s and seventies she confined her performances to the capital area and recorded infrequently. Exceptions were theme songs for the films *For Love of Ivy* and *Dandy in Aspic,* which Horn's producer, Quincy Jones, specially requested.

## Played by Her Rules

Those who criticized Horn for passing up important career opportunities in her early years failed to understand her dogged need to go her own way and cultivate her unique personal style. "That wonderful sense of drama," explained jazz critic Martin Williams in *Time,* "can turn any little song into a three-minute one-act play." Of her measured approach to singing, Horn divulged to *Time's* Cocks, "It's just the way I feel about a song. They call me the slowest singer in the world, but I don't talk fast either. You're trying to tell a story, paint a picture."

In the 1980s—by which time Horn's daughter had approached adulthood—the mood characterizing jazz became more receptive to the singer's unusual technique. It was then that Horn heeded the urging of Georgetown University professor Joel E. Siegel to resume her career. In the summer of 1981 she received a standing ovation at the North Sea Jazz Festival at The Hague, in the Netherlands. Later that year she accepted Siegel's invitation to perform in the concert series at the Corcoran Gallery in Washington. Her club circuit soon broadened beyond Washington to including jazz spots like Michael's Pub in New York City. Although reviewers were paying attention to her recordings of that period, Horn's albums had yet to garner significant royalties. A *Stereo Review* assessment of her 1989 effort, *Close Enough for Love,* read, "Though Horn has never reached the heights of success attained by Nina Simone or Roberta Flack, both of whom fall into roughly the same stylistic category, it is certainly not for lack of talent."

## Scored Big With *You Won't Forget Me*

In 1991 Horn released *You Won't Forget Me.* A collaboration with her trio regulars Charles Ables, on bass, and Steve Williams, on drums, the album rose to Number One on *Billboard's* jazz charts and provided Horn the stellar media treatment that had eluded her for decades. Jazz critics made much of her choice of support musicians—Branford and Wynton Marsalis, Toots Thielemans, and Miles Davis, who had not played sideman to a singer for the preceding 20 years. "*You Won't Forget Me* . . . should finally bring Ms. Horn acclaim as a jazz vocalist worthy of comparison with Billie Holiday, Ella Fitzgerald and Carmen McRae," predicted Stephen Holden in *The New York Times.* "It looked like an overnight success story," summed up John Leland in *Newsweek.* "But only now . . . is Horn enjoying the stature that must have seemed within easy reach thirty years ago." *Time* printed a particularly succinct appraisal: "It may also be read as an unconditional guarantee: Shirley Horn is indelible."

In the wake of her triumph with *You Won't Forget Me,* Horn commented to *Time* contributor Cocks on the media hype that had alluded her throughout her 40-year career. "It's been written that Shirley Horn is back on the scene," she said. "Well, I haven't been anywhere. And I've been busy." Horn has been busy, indeed, and—at long last—has reached the pinnacle of the jazz world on her own terms. "Horn's career," asserted *Newsweek*'s Leland, "come to fruition at its own pace, can now proceed under its own power."

## Selected discography

*Embers and Ashes,* Stereo-Craft, 1959.

*I Thought About You,* Verve, 1987.
*Close Enough for Love,* Verve, 1989.
*Loads of Love: Shirley Horn With Horns,* Mercury, 1990.
*You Won't Forget Me,* Verve, 1991.

## Sources

*Down Beat,* December 1990.
*Newsweek,* April 29, 1991.
*New York Times,* May 28, 1982; January 23, 1991.
*People,* March 25, 1991.
*Stereo Review,* August 1989.
*Time,* March 25, 1991.

—*Marjorie Burgess*

# Alberta Hunter

---

**Singer, composer**

---

Jazz singer Alberta Hunter, like many other early jazz musicians, had a turbulent childhood. Her father left the family soon after she was born, and he died a few years later. Poverty and hard times plagued much of Hunter's childhood in Memphis, Tennessee. Despite her upbringing, she went on to become one of the most famous jazz and blues performers of her time. Then, shocked by her mother's death in 1954, Hunter retired from the limelight and worked as a nurse for 20 years. In an unlikely turn of events, she reentered the music business at the age of 82, gaining as much fame as she had in the 1920s, '30s, and '40s.

Hunter's family moved frequently after her father abandoned them, and Alberta experienced turmoil during those years. She suffered the emotional ramifications brought on by her mother's ill-fated remarriage and coped with sexual abuse from a school principal and a landlady's boyfriend. While these events seemed to have an effect on her personality, they never stifled her will to survive and become a success. When she was only eight years old she escaped her stormy home life, sneaking off to Chicago with a former teacher.

Hunter recounted her journey in *Down Beat:* "My teacher, Mrs. Florida Cummings, had a train pass to Chicago, a child's pass. She asked me if I'd like to go to Chicago on the train and I said, 'Yeah, I'd like to go.' So she said, 'Run home and ask your mother and if she says you can go, you can go.' But I never did ask my mother, I just . . . hid between two houses until it was time to leave. My mother thought I was staying over at my friend's house or something."

### Began Performing in Chicago Clubs

In a fortuitous turn of events, Hunter's streetcar dropped her off right in front of the apartment building of the only person she knew in Chicago, a friend of her mother's named Helen Winston. She helped Hunter find a job peeling potatoes for six dollars a week and board, and the youngster always sent a good portion of her paycheck back to her mother. Walking the streets of Chicago after work, Hunter would peer into the windows of the clubs and "sporting houses" in the area, occasionally wandering in, only to be promptly thrown out. She was particularly attracted to a brothel known as Dago Frank's. One day she went in and began singing one of the only songs she knew, "Where the River Shannon Flows," and the inept piano player tried to accompany her. They threw her out again, but soon after she was offered a job there that paid ten dollars a week.

The prostitutes at Dago Frank's immediately took Hunter under their wing, encouraging her and coercing their clients to tip Hunter while waiting for services. Hunter commented: "People don't realize—prostitutes are good people. Prostitutes are the *best* people. People don't know what makes pimps and prostitutes what they are—it's *circumstances*. Circumstances lead to that way of life. . . . Prostitutes taught me to be a good girl . . . they *made* me be a good girl."

Hunter's voice was steadily improving; she soon graduated from Dago Frank's and began to sing at some of the nightclubs in the area—Hugh Hoskins's and the Panama Cafe—both a far cry from a run-down brothel. She even earned enough money to move her mother up from Memphis to Chicago. Gaining popularity, she was featured at the Dreamland Cafe and performed with King Oliver's Creole Jazz band, featuring Louis Armstrong; jazz greats Al Jolson and Sophie Tucker were among Hunter's audience. Also during her stint at the Dreamland, Hunter began composing and cut the album *Downhearted Blues,* which was a million seller in 1921. A few years later, newcomer Bessie Smith released her version of the album, and it achieved the same success.

## Became a Hit in Europe

Feeling the urge to move on again in the early 1920s, Hunter went to New York City. In 1923 she landed parts in two shows, *How Come* and *Change Your Luck.* When wanderlust hit the performer again, she went to London, singing at the London Pavillion to the likes of Jerome Kern and Oscar Hammerstein. Soon after, she starred with Paul Robeson in *Showboat.* "[Robeson's] voice," Hunter remarked in *Time,* "sounded like a bell in the distance, it had such resonance."

Following her appearance in *Showboat,* Hunter went to Paris, replacing Josephine Baker at the Casino de Paris. Denmark, Turkey, and Egypt marked Hunter's travel itinerary before she settled again in England, becoming a favorite of the Prince of Wales—the future King Edward VII and Duke of Windsor. Eventually returning to New York, Hunter worked in radio, and in 1939 she won a part in *Mamba's Daughters.*

The United Service Organization (USO) attracted Hunter in the 1940s, and she remained there through the Korean War. "They built a whole unit around me," Hunter noted in *Down Beat.* "I sang blues songs and some popular songs. I sang for General [Dwight D.] Eisenhower and General [Douglas] MacArthur." In the 1950s she returned to Chicago and New York, where she performed until her mother died in 1954. "My poor mother was the most important thing in my life," Hunter said. "She died on January 17, 1954 and that was the day I swore to give up singing and become a nurse. I went right to the YWCA [Young Women's Christian Association] and enrolled in their nursing program. I was accepted, by the goodness of God. I became a registered nurse and went to work at Goldwater Memorial Hospital on Roosevelt Island."

## An Amazing Comeback

Hunter told the hospital that she was 50 when she went to work there; she was actually 62. She worked there for the next 20 years, recording a few songs on the side, but basically showed no other interest in the music business. The hospital forced her to retire in 1977, believing she was at the mandatory retirement age of 70. In fact, she was 82.

At a party one day following her retirement from nursing, Hunter ran into Charlie Bourgeois, a publicist for the Newport Jazz Festival. He suggested she telephone Barney Josephson, who owned a club in Greenwich Village and would give her a job. Hunter declined, claiming to have enough money to live on. Bourgeois got her number and passed it on to Josephson. The club owner called Hunter immediately, begging her to come work for him. After some polite demurring, Hunter agreed.

The singer staged an amazing comeback, and Josephson's Cookery club suddenly became the scene of sold-out shows. Although seemingly frail, Hunter's sets were spirited and rollicking. She soon garnered a recording contract with Columbia and was commanding $10,000 a night for outside events. She was living proof of the line she had written herself in "Workin' Man": "There's plenty of good tunes, honey, left in an old violin." Hunter got a chance to travel to Brazil and was invited to sing at the White House, becoming a favorite of former President Jimmy Carter.

In the early 1980s, Hunter coped with health problems and was in and out of hospitals. After a while, she refused to take her medications and succombed to her illness in her Roosevelt Island apartment in 1984. Summing up the impact Hunter had on the music world, club owner Barney Josephson declared, "If I'm ever remembered for anything I have ever done in this business, I want you to remember me as the man who brought Alberta Hunter back to singing again."

## Selected discography

*Downhearted Blues*, Paramount, 1922.
*Jazzin' Baby Blues*, Paramount, 1922.
*Stingaree Blues*, Paramount, 1923.
*Young Alberta Hunter: The Twenties*, Stash.
*Classic Alberta Hunter: The Thirties*, Stash.
*The Legendary Alberta Hunter: The London Sessions—1934*, DRG.

(With Lucille Hegamin and Victoria Spivey) *Songs We Taught Your Mother*, Prestige Bluesville.
*Alberta Hunter With Lovie Austin's Blues Serenaders*, Riverside, 1961.
*Remember My Name* (original soundtrack recording), Juke Box.
*Amtrak Blues*, Columbia.
*The Glory of Alberta Hunter*.
*Look for the Silver Lining*.

### Other

*Alberta Hunter: Jazz at the Smithsonian* (video), Sony, 1982.

## Sources

### Books

Taylor, Frank C. and Gerald Cook, *Alberta Hunter: A Celebration in Blues*, McGraw-Hill, 1987.
*Black Pearls: Blues Queens of the 1920s*, Rutgers University Press, 1988.

### Periodicals

*Down Beat*, January 1980.
*Ms.*, March 1987.
*Time*, December 13, 1982; October 29, 1984.

*—Nancy Rampson*

# Ice-T

**Rapper, actor**

Ice-T appeared on the music scene in 1987 with a new style: gangster rap, which offered rhymes about crime and street life in general in unflinching detail. His tough, groundbreaking records paved the way for the wave of younger gangster-rappers that included Ice Cube and N.W.A. Before his arrival on the scene, rappers devoted most of their lyrics to partying. Ice-T, an ex-criminal from South Central Los Angeles trying to go straight by way of his music, sang about what he knew: robbery, murder, pimps, hustlers, gangs, and prison. In his own words: "I try to write about fun/And the good times/But the pen yanks away and explodes/And destroys the rhyme."

By the early 1990s, however, Ice-T had reached such a level of success as a recording artist and film star that his gangster image began to give way to that of a teacher. *Newsweek* referred to him as "a foulmouthed moralist." *Entertainment Weekly*'s James Bernard declared that "Ice-T has something to teach anyone concerned about the rotting core of America's cities." As his success broadened, Ice-T continued to sing about the street—but with a determination to help black kids escape the ghetto and make white kids understand it. He also considered his financial future a matter of strategy: "The name of the game is capitalism," reads a typical Ice-T quote from his publicity packet, "and I aim to win that game, too."

## From Crime to Rhyme

Ice-T was born Tracey Marrow in the late 1950s—he refused to release his birthdate—in Newark, New Jersey. By the time he was in the seventh grade both his parents had died, and he went to live with an aunt in Los Angeles. While at Crenshaw High School, he wrote rhymes for local gangs and was soon drawn by his friends into petty crime. At age 17 he left his aunt's home and, in his words, "starting hanging out in the 'hood with my friends." By the early 1980s, Ice was also drawn to rap music, thanks to the success of artists like Kurtis Blow. In 1982 he recorded "The Coldest Rap" for an independent label and was paid twenty dollars for it.

Naturally, this kind of money was nothing compared to what he and his friends could make illegally. Although he claimed to have never been a "gangbanger" himself, he was close enough to see that world as a dead end. Eventually his friends starting being sent to prison. "Then one of my buddies got life," he told *Musician*. "And they were all calling me from jail, saying, this ain't the place, homes. Stay with that rap. Stay down." He stayed with it, honing his style and landing a part as a rapper in the 1984 movie *Breakin'*.

## For the Record. . .

Real name, Tracey Marrow (some sources say Morrow); born during the late 1950s in Newark, NJ; parents deceased during childhood; raised by an aunt in Los Angeles, CA.

Recording artist and film actor. Wrote rhymes for Los Angeles gangs in 1970s; recorded "The Coldest Rap" in 1982 for independent label; made film debut in 1984 movie *Breakin'*; released first album, 1987; appeared in film *New Jack City*, 1991; cast in film *Ricochet*, 1991; joined Lollapalooza concert tour, 1991.

**Addresses:** *Record company*—Sire Records, 75 Rockefeller Plaza, 20th Floor, New York, NY 10019-6979. *Publicist*—Susan Blond, Inc., 250 West 57th St., Suite 622, New York, NY 10107.

In addition to the advice and admiration of his friends, Ice relied on his girlfriend Darlene, who stayed with him through the lean years and finally shared his success with him. "Even though we were broke," Ice told Scott Cohen in *Details,* "she knew that I could take five minutes out and go scam $20,000. I needed a girl who was ready to say, 'Don't do it, Ice. It's O.K.'" Darlene added that for a long time they were too broke to go to the movies: "We just lived in one little room and paid rent. We didn't have a car for two years."

By the mid-1980s rap had grown from an urban phenomenon to a national one, but New York City's rappers had a monopoly on street credentials. California, which had produced the good-natured surf pop of the Beach Boys and psychedelic rock bands like the Grateful Dead, hardly seemed a source of rhymes about urban strife. But Ice-T's 1987 debut, *Rhyme Pays,* put South Central Los Angeles on the nation's cultural map with its disturbing stories of inner-city warfare.

This new approach took the music community by storm; it also provoked charges from watchdog organizations like the Parents' Music Resource Center and from critics on the political left and right that Ice glorified violence, theft, and sexism. Subject matter aside, he drew fire—and the first warning sticker placed on a rap record, by his reckoning—for using "profanity." "No one has yet been able to explain to me the definition of profanity anyhow. . . . I can think of ways to say stuff— saying things using legitimate words but in a context— that makes a more profane comment than any bullshit swear words." The album's rap "6 in the Morning"

became particularly well-known, telling the story of a handful of gang members escaping the police.

Ice returned in 1988 with *Power.* The cover of the album featured a bikini-clad Darlene pointing a gun at the camera; Ice hadn't softened his approach. The album yielded two hits, "High Rollers" and "I'm Your Pusher." Ice's face began to appear more regularly on MTV, and he contributed the title song to the soundtrack of the 1988 film *Colors.* His high-profile gangsterism provoked more attacks from various authorities, particularly when he began speaking to students in schools. In a discussion with Arion Berger in *Creem,* Ice presented his imitation of an FBI agent opposed to his school tours: "'He has a record here called, um, "I'm Your Pusher."' 'Well, have you played it?' 'Oh, we don't have a phonograph here at the Bureau.'"

Ice's frustration at attempts to suppress his music motivated a change of direction on his next LP, *The Iceberg/Freedom of Speech . . . Just Watch What You Say,* released in 1989. A drawing of his face appeared on the cover with a gun to either side of his head and the barrel of another in his mouth. He enlisted punk politician and former Dead Kennedys lead singer Jello Biafra to deliver an announcement of right-wing martial law over a sampled piece of deathmetal guitar, setting the tone for a relentless counterattack on conservative thinking. The record also featured "Peel Their Caps Back," which Berger called Ice-T's "most vicious criminal record so far."

Ice later reflected that the *Iceberg* album was too preoccupied with censorship and free expression. "Sales were good on that album," he told Dennis Hunt of the *Los Angeles Times,* "but [I can see where] some of the raps made some people think I was going soft. I just got caught up in messages—about freedom of speech. People at the record company wanted me to do that and I'm sorry that I listened to them." In the meantime, he added, the rising stars of gangster rap had upped the ante of street-tough rhyming. In 1991, though, he would come roaring to the forefront of the scene once again.

### Original Gangster—and Actor

Ice-T landed the role of an undercover cop in the smash 1991 film *New Jack City* and his song "New Jack Hustler" appeared on the film's soundtrack. He received excellent reviews for his acting in the film; Alan Light of *Rolling Stone* called his performance "riveting." "It was scary," Ice told Dave DiMartino of *Entertainment Weekly.* "I didn't know how the actors were gonna react, and in music I'm in my own domain. But when I got there, the first thing I found out was that they were, like, in awe of me—they wanted, like, autographs and stuff." Soon he had signed on to play a drug dealer in another film, *Ricochet*.

Ice's 1991 album *O.G.–Original Gangster* contained twenty-four tracks of uncompromising and often violent raps. Rather than pursue the anti-censorship tack of the *Iceberg* album, *O.G.* returned to Ice-T's earlier turf with a vengeance. The album's themes are summed up by titles like "Straight Up Nigga," "Prepared to Die," and "Home of the Bodybag." Ice's raps, though laced with the "profanity" of earlier records, had become tougher and leaner; "Mic Contract" likened rap competition to gang warfare and suggested that Ice-T was ready to face off with young gangster-rappers. The album also included a rock and roll song, "Body Count," which was the name of the hardcore band he had assembled. Ice enlisted four different producers to work on the album, and DJ Evil E. provided the eclectic mix of beats and samples.

Reviews of *O.G.* were mostly very positive. *Entertainment Weekly*'s James Bernard declared that "Ice-T has something to teach anyone concerned about the rotting core of America's biggest cities," and gave the album an "A." Even as Jon Pareles of the *New York Times* acknowledged contradictions between Ice's "trigger-happy machismo and his increasing maturity," he remarked that "[*O.G.*] works to balance the thrills of action and the demands of conscience." "It's his candor that really draws blood," a notice in *Musician* commented, while *Stereo Review* insisted that "Ice-T raps in lightning-quick, non-nonsense rhymes that cut to the bone with lack of pretense or apology." In his *Rolling Stone* review, Mark Coleman noted that "*O.G.* can be heard as a careening, open-ended discussion. Of course Ice does tend to follow his sharpest points with defiant kiss-offs. . . . But get past his bluster and this guy is full of forthright, inspiring perceptions."

### Warnings and Promises

For its unsparing language and content, *O.G.* received a parental warning sticker; Coleman claimed that such warnings were "like sticking a Band-Aid on a gunshot wound." Ice-T's response to the sticker, in a quote which appeared in his publicity materials as well as ads for the album, was as follows: "I have a sticker on my record that says 'Parental Guidance is Suggested.' In my book, parental guidance is *always* suggested. If you need a sticker to tell you that you need to guide your child, you're a dumb f—kin' parent anyhow."

1991 also saw Ice-T join the ambitious traveling rock festival known as Lollapalooza. Organized by Perry Farrell—whose band, Jane's Addiction, was the head-lining attraction—the tour included such divergent acts as Black Rock Coalition founders Living Colour, the industrial dance outfit Nine Inch Nails, and British postpunk veterans Siouxie and the Banshees. As the only rapper on the tour, Ice-T faced Lollapalooza's predominantly white audiences with a positive attitude: "All I want them to do is come out and say 'I like him.' Not get the message, not understand a word I'm saying. Just think, 'Those black guys on the stage I used to be scared of, I like 'em.' I want to come out and say, 'Peace.' If I can do that, that's cool." His participation in Lollapalooza attested to his belief that rap had the same rebellious and unifying quality that rock and roll had when it first appeared: "White kids will continue to get hipper to black culture. With R&B, the kids didn't want to meet us, but this is rock & roll all over again—everybody chillin' together."

Ice-T began as a controversial rapper in the late 1980s, throwing around gangster slang and strong language

> *"White kids will continue to get hipper to black culture. With R&B, the kids didn't want to meet us, but this is rock & roll all over again—everybody chillin' together."*

and provoking anxiety in many listeners. By the early 1990s, however, he had matured into a thoughtful, charismatic performer with strong careers in at least two media. Despite his newfound success, though, Ice insisted that he still made a lot of people nervous: "Parents are scared because my record is Number One on the campus charts of Harvard for three months," reads a quote in his publicity packet. "These kids are being trained to grow up and become Supreme Court justices and politicians."

## Selected discography

*Rhyme Pays* (includes "6 in the Morning"), Sire, 1987.
*Power* (includes "High Rollers" and "I'm Your Pusher"), Sire, 1988.
(Contributor) *Colors* (motion picture soundtrack; includes "Colors"), Sire, 1988.

The Iceberg/Freedom of Speech . . . Just Watch What You Say
(includes "Peel Their Caps Back"), Sire, 1989.
(Contributor) New Jack City (motion picture soundtrack; includes
"New Jack Hustler"), Sire, 1991.
O.G.–Original Gangster (includes "New Jack Hustler," "Straight
Up Nigga," "Prepared to Die," "Home of the Bodybag," "Mic
Contract," and "Body Count"), Sire, 1991.

# Sources

## Periodicals

Billboard, June 8, 1991.
Creem, April/May 1991.
Details, July 1991.
Entertainment Weekly, May 24, 1991; May 31, 1991.
Los Angeles Times, April 21, 1991.
Musician, June 1991; August 1991.
Newsweek, July 1, 1991.
The New York Times, May 19, 1991.
Rolling Stone, May 16, 1991; June 13, 1991; September 19,
1991.
The Source, May 1991.
Spin, May 1991.
Stereo Review, August 1991.

## Other

Ice-T press release, Warner Bros./Sire, 1991.

—Simon Glickman

# The Jackson 5/
# The Jacksons

**Pop group**

The Jackson 5—Michael, Marlon, Tito, Jackie, and Jermaine—were a popular vocal group that achieved a string of Number 1 pop hits in the early 1970s. Signed to Motown Records by Berry Gordy in 1968, the Jackson 5's popularity eventually waned at Motown, and they left the label after their seven-year contract was up. The group joined the Epic label, a CBS subsidiary, in 1976, changing their name to the Jacksons for legal reasons.

Through the late 1970s and early 1980s, the group released several albums and toured extensively. At the same time, Michael Jackson's solo career was taking off, with two albums produced by Quincy Jones. The Jacksons' live performances and recording career culminated in the 1984 *Victory* tour and subsequent album. Following that difficult tour, the group disbanded, and Michael and his brothers were replaced on the record charts by their younger sisters, LaToya and, especially, Janet.

The Jacksons grew up in Gary, Indiana. Their father, Joe Jackson, was also born in Gary and worked as a crane operator at the Gary Works steel plant. He was a

musician on the side, and he taught his sons about music, later acting as their manager. His wife and matriarch of the Jackson family, Katherine, liked country and western music and that was the first music the young Jacksons were exposed to. Katherine was a Jehovah's Witness and raised her family in that religion. By all accounts, the Jackson family was very protective and strict with their children, and they led sheltered lives in the working-class neighborhood in which they grew up.

The Jackson 5, as a performing group, began with the three older sons, Tito, Jackie, and Jermaine. Rehearsing under their father's guidance, they were soon joined by Marlon (playing bongos) and Michael. Very precocious from an early age, Michael quickly became the group's lead singer. Around 1964 or 1965, the Jackson 5 won Gary's first city-wide talent show. Around 1966, they recorded seven sides for Gordon Keith's Steeltown Records, a small label based in Gary. One of the Steeltown singles, "Big Boy," was a regional success and was picked up by Atco for national distribution.

This moderately successful record gave the Jackson 5 an entree into Chicago nightclubs and the so-called "chitlin' circuit" of black theaters and nightclubs around the country. The chitlin' circuit really opened up for the Jackson 5 after they won the amateur talent show at Chicago's Regal Theater three weeks in a row. With the oldest Jackson, Jackie, about 15 years old and Michael only 8 or 9, the Jackson 5 were touring as the opening act for a string of notable black groups and singers, from the Temptations to Jerry Butler. At the end of 1967, the group was invited to Apollo Amateur Night in New York and were warmly received after coming in first place. Nine-year-old Michael's singing and dancing stole the show.

### Motown, or Michael, Diana, and Berry

Following their success at the Apollo, the Jackson 5 came to the attention of several Motown artists and talent scouts. Both Gladys Knight and Bobby Taylor praised the Jackson 5 to Motown executives after witnessing performances. According to some accounts, it was Diana Ross's enthusiasm for the group that captured Berry Gordy's attention and got the Motown president interested in them. When the Jackson 5 auditioned for Motown in 1968, it was videotaped at the label's Hitsville U.S.A. studio in Detroit for Berry Gordy to view at his offices in Los Angeles. Motown relocated the Jackson family to southern California after signing the group to an open-ended contract. Some of the family stayed with Berry Gordy, others with Diana Ross. By the end of 1970, they had moved into a house in Encino where Michael continued to live with his mother and sisters after the group disbanded.

Motown had relocated its operations from Detroit to Los Angeles in part to take advantage of film and television opportunities. The Jackson 5 made their television debut on October 18, 1969, on ABC's *Hollywood Palace,* in an episode hosted by Diana Ross and the Supremes. Motown's publicity machine had linked the Jackson 5 to the successful Supremes by calling their first album, *Diana Ross Presents The Jackson 5.* That same machinery would put the Jackson 5 on numerous television shows in conjunction with their record releases, and by the fall of 1971 the Jackson 5 had a Saturday-morning cartoon series that featured their music.

### Straight to the Top

Four of the group's first six singles for Motown, "I Want You Back," "ABC," "The Love You Save," and "I'll Be There,"—all released between late 1969 and mid-1971—went to Number 1 on the pop charts, and the other two, "Mama's Pearl" and "Never Can Say Goodbye," reached the Number 2 spot. "I Want You Back," "ABC," and "The Love You Save" were written and produced by the Corporation, a team consisting of Berry Gordy, Freddie Perren, Deke Richards, and Fonzie Mizell. The Jackson 5's next five singles, released in 1971 and 1972, only reached the Top 20 on the charts, but Michael picked up the slack with his solo releases.

His first on Motown, "Got To Be There," reached Number 4 and was followed by "Rockin' Robin," which went to Number 2. Jermaine also began his solo career in 1972, and his second release, "Daddy's Home," reached Number 9. "The Jackson 5 were then a very timely group for black Americans," Jackson employee Steve Manning told Dave Marsh in *Trapped*. "It was the time of the Afro and black pride. . . . The kids identified with them not as stars, but as contemporaries fulfilling their fantasies of stardom."

The Jacksons were growing up, and in 1972 Tito and Jackie both got married. On December 15, 1973, Jermaine married Hazel Joy Gordy, Berry Gordy's daughter. The Jackson 5 left Motown in 1975 following a decline in their record sales and their popularity. There was also speculation that the Jacksons wanted to write and produce their own material, or at least select their own producers. At Motown, they were part of a hitmaking system that left them with little control over the material they recorded. In 1974, the low point of their career at Motown, none of their albums cracked the Top 20, including solo albums by Michael and Jermaine.

When the Jacksons signed with Epic in 1975, Motown claimed legal rights to the Jackson 5 name. Several issues were fought in the courts between Motown and the Jacksons, in part because Motown hoped to promote Jermaine as a solo artist. It was a difficult decision for Jermaine to remain with Motown; but although it split him from his family, it left his career in the capable hands of his father-in-law, Berry Gordy. At Epic, the Jacksons replaced Jermaine with Randy, and the group enjoyed more artistic freedom and improved royalty terms.

The Jacksons' first two albums on Epic, *The Jacksons* and *Goin' Places,* featured songs by other writers and various producers, without notable results. In 1977 Michael went off to act in the film version of *The Wiz,* where he first met record producer and composer Quincy Jones. In May of 1977, the Jacksons played together for a royal command performance for Queen Elizabeth II's Silver Jubilee.

### Artistic Freedom at Last

The Jacksons regrouped in 1978 to begin their first self-written, self-produced album, *Destiny*. Standouts from that album include Randy and Michael's song, "Shake Your Body (Down To The Ground)," released in December of 1978. They began their world tour in January of 1979; upon their return, Michael recorded his first Quincy Jones-produced solo album for Epic, *Off The Wall*. 1980 saw the release of the Jacksons' fourth Epic album, *Triumph*, which was followed by a 36-city tour in

support of the album that grossed more than $5.5 million. As described by Dave Marsh in *Trapped*, "The show also incorporated video footage from the album, depicting the Jacksons as enormous unearthly godlings who revived a featureless mass of humans with a golden light radiating from their heads." A live album resulted from this tour, *The Jacksons Live!*

Michael began preparing a second solo album, the megahit *Thriller*, released in December of 1982. It eventually sold over 30 million copies worldwide, with the help of special videos, to become the best-selling album in the history of the record industry. Michael rejoined his brothers for a reunion tour in 1984, for which Jermaine also reunited with the Jacksons. Amid extensive hype and publicity, the *Victory* tour garnered a lot of negative publicity for the group. Charging $30 a ticket, double the standard concert fee at the time, the Jacksons were criticized for being greedy and uncaring about their biggest supporters, people who could not afford the price of admission. The Jacksons

---

*The Jackson family was very protective and strict with their children, and they led sheltered lives in the working-class neighborhood in which they grew up.*

---

countered charges of greed by donating some of their proceeds to various charities. Ultimately, the Jacksons could not survive the *Victory* tour as a group, even though the tour was seen by an estimated 2.3 million people and grossed nearly $70 million.

## Selected discography

**Singles; as the Jackson 5 unless otherwise noted**

"Big Boy"/"You've Changed," Steeltown, 1968.
"We Don't Have To Be Over 21 (To Fall In Love)"/"Jam Session," Steeltown, c. 1968.
"I Want You Back," Motown, 1969.
"ABC," Motown, 1970.
"The Love You Save," Motown, 1970.
"I'll Be There," Motown, 1970.
"Santa Claus Is Coming To Town," Motown, 1970.
(As the Ripples & Waves) "Let Me Carry Your School Books"/"I Never Had A Girl," Steeltown, c. 1971.

"Mama's Pearl," Motown, 1971.
"Never Can Say Goodbye," Motown, 1971.
"Maybe Tomorrow," Motown, 1971.
"Sugar Daddy," Motown, 1971.
"Little Bitty Pretty One," Motown, 1972.
"Lookin' Through The Windows," Motown, 1972.
"The Corner Of The Sky," Motown, 1972.
"Hallelujah Day," Motown, 1973.
"Get It Together," Motown, 1973.
"Dancing Machine," Motown, 1974.
"Whatever You Got, I Want," Motown, 1974.
"I Am Love," Motown, 1974.
"Forever Came Today," Motown, 1975.

**Singles; as the Jacksons**

"Enjoy Yourself," Epic, 1976.
"Show You The Way To Go," Epic, 1977.
"Goin' Places," Epic, 1977.
"Different Kind Of Lady," Epic, 1978.
"Blame It On The Boogie," Epic, 1978.
"Shake Your Body (Down To The Ground)," Epic, 1979.
"Lovely One," Epic, 1980.
"Heartbreak Hotel," Epic, 1980.
"Can You Feel It," Epic, 1981.
"Walk Right Now," Epic, 1981.
"State of Shock," Epic, 1984.
"Torture," Epic, 1984.
"Body," Epic, 1984.
"Nothin' (That Compares 2 U)," Epic, 1989.
"2300 Jackson Street," Epic, 1989.

**LPs; as the Jackson 5**

*Diana Ross Presents The Jackson 5*, Motown, 1969.
*ABC*, Motown, 1970.
*Third Album*, Motown, 1970.
*Christmas Album*, Motown, 1970.
*Maybe Tomorrow*, Motown, 1971.
*Goin' Back To Indiana*, Motown, 1971.

*Greatest Hits*, Motown, 1971.
*Lookin' Through The Windows*, Motown, 1972.
*Skywriter*, Motown, 1973.
*Get It Together*, Motown, 1973.
*Dancing Machine*, Motown, 1974.
*Moving Violation*, Motown, 1975.
*Anthology*, Motown, 1976.
*Joyful Jukebox Music*, Motown, 1976.
(CD only) *Compact Command Performances: 18 Greatest Hits*, Motown, 1984.

**LPs; as the Jacksons**

*The Jacksons*, Epic, 1976.
*Goin' Places*, Epic, 1977.
*Destiny*, Epic, 1978.
*Triumph*, Epic, 1980.
*Jacksons Live!*, Epic, 1981.
*Victory*, Epic, 1984.
*2300 Jackson Street*, Epic, 1989.

# Sources

### Books

Bianco, David, *Heat Wave: The Motown Fact Book,* Pierian, 1988.
Jackson, Katherine, *My Family, The Jacksons*, St. Martin's, 1990.
Marsh, Dave, *Trapped: Michael Jackson and the Crossover Dream,* Bantam, 1985.

### Periodicals

*Billboard*, September 22, 1984; December 22, 1984.
*Essence*, December 1990.
*People*, August 8, 1988.
*Rolling Stone*, August 16, 1984.
*Variety*, December 19, 1984.

—*David Bianco*

# Alan Jackson

Singer, songwriter

**B**illed in 1990 as "country music's new heartthrob"—a title that aptly describes the tall, blonde Georgian—Alan Jackson burst on the Nashville scene with his first album, *Here in the Real World.* The former construction worker and mail room clerk quickly found himself playing before crowds of 40,000 adoring fans. As Laurie Werner observed in a 1990 *USA Weekend* article, Jackson's overnight success "is due partly to Jackson himself, partly to his throwback musical style, partly to the accelerated new pop-style dynamics of country music. . . . Jackson's a guy you could swoon over *and* bring home to Mom. . . . In this tele-prompted age, a look like that in a music video or on an album cover can really move the merchandise."

Werner, however, may be stretching the point a bit; many up-and-coming Nashville stars are handsome, but it is unlikely that good looks alone would prompt the sale of almost a million copies of an album. Jackson's work, in fact, has been hailed as a refreshing dose of pure country, more traditional in theme and melody than many of the honky-tonkers of his time. His sinewy baritone voice masks little of his Georgia accent, and his favorite lyrics—extolling home, family, and marriage—are the very staples of country fare. Even with the spotlight on him, Jackson remains true to his small-town roots, and the result is a genuine, sincere country sound.

## Blue-Collar Roots

Alan Eugene Jackson was born in 1958 and raised in Newnan, Georgia, a town south of Atlanta. The youngest child and only boy in his family, Jackson had a very happy childhood even though money was scarce. From his mother he inherited a love of country and gospel music, while his father taught him how to repair and refurbish cars, a hobby he still enjoys. Growing up in Newnan, Jackson gave little thought to a career in music. He knew no one who had ever considered becoming a singer, and none of his family members were particularly musical. He seemed destined to settle in Newnan for life, especially after he married his high school sweetheart when he was 20 years old.

From the age of 12 Jackson held odd jobs, using his earnings to buy and restore old cars. While in his twenties he worked as a mechanic and a builder, but he gradually became bored by such jobs. He was inspired to try his luck in music by a friend who became an airline pilot, which "was a pretty big job to hope for in our little ol' town," Jackson mused in *Country Music.* "But four or five years later, [my friend] ended up as a pilot for a major carrier, making big money. That really made me

## For the Record. . .

Born Alan Eugene Jackson, October 17, 1958, in Newnan, GA; son of Eugene (a mechanic) and Mattie (a homemaker) Jackson; married; wife's name, Denise; children: Mattie Denise. *Education:* Attended South Georgia College.

Country singer and songwriter, 1985—. Worked variously as a car salesman, shoe salesman, construction worker, forklift operator, and as a mail room clerk at The Nashville Network (TNN), Nashville, TN. Signed with Arista Records, 1989, released first album, *Here in the Real World,* 1990. Has appeared on television programs, including *Grand Ole Opry, Hee Haw,* and *New West.*

**Awards:** Top New Male Artist of the Year award, Academy of Country Music, Horizon Award and Best Male Vocalist of the Year award, Country Music Association, Star of Tomorrow award, TNN/*Music City News,* Best New Artist of 1990, *R&R* magazine, and American Music Award nomination, all 1990.

**Addresses:** *Record company*—Arista Records, 6 West 57th St., New York, NY 10019.

young, attractive artists, Arista brought the same philosophy to its country division. Jackson fit the bill perfectly, and the fact that he wrote many of his own lyrics was an additional point in his favor. With Arista, he released his first album, *Here in the Real World,* early in 1990. The album's debut single was "Blue-Blooded Woman" and it went to Number One on the country charts in the summer of 1990. Subsequent Number One hits from *Here in the Real World* include "Wanted (One Good-Hearted Woman)," a spoken-sung love ballad, the up-tempo "Chasin' That Neon Rainbow," and the album's title cut.

It wasn't long before Jackson and his band had left behind their beat-up van and were touring in a plush bus, with technicians and security guards. The latter became necessary when an exuberant female fan literally tackled Jackson, knocking him off his feet. The singer spent much of the summer of 1990 opening for other country acts, but as he gained popularity he became a headliner in his own right, drawing impressive crowds in the southern and western United States. He was nominated for four Country Music Association awards late in 1990, including the coveted Horizon Award and Best Male Vocalist of the Year Award, and received the Top New Male Artist of the Year Award from the Academy of Country Music.

"I really didn't expect things to take off as fast as they did," Jackson reflected in *Country Music.* "Sometimes the whole thing just doesn't quite grab me. But then all of a sudden, I'll just be sittin' somewhere and it'll kinda sneak up on me, and I'll realize just how lucky I am."

### A Proponent of "Real" Country

With the 1991 Arista release of Jackson's second album, *Don't Rock the Jukebox,* the singer earned further praise. The LP displays the influence of George Jones, Jackson's protege who also lends vocals to the single "Just Playin' Possum." Reviewer Rich Kienzle declared in *Country Music* that "with *Don't Rock the Jukebox* Jackson has matured, setting a standard many of his contemporaries could emulate and a few of the old hands who've been off their game recently ought to remember." In addition, Lisa Shea writing in *People* found that the singer "has a knack for making middle-of-the-country-road music that never sounds self-satisfied or slick."

Jackson has also made music videos along with his albums, and the winsome performer has become one of the most requested acts on TNN. Opinions vary widely on Jackson's ability to maintain his popularity in the competitive Nashville music industry. If he does succeed in establishing himself as a major star, it will

look at my own life and decide that I needed to get on up to Nashville and try and do what I really wanted to do. But it was still a big jump for me, because I'd lived in that little town all my life and had never really traveled much. Just moving away from family was a big step." Despite such reservations, Jackson, who had performed with a band locally for years, moved with his wife to Nashville in 1985.

### Not Just Another Heartthrob

By that time Jackson had written a number of songs, most of them composed during a summer when his wife was away, working in North Carolina. Upon arriving in Nashville, he took a job in the mail room of The Nashville Network (TNN) and spent all of his spare time singing and trying to sell his songs. One day his wife, who was working as a flight attendant, ran into singer Glen Campbell in the airport at Atlanta. She asked Campbell for some musical advice on Jackson's behalf, and Campbell gave her his business card. Jackson subsequently took his songs to Glen Campbell Music and was given a publishing contract. That contract led to better bookings as well as a manager for the would-be star.

Jackson was one of the first artists signed at the Nashville office of Arista Records, which opened in the late 1980s. Known in the pop music business for recruiting certainly be on the strength of his songwriting and vocal delivery, not on his handsome appearance. Jackson's traditional songs, with their simple melodies and heartfelt lyrics, have been judged engaging enough in their own right to assure him an audience among those who love "real" country.

The successful singer, who has not forgotten his blue-collar past, "is at his best when singing about his own down-home roots," Cynthia Sanz noted in *People*. Describing himself to Sanz as "just a simple guy," Jackson told Werner in *USA Weekend* that he has enjoyed every minute of his success: "I caught up to all my goals so fast that I haven't had a chance to make new ones. I even got on the [television programs] *Grand Ole Opry* and *Hee Haw*. . . . When I was growing up, I thought that if you could be on *Hee Haw*, you'd made it. So I thought, 'Boy, here I am on *Hee Haw*, in the cornfield. I guess I really have made it.'"

## Selected discography

*Here in the Real World* (includes "Here in the Real World," "Blue-Blooded Woman," "Wanted (One Good-Hearted Woman)," and "Chasin' That Neon Rainbow,"), Arista, 1990.
*Don't Rock the Jukebox*, Arista, 1991.

## Sources

*Country Music*, July/August 1990; September/October 1990; July/August 1991; September/October 1991.
*People*, May 21, 1990; August 5, 1991; September 2, 1991.
*USA Weekend*, October 5-7, 1990.

—*Anne Janette Johnson*

# Mick Jagger

---

**Singer, songwriter**

In a career spanning nearly three decades, Mick Jagger has been characterized in many ways—from rock and roll's most demonic performer to one of its keenest business minds. The snarling, strutting lead singer of the Rolling Stones spent his early life in conventional, middle-class style, working hard in school and participating enthusiastically in sports. In 1962, he went to the London School of Economics to study for a career in business. There he met up with art student and guitarist Keith Richards, whom he had known when the two were five-year-olds attending school in Dartford, England. They discovered a mutual love of rhythm and blues and were quickly caught up in the musical revolution then sweeping England. After moving into a flat in Chelsea with guitarist Brian Jones, they began planning their own rock and roll band while Jagger prudently continued his business courses.

Their first public appearance was a spur-of-the-moment, unpaid show at a tiny jazz club called the Marquee. They had no name for their group, but impulsively decided to call themselves "Brian Jones and

114

Mick Jagger and the Rollin' Stones" after the title of a favorite Muddy Waters song. Jagger, Jones, and Richards were accompanied by drummer Charlie Watts and bassist Bill Wyman. For the next year, this line-up struggled through a series of dates in working-class bars, where audiences seemed not to know what to make of the band's long hair and unkempt appearance, or of Jagger's sneering and prancing. By 1963, though, they had begun to find their audience, and their popularity grew rapidly; by 1964 two different polls had named them England's most popular group, outranking even the Beatles.

### A Reputation for Rebellion

"In the beginning it was frightening," Jagger recalled to a *Newsweek* reporter. "It was dangerous. . . . We'd only do half an hour and then [the audience would] scream for half an hour and some of them would faint." By 1965 the Rolling Stones had stopped playing clubs in favor of large concert venues, and Jagger had quit economics school to devote himself full time to life as a Stone. The band's first recordings drew heavily on the music of their favorite performers, including Chuck Berry and Muddy Waters, but Jagger and Richards soon began collaborative songwriting and developed their own sound. Their first international hit, "Satisfaction," stands today as their signature song. It was considered the perfect expression of the defiant, raunchy image they seemed to be deliberately cultivating, per-

haps to differentiate themselves from the comparatively wholesome Beatles and their many imitators.

"I wasn't *trying* to be rebellious in those days," Jagger insisted, as quoted by Stephen Schiff in a 1992 *Vanity Fair* profile. "I was just being me. I wasn't trying to push the edge of anything. I'm being me and ordinary, the guy from suburbia who sings in this band, but someone older might have thought it was just the most awful racket, the most terrible thing, and where are we going if this is music?. . . But all those songs we sang were pretty tame, really. People didn't think they were, but I thought they were tame."

On the strength of such albums as *December's Children, Aftermath,* and *Between the Buttons,* Jagger and the Rolling Stones rose to the top, but their unsavory reputation led them into trouble with the law. In 1967 Jagger and two bandmates were arrested for drug offenses and given unusually harsh sentences. Jagger was handed three months for possession of four over-the-counter pep pills he had purchased in Italy. The punishment was eventually reduced, but their legal battles and internal conflicts seemed to leave the Stones demoralized. In 1967 they released *Their Satanic Majesties Request,* an album many critics dismissed as a flabby, pretentious attempt to copy the psychedelia of the Beatles' *Sgt. Pepper's Lonely Hearts Club Band.*

### Embarked on Solo Ventures

For the first time, Jagger began to look for creative outlets outside the group, playing lead roles in the films *Performance* and *Ned Kelly*. Reviews of his dramatic portrayals were mixed, but several critics expressed a certain fascination with the surly sexuality he projected on the screen, a style that became central to the performer's unique persona. "Before Mick Jagger," noted Schiff, "sexual iconography had reached a point that was both apotheosis and dead end. . . . Perhaps the enormous re-evaluation of sex and sexuality that dominated the sixties and seventies—the long hair, the unisex fashions, the so-called sexual revolution—would have taken place without him, but Mick Jagger's charged androgyny now looks at the very least hugely influential, and probably catalytic."

The Rolling Stones remained together, reestablishing their standing in 1968 with *Beggar's Banquet. Let It Bleed,* another classic, followed in 1969, the same year the band toured the United States after a three-year absence. They were met in city after city by frantic, hysterical audiences. A free concert was planned near San Francisco, California, as a way of thanking U.S. fans for their support. The ill-organized event turned nightmarish when a gang of Hell's Angels—hired by the Stones to provide security—attacked the crowd violently, beating one spectator to death. To the further detriment of the band's reputation, the murder was inadvertently captured on film and released to the general public as part of the documentary *Gimme Shelter*.

## Released First Solo Albums

The Stones stayed away from North America until 1972, but upon their return, they were met with as much enthusiasm as ever. Jack Batten praised Jagger in the Toronto *Globe and Mail* as "the single most exciting performer at work at this moment. He is charismatic, dynamic, glorious, riveting." Gradually, the media began to cast the Stones as superstars rather than outlaws. Each album they released was a sure bestseller, if not always a critical success. Though they continued to rock as hard as ever, the rise of the punk rock movement made the Stones's once outrageous behavior seem comparatively tame. Jagger recalled in *Rolling Stone* that the band lost "the whole idea of pushing the envelope open a little bit. We became a hard-rock band, and we became very content with it. . . . We lost a little bit of sensitivity and adventure."

That loss of adventure brought a sense of boredom and restlessness. Dissension among the Stones became quite intense, and Jagger and Richards began to snipe openly at each other in the rock press. Both eventually turned to solo projects. Jagger released the LP *She's the Boss* in 1985 and *Primitive Cool* in 1987; the albums had disappointing sales and Anthony DeCurtis noted in *Rolling Stone* that the songs "ranged from bad to ordinary."

## Despite Dissension, Stones Rock On

The Rolling Stones joined again to record *Dirty Work* in 1986, but Jagger refused to tour to support the album, a decision that infuriated Richards. "I was completely, 100 percent right about not doing that tour," Jagger avowed in *Rolling Stone* in 1989. "The band was in *no* condition to tour. . . . The album wasn't that good. It was *okay*. It certainly wasn't a great Rolling Stones album. The feeling inside the band was very bad, too. The relationships were terrible. The health was diabolical . . . so we had this long bad experience of making that record, and the last thing I wanted to do was spend another year with the same people." Such comments by Jagger had many fans predicting a Rolling Stones breakup.

Yet in May of 1988 Richards and Jagger set aside their differences to discuss the possibility of a new album and tour. Later that year they went to Barbados to begin writing new songs for *Steel Wheels*. Released in 1989, it was praised as "the best Rolling Stones album in at least a decade" by David Fricke in *Rolling Stone*. Both the album and the band's subsequent tour were widely touted as proof that the Stones were still a vital musical force. DeCurtis declared: "All the ambivalence, recriminations, attempted rapprochements and psychological one-upsmanship evident on *Steel Wheels* testify that the Stones are right in the element that has historically spawned their best music—a murky, dangerously charged environment. . . . Against all odds, and at this late date, the Stones have once again generated an album that will have the world dancing to deeply troubling, unresolved emotions."

## Starred in *Freejack*

In February of 1992, after nearly 30 productive years in the music business, Jagger was at work on a third solo

> *"Doing a solo album, it's more relaxed than doing the Rolling Stones. It's just free and easy."*

album and on the verge of signing a new three-record contract with Atlantic Records. "Doing a solo album, it's more relaxed than doing the Rolling Stones," Jagger admitted in to Schiff in *Vanity Fair*. "With a solo album, no one's going to get on my case. It's just free and easy." The singer also returned to his acting career, starring in *Freejack*—a science fiction film set in the year 2009—and he expressed an interest in writing and producing motion pictures. Though he has proven himself as a prolific solo performer, Jagger acknowledges the profound influence of his many years with the Rolling Stones. He told Schiff, "You know, I'm still me. . . . It's still going to sound like me. I'm the singer of the Rolling Stones. I can't completely change."

## Selected discography

### Solo singles

(With David Bowie) "Dancing in the Streets," 1985.

### Solo albums

*She's the Boss,* Columbia, 1985.

*Primitive Cool*, Columbia, 1987.

**With the Rolling Stones; on London Records**

*England's Newest Hit Makers—The Rolling Stones*, 1964.
*12 x 5*, 1964.
*The Rolling Stones Now!*, 1965.
*Out of Our Heads*, 1965.
*December's Children (and Everybody's)*, 1965.
*Big Hits (High Tide and Green Grass)*, 1966.
*Aftermath*, 1966.
*Got Live If You Want It!*, 1966.
*Between the Buttons*, 1967.
*Flowers*, 1967.
*Their Satanic Majesties Request*, 1967.
*Beggar's Banquet*, 1968.
*Through the Past Darkly (Big Hits, Vol. 2)*, 1969.
*Let It Bleed*, 1969.
*Get Yer Ya-Ya's Out*, 1970.
*Hot Rocks: 1964-71*, 1972.
*More Hot Rocks (Big Hits and Fazed Cookies)*, 1972.

**With the Rolling Stones; on Rolling Stone Records, except where indicated**

*Sticky Fingers*, 1971.
*Stone Age*, Decca, 1971.
*Gimme Shelter*, Decca, 1971.
*Milestones*, Decca, 1971.
*Exile on Main Street*, 1972.
*Goat's Head Soup*, 1973.
*No Stone Unturned*, Decca, 1973.
*It's Only Rock 'n' Roll*, 1974.
*Rolled Gold*, Decca, 1975.
*Metamorphosis*, Abkco, 1975.
*Made in the Shade*, 1975.
*Black and Blue*, 1976.
*Love You Live*, 1977.
*Some Girls*, 1978.

*Emotional Rescue*, 1980.
*Sucking in the Seventies*, 1981.
*Tattoo You*, 1981.
*Still Life*, 1982.
*Undercover*, 1983.
*Dirty Work*, Columbia, 1986.
*Steel Wheels*, Columbia, 1989.

Also recorded *Flashpoint*, 1991.

## Sources

*Entertainment Weekly*, January 31, 1992.
*Esquire*, June 1968.
*Globe and Mail* (Toronto), August 4, 1967.
*Guitar Player*, October 1989.
*Jet*, March 18, 1991.
*Life*, July 14, 1972.
*Newsday*, July 23, 1972.
*Newsweek*, January 4, 1971.
*New York Sunday News*, July 23, 1972.
*New York Times*, November 22, 1991; January 18, 1992.
*New York Times Magazine*, July 16, 1972.
*People*, March 25, 1985; June 3, 1985; April 28, 1986; November 2, 1987; June 13, 1988; December 18, 1989.
*Rolling Stone*, December 19, 1985; December 4, 1986; May 7, 1987; November 5, 1987; November 19, 1987; December 17, 1987; September 7, 1989; September 21, 1989; November 16, 1989; December 14, 1989; March 8, 1990; August 23, 1990; May 16, 1991; January 9, 1992.
*Time*, July 17, 1972; October 25, 1982; March 7, 1983; December 5, 1983; September 4, 1989.
*Vanity Fair*, February 1992.
*Vogue*, May 1985; May 1991.
*Wall Street Journal*, October 28, 1991.
*Washington Post*, July 5, 1972.

—Joan Goldsworthy

# David Johansen

**Singer, songwriter**

For two decades, the musical career of singer/ songwriter David Johansen has been shaped by his considerable versatility. In the early 1970s he was the flamboyant lead singer for the New York Dolls, a rock and roll band heralded as America's answer to the British group the Rolling Stones. With its male members sporting teased bouffants, outrageous makeup, and women's clothing, the New York Dolls became a prototype for the punk rock groups that emerged later in the decade. Since the mid-1970s Johansen has also performed as a solo act—without makeup or costumes—and has recorded both original compositions and old favorites in a variety of genres, including rock, rhythm and blues, and reggae.

While never a commercial smash, Johansen was consistently praised by critics and developed a fiercely loyal following; in a *High Fidelity* critique of his album *Live It Up,* Mitchell Cohen declared, "David Johansen simply has terrific taste in music, a belief in its capacity to merge passion and craft, and a gregarious ringmaster personality." In the mid-1980s Johansen adopted the persona of Buster Poindexter, a Las Vegas-style lounge singer, and performed a time-tested repertoire of saloon standards, including ballads, Latin songs, and blues. While seedy and slick, the tuxedoed, pompadoured Buster is more than a caricature; *Rolling Stone* writer Deborah Frost called Poindexter's act "timeless," adding, "wherever there's a piano bar, he'll have a home." "Buster can have this great life in the public eye and take the rap for everything, and then David can go home," Johansen told Margot Dougherty in *People,* "It's the most brilliant thing I've ever done."

## Formed the New York Dolls

Growing up in a large family on New York's Staten Island, Johansen took to music early, singing the rock and roll favorites of his older siblings. As an adolescent he would often sneak off to Greenwich Village and Times Square to hang out with other teens interested in the music scene; during high school he sang and played the guitar for such local bands as Fast Eddie and the Electric Japs and the Vagabond Missionaries. By late 1971 Johansen had joined musicians Johnny Thunders, Rick Rivets, Arthur Kane, and Billy Murcia— with the later addition of Sylvain Sylvain and Jerry Nolan—to form the New York Dolls, playing regularly at the Mercer Arts Center in lower Manhattan. A local cult following developed around the group, attracted to its outrageous look, offstage decadence, and searing rock songs about adolescent confusion and revolt.

The Dolls's music showed the influence of such groups as the Velvet Underground, the Stooges, and the Rolling Stones, with lead singer Johansen exhibiting some of the characteristics of the Stones's Mick Jagger. Obtaining a recording contract with Mercury Records, the group debuted with the album *New York Dolls* in 1973, followed by *Too Much Too Soon* a year later. Despite the band's stage popularity with young audiences, its recordings were largely unsuccessful; Jay Cocks suggested in *Time* that "sardonic anthems like 'Personality Crisis' and 'Vietnamese Baby' did not sit easy on a pop establishment that was still recovering from flower power [a 1960s movement advocating love, beauty, and peace] and cuddling up to the peaceful, easy feeling of the California sound." In addition, the group's unsettling appearance and trouble[d] reputation—Murcia died of a drug overdose while the Dolls were on tour—put off major club owners and led to its demise in 1975.

### Displayed Talent as a Solo Performer

For the next few years Johansen continued to perform, writing many of his own songs and searching for another recording contract. Blue Sky eventually released his 1978 album *David Johansen;* a reflection of his Dolls past, the album faltered commercially, but critics recognized in cult figure Johansen an accomplished songwriter and vocalist. The more successful *In Style* appeared in 1979 and delivered a soul-influenced rock. *New Rolling Stone Record Guide* contributor Wayne King noted, "From the opening Four Tops tribute, 'Melody,' through the beautifully rolling rhythms of 'Swaheto Woman,' Johansen sings with a passion and commitment unmatched by anything else in his career." And Cocks observed in *Time* that Johansen "sings as if he has a gun pressed to his temple."

*Here Comes the Night,* a collaborative effort with former Beach Boy bandsman Blondie Chaplin, preceded *Live It Up,* Johansen's most successful solo album. Capitalizing on the energy of Johansen's stage performances, *Live It Up* was recorded at Boston's Paradise Theater and featured a mix of Dolls material, solo originals, and pop/rock classics. His rollicking medley of such sixties Animals hits as "We Gotta Get Out of This Place," "It's My Life," and "Don't Bring Me Down" as well as a rendition of the Foundations's "Fill Me Up Buttercup" put the album on the charts in 1982.

### Poindexter: "Hot, Hot, Hot" Lounge Singer

According to Frost, Johansen's solo career suffered with the release of his 1984 album *Sweet Revenge,* a "jungle of lame synths, limp rap and conventional ambitions." The mid-1980s rise of Buster Poindexter "helped [Johansen] remember who he is," continued the *Rolling Stone* critic, who called him a singer of "exuberance and wit." "It's me, really," Johansen confirmed in *People.* "Sometimes I've found that by getting into a certain drag, or a certain feeling, you can cast off your mortal coil and really do something." In his personal collection of 1,500 albums, Johansen possesses a number of cabaret favorites not suited for his rock shows. Singing these songs at a neighborhood bar with a couple of backup musicians, he developed the Poindexter persona, using his showman's instincts to perfect the campy look and delivery.

With the 1987 album *Buster Poindexter* and its hit single "Hot, Hot, Hot," Johansen and his alter ego enjoyed widespread recognition, and *Rolling Stone* named the LP "party record of the year." Becoming a regular on national television and in print ads and continuing his live performances, the Poindexter persona has paved the way for chameleon Johansen to pursue a second career as a motion picture actor: he has made appearances in the films *Candy Mountain, Married to the Mob,* and *Scrooged.* Though the performer's rock and roll days with the New York Dolls are part of music history, the innovative group's impact on the punk rock movement will not soon be forgotten.

## Selected compositions

Has written and co-written numerous songs, including "French-ette," "Flamingo Road," "Swaheto Woman," and "Here Comes the Night"; collaborators include former New York Doll Sylvain Sylvain and former Beach Boy Blondie Chaplin.

## Selected discography

### With the New York Dolls

*New York Dolls,* Mercury, 1973.
*Too Much Too Soon,* Mercury, 1974.
*Lipstick Killers* (1972 studio demos), ROIR, 1981.
*Night of the Living Dolls: Best of the New York Dolls,* Mercury, 1985.

### Solo Albums

*David Johansen,* Blue Sky, 1978.
*In Style,* Blue Sky, 1979.
*Here Comes the Night,* Blue Sky, 1981.
*Live It Up,* Blue Sky, 1982.
*Sweet Revenge,* 1984.

### As Buster Poindexter

*Buster Poindexter,* RCA, 1987.

*Buster Goes Berserk,* RCA, 1989.

## Sources

### Books

*New Rolling Stone Record Guide,* edited by Dave Marsh and John Swenson, Random House, 1983.
*Rolling Stone Encyclopedia of Rock and Roll,* edited by Jon Pareles and Patricia Romanowski, Summit Books, 1983.
Stambler, Irwin, *Encyclopedia of Pop, Rock and Soul,* revised edition, St. Martin's, 1989.

### Periodicals

*High Fidelity,* September 1982.
*Los Angeles Magazine,* July 1990.
*People,* January 25, 1988; May 21, 1990.
*Rolling Stone,* August 27, 1987, November 19, 1987; July 13, 1989.
*Time,* August 20, 1979.
*Variety,* March 7, 1990.

—*Nancy Pear*

# Big Daddy Kane

## Rap singer, songwriter

**Q**uintessential rapper Big Daddy Kane captures the gritty realism of urban street life in his music while, at the same time, offering a hopeful message of humor and self-determination. Kane drew his inspiration from rap pioneers Grandmaster Flash and the Furious Five and Kool Moe Dee. He credits his development as a lyricist and performer to his friendships with rappers Biz Markie, Marley Marl, Roxanne Shante, and other early rappers he met at the Queensbridge Project in Queens, NY. Kane rode to rap stardom on the swelling tidal wave of tough, angry, urban rappers, which ultimately led to the much-publicized ascendancy of Public Enemy. After Public Enemy struck the mother lode of mainstream success, dozens of new urban rappers—including Kane—were ushered in to carry the baton.

Born Antonio M. Hardy on September 10, 1968, in Brooklyn, NY, Kane is a native of the rough Bedford-Stuyvesant section of Brooklyn. He met his first mentor, Biz Markie—the "Clown Prince" of rap—in downtown Brooklyn in 1984; Markie and other rappers were mounting a recording session outside of McCurry's department store. Kane was impressed with Markie's outrageous sense of humor, performance style, and gregariousness, and the two became fast friends. They were soon performing together at local high schools. Through Markie, Kane met Marley Marl and Roxanne Shante, among other up-and-coming rap artists. In 1985, when Shante emerged as the "Queen of Rap," Kane went on the road with her as a disc jockey, eventually writing some of her best-known material. Kane was also writing hits for the Juice Crew and Kurtis Blow at this time and even worked briefly with funk master Rick James.

### Signed by Cold Chillin'

After touring with Shante, Kane started working closely with Marl on recording sessions for Shante, Markie, and other rappers under the aegis of Cold Chillin' Records. The staff of Cold Chillin' was sufficiently enamored of Kane's songwriting ability to sign him on as an artist in his own right in 1987. The name "Kane" was adopted in 1982, but "Big Daddy" wasn't tacked on until 1985. A close friend jokingly referred to Kane as "Big Daddy"; Kane loved the sound of it and has sported the nickname as his professional tag ever since. Near the end of 1987 Kane and Marl spent a few weeks working on Kane's debut album, *Long Live the Kane*. The album sold well, and on the strength of its sales and the hit single "Ain't No Half Steppin'," Kane began touring the U.S., performing with rap acts Stetsasonic and Doug E. Fresh.

Born Antonio M. Hardy, September 10, 1968, in Brooklyn, NY. *Religion:* Member of the black Muslim sect the Five Percent Nation.

Began career as DJ for Roxanne Shante, *eventually writing material for her, the Juice Crew, and Kurtis Blow; signed to Cold Chillin' Records, Inc. and released first LP, Long Live the Kane,* 1987.

**Addresses:** *Record company*—Cold Chillin' Records, Inc., 1966 Broadway, Suite #47, New York, NY 10023-7001.

In January of 1990 Kane recorded a second album, *It's a Big Daddy Thing,* which featured the hits "Smooth Operator" and the lauded "I Get the Job Done." A string of coast-to-coast tour dates followed, Kane sharing the stage with rap giants Public Enemy and L.L. Cool J. Kane self-produced his third album, *Taste of Chocolate,* with some help from Prince Paul, who had served as producer for rap trio De La Soul. *Taste of Chocolate* proved funkier than Kane's previous albums, and featured a posse of special guests, including the inimitable, heavy-breathing 1970s soul crooner Barry White, and the daughter of black activist leader Malcolm X.

### Wry Wit Got the Job Done

Kane's style of rap belongs to a hard-edged school that reflects life on the street. "Pimpin' Ain't Easy" and "Calling Mr. Welfare," from the *It's a Big Daddy Thing* LP, are just two showcases for Kane's knowing, razor-sharp lyrics. But Kane is never far from humor either; he infuses many of his songs with his particular brand of wry, subtle wit. Kane relishes a clever play on words, as displayed in his classic dance hit, "I Get The Job Done." The song's chest-thumping beat builds to a rich crescendo while Kane's smooth lyrics buttress its high-energy pace and good-natured bravado.

To some, Kane's sartorial style typifies the upscale urban rapper: He sports white suits, enormous gold medallions and heavy link chains, fedoras, chunky gold and diamond rings, and a "Cameo flattop" hairstyle; his public appearances often feature a bevy of attractive, near-nude, fawning women who flank the rapper, suggestively stroking him periodically. The message his image presents is also evinced in Kane's first three albums: Big Daddy is clearly savoring the good life, which many feel is warranted by Kane's unique raps.

What sets Kane apart from other rap artists is the cleverness of his powerful "boasts"—one of the mainstays of rap lyrics. His rhyming style is solid and tightly woven; Kane also makes good use of familiar "samples," borrowed riffs from other well-known artists like James Brown and Public Enemy. With *Prince of Darkness,* Kane expanded his repertoire with sophisticated balladry and more actual singing, as opposed to rapping. Kane was quoted in a 1991 Cold Chillin' press release as saying, "I wanted to do songs that would appeal to both men and women. I think rap is still the strongest force in black music today, and it's moving straight ahead, but it's also expanding to take in lots of other styles."

### Member of the Five Percent Nation

While still in junior high school, Kane was introduced to a black Muslim sect, popular among rappers, called the Five Percent Nation. As an adult, Kane became a member of the sect at the behest of Rakim, a rapper he respects and admires. Kane points to Rakim's early influence on him as an example of how rap artists can inspire rap fans to better themselves. As a member of the Five Percent Nation, Kane tries to educate listeners about world affairs and their relevance to blacks. However, he has at times been criticized for seemingly contradicting his faith by extolling the virtues of materialism, hedonism, and sex appeal. Kane fueled this fire by posing partially nude in a June 1991 issue of *Playgirl* magazine. He responded to his detractors by telling *The Source's* Chris Wilder: "I may make a political song. I may make a heritage song. Then again, I may make 'Pimpin' Ain't Easy,' I have fun with my music because of the simple fact that that's what music is about; music is for enjoyment. And nobody wants to hear about problems all of the time."

In 1988, when Kane was just starting to burn in the firmament of rap, observer Martin Starkey commented in *The Ticker,* "The man can rap to any beat with a skill that hasn't been attempted or done since Kool Moe Dee and early L.L. Cool J. But while L.L. Cool J. relied upon a steady, relentless thrashing of lyrics, and Moe Dee upon a low baritone syncopation of rhyming words with strong, soundalike endings, Big Daddy Kane is simply a word manipulator. He does things to words that will make you stop, marvel, and wonder how he does it." Starkey went on to presage, "There is a new King of Rap in town, and long live the Kane."

## Selected discography

*Long Live the Kane,* Cold Chillin' Records, 1987.

*It's a Big Daddy Thing,* Cold Chillin,' 1990.
*Taste of Chocolate,* Cold Chillin,' 1991.
*The Prince of Darkness,* Cold Chillin,' 1991.

## Sources

*Billboard,* January 30, 1988.
*Black Radio Exclusive,* December 16, 1988.
*New York Amsterdam News,* March 16, 1991.
*New York Times,* July 15, 1988.
*Playgirl,* June 1991.
*Soul Underground,* February 1988.
*Source,* March/April 1991.
*Strictly Hip-Hop,* August 1988.
*Ticker,* August 30, 1988.

Other source material was gathered from an October, 1991, Cold Chillin' Records, Inc. press release.

—*B. Kimberly Taylor*

# Ben E. King

---

**Singer, songwriter**

---

When film director Rob Reiner was putting together the soundtrack to his nostalgic 1986 film about a group of boys growing up in the early 1960s, he remembered a song that perfectly captured the atmosphere of that period: "Stand by Me," a stark, soulful ballad by the early 1960s pop star Ben E. King, who had all but disappeared from the music scene by the 1980s. Reiner eventually titled his film *Stand by Me;* both film and song benefiting immensely from their union, as *Stand by Me* became a hit for the fledgling director, and King's "Stand by Me" enjoyed a huge resurgence in popularity on radio stations across America in 1986. A generation that had never heard of Ben E. King found themselves tapping their toes and humming the distinctive melody of the song some 16 years after it enjoyed its first success.

Born Benjamin Earl Soloman in Henderson, North Carolina, on September 28, 1938, King moved with his family at age 11 to New York City, where his father opened a luncheonette in Harlem. King had sung in church choirs throughout his childhood; at Harlem's James Fenimore Cooper Junior High he eagerly set out to start his own singing group, which was dubbed the Four B's, as all of its members' names started with the letter B. Accounts vary as to how King's professional career got started, but most agree that it began in his father's restaurant, where King often sang as he worked. Somehow, his smooth tenor attracted an authoritative ear, and King was asked to join the singing group the Crowns, with whom he immediately began touring on the rhythm and blues circuit.

Also cutting a swath through that circuit was a group called the Drifters; popular throughout the 1950s, the Drifters had cut 11 albums by 1958 when, with record sales slumping, the group disbanded. But George Treadwell, the Drifters' manager, was contractually obliged to deliver the group to audiences for years to come.

Scrambling to replace the old group, Treadwell discovered the Crowns and renamed them the Drifters, as he had retained legal use of the name. A complete overhaul was apparently just the ticket for the Drifters. Atlantic Records liked their new sound so much that its executives assigned ace producers Jerry Leiber, Mike Stoller, and Phil Spector to produce a string of new recordings. The new Drifters struck quickly with the Number Two hit "There Goes My Baby," which was sung and co-written by King, then only 20, and followed by "Save the Last Dance for Me"—with King again contributing lead vocals—which reached Number One on the pop charts in 1960.

Another 1960 release by the Drifters featured King singing lead over a background of Spanish guitars. The sound intrigued Spector and Leiber so much that they decided to try King as a soloist on a similar number, "Spanish Harlem." The song soared up the charts and King soon found himself performing solo as one of America's most favored balladeers. His eminence was cemented the following year when "Stand by Me"—his own composotion—made the Top Ten on the pop charts and Number One on rhythm and blues lists.

A versatile performer who seemed to please pop and R & B audiences equally, King became a headline act across the country in the mid-1960s, appearing at prestigious concert halls, on network television, and abroad. Among King's string of 1960s hit singles were "Don't Play That Song," "That's When It Hurts," and "I (Who Have Nothing)," which British sensation Tom Jones turned into a platinum-seller when he recorded it in 1970.

By the late 1960s, however, King's career seemed to have run its course; though he had earned so much respect and affection at Atlantic that the company may have carried him indefinitely, King left the his label in 1969. "I didn't really want to leave Atlantic," the singer explained in Bill Millar's book, *The Drifters,* as quoted in the *Encyclopedia of Pop, Rock, and Soul.* "But I find [performers and record] companies are like a husband and wife. Eventually you get to a point where there's really very little you can do for each other. . . . And one has to leave. So I had to."

King laid low for a period, trying to revive his career with the Mandala and Maxwell labels; but by 1974 he had seen enough and returned to Atlantic, where his career briefly flowered again with the 1975 Top Ten hit "Supernatural Thing—Part 1." Two years later King collaborated with the Average White Band, whose members had long idolized him, on the LP *Benny and Us,* which enjoyed mild success. King's later solo LPs, 1978's *Let Me Live in Your Life* and 1981's *Street Tough,* saw him regain a measure of prominence on the R & B charts, but he would never again see the tremendous crossover popularity he had enjoyed in his heyday—except, of course, when the impassioned and soulful simplicity of "Stand by Me" captivated late 1980s listeners with its infectious echoes of a simpler time.

## Selected discography

*Spanish Harlem,* Atlantic, 1961.
*Ben E. King Sings for Soulful Lovers,* Atlantic, 1962.
*Don't Play That Song,* Atlantic, 1962.
*Greatest Hits,* Atlantic, 1964.
*Seven Letters,* Atlantic, 1965.
*Beginning of It All,* Mandala, 1971.
*Supernatural Thing,* Atlantic, 1975.
*Ben E. King Story,* Atlantic, 1975.
*I Had a Love,* Atlantic, 1976.
(With the Average White Band) *Benny and Us,* Atlantic, 1977.
*Let Me Live in Your Life,* Atlantic, 1978.
*Music Trance,* Atlantic, 1980.
*Street Tough,* Atlantic, 1980.
*Rough Edges,* Maxwell.

## Sources

### Books

Futrell, John, *The Illustrated Encyclopedia of Black Music,* Harmony Books, 1982.
Hardy, Phil, and Dave Laing, *Encyclopedia of Rock,* Schirmer, 1982.
*The Rolling Stone Encyclopedia of Rock,* edited by Jon Pareles and Patricia Romanowski, Rolling Stone Press/Summit Books, 1983.
Stambler, Irwin, *Encyclopedia of Pop, Rock and Soul,* St. Martin's, 1974.

### Periodicals

*People,* February 3, 1986; September 14, 1987.
*Rolling Stone,* January 26, 1989.
*Stereo Review,* December 1980; August 1981; May 1986.

—David Collins

# King's X

## Christian heavy metal band

After the release of their first album in 1988, the hard-rock power trio King's X gathered a loyal cult following with their mixture of riff-heavy guitar, unusual song structures, rich vocal harmonies, and upbeat semi-evangelical messages. For several years, however, the band struggled to reach a wider audience; many critics who admired their sound had reservations about the preachiness of the lyrics, and few of the band's songs seemed appropriate for Top 40 radio. In 1991 they broke through with their single "It's Love," and joined a handful of other bands, in the words of *CD Review*'s Edward Murray, in "attempting to transform hard rock from its consistently stale glam/pop leanings."

Lead singer and bassist Doug Pinnick, whose vocals combine the wail of hard rock with the soulful croon of vintage rhythm and blues, is one of a handful of black heavy metal musicians; the biracial makeup of the band is yet another challenge to hard rock convention. Pinnick's influences serve to remind metal fans that this music developed out of several predominantly black

musical traditions—gospel has always been present in rock, perhaps the primary source of its uplift. According to *Rolling Stone's* David Fricke, the group, which also features Ty Tabor on guitar and Jerry Gaskill on drums, thinks of itself less as a Christian band than "a band of Christians, less interested in parroting dogma than in celebrating life and blowing minds." It hasn't been an easy road for a band with as much interest in the New Testament as the metal blast of bands like Black Sabbath. Unlike such easy-to-identify Christian metal acts as Stryper, King's X has always refused to play an evangelical version of commercial hard rock. The band has nothing but disdain for the Christian rock world's derivative nature, its tendency to seize on images from pop culture and "Christianize" them. In fact, Pinnick's vision crystallized when he heard "Gloria" by Irish rockers U2, a song that incorporates the words of a Latin hymn. "Here [U2 lead singer] Bono was singing in Latin this beautiful text," Pinnick recalled to Fricke. "And I thought, '*That dog!* He got away with it.' He did it in an artistic way. That was the day U2 changed my mind about a lot of things and encouraged me. Because if they could do it, we could do it."

### Musical Pilgrimage

Pinnick was born in the early 1950s in Joliet, Illinois, and was raised by his great-grandmother, a solemnly religious woman. He listened as a teenager to the classic rhythm and blues and soul records put out by Detroit's Motown label, but while attending college fell in love with the thunderous sounds of the legendary British hard rock group Led Zeppelin. It took many years of searching before he brought together his vision of a band that rocked as hard as Zeppelin but put across an upbeat spiritual message. Pinnick spent some years in a Christian community in Florida, arranging concerts that rarely drew crowds; finally he moved back to Joliet and put together a Christian rock band that gathered a large following. Soon the group and its followers formed a church called the Shiloh Fellowship, which Pinnick described to Fricke as "a hippie-community thing" that quickly wearied him with its inability to grow and change. "I had to move on, because these people weren't. So I said a prayer: 'Lord, open the doors and I am out of here.'"

The bassist found his opportunity as the 1970s drew to a close: He moved to Springfield, Missouri, to join the noted Christian rock band Petra. The group's drummer, Jerry Gaskill, had moved to Springfield from New Jersey, and though Petra disbanded within a month of Pinnick's arrival, Gaskill and Pinnick decided to continue working together. They worked for about a year as the rhythm section for Christian rocker Phil Keaggy, and then in 1980 set about forming their own band.

Pinnick heard guitarist and Pearl, Mississippi, native Ty Tabor—who had played with Gaskill in the past—playing at a local college and enlisted him in the project alongside guitarist Dan McCollom, who left the band shortly thereafter. Tabor, like Gaskill, had dropped out of Springfield's Evangel College, frustrated with the narrowness of the Christian university's environment. The new ensemble called themselves the Edge and embarked on the gritty road of rock and roll dues-paying, performing long nights in little clubs. Five years and many gigs later, the group relocated to Houston, Texas, because two promoters promised to finance them. Although the original offer fell through, the band had the good fortune to hook up with Sam Taylor, a fellow Christian and rock manager who had worked with the likes of Southern boogie masters ZZ Top. Taylor became something of a guru for the musicians, encouraging them to adopt the name King's X and taking on record producing, management, and video directing duties. "I'm a four-way partner. That's the way they wanted it," Taylor informed Fricke. He remarked that the band's name was "the name of the cool band in town when I was in high school. . . . I guess I was waxing philosophical at the time, too, thinking about the relationship between God and Christianity, and that we have a mark on us." Pinnick told *Rolling Stone's* Kim Neely that Taylor helped the band "to see that our art was more important than commercial success."

### Out of the Silent Fringe

Commercial success would prove elusive indeed. After

honing their chops for a while longer, King's X went into the studio to record their first LP, *Out of the Silent Planet,* which they released on Megaforce Worldwide records and distributed through Atlantic in 1988. Despite forceful jams like "Power of Love," they failed to convey to a large audience the promise they felt the band represented. The album generated a buzz among adventurous metal fans and a few critics, but King's X remained little-known, admired by other musicians—rock stars like Living Colour guitarist Vernon Reid and Mr. Big bassist Billy Sheehan have long spoken highly of them—but unfamiliar to the record-buying public.

The second album, 1989's *Gretchen Goes to Nebraska,* widened their popularity a bit more, garnering some impressive reviews and more publicity. *Rolling Stone* called *Gretchen* "a dizzying tapestry of smoldering guitar, ragged, soulful vocals and tight three-part harmonies . . . a feast for the senses." Something of a concept album, the record tells the tale of a young girl's adventures in a landscape the review described as "a sort of musical *Alice in Oz."* Pinnick characterized the band's lyrics to Neely as "psychedelic spiritual," and reviewers tended to question the point of some of the words. Even so, tracks like "Mission," with its soaring harmonies and crunch guitar, couldn't fail to convey their message: "What's the vision of the preacher man?/ Some are true, some do lie," roars Pinnick, asking if churchgoing means anything more than "a social get-together." This criticism of conventional religion recalls Pinnick's description, in his interview with Fricke, of his grandmother's "Pentecostal holiness attitude, where *everything* was wrong. Except sitting at home and reading your Bible all day and going to prayer meetings." Alongside the occasional sermon, however, King's X emphasized the sheer spiritual power of the sound, which Pinnick labeled "the Pound." The song "Over My Head" outlines a surrender to the force of rock: "Music, music/I hear music," soars the vocal, "Music over my head."

Though *Gretchen* won over some new fans, as did the group's impressive live shows, they still stood outside the sphere of Top 40 radio and MTV. At the time Pinnick told Neely, "Either people like us or they just don't get it, and that's the way it's always gonna be. We'd be stupid to think *everybody's* gonna like us." The band's tour in support of *Gretchen* pointed out not only their popularity abroad but their relative obscurity at home: "I enjoyed playing England better," Pinnick told *Mean Street* magazine. "Everywhere we played we sold out. When we come to America we can maybe pack a club out in maybe Chicago, New York, and L.A., but everywhere else it's like, 'King's X? Who?'"

## Third Album Proves Most Ambitious Yet

The band's recognition factor, however, was about to increase sharply. In 1990 they released *Faith Hope Love by King's X,* their most ambitious record, and the single "It's Love" became a hit, appearing frequently on Top 40 radio stations and MTV. Stylistically, *Faith Hope Love* has a lush feel, and its songs showcase the musicians' wildly diverse influences. "I'll Never Get Tired of You" has the richly melodic feel of folk-rock and psychedelia, while "We Are Finding Who We Are" is a churning mixture of funk and soul that displays Pinnick's affection for the vocal stylings of R&B master Sly Stone. Both Gaskill and Tabor took some lead vocals this time out, underlining the group's ensemble approach.

The group's newfound success did not translate into critical raves; many reviewers compared *Faith Hope Love* unfavorably to *Gretchen.* Even so, the most critical reviews had a few nice things to say. Janiss Garza of *Entertainment Weekly* referred to King's X as "A

---

*Alongside the occasional sermon, King's X emphasizes the sheer spiritual power of their sound.*

---

thinking man's metal band," applauding the sonic mixture of the trio's sound but taking issue with the album's "split personality," presumably divided between sixties nostalgia and nineties relevance. Murray spoke highly of the group's "soaring Beatlesque vocal harmonizing" as well as Pinnick's lead vocals and Tabor's riffing. "The problem here is ideas—or lack of them," the reviewer concluded, bemoaning the tendency of much of the material "to feel like a sermon." *Musician* was more positive, approving of the band's musical eclecticism: "Idiosyncratic? Sure, but irresistible, combining Def Leppard's pop smarts with Queensryche's ambitious invention. Prepare to be converted!" *Rolling Stone* reviewer Erik Davis, though irked by the album's "art-rock bloat" and the antiabortion stance of the songs "Legal Kill" and "Mr. Wilson," admired the band's singlemindedness: "Driven by conviction and fired by their music, the members of King's X wield the moldy art-rock sword and, despite some false moves, hone it to a hard, straight edge."

King's X continued honing their edge on tour, participating in the short-lived Gathering of the Tribes festival with EPMD, Fishbone, Primus, X, and others. In 1991 they contributed the song "Junior's Gone Wild" to the soundtrack of the film *Bill and Ted's Bogus Journey*. The days of obscurity have ended, and the band now confronts the issue that has daunted many an ambitious and thoughtful rock band: whether it should restrain its ideals for the sake of greater success. Pinnick, who has spent much of his life negotiating a path between the True Believers and the Devil Rockers, offered a humble summary of his artistic and spiritual mission in his interview with Fricke: "Rock & roll is very important in my life. But the most important thing is to give people things they need, like love and attention. We all need that friendly handshake or hug. That's what keeps us going, and that's what I want King's X to represent. I want people to be able to put one of our records on and feel like 'Yeah, I can deal with today.'"

# Selected discography

*Out of the Silent Planet* (includes "Power of Love"), Megaforce Worldwide/Atlantic, 1988.

*Gretchen Goes to Nebraska* (includes "Mission" and "Over My Head"), Megaforce Worldwide/Atlantic, 1989.
*Faith Hope Love By King's X* (includes "It's Love," "I'll Never Get Tired of You," "We Are Finding Who We Are," "Legal Kill," and "Mr. Wilson"), Megaforce Worldwide/Atlantic, 1990.
*King's X*, Atlantic, 1992.

**With other artists**

*Bill and Ted's Bogus Journey: Music from the Motion Picture* (contains "Junior's Gone Wild"), Interscope/Atlantic, 1991.

# Sources

*CD Review*, April 1991.
*Entertainment Weekly*, October 26, 1990.
*Guitar Player*, February 1991.
*Hijinx*, August 1991.
*Mean Street*, December 1990.
*Musician*, February 1991.
*Rolling Stone*, November 30, 1989; January 10, 1991; February 21, 1991.

—Simon Glickman

# Fela Kuti

**Musician, singer, political activist**

One of Africa's most acclaimed musicians, Nigerian Fela Anikulapo Kuti is "a peculiar late-twentieth-century mix of shaman, politician, ombudsman, activist and musical genius," according to Gene Santoro in the *Nation*. Kuti, or Fela, as he is popularly called, writes and performs political protest songs that have won him a large following both at home and abroad, to the frequent chagrin of government authorities. His music—dubbed "Afro-Beat"—is an amalgam of American blues and jazz blended with African rhythms, while his pointed lyrics—in pidgin English and African—confront government corruption, multi-national corporations, and police brutality. Larry Birnbaum in *Spin* described the Fela sound as "chicken-scratch guitar, vamping organ, massed brass, female chorus, jazzy horn solos, layered drumming—and antiestablishment doggerel," calling it "hypnotically persuasive" and commenting that "Fela's insinuating baritone is a potent preacher's tool." In a career that has spanned four decades Fela has recorded over 50 albums and performs frequently in concert.

Fela is a flamboyant singer and musician and his concerts—many held at his Lagos nightclub, The Shrine—are lengthy and infectious. Fela belts out his driving songs, gyrating as he performs on saxophone or keyboards, directing his thunderous 27-member band, Egypt 80. "[His] songs, which usually ride sloganlike lyrics over a densely woven web of cross-rhythms, have titles like 'Beasts of No Nation' (which deals with the way various governments abet South African repression) and 'Just Like That' (a sneeringly witty list of Nigeria's current shortcomings)," noted Santoro. John Darnton wrote in the *New York Times* that one of Fela's most popular songs, "Upside Down," describes a traveler who finds an organized, well-planned world everywhere except in Africa, where there are villages, but no roads, land, but no food or housing. "These things are the daily lot of all Lagosians," Darnton noted. " When Fela sings this song, . . . listeners nod their heads solemnly and look into their beers."

### Inspired by Black Power Movement

Fela's musical upbringing spanned three continents. Born and raised in Nigeria, he initially studied piano and percussion and, as a youth, led a school choir. In the late 1950s Fela moved to London—to study medicine, thought his middle-class parents—where he explored classical music and was exposed to American jazz artists Charlie Parker, John Coltrane, and Miles Davis. His music did not become political, however, until the late 1960s, when he visited the United States and was exposed to the black power movement. Influenced by the teachings of black activist leader

Malcolm X, Fela began to realize the implications for Africa of white oppression, colonialism, Pan-Africanism—the unity of African nations—and revolution. His new-found political consciousness inspired him to adopt the middle name Anikulapo—"having control over death"—and change his band's name from Koola Lobitos to Afrika 70 (later Egypt 80). The young musician's work would never be the same; as quoted by Jon Pareles in the *New York Times,* Fela said, "The whole concept of my life changed in a political direction."

Fela returned to Nigeria and began to write politically charged songs that rocked his country. Inspired by Pan-Africanism, he incorporated African instruments into his band, including Konga drums, klips sticks, and the sekere, a percussion instrument. "I'm playing deep African music," he said at the time, as Pareles noted. "The rhythm, the sounds, the tonality, the chord sequences, the individual effect of each instrument and each section of the band—I'm talking about a whole continent in my music." Fela's protest music became very popular among the ranks of Nigeria's unemployed, oppressed, and politically dissident. These groups remain a large part of his audience.

Fela's music and politics have made him a cult figure in Nigeria; he has run for the presidency twice. His openly confrontational messages have, however, repeatedly irked government authorities, who have found reason to jail Fela for a variety of offenses throughout his career. In 1977 official rancor turned violent when the Nigerian military—some say in response to Fela's

album *Zombie*—leveled his imposing Lagos residence after Fela had declared it an independent republic. Before burning down the house—including Fela's recording equipment and master tapes—soldiers went on a rampage in which Fela's 82-year-old mother, a prominent women's rights activist, was hurled from a second-story window. She later died from her injuries and her son, in protest, dumped her coffin at the house of then-president General Olusegun Obasanjo.

## Polygamy and Marijuana

Although such incidents have rallied support for Fela, he is notorious for a lifestyle that has alienated many Nigerians; he unabashedly preaches the virtues of sex, polygamy, and drugs, in particular the use of marijuana as a creative stimulant. In 1978 Fela shocked his countrymen when he married his harem of 27 women (whom he later divorced), in protest he said, against the Westernization of African culture. His commune, the Kalakuta Republic—established to protest the military rule of Nigeria—was reportedly itself run like a dictatorship. According to the *Times's* Darnton: "[Fela] ruled over the Kalakuta Republic with an iron hand, settling disputes by holding court and meting out sentences—cane lashings for men and a tin shed 'jail' for women in the backyard. . . . To some degree, these trappings of power account for his popularity among authority-conscious Nigerians." *Spin's* Larry Birnbaum elaborated on Fela's excesses, reporting, "Stories abound of his setting fire to hotel rooms, . . . firing penniless band members on overseas gigs, making interviewers cool their heels for days and then receiving them in his underwear. . . ."

## Toured United States

While Fela's politics and lifestyle are controversial, few quibble over the power of his music. In 1986—after the human rights organization Amnesty International helped free him from prison, where he had languished due to questionable currency-smuggling charges—Fela and Egypt 80 made their first tour of the United States, where their audience is limited but growing. He has influenced the work of reggae singer Jimmy Cliff and the Talking Heads' David Byrne. In 1991 he performed an epic gig at New York City's Apollo theater accompanied by 30 support players.

As Fela becomes better known outside Nigeria he feels that his music will increasingly hold an international message. He told *People's* Cathy Nolan: "America needs to hear some good sounds from Africa, man. The sanity of the world is going to be generated from Africa through art. Art itself is knowledge of the spiritual world. Art is information from higher forces, by those who are talented. I'm not jiving. I've been living with my art for 23 years. My music has never been a failure."

## Selected discography

*Army Arrangement*, Celluloid.
*Beasts of No Nation*, Shanachie.
*Black President*, Capitol.
*Coffin for the Head of State*.
*Fela*, Celluloid.
*Fela and Ginger Baker, Live*, Celluloid.
*Mr. Follow Follow*, Celluloid.
(With Roy Ayers) *Music of Many Colours*, Celluloid.
(With Lester Bowie) *No Agreement*, Celluloid.
*Overtake Done Overtake Overtake*, Shanachie.
*Shuffering and Shmiling*, Celluloid.
*Zombie*, Celluloid.

*Teacher Don't Teach Me Nonsense*, Mercury, 1987.
*Original Sufferhead*, Capitol, c. 1981, reissued, Shanachie, 1991.
(With wife, Sandra) *Upside Down*, Celluloid.

## Sources

### Books

Moore, Carlos, *Fela Fela*, Schocken, 1987.

### Periodicals

*Maclean's*, October 13, 1986.
*Nation*, August 13, 1990.
*New York Times*, July 24, 1977; November 7, 1986.
*People*, December 1, 1986.
*Spin*, November 1991.

—Michael E. Mueller

# Tom Lehrer

**Singer, songwriter**

"When Tom Lehrer's songs first surfaced in the 1950s, they seemed the last word in witty naughtiness," critic Frank Rich declared in the *New York Times*. The singer-songwriter has gifted audiences with famed novelty hits such as "Poisoning Pigeons in the Park," "The Masochism Tango," and the controversial "Vatican Rag." Despite the fact that Lehrer more or less retired from performing in the mid-1960s, he experienced a resurgence in popularity during the late 1970s and early 1980s primarily due to the efforts of nationally syndicated novelty disc jockey Dr. Demento. This new exposure for Lehrer's classics led to the adaptation of his work for an extremely successful stage review, "Tomfoolery."

Born Thomas Andrew Lehrer on April 9, 1928, in New York, New York, he took piano lessons from the age of eight. His parents decreed that he would focus solely on classical music, but he developed a taste for theater musicals in spite of this. But Lehrer also had more serious interests; he earned his bachelor's degree in mathematics from Harvard University by the time he was 18 and his master's degree, from the same institution, followed when he was 19. Nevertheless, Lehrer found time during his years at Harvard to amuse himself and his friends with his satirical songs. One of them, a sports fight song poking fun at his alma mater's upper-class reputation called "Fight Fiercely, Harvard," he eventually recorded.

Lehrer continued his education, completing everything towards his doctorate except the dissertation, and became a lecturer. He also spent time working for the Atomic Energy Commission at Los Alamos, and for Baird-Atomic, Inc. But he was unable to abandon his musical interests, and wrote clues in song form for a television quiz show in 1951. About the same time, friends began encouraging him to record his musical satires. Though the record companies Lehrer tried were not receptive, his acquaintances continued to egg him on, and he produced and recorded his first album independently.

### From Mathematics to Music

The result, aptly titled *Songs by Tom Lehrer,* included spoofs on such varied subjects as the American South—"I Wanna Go Back to Dixie"—faded love affairs—"I Hold Your Hand in Mine," and the Boy Scouts—"Be Prepared." Another of the tracks, "The Hunting Song," chronicles the misadventures of a sportsman who manages to kill everything in the area except the deer he sought. Yet another, "The Old Dope Peddler," Lehrer has conceded to be somewhat politically incorrect now that over thirty years have passed since its composition, but he originally intended it as a parody of nostalgic songs. With such content, *Songs by Tom Lehrer* quickly made a market for itself by word of mouth. It also brought about a demand for performance, and Lehrer made his professional singing debut at a nightclub called the Blue Angel in New York City. From this well-received start, he went on to play in clubs in Boston, San Francisco, and Los Angeles.

After a two-year hitch in the U.S. Army during the mid-1950s, Lehrer resumed his satiric musical efforts. He prepared new songs, and recorded a live performance of them in Cambridge, Massachusetts, for an album called *An Evening Wasted With Tom Lehrer.* Typical samplings from this disc include titles such as "Poisoning Pigeons in the Park" and the playfully kinky "Masochism Tango."

Also on the album are "The Elements," which celebrates the atomic periodic table to the tune of Gilbert and Sullivan's "I Am the Very Model of a Modern Major General"; and "We Will All Go Together When We Go," which points out the advantage of nuclear war—no one is left to grieve over loved ones. Lehrer recorded a studio version of these songs, called *More of Tom Lehrer,* in addition to a live version of his first album entitled *Tom Lehrer Revisited,* but neither of these is

now available in the United States. Then, shortly after the release of *An Evening Wasted With Tom Lehrer,* the songwriter dropped from public view for a time, furthering his career as a mathematics lecturer.

### Resumed Career

Lehrer resurfaced in 1964 and began writing tunes for a television news satire program, *That Was the Week That Was.* Though Lehrer did not perform on the show, he used some of his creations for it in a concert at the legendary hungry i club in San Francisco. The concert was recorded and became *That Was the Year That Was.* Lehrer's sense of satire was as apt as ever in cuts such as "National Brotherhood Week," which mocks hypocrisy about racism, and "Wernher von Braun," concerning the divorce of science and ethics.

But Lehrer found himself in the midst of controversy for "The Vatican Rag," a song that makes light of Roman Catholic ritual. Priests, ministers, and school boards called for the banning of Lehrer's record, but the composer contended that he had not intended to offend the religion, though he did confess to taking aim at the religion's ritual. Lehrer answered charges of sacrilege by arguing that war songs that imply that God favors one side killing another seem much more sacrilegious to him.

After the controversy died down Lehrer again retired to concentrate on teaching. He teaches at the University of California at Santa Cruz during half the year, and maintains a residence in Cambridge during the other half. During the 1970s, he contributed songs to the children's educational television program *The Electric Company.* In addition to instructing students in mathematics, Lehrer introduced a course in stage musicals. He inadvertently became popular again, however, when disc jockey Dr. Demento's nationally syndicated radio novelty show introduced his work to a whole new generation of listeners.

### Eighties Revival

Coupling that phenomenon with Lehrer's own explanation in the *Washington Post* that completely original musical theater productions were on the decline may explain the fact that in 1980 Cameron Mackintosh and Robin Ray adapted much of Lehrer's repertoire into a musical revue, "Tomfoolery." Citing revues of other songwriters' works, such as those of Duke Ellington and Jacques Brel, Lehrer joked: "It was inevitable . . . that someone would peer into the almost empty barrel and notice me down there." *Variety* called "Tomfoolery" "a charming and witty revival" of a "special brand of lunacy."

The show—successful on both the West End and off-Broadway—provoked speculation on whether Lehrer would take up his piano again. Reports varied; *Newsweek* quoted him as saying: "I don't want to perform, I have no desire for anonymous affection." Gail Jennes in *People* claimed, however, that "Lehrer has no trouble with the thought of performing again." Whatever the case, satire is doubtful—he told Jennes that his "mind doesn't run that way anymore."

## Selected discography

### LPs

*Songs by Tom Lehrer* (includes "The Irish Ballad," "The Wiener Schnitzel Waltz," "Be Prepared," "I Wanna Go Back to Dixie," "The Hunting Song," "My Home Town," "I Hold Your Hand in Mine," and "The Old Dope Peddler"), Reprise, 1953.
*An Evening Wasted With Tom Lehrer* (includes "Poisoning Pigeons in the Park," "The Masochism Tango," "A Christmas Carol," "The Elements," "She's My Girl," and "We Will All Go Together When We Go"), Reprise, 1959.
*More of Tom Lehrer,* Decca, 1959.
*Tom Lehrer Revisited,* Decca, 1960.
*That Was the Year That Was* (includes "National Brotherhood Week," "Smut," "So Long Mom: A Song for World War III," "Wernher von Braun," and "The Vatican Rag"), Warner Bros., 1965.
(With others) *Dr. Demento Presents the Greatest Novelty Records of All Time,* Rhino Records, 1986.

## Sources

*Esquire,* February 1986.
*Newsweek,* November 23, 1981.
*New York Times,* December 15, 1981.
*People,* January 11, 1982.
*Variety,* June 18, 1980.
*Washington Post,* January 3, 1982.
*Washington Post Book World,* December 12, 1981.

—Elizabeth Wenning

# Living Colour

Rock band

The New York rock and roll band Living Colour, with its hard-hitting songs and expert musicianship, had all the ingredients for success when it first approached the music industry. Yet record labels didn't know what to do with the band, for the simple reason that all four of its members were black. Despite music-business stereotyping, Living Colour proceeded to banish all doubt with their 1988 debut album *Vivid,* which went gold, and their 1990 follow-up *Time's Up,* spearheading a wave of eclectic and critically-acclaimed bands who challenged racial conventions.

Guitarist Vernon Reid, who started the band in 1985, struggled for years to realize his dream of an all-black, all-rock band. An early inspiration was rock guitar giant Jimi Hendrix, whose trailblazing songs remain some of the most popular music of the late sixties. For Reid, Hendrix provided an example of a black musician fusing traditionally black forms like the blues with psychedelia and other new styles. Yet the popular tendency to deemphasize Hendrix's blackness frustrated Reid. When he was in high school, Reid told Charles Shaar

Bad Brains (to name but a few), with the muscle and volume of Led Zeppelin."

That same year he co-founded the Black Rock Coalition (BRC), an organization designed to support African-American musicians hoping to break out of the straitjacket of "black" and "white" music categories. By 1990, the organization had a membership of 175 individuals and 30 bands, though Living Colour was the first to achieve mainstream success.

At a BRC meeting Reid met bassist Muzz Skillings, and soon thereafter ran into drummer Will Calhoun, who was playing for Harry Belafonte at the time. Glover left the band briefly to act in the film *Platoon,* and singer Mark Ledford fronted the band for its appearance at the Moers Jazz Festival in Europe in 1986. When Glover returned, the band played club dates in the New York area in 1987 and 1988.

Murray, author of the book *Crosstown Traffic: Jimi Hendrix and the Rock 'n' Roll Revolution,* that he heard a white Florida deejay say "that Hendrix was black, but the music didn't sound very black to him [the DJ]. . . . and I flipped out. At the time I was very culturally aware of the race issues because of [black activists] Martin Luther King [Jr.] and Malcolm X and all the ferment that was happening in the Black Power movement. I didn't really connect it all so much with *music,* but that really threw it in my face. It was a phone-in show, and I spent all night trying to call in. I fell asleep with the phone in my hand." This early incident focused Reid's attention on the attitudes he would eventually challenge.

### Assembled First Band in 1983

Reid was born in London to West Indian parents and raised in Brooklyn. He assembled the first version of his band in 1983, while still playing with drummer Ronald Shannon Jackson's jazz-fusion band The Decoding Society. Several different musicians played with early versions of the band, which would be named Living Colour in 1986, including jazz pianist Geri Allen. Reid met vocalist Corey Glover at a party during this period, and their common interests led them to collaborate. Reid left The Decoding Society in 1985 with the determination to form what *Rolling Stone's* David Fricke termed "a full-tilt *rock* band celebrating the continuing vitality and enduring promise of Robert Johnson, Billie Holiday, Bo Diddley, Sly Stone, Ornette Coleman, and

### Assisted by Mick Jagger; Made "Cult" Video

Mick Jagger, lead singer of the pioneering British rock band The Rolling Stones, heard Living Colour at a club date and was sufficiently impressed to produce two songs for the band, "Glamour Boys" and "Which Way to America." The songs served as demos that helped them secure a record deal with the Epic label and were remixed for the LP *Vivid,* which was released in 1988. The album was slow to take off, and the first video, "Middle Man," aired only scantily on MTV. The second video, for the song "Cult of Personality," marked a breakthrough for the band, inspiring heavy radio airplay and increased record sales.

The video for "Cult," a metallic rock tune with lyrics about blind obedience to leaders, featured film clips of politicians as diverse as Italian fascist Benito Mussolini and U.S. president John F. Kennedy, interspersed with energetic footage of the band onstage. Other songs from *Vivid* that fared well on radio and MTV were "Glamour Boys," which, like "Cult," became a Top 40 hit, "Open Letter (to a Landlord)," and "Funny Vibe," a song about racism which included a guest appearance by the rap group Public Enemy. The LP went gold, then double platinum. Living Colour won a 1989 Grammy for best hard rock performance for "Cult," and numerous trophies at the MTV Video Music Awards, among them best new artist. *Rolling Stone's* Alan Light referred to *Vivid* as "one of the most promising—and with over one and a half million copies sold, one of the most successful—rookie efforts in years." Reid's band had answered industry concern that, in Fricke's words, "black rock was a contradiction in terms."

### Opened for Stones on Tour

Shortly thereafter, Jagger invited the band to join the Rolling Stones on their 1989 *Steel Wheels* tour. Backstage after one of these shows, Living Colour was approached by Little Richard, one of the first black rock and roll artists to gain mainstream success in the fifties. "Hi!" Richard greeted the band. "I'm one of those glamour boys you been singin' about!" For the band, Richard's encouragement was stunning and uplifting. "That was *the* moment," Reid told Fricke. "Having Little Richard say 'You guys are doing the right thing'—if I needed validation, that's it."

Little Richard contributed a rap to the song "Elvis Is Dead" on the band's next album, *Time's Up*. This song both ridiculed the host of "Elvis sightings" publicized in tabloid newspapers and reminded listeners that Elvis Presley was a white singer making use of a black musical tradition. The song also featured a saxophone solo by former James Brown sideman Maceo Parker. A host of other noted musicians contributed to the LP, including rappers Queen Latifah and Doug E. Fresh. The album's first single, "Type," made the Top Ten with radio airplay, and its video fared well on MTV. Epic shipped 400,000 copies of the album to stores initially, and within a week the company was taking reorders. *Time's Up* entered *Billboard*'s album chart at Number 82, and reached the Top 20 the next week.

### *Time's Up* Explored Timely Issues

The second LP was, as Reid remarked to *Interview*'s Charlie Ahearn, "a few steps removed from where we were when we did *Vivid*." Indeed, *Time's Up* explored a wide range of musical styles, including rap, soul, and African "High Life" music, and also included spoken-word passages about black experience on "History Lesson" by noted actors Ossie Davis, Ruby Dee, and James Earl Jones. Among the subjects treated in the lyrics were sexuality in the age of AIDS, information technology, and the motivations of drug dealers. According to *Rolling Stone*'s Light, the album "represents the fulfillment of the band's promise. . . . The challenge of a second record is to avoid formula, and this spectacular album is a tribute to Living Colour's bravery." *Time's Up* was voted one of the best albums of the year in a *Rolling Stone* reader's poll, and Living Colour voted one of the best bands.

In 1991 Living Colour joined the massive Lollapalooza concert tour, along with such diverse performers as hard rockers Jane's Addiction, rapper Ice-T, and punk mischief-makers The Butthole Surfers. At the outset of the tour, the band released an EP, *Biscuits*, which included covers of Hendrix's "Burning of the Midnight Lamp," soul great Al Green's "Love and Happiness," and James Brown's "Talkin' Loud and Saying Nothing," as well as an outtake from *Time's Up*, "Money Talks," and two live tracks. Yet *Entertainment Weekly*'s David Brown called the record "overambitious . . . Living Colour may indeed be the successors to Hendrix and Brown, but they need to make their biscuits with a simpler recipe."

These criticisms still acknowledged Living Colour as the fulfillment of Reid's ambitions: a successful modern black rock group with a solid connection to a black rock tradition. After years of frustration, the band had become rock heavyweights.

## Selected discography

*Vivid* (includes "The Cult of Personality," "Glamour Boys," "Open Letter (to a Landlord)," "Middle Man," "Funny Vibe," and "Which Way to America"), Epic, 1988.
*Time's Up* (includes "Type" and "Elvis Is Dead"), Epic, 1990.
*Biscuits* (includes "Burning of the Midnight Lamp," "Love and Happiness," "Talkin' Loud and Saying Nothing," and "Money Talks"), Epic, 1991.

## Sources

### Books

Murray, Charles Shaar, *Crosstown Traffic: Jimi Hendrix and the Rock 'n' Roll Revolution,* St. Martin's Press, 1989.

### Periodicals

*Down Beat,* October 1990.
*Entertainment Weekly,* July 19, 1991.
*Interview,* September 1990.
*Rolling Stone,* September 6, 1990; November 1, 1990; December 13-27, 1990; March 7, 1991.

—Simon Glickman

# Neville Marriner

**Conductor, violinist**

Sir Neville Marriner—perhaps the most recorded of all classical conductors, especially of Mozart pieces—is in large part responsible for maintaining the renaissance of interest in baroque music that developed shortly after World War II. He founded and directs the Academy of St. Martin-in-the-Fields, one of the most highly respected and recorded classical ensembles in the world. Marriner's recordings are so numerous that his name is known by even those on the periphery of the classical music audience. Consider Eve MacSweeney's ingenuous observation in *Harper's Bazaar:* "Every American brushing his teeth in the morning to a classical station hears [Marriner's] music and his orchestra's mouthful of a name." Millions previously unexposed to classical music, Dennis Rooney pointed out in *The Strad,* came to know his name through his musical direction of the Academy Award-winning 1984 film *Amadeus,* about the life and times of eighteenth-century Austrian composer Wolfgang Amadeus Mozart. Marriner's focus, however, has never been on popularity, but on an artistic love of the subject and the freedom to produce music that is attentive to details, vital, and clear.

These traits were developed during childhood. Born in Lincoln, England, in 1924, Marriner began playing the violin at the age of five. His father—a carpenter by trade, an amateur musician by desire—and his mother filled the family's home with music. "This was our entire home entertainment," Marriner told Rooney, "so that having gone to sleep for the first four or five years of my life with this noise going on, it seemed completely natural that when it became possible for me to play an instrument, I should be given one to play." Spurred on by his father and his own growing talent, Marriner won local competitions and eventually a scholarship to the Royal College of Music in London when he was 16. Shortly thereafter, however, he was drafted for service into World War II and subsequently wounded. During his convalescence, Marriner met Robert Thurston Dart, a mathematician and baroque musician who greatly influenced the young Marriner's approach to and expectations of music.

Marriner's view of the baroque's joyous, expansive, ornamental music was enhanced through Dart's vision. He explained to Rooney, "[Dart] persuaded us that an ornament was just what it said it was, an *ornament*, an embellishment, something that should sit comfortably within the music as part of your own expressive intention toward the composer. There had to be something of yourself."

After his recovery, Marriner studied for a year at the Paris Conservatory, then returned to England to teach for a year at Eton College and for ten years at the Royal

Born April 15, 1924, in Lincoln, England; son of Herbert Henry (a carpenter) and Ethel May (Roberts) Marriner; married Diana Margaret Corbutt, 1949 (died, 1957); married Elizabeth Sims, 1957; children: (first marriage) Susan Frances, Andrew Stephen. *Education:* Received degree from Royal College of Music, London; attended Paris Conservatory for one year.

Orchestra conductor. Taught music at Eton College, 1947; professor of music at the Royal College of Music, 1949-59; violinist with Martin String Quartet, 1946-53, Virtuoso String Trio, 1950, Jacobean Ensemble, 1952, London Philharmonic, 1952-56, and London Symphony Orchestra, 1956-1968; founder and member of board of directors of the Academy of St. Martin-in-the-Fields, 1959—; conductor of the Los Angeles Chamber Orchestra, 1969-77; music director of the Minnesota Orchestra, 1980-86. Guest conductor with the Berlin Philharmonic, New York Philharmonic Orchestra, Concertgebouw, Boston Symphony, French National Orchestra, Cleveland Orchestra, and others; artistic director of the South Bank Festival of Music, 1975-78, Meadow Brook Festival, 1979-84, and Barbican Summer Festival, 1985-87; music director of the Stuttgart Radio Symphony Orchestra, 1986-89. Honorary fellow of the Royal Academy of Music.

**Awards:** Named commander of the Order of the British Empire, 1979; Grammy Award for best choral performance other than opera for *Haydn—The Creation,* 1981; *Amadeus—Original Soundtrack* was named classical album of the year, 1984; Marriner was knighted by Queen Elizabeth II, 1985; Grand Prix du Disque; Edison Award; Mozart Gemeinde Prize; Tagore Prize.

**Addresses:** *Office*—Academy of St. Martin-in-the-Fields, 109 Boundary Rd., London NW8 0RG, England; and c/o Harold Holt Ltd., 31 Sinclair Rd., London W14 0NS, England. *Agent*—IMG Artists, Media House, 3 Burlington Ln., Chiswick, London W4 2TH, England.

Conservatory of Music. During this time Marriner played as a free-lance violinist with numerous quartets, ensembles, and chamber groups before joining the London Symphony Orchestra in 1956.

### Founded Academy of St. Martin-in-the-Fields Ensemble

But a desire for more emotional rewards from playing music led Marriner and a group of other string players to meet at an eighteenth-century Anglican church in London's Trafalgar Square, St. Martin-in-the-Fields. What began as a group of individuals seeking an artistic outlet soon coalesced into a vigorous performing ensemble whose view toward its players, Marriner told Andrew Keener in *Gramophone,* "was that no one was indispensable but everyone was immensely valuable. Therefore we try to keep the highest grade of player interested in us by allowing them as much freedom as possible."

Having taken conducting lessons from Pierre Monteux, the conductor of the London Symphony Orchestra, Marriner was forced out of the concertmaster's chair and onto the podium to lead the growing ensemble. Although he felt his position was only to provide a framework—"The flesh and character must come from the musicians themselves," he explained to *People*'s Giovanna Breu—Marriner nonetheless desired to create a certain sound with the ensemble, a vibrant clarity that has since become the Academy of St. Martin's trademark. "I like a certain *whiteness* in the sound," he told Rooney. "I find that too much individual colour in an ensemble—too wide a vibrato, a too-flat placement of the bow on the string, too much forearm in the stroke, too much wrist in the vibrato, too much arm—always means that individuals will stick out."

### Acclaimed for Insightful Approach to Conducting

This uniformity and cleanness of sound won Marriner and the Academy critical praise. Christopher Porterfield noted in *Time* that Marriner "has built an international reputation for graceful, lively, intelligently shaped performances, especially of the Baroque composers and Mozart and Haydn." Richard Freed concurred in *Stereo Review* in a critique of a recording of Mozart symphonies 30, 32, and 33: "Everything about these stylish performances seems just right: they are alert and crisp, yet as lilting as anyone could wish in the appropriate sections. This is the sort of thing Marriner does best."

In addition to the Academy performers' virtuosity and Marriner's gifted vision, it was his own attentiveness to the details of recording that brought praise. "Perhaps no other conductor in history except Leopold Stokowski has studied as intensively the special demands of the recording process on performing musicians," Rooney pointed out. "Although his interest in a recording ends as soon as it is released, up to that point no detail escapes his attention."

## Focused Energies on Larger Vision

Because of his growing reputation, Marriner was asked in 1967 to form the Los Angeles Chamber Orchestra. Up until then, he was still connected with the London Symphony Orchestra and the Academy. However, since he felt his greatest impact could be as a conductor, he resigned from the London Symphony but remained on the board of directors of the Academy, maintaining his recording abilities with it.

Soon thereafter, Marriner began guest-conducting with large symphonic ensembles such as the Concertgebouw, the Boston Symphony, the National Symphony Orchestra, and the French National Orchestra. "His intention," John Rockwell extrapolated in the New York Times, "was in part to escape the typecasting inherent in his role as a chamber-orchestra specialist, and in part simply to learn the basic 19th-century repertory. He played it all during his days as an orchestral musician." Another reason for his shift from the baroque to larger works of the classical and romantic periods was his desire to keep his perspective vital. "It got to the stage with the Academy," Marriner explained to Stephen Johnson in Gramophone, "that I felt we were jumping through the same hoop over and over again, and it eventually got immensely tedious."

Marriner's appointment in 1980 as music director of the Minnesota Orchestra signaled his immersion in the large-scale symphonic world. Critics, however, did not uniformly hail his work in this area. Of an early concert performance piece, a reviewer for High Fidelity/Musical America noted that "the successive tonal portraits of Mussorgsky's gallery were etched with a keen eye for detail and atmospheric effect. Witty caricature rather than dark colors seemed foremost in [Marriner's] mind." But Michael Anthony, writing in Ovation, felt that "in works of the second half of the 19th century, [Marriner] can on occasion seem too cool, too controlled, as though he were looking at the scores through a monocle." And of his foray into the American music of Aaron Copland with the Minnesota Orchestra, Noah Andre Trudeau wrote in High Fidelity/Musical America that Marriner's interpretation of El Salon Mexico was "superb," but that Appalachian Spring "missed the warmth I know to be in the score, . . . the occasional 'kick' a more balletic conception would have provided."

Despite this early criticism, Marriner has continued to seek out and record works of the later periods, leading the Stuttgart Radio Symphony Orchestra (he served as music director from 1986 to 1989), and the Academy, with whom he continues to record. The subsequent critical reaction has returned to the glowing accolades he received for his early baroque work. In a recording of Schumann pieces with the Academy, Marriner, according to Freed, "is here not merely persuasive but unarguably authoritative. . . . [He] gives them readings that are suitably large-scaled but youthful at the same time, realizing all their Schubertian warmth, charm, and vigor." And Lawrence Hansen, writing in American Record Guide, said of the Stuttgart's recording of two orchestral suites of Tchaikovsky: "I have no higher praise to give than to call this disc 'beautiful.'. . . I don't mean surface prettiness, but down-to-the-very-core, heart-and-soul beauty shining through the pain, anxiety, and sadness."

# Selected discography

### With the Academy of St. Martin-in-the-Fields

Amadeus: Original Soundtrack, Fantasy, 1984.
J. C. Bach: Sinfonias (6), Op. 6, MHS, 1988.
J. S. Bach: Brandenburg Concertos Nos. 1, 2 & 3, Philips, 1981.
Baroque Concertos: Avison, Manfredini, Albinoni, Handel, Telemann, London, 1982.
Beethoven: Symphony No. 9, Philips, 1990.
English Music for Strings: Holst, Delius, Britten, Vaughn Williams, Walton, Purcell, Angel, 1972.
Faure: Pavanne; Pelleas et Melisande; Masques et Bergamasque Suite; Fantasie for Flute, Argo/Decca, 1982.
Handel: Arias, Angel, 1990.
Handel: Music for the Royal Fireworks; Concerto Grosso in C; Overture in D, Philips, 1980.
Haydn: Cello Concertos in C and in D, Philips, 1989.
Herbert: Cello Concertos No. 1 in D Major and No. 2 in E Minor, London, 1989.
Mendelssohn: Violin Concerto in E Minor, and Bruch: Violin Concerto in G Minor, London, 1988.
Mozart: Cosi fan tutte, Philips, 1991.
Mozart: Horn Concertos (4); Rondo for Horn and Orchestra in E-flat Major, Philips, 1989.
Mozart: Sacred Arias, Angel/EMI, 1988.
Mozart: Symphonies 30, 32, 33; Adagio Maestoso, Philips, 1982.
Mozart: Symphonies 34 and 38; Minuet in C, Philips, 1982.
Paganini: Violin Concerto No. 1, and Vieuxtemps: Violin Concerto No. 5, Philips, 1990.
Respighi: The Birds; Three Botticelli Pictures, Angel/EMI, 1977.
Rossini: La Cenerentola, Philips, 1989.
Schubert: Symphonies 1 and 4, Philips, 1984.
Suppe: Overtures, Angel/EMI, 1990.
Trumpet Concertos: Haydn, Hertel, Hummel, Stamitz, Philips, 1988.
Vaughn Williams: Fantasia on a Theme by Thomas Tallis; Fantasia on Greensleeves; The Lark Ascending; Five Variants of "Dives and Lazarus," Argo, 1972.

**With the Minnesota Orchestra**

Copland: *El Salon Mexico; Four Dance Episodes from "Rodeo"; Suite from "Appalachian Spring,"* Angel, 1984.
Paulus: *Symphony in Three Movements,* and Larsen: *Symphony: Water Music,* Electra/Nonesuch, 1988.
Wagner: *Die Meistersinger; Siegfried's Rhine Journey; Rienzi; The Flying Dutchman,* Telarc, 1983.

**With the Stuttgart Radio Symphony Orchestra**

Schumann: *Symphony No. 1; Overture, Scherzo & Finale; Manfred Overture,* Capriccio, 1988.
Schumann: *Symphony No. 2; Symphony in G Minor,* Capriccio, 1988.
Schumann: *Symphonies 3 and 4,* Capriccio, 1988.
Strauss: *Metamorphosen; Oboe Concerto,* Capriccio, 1989.
Tchaikovsky: *Suites for Orchestra: No. 1 in D, No. 2 in C,* Capriccio, 1989.

Tchaikovsky: *Suites for Orchestra: No. 3 in G, No. 4 in G, Capriccio,* 1988.

## Sources

*American Record Guide,* March/April 1988; May/June 1988; July/August 1988.
*Gramophone,* November 1984; April 1987.
*Harper's Bazaar,* September 1989.
*High Fidelity/Musical America,* February 1980; December 1984.
*New York Times,* May 6, 1979; October 21, 1990.
*Ovation,* January 1984.
*People,* August 24, 1981.
*The Strad,* October 1986.
*Stereo Review,* March 1982; March 1984.
*Symphony Magazine,* October/November 1984.
*Time,* March 17, 1980.

*—Rob Nagel*

# Hugh Masekela

---

**Musician, composer, singer**

---

**S**outh African trumpeter, fleugelhornist, composer, and singer Hugh Masekela is an acknowledged master of African music. He is also one of his country's most recognizable freedom fighters in the battle against the racist rule of apartheid. Masekela was born on April 4, 1939, in Witbank, a coal mining town near Johannesburg, South Africa. Although his father was a health inspector and acclaimed sculptor, the Masekela home was a modest one, and young Hugh was raised by his grandmother. By age six Masekela was singing the songs of the street and at age nine began attending missionary schools, where he learned to play the piano.

Masekela first became interested in playing the trumpet after seeing the 1949 film *Young Man With a Horn,* the story of Bix Beiderbecke. Initially Masekela's greatest influences were the performers of American swing. Later he became interested in be-bop jazz and the music of Dizzy Gillespie and Charlie Parker, whom Masekela credits with the development of his talent. As a teenager Masekela began playing trumpet with South African dance bands, some of which toured major African cities. In 1958 he joined Alfred Herbert's African Jazz Revue and the following year formed his own band, the Jazz Epistles, with pianist Dollar Brand, drummer Makaya Ntshoko, trombonist Jonas Gwanga, and alto saxophonist Kippie Moeketsi.

### Studied Music Abroad

As a black man, South African music schools were closed to Masekela; he was forced to go abroad to continue his musical training. He studied at London's Guildhall School of Music and received a scholarship from American calypso star and human rights activist Harry Belafonte to the Manhattan School of Music, in New York City, which he attended from 1960 to 1964. Staying on the the U.S., Masekela also worked with Belafonte's Clara Music and arranged the music on several albums for his then-wife, African folksinger Miriam Makeba, from whom he was divorced in 1966.

In 1964 Masekela teamed with fellow student Stewart Levine to found Chisa Records. *The Emancipation of Hugh Masekela* was the first of 11 albums the duo produced. In 1968 Masekela became one of the first African artists to pierce America's pop music world when his song "Grazing in the Grass" topped *Billboard's* singles chart for two weeks. Written in the style of *mbaqanga*—a combination of traditional Zulu music and black American pop—"Grazing in the Grass" clearly reflected Masekela's African heritage. Masekela toured parts of Africa in 1973, playing with a variety of African musicians. In Ghana he met Nigerian "Afro-beat" purveyor and protest singer Fela and the Ghanian group Hedzoleh Soundz. He became the group's leader and recorded *Masekela: Introducing Hedzoleh Soundz* with them in 1973. The following year Masekela and Hedzoleh Soundz toured the United States.

Having spent the better part of the 1960s and 1970s in the U.S., Masekela moved back to Africa in 1980, eventually settling in Botswana, where he lived for four and a half years—though he would later return to the U.S. He arranged for a mobile recording studio to be shipped from California, and working with Jive Afrika Records, released the album *Technobush.* The single "Don't Go Lose It Baby," topped dance charts in the U.S. In 1986 Masekela founded the Botswana International School of Music, a nonprofit institute dedicated to training African musicians. The following year he signed on a guest star with American singer-songwriter Paul Simon's *Graceland* tour, which was a popular and critical success, though accompanied by criticism from some who claimed that Simon had violated a United Nations cultural boycott of South Africa when he recorded parts of the album *Graceland* in Johannesburg. Masekela, however, had not performed on the record.

### Collaborated With Playwright Ngema

Earlier, in 1983, Masekela had met South African playwright Mbongemi Ngema, author of several critically acclaimed plays. One of them is *Woza Albert,* in which

Ngema used Masekela's song "Coal Train." After seeing a performance of the play, Masekela went backstage to meet Ngema. They became friends and decided to collaborate on a piece of theater. Winnie Mandela, wife of then-imprisoned South African political activist Nelson Mandela, suggested that they portray the children of South Africa and their resistance to *bantu* education, which prepares them to serve the white minority in their country.

Ngema wrote the book and some of the music for what was to become *Sarafina!,* titled for the main character, who bears a woman's name common in the townships around Johannesburg. He asked Masekela to compose additional music. Loosely structured, the play is more like a series of choral set pieces than musical theater, but the songs and dances are all tied together thematically by the famed Soweto uprising; the action takes place in the schoolyard of the Morris Issacson High School, the site of the 1976 uprising in which nearly 600 students were killed and many more shot by police for protesting the teaching of Afrikaans—considered by them the language of white colonialist oppression—instead of English. In *Sarafina!,* the students at the school, inspired by their student leader, Sarafina, produce a play that depicts the release of the imprisoned Mandela.

Ngema auditioned and rehearsed about 20 young South Africans from the townships for roles in *Sarafina!* The members of the ten-piece band that provided the production's energetic *mbquanga* music are dressed as soldiers; they play on a set made up of a chain link fence and a tank. At the beginning of the piece, the performers are dressed in the trouser-and-blouse uniforms of the school, but by the end, they appear in tribal costumes, dancing, singing about their heritage, and protesting their oppression.

### *Sarafina!* an International Hit

At its 1987 premier in South Africa *Sarafina!* was an immediate hit. It went from Johannesburg to New York City's Lincoln Center later that year, and in January 1988 moved to Broadway, where, an instant success, it played for two years to sell-out crowds before beginning a national tour. A second troupe was formed to perform the Tony Award-nominated musical in Europe. "I think it's one of the most rewarding projects I've done," Masekela told *Detroit News and Free Press* contributor Cassandra Spratling.

When Masekela left South Africa to study music, he began what was to become a roughly three-decade self-imposed exile in protest of apartheid. Despite his physical separation, however, he never lost his emotional and cultural ties to his country, or the desire to see his homeland freed from racial inequality. "I'm not the kind of musician you hear saying 'my music,'" Masekela told the *Washington Post*'s Donna Britt. "I don't think I have music. I think everybody gets music from the community they come from. . . . And every note that I play, every song that I've ever worked on is really from the people. And their freedom will usher in a place where I can say, 'Now I'm an artist.'"

In late 1990 Masekela returned to a slowly changing South Africa to visit his mother's grave for the first time. He also established a residence to use during part of the year, thus effectively ending his exile. Masekela spoke hopefully in the *Boston Herald* of his plan to spend time in his country. "I will go back a lot now I think. There is no doubt in our minds that we will be free one day soon and that South Africa will become a normal society. There's a lot of work to be done with the reconstruction that will be coming up. We'll all have to be a part of it."

## Selected discography

*Trumpet Africaine*, Mercury Records, 1960.
*Home Is Where the Music Is*, Chisa Records, 1972.
*Masekela: Introducing Hedzoleh Soundz*, 1973.
*I Am Not Afraid*, Chisa Records, 1974.
(With Herb Alpert) *Main Event*, A&M, 1978.
*Technobush* (includes "Don't Go Lose It Baby"), Jive Afrika Records, 1984.
*Waiting for the Rain*, Jive Afrika Records, 1985.
*Uptownship*, Novus/RCA, 1990.
*The Emancipation of Hugh Masekela*, Chisa Records.

## Sources

*Africa Report*, July/August 1987.
*American Visions*, April 1990.
*Boston Globe*, October 26, 1990.
*Boston Herald*, March 6, 1988; October 26, 1990.
*Chicago Sun Times*, August 5, 1990.
*Detroit News and Free Press*, June 3, 1990.
*Down Beat*, March 1992.
*Jet*, August 5, 1991.
*Record* (Hackensack, NJ), October 26, 1987.
*Hartford Courant* (CT), April 24, 1988; March 21, 1990.
*Times* (Madison, WI), April 4, 1989.
*Milwaukee Journal*, July 29, 1990.
*Star-Ledger* (Newark, NJ), October 3, 1989; January 24, 1988.
*New York Post*, October 24, 1987; October 26, 1987.
*New York Tribune*, February 12, 1988.
*Philadelphia Inquirer*, November 22, 1987.
*Pittsburgh Press*, June 1, 1989.
*Providence Journal* (RI), July 20, 1990.
*Rolling Stone*, June 10, 1982; July 2, 1987.
*San Francisco Examiner*, June 14, 1990.
*Stereo Review*, June 1990.
*Sunday Republican* (Springfield, MA), January 24, 1988.
*Variety*, April 1990.
*Washington Post*, April 27, 1990.

—*Jeanne M. Lesinski*

# John Mayall

**Bandleader, instrumentalist, singer**

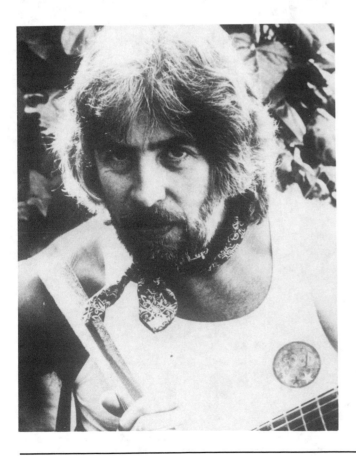

John Mayall's Bluesbreakers were without a doubt *the* seminal British blues band, a major catalyst in the musical revolution that swept England in the 1960s and gave birth to blues rock. Countless musicians hold Mayall in highest regard for both his talent and his integrity; nonetheless, he is best known primarily for the caliber of musicians who learned their craft in his band. Many Bluesbreakers alumni have gone on to a star status greater than anything Mayall has achieved simply because they branched out into pop music, while Mayall's dedication to pure blues remains greater than his desire for a chart-breaking hit.

Mayall's father played in many amateur dance bands, and his large collection of jazz recordings was his son's first inspiration. He never made a living at music, however, and John had no intention of pursuing that trade either, though he learned to play piano, guitar, and ukelele while in his early teens. Mayall's natural talent in art led him to the Manchester Junior Art School at age 13, about the same time he discovered and fell in love with American blues. He taught himself to play harmonica while going through the school's two-year course. At 15 he went to work as a window dresser in a Manchester department store, moving his way up to a position in the art offices before being drafted into the British Army. He spent two years in the service, including some time in Korea. Upon returning to England in 1955, he continued his education at the Regional College of Art in Manchester, where he formed his first band, the Powerhouse Four. Graduating in 1959, he landed a job with an advertising agency and quickly established a reputation as one of the best typographers and graphic artists in the region.

### Formed Bluesbreakers at 29

The legendary Mississippi-born Muddy Waters had toured England in 1958 with an electric band featuring Chicago's best bluesmen. The tour is often credited with sparking a British music revolution as it unified the country's scattered blues followers and gave them a common vision. Mayall is often referred to as "The Father of British Blues," but he told *Down Beat*'s Dan Ouellette that the title properly belongs to "Alexis Korner and Cyril Davies, [who] triggered the transformation of London's club scene from traditional jazz of the '50s to electric blues in 1960 with their six-piece band influenced by Muddy Waters." Korner and Davies convinced Mayall that if he left Manchester—where he'd put together an amateur group, the Blues Syndicate—and went to London, he could make it as a professional musician. In 1963, at the age of 29—old by most rock and roll standards—he took up residence in London and formed his dream group, the Bluesbreakers.

Mayall worked days as a draftsman for about a year; but by early 1964 the Bluesbreakers were doing well enough for Mayall to become a full-time musician. The band backed American greats John Lee Hooker and Sonny Boy Williamson on their tours of the United Kingdom and played dates in small clubs six nights a week. Before long the Bluesbreakers were acknowledged as the best blues band in England; their success, however, was overshadowed by the mass popularity of new rhythm-and-blues-influenced groups like the Rolling Stones. The situation changed rapidly when guitarist Eric Clapton became a Bluesbreaker in April of 1965. Clapton had already made a name for himself with the Yardbirds, but decided leave that group when they began developing what he considered too pop-oriented a sound. Mayall's purist philosophy suited Clapton perfectly, and his talent blossomed in the group. It was at this time that the famous graffito "Clapton is God" began to appear in London. With "God" in the lineup, the Bluesbreakers became the hottest ticket around.

### Band an Incubator of Talent

Clapton was a restless musician, however; he abruptly left the Bluesbreakers in August of 1965, returned in November, then left for good in July of 1966 to form Cream with drummer Ginger Baker and ex-Bluesbreaker Jack Bruce. Mayall was unruffled. He understood from the start that some musicians would feel constrained by his strict adherence to classic blues forms, and he frequently encouraged them to leave and explore new directions. He also let many excellent players go simply because he had conceived a new sound for the band and didn't feel they could contribute what he needed.

Still other musicians were thrown out of the group for breaking their leader's absolute prohibition against drinking on the job. Each time a great player moved on, Mayall found a replacement capable of bringing a new dimension to his band. Some of the musicians who developed their talents in the Bluesbreakers are John McVie, Mick Fleetwood, and Peter Green, who went on to form Fleetwood Mac; Aynsley Dunbar, who became a part of the Jeff Beck Group, the Mothers of Invention, and Journey; Jon Hiseman and Tony Reeves, who formed the pioneer jazz rock group Colosseum II; and Mick Taylor, who would later go on to fame as a Rolling Stone.

In 1967 Mayall and the Bluesbreakers made their first U.S. tour. American audiences greeted them with great enthusiasm—so much so that Mayall soon moved to Laurel Canyon, California. He continued to be a blues purist, but that didn't keep him from exploring all the possibilities of the music. At a time when heavy amplification was common, he recorded *The Turning Point,* a subtle, wholly acoustic album that was notable particularly for its lack of drums. The absence of percussion instruments, however, did not keep Mayall and his sidemen from creating a driving, accessible sound; in fact, the record yielded what is probably Mayall's best-known tune, "Room to Move." *The Turning Point* became his best-selling album and was eventually certified gold. As Mayall entered the 1970s he disbanded the many-peopled Bluesbreakers and instead hired free-lance musicians to support him on his tours and recording projects.

### 1970s Proved Difficult

As the 1970s wore on, Mayall entered a slow decline; he still played roughly 120 live dates a year, but as he revealed to Ouellette in *Down Beat,* he saw his recording career "dwindle and finally die out" after several label changes. The abstemious musician who'd once fired sidemen for having a drink before playing now developed his own alcohol problem. "Throughout the '70s, I performed most of my shows drunk," he admitted in *Down Beat.* Other bad luck plagued him as well, including the complete destruction of his house in a 1979 fire, and a serious injury sustained when he jumped from a balcony and missed the swimming pool for which he was aiming. "That was one incident that got me to stop drinking," he told Ouellette.

Things began to turn around for Mayall in the early 1980s. In 1982 he recreated one of the earlier incarnations of the Bluesbreakers with Mick Taylor and John McVie, playing a series of well-received club dates. Although that reunion didn't last, the idea of getting back to the original Bluesbreakers sound did. In 1984 Mayall put together a new edition of the Bluesbreakers featuring guitarist Coco Montoya and drummer Joe Yuele. This lineup toured Eastern Europe and released some small-label recordings, including *Behind the Iron Curtain, The Power of the Blues,* and *Chicago Line.* Island Records eventually re-released *Chicago Line* in the U.S. and signed Mayall to a recording contract, which led to his 1990 release, *A Sense of Place. Down Beat* contributor David Whiteis stated that the album "shows that Mayall is capable of exploring new directions with sensitivity and imagination."

## Selected discography

*John Mayall Plays John Mayall,* London, 1965, reissued, Polydor, 1988.
*The Bluesbreakers,* London, 1967.
*A Hard Road,* London, 1967, reissued, 1987.
*The Blues Alone,* London, 1968.
*Crusade,* London, 1968.
*Bare Wires,* London, 1968.
*Raw Blues,* London, 1969.
*Looking Back,* London, 1969.
*Blues From Laurel Canyon,* London, 1969, reissued, 1990.
*The Turning Point* (includes "Room to Move"), Polydor, 1969.
*Empty Rooms,* Polydor, 1970.
*Diary of a Band* (Volume 1), London, 1970.
*U.S.A. Union,* Polydor, 1970.
*Live in Europe,* London, 1971.
*Back to the Roots,* Polydor, 1971, revised as *Archives to Eighties,* 1988.
*Thru the Years,* London, 1971, reissued, Deram, 1991.
*Memories,* Polydor, 1971.
*Jazz Blues Fusion,* Polydor, 1972.
*Diary of a Band* (Volume 2), Decca, 1972.
*Moving On,* Polydor, 1972.

*Down the Line,* London, 1973.
*Ten Years Are Gone,* Polydor, 1973.
*The Latest Edition,* Polydor, 1974.
*The Best of John Mayall,* Polydor, 1974.
*New Year, New Band, New Company,* Blue Thumb, 1975.
*John Mayall,* Polydor, 1976.
*Notice to Appear,* ABC, 1976.
*A Banquet in Blues,* ABC, 1976.
*Primal Solos,* London, 1977.
*The Hard Core Package,* ABC/MCA, 1977.
*Lots of People,* ABC, 1977.
*Last of the British Blues,* ABC/MCA, 1978.
*Bottom Line,* DJM, 1979.
*Behind the Iron Curtain,* Crescendo, 1986.
*Some of My Best Friends Are Blues,* Charly, 1986.
*Crusade,* London, 1987.
*Chicago Line,* Island, 1988.
*The Blues Alone,* Polydor, 1988.
*A Sense of Place,* Island, 1990.

Also recorded *The Power of the Blues* and *No More Interviews.*

## Sources

### Books

Fleetwood, Mick, with Stephen Davis, *Fleetwood: My Life and Adventures in Fleetwood Mac,* Morrow, 1990.

### Periodicals

*Down Beat,* July 1990.
*People,* August 6, 1990.
*Playboy,* October 1990.
*Rolling Stone,* September 10, 1987; September 24, 1987; August 23, 1990; December 13, 1990.
*Variety,* July 8, 1987.

—Joan Goldsworthy

# Don McLean

## Singer, songwriter, guitarist

In 1971 folk balladeer Don McLean released "American Pie," an infectious, though puzzling, eight-and-a-half-minute portrait of the history of rock and roll—and of its gradual despoilment by commercialism. Beginning with rock musician Buddy Holly's tragic plane crash in 1959, the song alludes to musical and popular figures and symbols of the late 1950s and sixties, its final verses suggesting the disaster at Altamont, when a Rolling Stones open-air concert ended in bloodshed. Mirroring the nation's own feelings of malaise and lost innocence as the Vietnam War dragged on, "American Pie" became an enormous success, selling three million copies and topping the singles charts for months.

The solitary, introspective McLean was thrust into the spotlight, exulted at concerts, and pressed to explain his lyrics line for line. "It was like a complete creative life lived with the release of one song," McLean told Richard Hogan in *People,* recalling how "American Pie" overshadowed all his achievements before or after; for several years following the "American Pie" phenomenon the performer refused to play the song that had assured his fame and fortune. Strident about the neglect his other compositions and their messages received, he antagonized the American music press and his career faltered. McLean continued to enjoy musical success abroad, though, earning many gold records in Israel, Australia, Brazil, and Italy. By 1980 a more mellow and resigned McLean—intent on finding a balance between the anonymity he craved and the notoriety required to maintain an audience for his music—had his first U.S. hit single since the mid-1970s, a remake of "Crying," the classic Roy Orbison composition. "Adaptability," he ceded to Hogan, "is the keynote to survival."

### Remained Aloof From Folk Scene

McLean was sickly and asthmatic as a child; his frequent absences from school were spent listening to records and the radio. Rock and roll pioneer Buddy Holly was his idol. During high school McLean played guitar in rock bands, but was gradually drawn to folk music. The choice was a natural fit with his solitary nature; he didn't like "the problems of working with other musicians," revealed a *New York Times* interview with Don Heckman, or being "saddled with a lot of equipment." After graduation McLean hitchhiked across the East and Midwest, performing at small folk clubs and coffeehouses, avoiding large cities and popular folkie hangouts like New York City's Greenwich Village. "I just wanted my own little niche," he explained to Bruce Pollock in *Rock,* "and I just wanted to be by myself."

their voyage chronicled for television and in a book edited by McLean. His public profile significantly heightened, McLean began to appear at folk and rock festivals with fellow folk artists Seeger, Arlo Guthrie, and Janis Ian; he shared billing with pop performers like Laura Nyro and Dionne Warwick as well. McLean had less luck landing a recording contract, though, and his first album, *Tapestry*—filled with lyrical social-protest songs—caused barely a stir when it was released by Mediarts in 1970.

### "American Pie" Actually a Protest

As McLean became better acquainted with the music industry he realized that genuine talent mattered far less than a carefully packaged image. In "American Pie" he lamented this state of affairs: the fate of music in the hands of the tastemakers. His message in that song was so hidden by complex metaphors that few discerned it—including the industry he indicted. Ironically, McLean's new record company, United Artists, marketed the single vigorously. In a genius stroke of promotion, the song was leaked to New York City rock radio station WPLJ-FM on the day the celebrated Fillmore East rock theater closed its doors, making the refrain "the day the music died" especially memorable. "American Pie" became the title of McLean's next album, which sold five million copies and made him an international star. Although it was overshadowed by the sensation of "American Pie," the record contained a second hit single, a tender ode to Dutch artist Vincent Van Gogh. Titled simply "Vincent," the song is remembered by many for its opening phrase: "Starry, starry night." The ballad has played daily at the Van Gogh Museum in Amsterdam, the Netherlands, since its release.

With his runaway success, McLean felt a loss of control—over his career, his music, and its meaning. "Dreidel," a cut from the singer's next album, dolefully reflected on his struggle to keep former values and convictions alive. The performer ceased concert work and songwriting while coming to grips with the commercialization of his art; in a year's time he had refocused his energies on his original love, folk music, and looked abroad for performance opportunities.

### Mix of Originals and Standards Refreshed Career

While McLean's new songs reflected familiar themes about social injustice and life's bittersweet challenges, the singer had added a number of old standards to his repertoire, favorites by such diverse artists as Hank

Nonetheless, McLean's warm, easy, and often compelling sound, poetic lyrics, and keen observations on the human condition did not escape the appreciation of folk devotees and other musicians; in 1968 the budding singer-songwriter was brought to the attention of the New York State Council on the Arts and became its Hudson River troubadour, presenting ecology and community-oriented free concerts in more than 50 river towns. Veteran folksinger Pete Seeger was among those who heard McLean perform at that time; he is said to have declared the young folk artist the finest singer and songwriter he had met since Bob Dylan.

In 1969 McLean joined the folksinging crew members of the sloop Clearwater, Seeger's ecological project designed to raise public awareness and funds to halt industrial pollution of eastern rivers. The group gave dockside concerts in 27 cities from Maine to New York,

Williams, Bing Crosby, and Roy Orbison. The mix of old and new proved a winning formula; McLean's 1979 album, *Chain Lightning,* sold 1.5 million copies worldwide. Discussing a second album of original compositions and new renditions of classic songs—1981's *Believers*—*Stereo Review* contributor Noel Coppage admired McLean's new "range and eclecticism" and "spirit of experimentation." Perhaps like many music observers of the day, however, Coppage missed the younger, pithier McLean, writing: "I keep wanting McLean to go deeper into certain things, partly because he's one of the few troubadours working now who seems able to." McLean's fans the world over—despite any critical misgivings about his recorded output—have nonetheless continued to delight in this musical survivor's stage appearances throughout the 1980s and into the 1990s.

## Selected discography

*Tapestry* (includes "And I Love You So"), Mediarts/United Artists, 1970.
*American Pie* (Includes "American Pie" and "Vincent"), United Artists, 1971, reissued, EMI.
*Don McLean,* United Artists, 1972.
*Playin' Favorites,* United Artists, 1973.
*Homeless Brother,* United Artists, 1974.
*Solo,* United Artists, 1976.
*Prime Time,* Arista, 1977.
*Chain Lightning,* Millennium, 1979.

*Believers,* Millennium, 1981.
*The Best of Don McLean,* EMI America, 1987.
*Don McLean's Greatest Hits, Then & Now,* Capitol, 1987.
*Love Tracks,* Capitol, 1988.
*For the Memories* (two volumes), Gold Castle, 1989.
*Don McLean's Greatest Hits: Live,* Gold Castle, 1990.

McLean has written more than 200 songs, several recorded by other artists, including Perry Como's popular version of "And I Love You So."

## Sources

### Books

*The New Rolling Stone Record Guide,* edited by Dave Marsh and John Swenson, Random House, 1983.
Stambler, Irwin, *The Encyclopedia of Pop, Rock & Soul,* revised edition, St. Martin's, 1989.

### Periodicals

*New York Times,* February 13, 1972.
*People,* April 27, 1981; February 26, 1990.
*Rock,* April 23, 1973.
*Rolling Stone,* September 20, 1990.
*Stereo Review,* April 1982.

—*Nancy Pear*

# Metallica

**Heavy metal band**

"In a world of hairspray-and-mascara glam rock, Metallica sticks out like a junkyard mongrel at a poodle show," wrote Karl Coryat of *Bass Player* magazine. The San Francisco Bay Area's Metallica, a flagship speed-metal—or "thrash"—band has emerged as one of America's most popular heavy metal outfits, a result, no doubt, of the group's steady maturation during the dues-paying 1980s. Metallica's self-named 1991 release addressed the decidedly adult topics of nuclear holocaust, mental illness, suicide, and the dangers of drug addiction. Yet despite these grim themes, Metallica's music runs contrary to heavy metal's one-dimensional image; their sound involves more than just bone-breaking chords and fire-and-brimstone lyrics. The band has distinguished itself with a grungy sophistication well beyond the work of its predecessors. Members of Metallica are rude and cheeky, but they're proficient. *Bass Player*'s Coryat attested, "Their famous 'Metal Up Your Ass' T-shirt ensured Metallica a notorious place in rock-and-roll history." Taste in merchandising notwithstanding, *Spin* magazine's Alec Foege called Metallica "a burnished black gem."

## For the Record. . .

**K**irk Hammett (lead guitar; raised in San Francisco, CA; studied guitar with Joe Satriani, 1983; replaced **Dave Mustaine,** 1983, who had replaced **Lloyd Grant**), **James Hetfield** (vocals, rhythm guitar), **Jason Newsted** (bass; raised in Niles, MI; replaced **Cliff Burton,** who died in a tour bus accident, 1986), **Lars Ulrich** (drums).

Group formed in 1981; recorded *Kill 'Em All* on Elektra/Asylum Records, 1983; toured with heavy-metal Monsters of Rock arena show.

**Awards:** Gold record for *Ride the Lightning,* platinum record for . . . *And Justice for All,* and double-platinum record for *Metallica;* Grammy Award nomination for best hard rock/metal performance, 1989, and Grammy Awards for best hard rock/metal performance, 1990, for "One," and 1991, for "Stone Cold Crazy."

**Addresses:** *Record company*—Elektra Entertainment, 75 Rockefeller Plaza, New York, NY 10019.

Metallica coalesced in 1981 with singer-guitarist James Hetfield, drummer Lars Ulrich, bass player Cliff Burton, and lead guitarist Dave Mustaine. Mustaine, who had taken over for early collaborator Lloyd Grant, was replaced in 1983 by Kirk Hammett. Their first album, *Kill 'Em All,* attracted droves of "head-banging" fans. The follow-up releases *Ride the Lightning* and *Master of Puppets* were greeted with even more enthusiasm by the world's heavy metal constituency, which enabled the band to strut their stuff with fellow "metalheads" on the enormous Monsters of Rock Tour. That outing featured a free concert in Moscow that was attended by 500,000 Soviet metal fans. Infamous spitoon in tow for this tour and others—band members needed a place to deposit their chewed tobacco—Metallica was increasingly credited with single-handedly revitalizing heavy metal music, paving the way for other thrash bands like Slayer and Megadeath.

### Bass Player Killed in Tour Bus Accident

Tragedy struck Metallica on September 27, 1986, when the band's tour bus went into a ditch in Sweden, killing bassist Cliff Burton. After a brief hiatus the band reassembled and began looking for a replacement for Burton. Attempting to fill the bass player's shoes and duplicate his eccentric, unbridled style seemed impossible. Burton had never been a particularly smooth player, but other band members had not attempted to reign him in. They did try once, however, to persuade him to forego his bell-bottom jeans in favor of more traditional heavy metal garb, but quickly realized the attempt was futile; Burton was set in his ways and rarely influenced by others. In truly bizarre heavy metal fashion, one of his dreams had been to invent a gun that shot knives instead of bullets.

To refurbish their lineup, the members of Metallica decided to settle on someone completely different from Burton: Jason Newsted, then with the Phoenix band Flotsam & Jetsam. Newsted was raised in Niles, Michigan, and had decided to turn professional after playing in bands throughout high school. He told Coryat, "I heard Cliff (Burton) had died the day after the accident. . . . I was a huge Metallica fan at the time. When I was looking at the blurb in the paper, I was sad, but things started flashing through my mind. . . . I just thought if I could play 'Four Horsemen' once with those guys, I'd be really happy."

### New Sound Signaled Turning Point

Burton had been a remarkable soloist, but Newsted provided Metallica with a more cohesive sound. Burton's sound had not been well-defined, particularly when he played low on the guitar's neck. Newsted chose to mirror the band's guitar riffs precisely instead, producing a newly unified guitar effect. This sound dominated the new band's 1988 double album. Titled . . . *And Justice for All,* the record went platinum and earned a Grammy Award nomination, despite a dearth of radio airplay. The release of *Justice* coincided with Metallica's return to its musical roots: the groundbreaking metal stylings of 1970s rock giants Led Zeppelin and Black Sabbath. This resolve became the cornerstone for the 1991 release, *Metallica.*

Still steely, but a little slicker, *Metallica* was produced by Bob Rock, who had also worked with metal acts Motley Crue, Loverboy, and Bon Jovi. Buoyed by the dark, driving single "Enter Sandman," *Metallica* sold 2.2 million copies in its first week. Metallica's hard-won versatility is showcased on the record with guitarist Hammett's winsome wah-wah, and open-throated, more melodic vocals from Hetfield. The band earned Grammys in both 1990 and 1991 and effectively ascended to a new strata of heavy metal superstardom. Featured on the covers of both *Rolling Stone* and *Spin,* Metallica's popularity seemed to know no bounds. With increased media coverage, it became clear that the band's appeal was not narrowly bohemian, political, or reflective of any trend—except perhaps anger. *Village Voice* contributor Erik Davis wrote that "Metallica's 'image'—dark shades, frowns, and poorly conceived facial hair—allies them with a musical culture of refusal. They haven't stopped dragging mud onto the carpet and slamming their bedroom doors without saying hello. 'Enter Sandman' has touched the brains of fry cooks and Bud guzzlers across the land."

### Mythic Syntax and "Rigorous Minimalism"

Analysis of Metallica's lyrics reveals the band's unique penchant for conjuring up the timeless grandiosity of myth by placing the object of a line before its subject: "This fight he cannot win," and "Off the beaten path I reign" are two examples. The band's head-banging thrash metal songs are short, but not sweet; they're delivered with grim, tight expressions, and a minimum of emotion, which gives the impression that the entire band is grimacing. Metallica's albums have few tender spots; songs range from the brutal "Sad But True" to the sweet and gritty "Ride the Lightning," from the praised pagan slant found on "Of Wolf And Man" to the metaphysical musings of "Through the Never." Commenting on their larger musical style—"Metallica's riffs crack like glaciers"—the *Village Voice*'s Davis said of the band, "They hew thrash to a rigorous minimalism."

*Spin*'s Foege waxed mathematic in his assessment of Metallica, writing, "At turns algebraically elegant and geometrically raucous, present-day Metallica can stop and start on a dime." With their popularity showing no signs of flagging, their musical and lyrical virtuosity on the upswing, and their fans more crazed than ever, Metallica is a speeding bullet heading perilously close to the heads of those adults with barely tolerant, thin-lipped expressions molded onto their faces. The band's motto, after all, is "Bang Those Heads That Don't Bang."

## Selected discography

*Kill 'Em All,* Elektra, 1983.
*Ride the Lightning,* Elektra, 1984.
*Master of Puppets,* Elektra, 1986.
*. . . And Justice for All,* Elektra, 1988.
*Metallica,* Elektra, 1991.
*Garage Days Re-visited,* Elektra.

## Sources

*Bass Player,* September/October 1991.
*Newsweek,* September 23, 1991.
*Rolling Stone,* November 14, 1991; March 19, 1992.
*Spin,* October 1991; December 1991.
*Village Voice,* September 18, 1991.
*Wilson Library Bulletin,* January 1992.

*—B. Kimberly Taylor*

# Midori

**Violinist**

At age twenty Japanese violinist Midori Goto, who performs under the name Midori, is no longer considered a mere child prodigy. With her virtuoso technique, pure tone, and artistic interpretations, she is quickly dispelling doubts about her future as a violinist. Midori has appeared with many of the world's best orchestras, including those in Berlin, Chicago, Cleveland, Philadelphia, Boston, Montreal, and London, performing some of the most technically difficult works in the solo violin repertoire.

Born in Osaka, Japan, on October 25, 1971, Midori demonstrated her musical ability at an early age. Her mother, a violinist, regularly took young Midori with her to orchestra rehearsals, and one day she noticed that the toddler was humming a piece that the orchestra had been practicing several days earlier. Midori, fascinated by her mother's violin, often tried to touch the instrument, so on her third birthday, her mother gave her a one-sixteenth-size violin and began to teach her to play it. Later Midori maintained that learning to play the violin was as natural as learning to talk.

### Talent Discovered

At age six, Midori gave her first public recital with a performance of a free form instrumental piece by Niccolo Paganini. She progressed rapidly during the next few years, practicing diligently, and she often went with her mother to the auditorium where orchestra rehearsals were conducted, practicing in one of the hall's empty rooms. An American colleague of Midori's mother chanced to hear the young girl play and, astonished by her technique, took a recording to renowned violin instructor Dorothy Delay at New York City's Juilliard School of Music.

Delay, who taught at the music festival in Aspen, Colorado, during the summer of 1981, invited Midori to participate and arranged for a scholarship. Midori's performances that summer confirmed Delay's estimation of her talent, and a year later Midori and her mother moved to New York City so that Midori could enroll on a full scholarship at Juilliard in the precollege division.

After enduring years of an unhappy, arranged marriage, Midori's parents divorced. Midori and her mother began a new life in the United States. Remembering those early years in New York, Midori told *Los Angeles Times* contributor Donna Perlmutter, "When she decided to bring me here—for the study opportunities, for a school like Juilliard—we had no money and could not even speak English. . . . It took amazing conviction to come alone to a foreign country with a little kid, and to go against the family wishes. I like to think I have some

## For the Record. . .

**B**orn Midori Goto, October 25, 1971, in Osaka, Japan; given name pronounced "Mee-dor-ee"; daughter of an engineer and a violinist; single. *Education:* Attended Juilliard School of Music, New York City.

Violinist. Has performed with orchestras and in recital throughout the United States and in Japan, 1981—.

**Awards:** Named Best Artist of the Year by the Japanese government, 1988; Dorothy B. Chandler Performing Arts Award, Los Angeles Music Center, 1989; Crystal Award, *Ashani shimbun* newspaper, for contributions to the arts.

**Addresses:** *Home*—New York, NY. *Agent*—ICM Artists Ltd., 40 West 57th St., New York, NY 10019.

of that strong-mindedness." Midori's mother obtained a position at the Hebrew Arts School in Manhattan, teaching violin to support the family. While studying at Juilliard, Midori attended the nearby Professional Children's School for academic subjects. She also began performing with the New York Philharmonic Orchestra for young people's concerts and galas, but her agent strictly limited her schedule.

In the summer of 1986, fourteen-year-old Midori took the stage with the Boston Symphony at Tanglewood, in the Berkshire Mountains of Massachusetts. She performed Leonard Bernstein's *Serenade* until a string on her violin broke. As is the custom, Midori calmly approached the concertmaster and borrowed his violin, a much larger one than her own. A short while later a string on this instrument broke. After Midori borrowed the associate concertmaster's violin and finished the performance, the audience, orchestra members, and Bernstein, who was conducting that night, burst into hearty applause. The next day Midori's photograph appeared on the front page of the *New York Times.*

### Leap to Fame

Despite the sudden fame, the number of Midori's annual performances was increased gradually. By 1990 she was appearing in a total of ninety concerts or recitals per year. Midori claims she does not suffer from stage fright. "I never get nervous or anything," she told Michael Fleming of the *St. Paul Pioneer Press-Dispatch.* "For me it is such fun and so comfortable to play the violin. When I am on stage, those are some of the happiest times of my life." Surprisingly, however, Midori maintains that she is always a bit disappointed with her

performances, insisting that she will do better the next time. "I'm always fighting to be better, to improve, to express new ideas with my violin," she explained to *Denver Post* writer Marian Christy. "After a concert I rate my performance: What was good? What was not so good? Then I tell myself that I'm not a robot." While traveling, Midori practices several hours each day, and until she graduated from the Professional Children's School in June of 1990, she also did several hours of homework daily.

Earlier—in 1987—Midori left Juilliard because of personal differences with Delay, which she declines to discuss. "Between school homework, rehearsals and practice there was no time for anything else," Midori explained to Perlmutter. "Since dropping out of Juilliard the world has opened. I go to concerts and movies and have a special curiosity to hear how this one plays and that one plays. I love it." Midori enjoys reading, writing short stories, studying karate, and attending concerts. In addition, she regularly contributes a column on life in the United States to a Japanese teen magazine.

### Budding Recording Career

Midori has successfully ventured into the recording industry as well, releasing double concertos of Johann Sebastian Bach and Antonio Vivaldi with Pinchas Zuckerman, two violin concertos by Bela Bartok, the violin concerto of Antonin Dvorak, and caprices by Paganini. Under an exclusive contract with CBS Masterworks, Midori chooses her own repertory for recordings and also selects the conductor and orchestra, though some orchestras and conductors are unavailable because of contracts with other record companies. After listening to some of the records she made in the 1980s, Midori confessed to Fleming: "I sound like a little girl. But now . . . I'm different; I'm sure I will sound different when I'm forty. That's the great advantage of playing from an early age, that you get to see yourself change."

# Selected discography

J. S. Bach: *Concerto No. 2,* Philips.
J. S. Bach: *Concertos for Two Violins and Orchestra in D Minor,* Philips.
Dvorak: *Concerto for Violin and Orchestra in A Minor,* Columbia Masterworks.
Dvorak: *Romances for Violin and Orchestra in F Minor,* Columbia Masterworks.
*Live at Carnegie Hall,* Sony Classical.

Paganini: *Complete Caprices for Unaccompanied Violin*, Columbia Masterworks.

Paganini: *Violin Concerto No. 1*, Philips.

Tchaikovsky: *Serenade melancolique*, Philips.

Tchaikovsky: *Valse-Scherzo*, Philips.

Vivaldi: *Concertos for Violins and Orchestra*, Op. 3 No. 8, Philips.

## Sources

*Atlanta Journal*, April 12, 1989.

*Berkshire Eagle* (Pittsfield, MA), August 26, 1988.

*Boston Herald*, July 22, 1988.

*Buffalo News*, March 26, 1989.

*Denver Post*, March 21, 1991.

*Los Angeles Times*, April 8, 1990.

*New York Times*, July 28, 1986.

*Ovation*, August 1987.

*Reader's Digest*, March 1987.

*St. Paul Pioneer Press-Dispatch*, September 8, 1990.

*San Francisco Examiner*, February 7, 1991.

*Strad*, May 1987.

*Washington Post*, January 24, 1988.

—*Jeanne M. Lesinski*

# The Monkees

**Pop group**

The advertisement in *Variety* in the summer of 1965 read: "MADNESS!! Auditions. Folk & Roll Musicians-Singers. For acting roles in new TV series. Running parts for 4 insane boys, age 17-21." 437 young men auditioned. According to *People* magazine, the winners—Micky Dolenz, Davy Jones, Michael Nesmith, and Peter Tork—were expected to "clown on camera and sing catchy tunes written by some of the top professionals in the business." They were the American answer to the Beatles—playful, cute, hilarious; thus, the "pre-fab" four, as they were called, were born. Two television seasons and a movie later, the group disbanded, leaving behind some small-screen glory, several albums of varying success, and a host of solid pop tunes.

An elaborate campaign was launched in September of 1966 to give the Monkees their chance. Their first single, "Last Train to Clarksville," was vigorously promoted, resulting in sales of over 500,000 copies in only three weeks. Even before their television debut, over 2,000 teenagers—mostly girls, described by the *New*

*York Times* as "too old for Barbie dolls and too young for miniskirts"—crowded the Broadway Theater in New York City to see the group perform. An album, *The Monkees,* followed, the group providing vocals on a variety of catchy tunes. The instrumentation, however, maintained several sources, was provided by studio musicians, for which the group would later be criticized, though by then all could in fact play their instruments. From the beginning, both Nesmith and York were capable guitarists. The former became known as an accomplished songsmith for both the Monkees and other performers; Nesmith penned "Different Drum," the song that would make a star of Linda Ronstadt.

## Criticized as "Manufactured"

While teens across America embraced the Monkees' wacky, song-filled television program, critics gave them mixed reviews, almost unanimously agreeing that they would have little if any impact on the music industry—even if the show itself was good, clean fun. Said the co-manager of the English band Herman's Hermits, as reprinted in *People,* who themselves were called Beatles imitators, "The Monkees don't rate at all as musicians. They have been artificially created and nothing in show business sticks around very long if it's false." Even Beatles manager Brian Epstein deigned to comment, again as recalled in *People,* "I can't see a synthetic talent lasting."

But Richard Goldstein, writing in the *New York World Journal Tribune,* recognized something significant about the Monkees. Though "as unoriginal as anything yet thrust upon us in the name of popular music," the Monkees seemed to have power in the very fact that they were created in the image of something great. For "ultimately," Goldstein pointed out, the group was "a tribute to the originals. . . . The Beatles are so good, even their imitators are interesting." Equally important were the actors themselves. All four were gifted with the ability to project their natural qualities on screen and connect with their audience. Said the show's co-producer, Robert Rafelson, in the *New York Times,* "It's important to listen to what they're saying and not just tune them out because they have long hair."

In their first season, 1966-67, the Monkees won an Emmy Award for outstanding comedy series, an event that foreshadowed the craze for "music television" that would take American youth by storm 15 years later. Tom Freston, general manager of cable network MTV, said in *Rolling Stone,* "They were the first video band. We all made fun of their music back in the Sixties, but they're classics." Monkees albums, the covers of which shamelessly mimicked early Beatles albums, contained a mixture of hits and misses. Years later, however, many of these songs remain fresh, despite their relatively primitive origins.

The television series helped propel six of the Monkees' singles into the Top 10 during the show's first season. While their first album was considered weak by some critics, *Cream* contributor Bill Holdship called their second, *More of the Monkees,* a "pop lover's dream feast, ranging from the inspired Tommy Boyce & Bobby Hart classics '(I'm Not Your) Steppin' Stone' and 'She' to Neil Sedaka's Buddy Holly-ish 'When Love Comes Knockin' (at Your Door),' one of the happiest love songs ever recorded." The record also included the popular numbers "I'm a Believer"—written by Neil Diamond— "Auntie Grizelda," and "Mary, Mary." The band's third effort, *Pisces, Aquarius, Capricorn & Jones,* was a surprising combination of synthesizer and psychedelic leanings that featured the hit "Pleasant Valley Sunday." *Pisces* was followed by *Headquarters,* which *Cream* termed a "hodge-podge of styles, ranging from the exciting Little Richard/Chuck Berry-influenced 'No

Time' . . . to the beautiful, moving, magnificent, splendid, wonderful 'Shades of Gray,' which rates as one of the '60's best compositions—and sounds as beautiful etc. today as it did then." The Monkees mounted well-attended worldwide tours in both 1967 and 1968. Guitar hero Jimi Hendrix even opened for them on a few domestic dates in 1968, though the pairing was a mismatch, Monkees fans making their negative opinion of Hendrix quite clear.

### Show Canceled After Two Seasons

Despite these heady accomplishments, by late 1968 the popularity of the Monkees began to fade and their television show was canceled. They had nothing to lose when they launched a feature film project, aided by actor and screenwriter Jack Nicholson and director Robert Rafelson. The result was *Head,* the overall effect of which was something like a typical Monkees episode "laced with a bit of R-rated cynicism and worldliness," according to *Stero Review.* The Monkees, like the Beatles they had been cast to imitate, were growing up, changing in response to the turbulent times, as was their audience. The group's 1968 album, *The Birds, the Bees and the Monkees,* was disappointing. Uneven at best and lacking focus, the record nonetheless showcased Nesmith's electric "Valleri," with its sharp guitar licks, and Jones's memorable rendition of "Daydream Believer."

Tork had departed immediately following the demise of the television series. Dolenz, Jones, and Nesmith continued to perform without him for a few years, but eventually the four actor-musicians went their separate ways. As reported in *People,* Tork has little memory of the period between 1969 and 1971. Plagued by substance abuse, he found failure at almost every turn. Three marriages ended; all attempts to form musical groups were unsuccessful. He taught for a short time, finally finding his niche in modest performances at folk festivals and small clubs, and coaching pop and rock performers. "The 60's were a very schizoid period," he told *People* in 1985. "We had, on the one hand, a lot of hope and good cheer and gentility going on, and on the other, a lot of pretty brutal stuff. I think in some ways the Monkees were the distillate of the cheery side. They were the epitome: ultrasharp, ultragood cheer, ultraharmless."

Dolenz too needed a period of recuperation after the Monkees' heyday. The Monkees' initial success, he recalled in *People,* was mind-boggling and exhausting. "It was a devastating experience for anyone. I don't remember much about it, subjectively. I'm told I had a great time. But so much happened so quickly, I think I was probably quite an ass at times." Rising above the ashes of his Monkees career and a failed marriage, Dolenz, currently remarried and the father of four, went on to become a television and theatrical director and producer in England.

Unlike Tork and Dolenz, Jones emerged from the Monkees experience and his own divorce ready to play it all again. "That was a real important time for me and a real fun time in my life," he admitted in *People.* "I have no regrets whatsoever. We went straight to the top with a million dollars worth of publicity, stayed there three years and sold millions of records." Reuniting the Monkees, to Jones, had seemed a wonderful idea for years. "There are only a few groups that can generate that kind of nostalgia," he said in 1985. "A good thing is worth repeating, but time is running out."

Running out of time seems never to have mattered to Michael Nesmith. Perhaps the most talented of the Monkees, Nesmith has thrown himself into his music, feature-film writing and producing, and television video production, the latter of which garnered him a Grammy Award. Nesmith has shown no inclination to discuss his affiliation with the Monkees, nor has he ever considered a reunion. "We were totally a video group," he commented in a 1985 *People* feature. "We were no more a rock group than Marcus Welby is a real doctor. It was all an illusion."

### Reunion Tour a Success

Back in 1975 Jones and Dolenz had gone on tour with Tommy Boyce and Bobby Hart, the principal songwriters for the Monkees. They toured fruitfully for several years, even releasing an album of original material. When that foursome split, interest remained. Finally, in 1986, after much talk from promoter David Fishoff, Dolenz, Jones, and Tork were convinced that a Monkees reunion was worth undertaking.

Be it the comfort of nostalgia or the timelessness of their pop hits, the Monkees' performances in the latter half of the 1980s were a success. They reunited without Nesmith—who sent a stuffed dummy of himself to join his former cohorts at the press conference heralding the reunion—and hammed it up across the United States and Canada, shamelessly parodying their television personas and proving to unbelievers once and for all that they could indeed sing and play. Audiences were divided between adults who, as youngsters, had watched the Monkees' slapstick television program, and their children, who were catching the pre-fab four for the first time in syndication. A new song "That Was Then, This Is Now" seemed to please both. Although

*Spin* contributor Mark Blackwell later deemed the reunion "very unfortunate," *Cream*'s Holdship said of the reunited Monkees, "They were better than the last two times I saw the [Rolling] Stones and the last five times I saw the Kinks."

## Selected discography

*The Monkees*, RCA, 1966.
*More of the Monkees*, RCA, 1967.
*Headquarters*, RCA, 1967.
*Pisces, Aquarius, Capricorn & Jones*, RCA, 1967.
*The Birds, the Bees and the Monkees*, RCA, 1968.
*Then and Now . . . The Best of the Monkees*, RCA, 1968.
*Live 1967*, Rhino, 1987.
*Pool It!*, Rhino, 1987.
*Listen to the Band*, Rhino, 1991.

Dolenz and Jones also recorded *Dolenz, Jones, Boyce and Hart*, Capitol, 1976.

## Sources

*American Film*, July/August 1985.
*Creem*, December 1986; November 1987.
*New York Times*, September 10, 1966; September 19, 1966; October 2, 1966; November 7, 1968.
*People*, August 12, 1985.
*Rock Express*, #106, 1986.
*Rolling Stone*, September 25, 1986.
*Spin*, January 1992.
*Stereo Review*, March 1987.

—*Meg Mac Donald*

# Melba Moore

**Singer, actress**

**M**elba Moore's enduring beauty and strong, four-octave voice have assured her a rewarding career in theater, television, and film. Finding fame in the offbeat hippie musical *Hair* in the late 1960s, the singer has not been out of work since. As a chanteuse, Moore has been at home in a variety of genres, including rhythm and blues, gospel, rock and roll, and pop. *Newsday* contributor Bill Kaufman described the versatile entertainer as "a superb stylist who bounces on stage looking like a lithe African princess. . . . One gets the feeling that Miss Moore can become anyone she wants. She's a belter. Then she transforms into a sultry song goddess."

Melba Moore was born Beatrice Hill in New York City on October 27, 1945. Her parents, Bonnie and Ted Hill, were both successful entertainers; Bonnie was a singer and Ted played jazz saxophone. While Melba was still a baby her mother remarried, this time to a pianist/singer named Clem Moorman. As the daughter of professional musicians, Moore was often left in the care of a nanny named Lulu Hawkins while her parents toured. Although she remembers Hawkins fondly, Moore has admitted that she was often beaten by her old-style nursemaid. She noted that the corporal punishment made her "tough," and as a result, she never felt particularly out of place on the harsh streets of Harlem where she lived.

## Played the Lead in *Hair*

Moore's family eventually moved to Newark, New Jersey, where she attended a special high school for the performing arts; she studied voice and piano, planning to follow a career on stage. After high school she entered nearby Montclair State Teachers College and majored in music education. She received her bachelor's degree and, on her parents' advice, began a teaching career. But she soon found herself regretting the decision to set aside her original goal of being a performer: "I had been singing since I was four years old," she told the New York *Sunday News*. "God gave me an opera voice and I wanted to use it."

Turning to show business in the mid-1960s, Moore took work as a singer/pianist with a group called Voices, Inc., and also did solo shows at clubs in New Jersey and the Catskills. In addition, she was able to supplement her income by doing background vocals for several Manhattan recording studios. At one such recording session in 1968 she met the composer of the Off-Broadway musical *Hair*. He encouraged her to audition for the new production of the show that was being planned for Broadway. On the strength of her

## For the Record. . .

B orn Beatrice Hill, October 29, 1945, in New York, NY; daughter of Melba (a singer; professional name, Bonnie) and Ted (a jazz saxophonist) Hill. *Education:* Received bachelor's degree from Montclair State Teachers College.

Singer and actress, 1968—. Solo singer and singer/pianist for group Voices, Inc., 1965-68; signed with Mercury Records and released first album, *Learning to Give,* 1970. Original cast member of *Hair,* 1968, became lead, 1969; has appeared in other Broadway musicals, including *Purlie,* 1970, and *Inacent Black,* 1981. Actress appearing in motion pictures, including *Lost in the Stars,* 1974, *Hair,* 1979, and *Flamingo Road,* 1980; and on television programs, including the *Melba Moore-Clifton Davis Show,* 1972, *Ellis Island,* 1984, and *Melba,* 1986.

**Selected awards:** Tony Award for best supporting actress in a musical, 1971, for *Purlie.*

**Addresses:** *Record company*—Capitol Records, Inc., 1750 N. Vine St., Hollywood, CA 90028.

audition Moore was offered a role in the play, which opened on April 29, 1968.

*Hair,* a no-holds-barred exploration of the 1960s hippie culture, proved extremely popular with Broadway audiences. Moore remained with the show for 18 months, moving from role to role until she finally found herself in the lead. It was the first time in the history of Broadway that a black actress had replaced a white, and critics hailed Moore for her groundbreaking performance. Moore found the work in *Hair* liberating; she declared in *Newsweek,* "I had been a misfit, a rule-breaker. . . . But the *Hair* experience informed and reformed my deepest feelings. . . . What *Hair* taught me was to take a chance, to try."

### Won a Tony for *Purlie*

From *Hair* Moore moved to another Broadway show, *Purlie,* a musical recounting the experience of blacks on plantations in the southern United States. Moore took the role of Lutiebelle, an innocent Georgia domestic who falls in love with a fast-talking preacher named Purlie. Reviews of the show invariably pointed to Moore's outstanding performance, and she was awarded a Tony in 1971 for her work in the musical. *Newsday* critic George Oppenheimer, for example, praised the singer as "enchanting in her wide-eyed looks, her infectious personality, her comic ability, and her singing and dancing."

Moore was at the height of her career in the mid-1970s when she toured as a singer and made appearances on numerous television programs. She has also been the star of network variety shows, including the *Melba Mocre-Clifton Davis Show* in 1972 and *Melba* in 1986. Ironically, Moore has often found herself cast as an unsophisticate in dramas, a trend she has sought to reverse since 1984 when she starred as a wealthy and dignified singer in the television miniseries *Ellis Island.*

That stereotype, though, has never followed Moore in her club appearances. There she projects a sophisticated and contemporary image and an unforced vitality. While she has never had a huge hit, her albums—most of them with Mercury and Capitol Records—have consistently sold well within the rhythm and blues market. *Essence* correspondent Herschel Johnson contended that through her extraordinary vocal work, Moore has "established herself as a powerhouse of an entertainer."

### Established the Melba Moore Foundation

In the 1980s, Moore added a new dimension to her public image: she began donating a portion of her earnings to the Melba Moore Foundation for Children, a nonprofit organization that funds a variety of charities for needy youth. Now a born-again Christian who has added gospel numbers to her repertoire, Moore told the *Detroit Free Press:* "I see my work as an entertainer and my work for the foundation and other charities as connected. With every show I do, I want some part of the proceeds to go to something worthwhile." That attitude has sparked Moore's biggest single hit to date, a version of "Lift Every Voice and Sing," unofficially recognized as the black national anthem.

Moore further explained in the *Detroit Free Press* that she sees her work with children's charities as "God's will" and added, "He said, 'If you love me, feed my sheep.' I think each of us has a calling . . . and if each of us does our little part, our life is worthwhile. I want my life to be worth something."

## Selected discography

*Learning to Give,* Mercury, 1970.
*Look What You're Doing to the Man,* Mercury, 1971.
*Melba Moore Live!,* Mercury, 1972.
*Living to Give,* Mercury.
*This Is It,* Buddah.

*Melba*, Epic.
*What a Woman Needs*, Capitol.
*A Lot of Love*, Capitol, 1986.
*Soul Exposed*, Capitol, 1990.

Also recorded *The Other Side of the Rainbow, Never Say Never, Read My Lips, Peach Melba,* and *A Portrait of Melba.*

## Sources

*Detroit Free Press,* May 11, 1990.
*Essence,* September 1984.
*Jet,* May 6, 1991.
*Newsday,* March 16, 1970; October 12, 1971; October 13, 1971.
*Newsweek,* March 30, 1970; June 28, 1971.
*People,* May 28, 1990; September 10, 1990.
*Stereo Review,* June 1971.
*Sunday News* (New York), July 2, 1972.

*—Anne Janette Johnson*

# Jelly Roll Morton

---

**Pianist, composer, bandleader**

---

When one hears of jazz having its roots in New Orleans, some of the first jazz musicians that come to mind are Louis Armstrong and Jelly Roll Morton. While jazz historian Gunther Schuller considered Armstrong "the first great soloist," he called Morton "the first great composer" in his book *Early Jazz: Its Roots and Musical Development*. In addition to being a composer, Morton was a vocalist, pianist, arranger, and ensemble leader. His contributions to the development of jazz were improvisational as well as compositional and his legacy endures in spite of the fact that he didn't make his first commercial recordings until 1923, twenty years after he first appeared on the New Orleans musical scene.

Much of what we know about Morton's early years is the result of contemporary accounts and Morton's own reminiscences, both of which vary in reliability. In his late-in-life Library of Congress Recordings (1938), he recalled his musical past and recreated many of the styles from the first two decades of the twentieth century. Morton's personality has also tended to obscure his very real contributions to jazz. As Waldo Terry observed in *This Is Ragtime,* Morton was "a complete singing, joke-telling, piano-playing entertainer, but he was also a key figure in the development of jazz music." In *The Jazz Tradition,* Martin Williams noted "the colorful character of Jelly Roll Morton seems to be one of the abiding cliches of jazz history."

### A Colorful Character

Morton was at various times in his life a gambler, pool-hall hustler, procurer, nightclub owner, and itinerant piano player. He traveled around the country, and his piano playing was heard all the way from Los Angeles to New York. He was known as a braggart and a liar and claimed to have invented jazz in 1902. Williams confessed that one of the problems biographers face when researching Morton is that "he had a large and fragile ego that hardly encourages one to try and understand the man." Summing up Morton's personality in *The Real Jazz, Old and New,* Stephen Longstreet concluded that "he was no easy man to get along with. He knew he was good and his bump of ego was salted with genius. He was a creative jazz man, not just a performer; part naive, part mean."

Morton was known to have arrived on the New Orleans scene around 1902. To understand the context in which Morton worked, it is necessary to learn a little about New Orleans geography. Two sections of the city—one uptown and the other downtown—had been partitioned, so to speak, into areas where all kinds of vice were allowed. Music was played in the bordellos, which ranged from converted mansions to the lowest "cribs," as well as in gambling dens and other types of clubs. Each section had its own style of music, with the uptown style characterized as hot and emotional and largely played by blacks. The downtown section was the legendary Storyville, a bawdy, sinful area nestled in the French Quarter. Storyville was named after New Orleans Alderman Sidney Story, who initiated the city ordinance that set up the two areas where prostitution could be carried on legally. Down in Storyville, there were primarily Creoles playing a more controlled type of music, and this is the area where Morton lived and played.

### Pioneered Jazz Style

New Orleans around the turn of the century was bursting with music, and ragtime was the music of the period. In Morton's early New Orleans days, from about 1902 to 1907, contemporary accounts indicate that he was playing something different. According to Schuller, "It takes only a few moments of comparative listening to any early ragtime recording to hear the marked difference between Jelly Roll's jazz style and the more rigid, conservative ragtime." He loosened up the rhythmic tightness of ragtime with his left hand, and he made right-hand improvisation the keynote of his piano style. By means of embellishments and improvisations, he gave melodic lines a freer, looser feeling.

Ragtime, within a decade of its emergence around 1899, was overtaken by "exploitation, excess, popularization, decadence, and its own implicit limitations," according to Williams. Calling Morton a "modernist" for

the moment he represents, Williams further noted that "Morton was part of a movement which saved things from decadence. Ragtime was structurally, rhythmically, and emotionally limited, and Morton seems to have known it."

An overlapping movement in American popular music in the first decade of the century was "the blues craze," announced by the publication of W.C. Handy's songs, "St. Louis Blues" and "Beale Street Blues." As a composer, Morton considered ragtime and blues not just musical styles, but specific musical forms. Ragtime was a multi-thematic structure, while the blues was a single-theme form with a predetermined chord progression. According to Schuller and other writers, Morton distinguished between ragtime, blues, and jazz before leaving New Orleans in 1907.

Schuller is one writer who appears willing to accept, at least in part, Morton's claim to have invented jazz, noting the variety of sources Morton used in his music: ragtime, opera, and French and Spanish popular songs and dances. To these musical materials, Schuller concluded, Morton "applied a smoother, more swinging syncopation and a greater degree of improvisational license." Schuller also credited Morton with "blending the more technically controlled playing of Downtown with the hot, unabashedly emotional playing of Uptown." He characterized Morton's improvisational style as one based on themes or melodies, rather than improvisations over a chord structure, as in later jazz. Finally, Schuller pointed out that Morton took the "vertical" harmonic emphasis of ragtime and turned it into a "horizontal" music with a "rhythmic forward momentum . . . without which, either in Morton's or subsequent players' terms, there could be no jazz."

### Eclectic Musical Influences

Morton's innovations as a piano player, and later as an ensemble leader, reflect his compositional genius. By means of melodic improvisation, Morton would give songs variations over chorus-like patterns, combining several strains into larger complete ideas. In addition to ragtime, with its multi-thematic structure, blues influenced Morton's style of play and composition. It was likely the blues, being essentially improvised, that allowed Morton "the improvisational freedom and emotional expressiveness that one side of his nature demanded," according to Schuller.

He also absorbed Italian and French opera, as did other trained Creole musicians of the day. His solo and ensemble playing has been praised by critics for his use of countermelodies, in ensemble to accompany soloists and in his orchestral-like compositions played on solo piano. It was likely his opera influences that gave him an appreciation of unity of form and allowed him to introduce countermelodies and embellish his melodies by repetition. Schuller believes that through his exposure to opera, "Morton learned to value the sense of enrichment and complexity contributed by such counterlines."

Morton may have also invented the jazz break, typically two bars of improvisation inserted into a composition. Again quoting Schuller, "Morton was certainly the first jazz musician to insist upon inclusion of particular compositional details [such as riffs and breaks] in an otherwise improvised performance." He constantly sought variety and contrast in his formal compositions. "When the composition did not already contain sufficient formal contrast," Schuller continued, "Morton would intersperse blues choruses at just the proper moments."

### Recorded Musical Legacy After the Fact

Ironically, when Morton hit his peak in the Red Hot Peppers ensemble recordings of 1926-28, his particular mixture of ragtime and blues and his strong sense of form in his compositions had become "old-fashioned." According to Schuller, Morton was "an anachronistic figure in mid-career." By the late 1920s popular music had strongly influenced jazz, and Louis Armstrong's innovations had left the New Orleans tradition of collective improvisation way behind. Nevertheless, Schuller stated, that "the most perfect examples of this kind of improvised-ensemble organization were produced by Jelly Roll and his Red Hot Peppers, where contrasting individual lines attain a degree of complexity and unity that jazz had not experienced before."

It is Williams's belief that Morton's Red Hot Peppers recordings, done in Chicago and New York, form the basis of his musical reputation. The recording sessions were successful for several reasons. For one, they were carefully rehearsed. Morton wrote out or dictated the arrangements, and he discussed with the players where the solos and breaks should occur. The sessions combined improvisation and pre-arranged compositions in a perfect example of the New Orleans style of collective improvisation. Some of the best cuts from these sessions, according to Schuller, are "Black Bottom Stomp," "Smoke House Blues," "Dead Man Blues," "Grandpa's Spells," and "Original Jelly Roll Blues." Later sessions, often with other musicians, would not be as memorable.

The musical record left by Jelly Roll Morton is incomplete, leaving out as it does the first 20 years of his career. However, all is not lost, and through Jelly Roll's genius he was able to recreate the piano styles of Storyville in the first decade of the twentieth century. Listening to his solo piano on songs like "Sporting House Rag" and "Naked Dance" from the 1939 sessions for *General* (later released as *New Orleans Memories*), one understands and hears that Morton's piano

---

*Morton was at various times in his life a gambler, pool-hall hustler, procurer, nightclub owner, and itinerant piano player. He was known as a braggart and a liar and claimed to have invented jazz in 1902.*

---

playing was characterized by rhythmic variety, shifted accents, delays and anticipations, and melodic embellishments, all leading to a sense of fantastic and frenzied variation. His most successful solo and ensemble recordings reveal his vision of jazz as requiring contrast and variety at all levels.

## Selected discography

### Single releases; as unaccompanied soloist

"King Porter Stomp"/"Wolverine Blues," Gennett, 1923.
"Perfect Rag"/"New Orleans Joys (New Orleans Blues)," Gennett, 1923.
"Grandpa's Spells"/"Kansas City Stomp," Gennett, 1923.
"The Pearls," Gennett, 1923.
"Bucktown Blues"/"Tom Cat Blues," Gennett, 1924.
"Jelly Roll Blues"/"Big Fat Ham," Gennett, 1924.
"Shreveport Stomp"/"Stratford Hunch," Gennett, 1924.
"Mamanita"/"35th Street Blues," Paramount, 1924.
"London Blues (Shoe Shiner's Drag)," Rialto, 1924.
"Mr. Jelly Lord," Vocal Style Song Roll (piano roll), 1924.
"Dead Man Blues," QRS (piano roll), 1926.
"Fat Meat and Greens"/"Sweetheart O' Mine," Vocalion, 1926.
"King Porter Stomp"/"The Pearls," Vocalion, 1926.
"Seattle Hunch"/"Freakish," Victor, 1929.
"Pep"/"Fat Frances," Victor, 1929.
"Winin' Boy Blues"/"Honky Tonk Music," Jazzman, 1937.
"Finger Buster"/"Creepy Feeling," Jazzman, 1937.
"Original Rags"/"Mamie's Blues," General, 1939.
"The Naked Dance"/"Michigan Water Blues," General, 1939.
"The Crave"/"Buddy Bolden's Blues," General, 1939.

"Mister Joe"/"Winin' Boy Blues," General, 1939.
"King Porter Stomp"/"Don't You Leave Me Here," General, 1939.

### Single releases; as leader of the Jelly Roll Morton Stomp Kings

"Muddy Water Blues"/"Big Fat Ham," Paramount, 1923.
"Someday Sweetheart"/"London Blues," OK, 1923.
"Mr. Jelly Lord"/"Steady Roll," Paramount, 1923.
"Tom Cat Blues"/"King Porter Stomp," Autograph, 1924.
"High Society"/"Fish Tail Blues," Autograph, 1924.
"Tiger Rag"/"Weary Blues," Autograph, 1924.

### Single releases; as leader of the Red Hot Peppers (unless otherwise noted)

"Black Bottom Stomp"/"The Chant," Victor, 1926.
"Smoke House Blues"/"Steamboat Stomp," Victor, 1926.
"Sidewalk Blues"/"Dead Man Blues," Victor, 1926.
"Someday Sweetheart"/"Original Jelly Roll Blues," Victor, 1927.
"Doctor Jazz," Victor, 1927.
"Grandpa's Spells"/"Cannon Ball Blues," Victor, 1927.
"Billy Goat Stomp"/"Hyena Stomp," Victor, 1927.
"Jungle Blues," Victor, 1927.
"The Pearls"/"Beale Street Blues," Victor, 1927.
"Georgia Swing"/"Mournful Serenade," Victor, 1928.
"Kansas City Stomps"/"Boogaboo," Victor, 1928.
"Shoe Shiner's Rag," Victor, 1928
"Red Hot Pepper"/"Deep Creek Blues," Victor, 1929.
"Burning The Iceberg"/"Tank Town Bump," Victor, 1929.
"New Orleans Bump (Moravia Blues)"/"Pretty Lil," Victor, 1929.
"Courthouse Bump"/"Sweet Anita Mine," Victor, 1929.
"Try Me Out"/"Down My Way," Victor, 1929.
"Mint Julep"/"Low Gravy," Victor, 1930.
"Sweet Peter"/"Jersey Joe," Victor, 1930.
"Mississippi Mud"/"Primrose Stomp," Victor, 1930.
"I'm Looking For A Little Bluebird"/"Mushmouth Shuffle," Victor, 1930.
"That'll Never Do"/"Fickle Fay Creep," Victor, 1930.
"If Someone Would Only Love Me"/"Oil Well," Victor, 1930.
"Each Day"/"Strokin' Away," Victor, 1930.
"Little Lawrence"/"Harmony Blues," Victor, 1930.
"Fussy Mabel"/"Pontchartrain Blues," Victor, 1930.
"Crazy Chords"/"Gambling Jack," Victor, 1930.
"Load Of Coal," Victor, 1930.
"Blue Blood Blues," Victor, 1930.

### Single releases; with his trio

"Wolverine Blues"/"Mr. Jelly Lord", Victor, 1927.
"Shreveport," Victor, 1928.

### Single releases; as Jelly Roll Morton and His Orchestra

"Didn't He Ramble"/"Winin' Boy Blues," Bluebird, 1939.
"High Society"/"I Though I Heard Buddy Bolden Say," Bluebird, 1939.
"Climax Rag"/"West End Blues," Bluebird, 1939.

"Don't You Leave Me Here"/"Ballin' The Jack," Bluebird, 1939.

### Single releases; with the Morton Sextet

"Why"/"Get The Bucket," General, 1940.
"If You Knew"/"Shake It," General, 1940.

### Single releases; with the Jelly Roll Morton Seven

"Sweet Substitute"/"Panama," General, 1940.
"Good Old New York"/"Big Lip Blues," General, 1940.
"Mama's Got A Baby"/"My Home Is In A Southern Town," General, 1940.
"Dirty, Dirty, Dirty"/"Swinging The Elks," General, 1940.

### LPs

*Stomps and Joys,* RCA Victor.
*Hot Jazz, Hokum and Hilarity,* RCA Victor.
*The King of New Orleans Jazz,* RCA Victor.
*Jelly Roll Morton Classic Piano Solos,* Riverside.
*The Incomparable Jelly Roll Morton,* Riverside.
*Ferd "Jelly Roll" Morton* (contains 19 of the 1923-24 piano solos), Fountain.
*Piano Rolls,* Biograph.
*Jelly Roll Morton* (recorded from 1924 piano rolls), Everest.
*New Orleans Memories,* Atlantic.
*The Library of Congress Recordings,* Volumes 1-12, Circle, 1948; reissued, Riverside, 1957.
*New Orleans Memories Plus Two* (contains piano solos and vocals from 1939), Commodore, 1979.
*N.O.R.K., New Orleans Rhythm Kings with Jelly Roll Morton,* Riverside.
*The Pearls* (contains 1926-28 Red Hot Peppers and trio sides), Bluebird, 1988.
*And His Red Hot Peppers,* Volumes 1-8, RCA Victor (France).
*Morton Sixes and Sevens* (contains last commercial recordings from 1940), Fontana.
*1923/1924* (contains the 1923-24 piano solos), Milestone, 1992.

## Sources

### Books

Delauney, Charles, *New Hot Discography: The Standard Directory of Recorded Jazz,* Criterion, 1948.
Lomax, Alan, *Mister Jelly Roll: The Fortunes of Jelly Roll Morton,* Duell, Sloan and Pearce, 1950; reprinted by Grove Press, 1956; 2nd edition, University of California Press, 1973.
Longstreet, Stephen, *The Real Jazz, Old and New,* Louisiana State University Press, 1956.
*The New Grove Dictionary of Jazz,* edited by Barry Kernfeld, Macmillan, 1988.
Schuller, Gunther, *Early Jazz: Its Roots and Musical Development,* Oxford University Press, 1968.
Waldo, Terry, *This Is Ragtime,* Hawthorn Books, 1976.

Williams, Martin, *The Jazz Tradition,* Oxford University Press, 1970; new and revised edition, 1983.

**Other**

Liner notes from *New Orleans Memories Plus Two,* Commodore, 1979.

—*David Bianco*

# Jessye Norman

---

**Opera and concert singer**

---

American soprano Jessye Norman is hailed as one of the world's greatest opera and concert singers and performers. Since the early 1970s she has starred at leading opera houses, concert halls, and music festivals throughout Europe, North America, and three other continents, and has also enjoyed a prolific recording career with over 40 albums and several Grammy Awards to her credit. Norman's voice has been resoundingly praised for its mastery of expression, technical control, and sheer power, while her diverse song repertoire spans standard and obscure operas to German lieder, avant-garde works, and even popular ballads. As a performer, she is known for her magnetic and dramatic personality, and, with her imposing physical presence, cuts an impressive figure before audiences. According to Curt Sanburn in *Life,* Norman on stage creates the perception of one who "veritably looms behind her lyrics."

Born into a musical family in Augusta, Georgia, Norman early on found encouragement to be a singer. Her mother, an amateur pianist, saw that all the children in the family took piano lessons, while Norman's father, a successful insurance broker, was a frequent singer in the family's Baptist church. As a young girl Norman loved singing and performed wherever she had the opportunity—in church, school, Girl Scout meetings, even a supermarket opening; yet she never formally studied voice until college. Norman fell in love with opera the first time she heard a Metropolitan Opera radio broadcast and soon mastered her first aria, "My Heart at Thy Sweet Voice," from Saint-Saens's *Samson and Delilah.* At 16 Norman traveled to Philadelphia with her school choral director for the Marian Anderson Scholarship competition and, while most of the participants were much older and she failed to win, received positive comments from the judges. On her return trip to Georgia she visited the music department of Howard University in Washington, D.C., and sang for Carolyn Grant, who would later become her vocal coach. After hearing Norman's voice, Grant recommended the budding soprano for a full-tuition four-year scholarship to the university when she came of college age.

### Graduated From Howard With Honors

Norman graduated from Howard with honors in 1967 and during her university career won many fans who heard her sing in the university choral group and local church choirs. Norman went on to complete a summer of postgraduate study at the Peabody Conservatory in Baltimore, Maryland, followed by her master's degree at the University of Michigan in Ann Arbor. While at Michigan Norman worked with two renowned teachers of voice, French baritone Pierre Bernac—a famous teacher of the art song—and Elizabeth Mannion. To finance her graduate school studies Norman auditioned for and received grants from various musical foundations and in 1968 received a scholarship from the Institute of International Education that allowed her to enter Bavarian Radio's International Music Competition in Munich, Germany. When Norman was on a U.S. State Department musical tour of the Caribbean and Latin America that year she received word that she had won the prestigious European contest. Subsequently, she received offers to perform and work in Europe and moved overseas in 1969, following the path of many American singers who began their careers in the celebrated concert and opera halls of Europe.

Norman enjoyed rapid success in Europe. In Decem-

ber of 1969 she signed a three-year contract with the venerable Deutsche Oper in West Berlin and was a sensation in her debut—at the age of 23—as Elisabeth in Wagner's *Tannhauser.* Norman thereafter received other primary roles with the opera company, in addition to numerous offers to sing concerts and operas throughout Europe. In 1970 she made her Italian debut in Florence in Handel's *Deborah* and the following year her busy opera schedule included performances in Mozart's *Idomeneo* in Rome, Meyerbeer's *L'Africaine* in Florence, and Mozart's *The Marriage of Figaro* at the Berlin Festival. Later in 1971 Norman auditioned for and won the opportunity to sing the role of the Countess in a Philips recording of *Figaro* with the BBC Orchestra under the direction of Colin Davis. The recording was a finalist for the prestigious Montreux International Record Award competition and brought Norman much exposure to music listeners in Europe and the U.S.

In 1972 Norman performed in a Berlin production of Verdi's *Aida,* a role in which she debuted later that year at the famed Italian opera stage, La Scala, in Milan. Also in 1972 she sang in a concert version of *Aida* at the Hollywood Bowl in California, followed by a performance at Wolf Trap in Washington, D.C., with the National Symphony Orchestra, and an acclaimed Wagner recital at the prestigious Tanglewood Music Festival in Massachusetts.

Norman's triumphs of 1972 continued when she returned to Europe in the fall and debuted at the Royal Opera House in Covent Garden, England, as Cassandra in Berlioz's *Les Troyens.* She also made her debut at the prestigious Edinburgh Music Festival that year. As a result of these victories much acclaim and excitement awaited her first-ever New York City recital the following year when she appeared as part of the "Great Performers" series at Alice Tully Hall in Lincoln Center. Norman's performance, which included songs by Wagner, Strauss, Brahms, and Satie, was hailed by Donald Henahan in the *New York Times* as one of "extraordinary intelligence, taste and emotional depth."

### Took Temporary Leave of Opera

In the mid-1970s, wanting to more fully develop her vocal range, Norman made the decision to stop performing operas temporarily to concentrate on concert performances. She commented to John Gruen in the *New York Times* on her desire to master a broad repertoire. "As for my voice, it cannot be categorized— and I like it that way, because I sing things that would be considered in the dramatic, mezzo or spinto range. I like so many different kinds of music that I've never allowed myself the limitations of one particular range."

Over the years Norman's technical expertise has been among her most critically praised attributes. In a review of one of her recitals at New York City's Carnegie Hall, *New York Times* contributor Allen Hughes wrote that Norman "has one of the most opulent voices before the public today, and, as discriminating listeners are aware, her performances are backed by extraordinary preparation, both musical and otherwise." Another Carnegie Hall appearance prompted these words from *New York Times* contributor Bernard Holland: "If one added up all the things that Jessye Norman does well as a singer, the total would assuredly exceed that of any other soprano before the public. At Miss Norman's recital . . . tones were produced, colors manipulated, words projected and interpretive points made—all with fanatic finesse."

Norman returned to the operatic stage in 1980 in a performance of Strauss's *Ariadne auf Naxos* in Hamburg, Germany, and in 1983 made her debut with New York City's Metropolitan Opera Company in its gala centennial season opener of *Les Troyens*. Norman shone among the star-studded cast, as the *Times's* Henahan wrote in his review. "Miss Norman . . . is a soprano of magnificent presence who commanded the stage at every moment," he declared. "As the distraught Cassandra she sang grippingly and projects well, even when placed well back in the cavernous sets."

Although Norman has had great success performing in full-scale opera productions, her formidable physical stature has somewhat limited the availability of stage roles to her and she has increasingly directed her opera singing to condensed concert versions. A standard in her repertoire has become "Liebestod" ("Love of Death"), the finale from Wagner's *Tristan and Isolde*, in which a despondent and soon-to-expire Isolde sings to her dead beloved, Tristan. Henahan reviewed Norman's performance of "Liebestod" at the 1989 New York Philharmonic season opener: "Although she has never sung the complete role on any stage, she has handled this fearsome 10-minute challenge with increasing vocal authority and dramatic insight. . . . Hers is a grandly robust voice, used with great intelligence and expression."

### Ten Minutes of Applause

Another pinnacle of Norman's career came in 1987 with the Boston Symphony Orchestra at Tanglewood; her program of Strauss songs, which featured the final scene from Strauss's opera *Salome*, prompted more than ten minutes of applause and ovations. Michael Kimmelman wrote in the *New York Times* on the power of her performance: "Ms. Norman's voice seems to draw from a vast ocean of sound. . . . No matter how much volume Sieji Ozawa requested from his orchestra during the fiery scene from 'Salome,' it seemed little match for her voice. Yet, as always, what made the soprano's performance particularly remarkable was the effortlessness with which she could hover over long, soft notes. . . . And there is also the quality of sound she produces: even the loudest passages are cushioned by a velvety, seductive timbre."

Over the years Norman has not been afraid to expand her talent into less familiar areas. In 1988 she sang a concert performance of Poulenc's one-act opera *La Voix Humaine* ("The Human Voice"), based on Jean Cocteau's 1930 play of the same name, in which a spurned actress feverishly pleads to keep her lover on the other end of a phone conversation. Although Henahan noted in the *Times* that Norman's "characteristic . . .

> *Norman's Tanglewood program of Strauss songs prompted more than ten minutes of applause and ovations.*

style puts great emphasis on tragic dignity," and that the role perhaps called for less restraint, he nonetheless admired her as among those artists "driven to branch out into unlikely roles and whole idioms that stretch their talents interestingly, if sometimes to the breaking point."

Other of Norman's diverse projects have included her 1984 album, *With a Song in My Heart*, which contains numbers from films and musical comedies, and a 1990 performance of American spirituals with soprano Kathleen Battle at Carnegie Hall. Norman commented to William Livingstone in *Stereo Review* that one of her objectives as a performer is "to communicate, to be understood in many ways and on many levels." In 1989 she was invited to sing the French national anthem—"La Marseillaise"—in Paris during the celebration of the bicentennial of the French Revolution. Norman, who sings nearly flawless French, in addition to German and Italian, was particularly honored by the opportunity. "It makes you feel really good that people at home think you are worth their interest, but it's incredible to be so warmly received in a foreign country," she told Livingstone. "I love watching the faces of the people who are listening as I sing these songs and know that they understand."

Norman described to *New York Times* contributor Gruen the reverence with which she approaches her work. "To galvanize myself into a performance, I must be left totally alone. I must have solitude in order to concentrate—which I consider a form of prayer. I work very much from the text. The words must be understood, felt and communicated. . . . If you look carefully at the words and absorb them, you're half-way home already. The rest is honesty—honesty of feeling, honesty of involvement. If a performer is truly committed, then the audience will be the first to know and will respond accordingly. Of course, love is the thing that propels us all. It's what carries us along—*that's* the fuel!"

# Selected discography

Beethoven, Ludwig van, *Symphonie No. 6, op. 68: "Pastorale,"* Deutsche Grammophon, 1981.
Beethoven, *Symphony No. 9 in D minor,* London, 1987.
Beethoven, *Fidelio.*
Berg, Alban, *Lulu Suite* [and] *Der Wein,* CBS Masterworks, 1979.
Berlioz, Hector, *Les nuits d'ete,* Philips, 1980.
Berlioz, *Les nuits d'ete* [and] *La mort de Cleopatre,* Deutsche Grammophon, 1982.
Berlioz, *Romeo et Juliette,* Angel, 1986.
Bizet, Georges, *Carmen,* Philips, 1989.
Brahms, Johannes, *Lieder,* Deutsche Grammophon, 1983.
Brahms, *A German Requiem,* Angel, 1985.
Brahms, *Symphony No. 3 in F; Alto Rhapsody.*
Bruckner, Anton, *Symphonie nr. 8 c-moll* [and] *Te Deum,* Deutsche Grammophon, 1981.
Bruckner, *Te Deum* [and] *Helgoland* [and] *150 Psalm,* Deutsche Grammophon, 1983.
Chausson, Ernest, *Poeme de l'amour et de la mer: op. 19* [and] *Chanson perpetuelle: op. 37* [and other selections], Erato, 1983.
*Les chemins de l'amour,* Philips, 1977.
*Christmastide,* Philips, 1987.
Debussy, Claude, *L'enfant prodigue* [and] *La damoiselle elue,* Pro-Arte, 1982.
Faure, Gabriel Urbain, *Penelope,* Erato, 1982.
Gluck, Christoph Willibald, *Alceste,* 1982.
Haydn, Joseph, *La vera costanza,* Philips, 1977.
Haydn, *Armida,* Philips, 1979.
*Jessye Norman Live,* Philips, 1988.
*Jessye Norman Sings Duparc, Ravel, Poulenc, Satie,* Philips, 1977.
*The Last Night of the Proms,* Philips, 1969.
*Lieder* (various composers), Philips, 1988.

*Lucky To Be Me,* Polygram, 1992.
Mahler, Gustav, *Das Lied von der Erde,* Philips, 1982.
Mahler, *Symphony 2: "Resurrection,"* CBS, 1984.
Mahler, *Symphony No. 6 in A Minor; Songs of a Wayfarer.*
Mahler, *Symphony No. 7 in E Minor; Kindertotenlieder.*
Mozart, Wolfgang Amadeus, *Die Gaertnerin aus Liebe,* Philips.
Mozart, *The Marriage of Figaro,* Philips, 1971.
Offenbach, Jacques, *La belle Helene,* Angel, 1985.
Offenbach, *Les contes d'Hoffmann,* Angel, 1988.
Purcell, Henry, *Dido and Aeneas,* Philips, 1986.
Ravel, Maurice, *Sheherazade,* Philips, 1980.
Ravel, *Songs of Maurice Ravel,* CBS Masterworks, 1984.
*Sacred Songs,* Philips, 1981.
Schonberg, Arnold, *Gurre-Lieder,* Philips, 1979.
Schubert, Franz, *Lieder,* Philips, 1973.
Schubert, *Lieder,* Philips, 1985.
Schumann, Robert, *Frauenliebe und Leben, op. 42* [and] *Liederkreis, op. 39,* Philips, 1976.
*Spirituals,* Philips, 1979.
Strauss, Richard, *Four Last Songs,* Philips, 1983.
Strauss, *Lieder,* Philips, 1986.
Strauss, *Ariadne auf Naxos,* Philips, 1988.
Stravinsky, Igor, *Oedipus Rex,* Orfeo, 1983.
Tippett, Michael, *A Child of Our Time,* Philips, 1975.
Verdi, Giuseppe, *Un giorno di regno,* Philips, 1974.
Verdi, *Il corsaro,* Philips, 1976.
Wagner, Richard, *Tristan and Isolde* [and] *Five Poems by Mathilde Wesendonk,* Philips, 1975.
Wagner, *Wesendonk Songs,* Angel, 1986.
Wagner, *Lohengrin,* London, 1987.
Wagner, *Scenes From Tristan and Isolde, Tannhauser, Der fliegende Hollander, Gotterdammerung,* EMI, 1988.
Wagner, *Die Walkure,* Deutsche Grammophon, 1988.
Weber, Carl Maria von, *Euryanthe,* Angel, 1975.
*With a Song in My Heart,* Philips, 1984.

# Sources

### Books

Greenfield, Edward, Robert Layton, and Ivan March, *The New Penguin Guide to Compact Discs and Cassettes,* Penguin, 1988.
Hunt, Adam Paul, *Jessye Norman, Singer: Portrait of an Extraordinary Career,* 1991.
*The International Encyclopedia of Music and Musicians,* 10th edition, edited by Oscar Thompson, Dodd, 1975.

### Periodicals

*Ebony,* March 1988; July 1991.
*Life,* March 1985.
*Musical America,* January 1991; July 1991; September/October 1991; November/December 1991.
*Music and Musicians,* August 1979.
*Newsweek,* December 6, 1982.

*New York,* April 1, 1991; April 29, 1991; May 20, 1991.

*New Yorker,* April 1, 1991; May 20, 1991.

*New York Times,* January 21, 1973; January 23, 1973; December 15, 1982; September 18, 1983; September 27, 1983; November 24, 1983; January 26, 1986; August 25, 1987; February 20, 1988; March 6, 1989; September 22, 1989; March 19, 1990.

*Opera News,* June 1973; February 18, 1984; February 16, 1991; July 1991.

*Stereo Review,* October 1989; February 1991; July 1991; August 1991; September 1991.

*Washington Post,* August 7, 1972.

*—Michael E. Mueller*

# The Oak Ridge Boys

**Country group**

"The pop-country and former gospel aggregation," wrote Jack Hurst in the *Chicago Tribune*, describing the 1990s re-emergence of perennial crowd-pleasers the Oak Ridge Boys, "thus demonstrated yet again that it has more lives than a yardful of cats. And now it seems that the new configuration's real rebirth hasn't even occurred yet." Rooted in the gospel traditions of Tennessee, the Oak Ridge Boys are a prime example of the pre-eminence of musical harmony in country music; richly textured bass, baritone, and tenor voices have graced the band for more than four decades. Enlisted to sing gospel music to staff members restricted during World War II to a nuclear research plant at Oak Ridge, near Knoxville, Tennessee, the group originated as the Country Cut-Ups. Although none of its earliest members are represented among today's Oak Ridge Boys—Duane Allen, Joe Bonsall, Steve Sanders, and Richard Sterban—the permanence of the gospel, country, pop, Cajun, and blues group as a whole remains assured by their dynamic sound.

## For the Record. . .

**M**embers include **Duane Allen** (baritone; born April 29, 1943, in Taylortown, TX; joined group in 1966), **Joe Bonsall** (tenor; born May 18, 1948, in Philadelphia, PA; joined group in 1973), **Steve Sanders** (baritone; born September 17, 1952, in Richland, GA; joined group in 1987; replaced **William Lee Golden,** born January 12, 1939, in Brewton, AL; joined group in 1964), and **Richard Sterban** (bass; born April 24, 1943, in Camden, NJ; joined group in 1972). Quartet backed by the Oaks Band: Dewey Dorough, Ron Fairchild, Fred Satterfield, Dave Watson, and Kent Wells.

Originally gospel performers; group descended from the Country Cut-Ups, late 1940s, and their offspring, the Oak Ridge Quartet, late 1950s; group renamed the Oak Ridge Boys, c. 1960. Crossed over to country-pop market with hit single "Y'All Come Back Saloon," 1977. Secular country music group, 1977—. Have appeared at prestigious festivals and performance halls, including Switzerland's Montreux International Jazz Fest, New York City's Carnegie Hall, and London's Royal Albert Hall. Performed at President George Bush's inaugural gala, and at several command performances for American presidents and European royalty.

**Awards:** Numerous gold and platinum albums; 12 Dove Awards, 1969-73; four Grammy Awards, 1971-81; cited by the Academy of Country Music as best vocal group, 1977 and 1979, for best album, Y'All Come Back Saloon, 1977, and for single of the year, "Elvira," 1981; four Country Music Association Awards, 1978-86; two American Music Awards, 1982 and 1985.

**Addresses:** Fan club—329 Rockland Rd., Hendersonville, TN 37075.

The Oak Ridge Boys first came to national attention when they left gospel singing to record secular music. Until the pivotal 1977 album Y'All Come Back Saloon, the ever-changing ensemble lived hand-to-mouth on the white gospel circuit. Called the Oak Ridge Quartet during the late 1950s, the group changed its name to the Oak Ridge Boys around 1960. Although the Oak Ridge Boys earned several Dove and Grammy Awards in the gospel category, financial success eluded them. Members were ready to disband the group during the mid-1970s. "We had reached the height of gospel success," former Oak Ridge baritone William Lee Golden commented to Dolly Carlisle in People. Golden sought to preserve the group by persuading his colleagues to enter the lucrative country-pop market. The Oaks, who already sported long hair and beards, did

not fit the image of gospel singers, nor did their rock drummer meet with approval. They began the crossover from religious to secular music—dubbed the "Nashville Syndrome"—during the late seventies. Their only real competition in the area at the time was country's highly popular Statler Brothers.

### From Gospel to Country

The transition to both a financially and artistically successful career for Oaks members Golden, Allen, Bonsall, and Sterban was aided by country legend Johnny Cash; he made the quartet a loan and hired them to open his Vegas nightclub act. When singer-songwriter Paul Simon used the group as backup singers on his single "Slip Slidin' Away," the Oaks became full-fledged members of the pop market. By the end of the decade they had produced five straight Number One country hits, including "Y'All Come Back Saloon" and "You're the One." Golden revealed to People's Carlisle, "We've learned one thing through this change. A change of style doesn't cancel off fans. They stay with you and new fans pile up. Inevitably our music will cross all borders and all labels."

During the early 1980s the Oaks found their niche in country music with "catchy and commercial" songs like the material described in Stereo Review from the album Bobbie Sue. "There's a fairly good mixture of songs, if you don't require that the songs be very deep, and most of the performances have a certain amount of zest. . . . This is a fair sampler of the Oak Ridge Boys' activities— a bouncy little record for your bouncy little moods." In 1983 People contributor Cheryl McCall reported, "The band has to its credit 10 No. 1 country hits, seven gold and two platinum LPs, and such spectacular pop breakthroughs as the singles 'Elvira' and 'Bobbie Sue.'" Oaks lead singer Duane Allen told McCall, "We don't do any cheatin' or drinkin' songs," indicating that the group has been able to hold on to their principles without sacrificing popularity. In fact, the Oaks have refused opportunities to do cigarette and beer commercials as well as movie appearances they considered racy, including one in the film The Best Little Whorehouse in Texas. Bass singer Richard Sterban divulged to McCall, "We don't want to do anything that's going to offend our audience."

Of one mind about music, the Oaks were less united on other matters. When Golden—then the longest-standing member of the group—donned beaded buckskin and grew hair and beard similar to that of his fellows in the American Mountain Man Association, the rest of the Oaks became concerned. Rumors abounded that Golden was leaving the group to pursue a solo career during the recording of the gold record *American Made*. In partnership for 17 years by 1983, Golden and Allen landed in the middle of a legal confrontation whereby Golden was instructed through a "letter of reprimand" to conform to the Oaks' standards of appearance. "He doesn't have to change, but the Oak Ridge Boys have an identity that we must keep up," disclosed Allen in *People*. "If Golden's personal tastes are stronger than his commitment to his job, then he can dress or look however he wants—but the Oak Ridge Boys won't go on." A few months later, though, Golden, Allen, and the rest of the group were back on speaking terms. In 1984, when the Oak Ridge Boys released another gold record—*Deliver*—*Stereo Review* glowingly called the album "the most diversified LP they've ever done" with "more emphasis on music than hits"; the split had seemingly been repaired.

### Golden Voted Out

That year's *Greatest Hits Two* added another platinum award to the Oaks' previous million-sellers, *Greatest Hits* and *Fancy Free*. With the appearance of 1986's *Seasons*, *People* called the ensemble "one of country music's most durable groups." But the real test of the Oaks' durability came a year later when William Lee Golden filed suit to dissolve the group. Replaced by Steve Sanders, who had been a member of the Oaks Band during the previous five years, Golden sought millions in monetary compensation after the Oaks voted him out of the group in the spring of 1987. Allen recounted to the *Chicago Tribune*'s Hurst, "I feel we chose the way we wanted to go and that, in one way or another, he did, too. If he couldn't see the handwriting on the wall, he was not looking at the wall; the writing had been there for years. I wish there had been a more graceful way to make an exit, but I've never been good at that. I don't know how to quit—or to tell somebody else to."

For his part, Golden in late 1990 "[professed] not to understand" the split. *Country Music*'s Rich Kienzle reported that Golden "and the Oaks recently reached a legal settlement which involved, among other things, William Lee forfeiting all future royalties on recordings made during his time with the group." Kienzle quoted Golden as saying, disappointment creeping into his voice, "Things happen like that sometimes. When greed takes over, sometimes it can mess up a good team." Of his ouster, Golden went on to reveal, "I didn't even know what was going on for awhile. So all I knew is what I was readin' every day [in the papers] when it all went down."

Golden's appearance on the Oaks' 1987 album *Where*

*the Fast Lane Ends* was one of his last with the group. Oaks record sales were already on the decline when *Stereo Review* called the album "hardly the stuff to make you sit up and take notice. Unless you're just enthralled with the blend of the Oaks' voices—which, admittedly, accounts for whatever spark there is here—you might want to wait 'til they get their energy back."

During the four years following Golden's departure the quartet did not produce a single gold or platinum album. In 1991 the ensemble made the decision to leave MCA—their record company for 13 years—to join RCA. They also changed musical direction, returning to the up-tempo melodies that had marked earlier Oak Ridge Boys records. "Although the group's style has always leaned toward the pop side of the country spectrum," wrote *Chicago Tribune* contributor Hurst, "Allen, Bonsall and Sterban preferred to remain under the Nashville field's broad and friendly umbrella, where they had carved out a name. The disagreement with

---

*"We did things no other group has done before or since— went to the top of three fields. That's kind of hard for any country musician or singer to do."*
—*William Lee Golden*

---

Golden degenerated into lack of communication, after which the rest of the group finally divorced itself from Golden, hired Sanders and went back on the country concert trail."

After recovering from his break with the group he had helped lead for nearly a quarter century, Golden embarked on a solo career. He began recording with Polygram Records and went on the road with his band; appropriately named the Goldens, the support ensemble features Golden's oldest son, Randy, on piano, and his youngest, Chris, on drums. Despite the unpleasantness with the Oaks, Golden remains rightly proud of the band's impressive history. He told *Country Music*'s Kienzle, "We did things no other group has done before or since. As young singers we went to the top of three fields. In gospel music we won a Grammy, then went to the top of country music and also had two crossover Top Five pop records. That's kind of hard for any country musician or singer to do."

**Entered 1990s With Return to Vintage Style**

The new Oak Ridge Boys, too, eventually picked up the pieces and moved on. Reviewing the Oaks' 1991 release, *Unstoppable,* Hurst characterized the album as "full of the kind of gospel-hot melodies, Middle-American lyrics and pop-ish instrumentation that first took the Oaks to the top of the country charts and into the pop charts beginning in the late 1970's. . . . Lyrically, the new album's material seems well above the group's norm in recent years, and musically it is supercharged with the heat, harmony and below-the-belt bass notes of the old Oaks." When Michael Bane interviewed the Oaks in *Country Music* after the release of *Unstoppable,* he called their success "legendary. . . . The Oak Ridge Boys—Joe Bonsall, Duane Allen, Richard Sterban and newest member Steve Sanders—have set the standard for vocal groups, crossing over not only into country, but pop as well."

Accompanying the success of *Unstoppable* was an improved relationship with former partner Golden, Allen revealed to Hurst. "We don't talk often, but when we do it's good. There's no bitterness in our tones of voice now. There still is bitterness there in all of us, I'm sure, if we want to cultivate it. But I choose to go forward from here." Forward is the direction for all the Oak Ridge Boys, Sterban disclosed to *Country Music*'s Bane. "We won't go away." Bonsall seconded Sterban, explaining "That's why Duane named the new album *Unstoppable.* It was his idea, and it's a great name for us, because by God, we are."

## Selected discography

*Sky High,* Columbia.
*Oak Ridge Boys,* Columbia.
*Old Fashioned Music,* Columbia.
*Super Gospel Hits,* two volumes, Columbia.
*The Sensational Oak Ridge Boys,* Starday.
*The Oak Ridge Boys,* Power Pak.
*Old Fashioned, Down Home, Hand Clappin', Foot Stompin', Southern Style, Gospel Quartet Music,* Columbia.
*Y'All Come Back Saloon,* MCA, 1977.

*Room Service,* MCA, 1978.
*Oak Ridge Boys Have Arrived,* MCA, 1979.
*Together,* MCA, 1980.
*Greatest Hits,* MCA, 1980.
*Fancy Free,* MCA, 1981.
*Bobbie Sue,* MCA, 1982.
*Oak Ridge Boys Christmas,* MCA, 1982.
*American Made,* MCA, 1983.
*Deliver,* MCA, 1984.
*Greatest Hits Two,* MCA, 1984.
*Step On Out,* MCA, 1985.
*Seasons,* MCA, 1986.
*Christmas Again,* MCA, 1986.
*Where the Fast Lane Ends,* MCA, 1987.
*Heartbeat,* MCA, 1987.
*Monongahela,* MCA, 1988.
*Greatest Hits Volume Three,* MCA, 1989.
*American Dreams,* MCA, 1989.
*Unstoppable,* RCA, 1991.

## Sources

### Books

*The Illustrated Encyclopedia of Country Music,* Harmony, 1977.
Stambler, Irwin, and Grelun Landon, *The Encyclopedia of Folk, Country & Western Music,* St. Martin's, 1983.
Widner, Ellis and Walter Carter, *The Oak Ridge Boys: Our Story,* Contemporary, 1987.

### Periodicals

*Chicago Tribune,* January 27, 1991.
*Country Music,* November/December 1990; May/June 1991.
*Library Journal,* July 1987.
*People,* May 28, 1979; April 4, 1983; April 25, 1983; June 9, 1986.
*Stereo Review,* July 1982; April 1984; October 1987.
*Variety,* May 13, 1987.

Additional information for this profile was obtained from a Kathy Gangwisch & Associates, Inc., press packet, 1991.

*—Marjorie Burgess*

# Phil Ochs

---

**Singer, songwriter, activist**

---

Phil Ochs was a man of apparent ironies and contradictions. To many, he was radically un-American; his left-wing politics inspired death threats and an F.B.I. file 410 pages long. Yet, he was a patriot, a man who John Poses of *Spin* described as "the uncompromising patriot, the rebel with causes," who loved the U.S. and was determined to see that it live up to the ideals upon which it was founded. He admired John F. Kennedy and quintessentially American actor John Wayne, but also Fidel Castro and Latin American revolutionary leader Che Guevara. Throughout the sixties he feared his dedication to left-wing politics would get him killed; but in the end, it was he who killed himself.

Ochs was arguably the greatest of the sixties protest singer-songwriters. Leon Wieseltier of the *Washingtonian* stated that "it was *he* who was the most brilliant and serious and moving and funny singer of the '60s, the movement's most intelligent contribution to American popular music." At root an activist and journalist, he lived by the words of union organizer and songwriter Joe Hill, who said "a pamphlet, no matter how good, is never read more than once, but a song is learned by heart and is repeated over and over." According to Wieseltier, Ochs "was never, in his criticism of the United States, uninformed or unsophisticated." He studied papers and journals and was committed to communicating what he learned, and righting the injustices he saw. In the words of *Spin*'s Poses, he was "an astute, acerbic journalist who knew rhythmically and lyrically how to couch his sarcastic wit in meter." Nonetheless, Ochs was not simply a singing journalist; he was capable of writing beautiful, lyrical songs, combining, in *Rolling Stone*'s words "a poet's soul with the gutsy bravado and knife-point writing of a seasoned press hound." British folk musician and political activist Billy Bragg has said, "America has yet to produce another songwriter like him."

### Discovered Folk Music in College

Ochs's upbringing in New York and Ohio was rocky. His doctor father suffered from manic depression. In and out of hospitals, Jacob Ochs was unable to maintain a medical practice. Ochs was a particularly dreamy child who often appeared to be in another world; his favorite escape was the movies. As a teenager he attended Staunton Military Academy in Virginia—an unusual place for a future leader of an antiwar movement. In *The Encyclopedia of Folk, Country and Western Music,* Ochs's brother, Michael, told Irwin Stambler that Phil "probably decided to go [to Staunton] because of the way the movies portrayed military schools and an identification with John Wayne." During high school Ochs took up the clarinet and his teachers discovered he was an exceptional musician. It wasn't until he attended Ohio State University, however, that he became interested in folk music and started writing songs. Ochs's roommate, Jim Glover, who introduced him to folk music, taught him to play guitar, and actually gave him his first guitar after losing a bet on the Kennedy-Nixon election of 1960.

It was also as a student that Ochs became interested in journalism. According to *Rolling Stone,* after two years in college he was jailed in Florida for vagrancy; the experience motivated him to become a writer. Upon his return to Ohio State, he started publishing a radical newspaper and soon found himself in line for the editorship of the school's publication, *The Lantern.* School authorities eventually blocked him from taking that post, however, probably the result of his statement that communist Cuban leader Fidel Castro was the greatest figure in the Western Hemisphere in the twentieth century. Michael Ochs told Stambler that disappointment over this rejection prompted Ochs to quit school a few months before graduation.

Instead of obtaining his degree, Ochs formed a duo with roommate Glover and began playing bars in Cleveland. In 1961 he moved to New York City, landing in the middle of the thriving Greenwich Village folk scene. He began writing protest songs in the company of some of folk music's greats—Bob Dylan, Joan Baez, Tom Paxton, and Dave Van Ronk. Ochs and Dylan shared a close but volatile personal and professional relationship in the early 1960s. Clearly, Dylan was the star of the folk scene, but most agree that Ochs ran a close second.

Ochs began to draw widespread attention when he performed in Rhode Island at the Newport Folk Festival in 1963. Elektra records signed him, and in 1964 released his debut album, *All the News That's Fit to Sing,* its title reflecting Ochs's brand of journalism. When it was re-released in 1987, *Sing Out!* magazine called the album "clearly one of the most important debuts of the 'folk boom'" and *Rolling Stone* described it as "a manifesto of social urgency; Ochs sounds the alarm in a strident clarion voice with acidic humor, noble rage and at times, priestly tenderness." Ochs followed *All the News* with *I Ain't Marchin' Anymore,* which introduced on vinyl some of his most popular songs, including "Here's to the State of Mississippi," "Draft Dodger Rag," and the title cut—the anthem of the period, according to the *Penguin Encyclopedia of Popular Music.* This second album, according to *Rolling Stone* "firmly established Ochs as the leading protest singer/songwriter." By this time Dylan had moved away from protest music and had begun to alienate many in folk circles; *Sing Out!* proclaimed that the crown had been passed to Ochs.

Ochs's third album, *Phil Ochs in Concert,* put him on the *Billboard* charts; Joan Baez's recording of one of its songs, "There But for Fortune," was also a hit. As Ochs's talent began to mature, he added some personal subjects to his songs. "Musically," read the liner notes to *The War is Over,* "this entailed a greater emphasis on melody and arrangement. Lyrically, it meant that Ochs was striving for something deeper than making a point."

## Dedicated to Antiwar Movement

During this time, and throughout the sixties, Ochs was deeply involved in the anti-Vietnam War movement. He played rallies, often for free, and expressed his objections to the combat in Southeast Asia at folk festivals across North America. His outspoken politics across the board won him more than a handful of enemies; he alienated much of the South with civil-rights songs like "Talking Birmingham Jam," and "Here's to the State of Mississippi." Because of his views, according to *Melody Maker,* Ochs was banned from performing on television or radio in the United States for several years. Ironically, the folksinger was even attacked by one of his heroes, John Wayne. As recalled by *Spin's* Poses, Wayne told *Playboy* that he made his film *The Green Berets* "to counteract the lies that Phil Ochs and Joan Baez were spreading." Nonetheless, Ochs considered this the high point of his career: John Wayne actually knew who he was!

As radical as Ochs was, he was not blind to the

problems and hypocrisy of the Left. Many of the songs he wrote in the late sixties—"Love Me, I'm a Liberal," "Outside of a Small Circle of Friends, and "Flower Lady"—chide and even indict many of those in his own camp. As that decade wore on, Ochs became increasingly disillusioned with American society. His popularity began to wane. Michael Ochs and Billy Bragg cite the tumultuous Democratic National Convention, held in Chicago in 1968, as the primary catalyst of Ochs's decline. "Something inside Phil died in Chicago in 1968. He'd witnessed the country he loved devouring its own children and realized that the U.S.A. was no place for heroes," wrote Bragg in the liner notes to Ochs's record There & Now: Live in Vancouver, 1968. Ochs's optimism began to fail and his recordings reflected a growing bitterness. He recorded his last studio album in 1970. As the times changed, Ochs had trouble adapting; his friend David Blue told Rolling Stone that "Phil was totally a child of the Sixties. He was a political animal and that political energy was his only source. When that started to go, he started to wither."

The 1970s were hard on Ochs; his creativity began to dry up and he turned to alcohol. In 1970 he recorded a performance at New York's Carnegie hall that is remembered for a bomb scare and a jeering audience shouting "Phil Ochs is dead." Ochs told Tom Nolan in Rolling Stone that he thought it was great. "You can hear the whole audience thing, at first they're booing me, then I win them over and they come around, at the end they're cheering." His record label—by this time A&M—however, was not so pleased. At first it would not release the album, and then did so only in Canada, and not until 1974.

### Lost Confidence in Talent

As musicians turned introspective in the seventies, Ochs was not able to follow suit; he lost confidence and inspiration. His brother told Poses that Ochs "never developed his personal stuff. He always thought of the greater good and never thought about himself. Frankly, he never grew emotionally; he wasn't equipped to deal with the me generation. It wasn't part of his psyche." Ochs stopped writing and sank deeper into drinking and depression, producing one single in the seventies, a rewrite of "Here's to the State of Mississippi" entitled "Here's to the State of Richard Nixon." Still, Ochs did not lose his dedication to the causes of freedom and justice. He wrote for the Los Angeles Free Press and organized benefit concerts. He also tried to take his message to different parts of the world, touring Chile, Australia, and Africa. In Kenya tragedy struck: Ochs was mugged and almost strangled to death. His vocal chords were damaged beyond repair. Already unable to write, he was then barely able to sing.

In 1975 Ochs appeared at a rally in New York's Central Park that celebrated the end of the Vietnam War. He performed "The War Is Over." To Chet Flippo of Rolling Stone, it was clear that Ochs's career was also over: "Reality had finally caught up with his ten-year-old song and it was pathetically clear that antiwar songs and singers were relics from the past. Ochs went downhill fast after that." Suffering, as his father had, from manic depression, he continued drinking and drifting, staying with friends in cheap hotels and even on the street. He started calling himself John Butler Train, and according to Flippo, as Train was charged with assaulting a woman friend and arrested for drunkenness. Ochs eventually went to stay with his sister in Far Rockaway, New York. It was there that he hanged himself, on April 9, 1976. Three months later, a sell-out crowd of 4,500 filled Madison Square Garden's Felt Forum in New York City for a six-and-a-half-hour tribute concert in Ochs's memory.

> "America has yet to produce another songwriter like him."
> —Billy Bragg

Fortunately for younger generations, Ochs's music did not die with him. He has continued to influence musicians, especially folk singers. The folk music renaissance of the late 1980s brought a resurgence in his popularity; a handful of record companies re-released some of Ochs's albums and produced new compilations. In reference to the new releases, Sing Out!'s Mark Moss affirmed that "much of the material, though over two decades old, speaks just as loudly and truly as when it was first recorded." The Washingtonian's Wieseltier agreed: "These songs sound strong today because they had the strength of the particular. Nothing gauzy here, nothing pompous, nothing metaphysical, nothing for the ages, nothing general. Only a natural bard with a devotion to the affairs of the day, a poet of political details."

## Selected discography

### Singles

"The Bells," Elektra, 1964.

"The Power and the Glory," Elektra, 1964.
"Draft Dodger Rag," Elektra, 1965.
"Here's to the State of Mississippi," Elektra, 1965.
"I Ain't Marchin' Anymore," Elektra, 1965.
"In the Heat of the Summer," Elektra, 1965.
"There But for Fortune," Elektra, 1965.
"Canons of Christianity," Elektra, 1966.
"The Ringing of Revolution," Elektra, 1966.
"Santo Domingo," Elektra, 1966.
"Crucifixion," A&M, 1967.
"Miranda," A&M, 1967.
"The Party," A&M, 1967.
"Outside of a Small Circle of Friends," A&M, 1967.
"Joe Hill," A&M, 1968.
"The War Is Over," A&M, 1968.
"When in Rome," A&M, 1968.
"My Life," A&M, 1969.
"Where Were You in Chicago," A&M, 1969.
"Here's to the State of Richard Nixon," A&M, 1974.

## Albums

*All the News That's Fit to Sing,* Elektra, 1964.
*I Ain't Marchin' Anymore* (includes "Draft Dodger Rag," "Talking Birmingham Jam," and "Here's to the State of Mississippi"), Elektra, 1964.
*Phil Ochs in Concert* (includes "There But for Fortune" and "Love Me, I'm a Liberal"), Elektra, 1966.
*Pleasures of the Harbor* (includes "Flower Lady" and "Outside of a Small Circle of Friends"), A&M, 1967.
*Tape From California* (includes "The War Is Over"), A&M, 1968.
*Rehearsals for Retirement,* A&M, 1969.
*Greatest Hits,* A&M, 1970.

*Gunfight in Carnegie Hall,* A&M, 1971.
*Chords of Fame,* A&M, 1976.
*A Toast to Those Who Are Gone,* (songs recorded before 1964), Rhino, 1986.
*The War is Over: The Best of Phil Ochs,* A&M, 1988.
*The Broadside Tapes I,* Smithsonian Folkways, 1989.
*There But for Fortune,* Elektra, 1989.
*There & Now: Live in Vancouver, 1968,* Rhino, 1990.

# Sources

### Books

Eliot, Marc, *Death of a Rebel,* Anchor Press, 1979.
*The Penguin Encyclopedia of Popular Music,* edited by Donald Clarke, Viking, 1989.
Stambler, Irwin, and Grelun Landon, *The Encyclopedia of Folk, Country and Western Music,* St. Martin's Press, 1983.

### Periodicals

*Crawdaddy,* July 1976.
*Melody Maker,* April 17, 1976.
*Rolling Stone,* May 27, 1971; May 20, 1976; July 15, 1976; March 12, 1987.
*Sing Out!,* Spring 1976; Spring 1987.
*Spin,* April 1991.
*Washingtonian,* July 1989.

Other sources include album liner notes to *The War is Over* and *There & Now: Live in Vancouver, 1968.*

—Megan Rubiner

# Odetta

**Folksinger, songwriter, guitarist**

The name Odetta is probably unfamiliar to most people in the generation raised on MTV, yet she is one of the pillars of twentieth-century music. A folksinger distinguished by the power and clarity of her voice as well as the richness and intensity of her delivery, Odetta has also functioned as a living archive of music. By tirelessly researching, recording, and touring, and drawing on a variety of musical genres, she has kept alive the legacy of early folk and blues singers, including Bessie Smith and Leadbelly. Odetta has had a significant influence on modern music, providing inspiration for such performers as Janis Joplin and Joan Armatrading.

The singer was born Odetta Holmes on December 31, 1930, in Alabama. Her father died when she was quite young, and her mother remarried, giving the children their stepfather's surname, Felious, and moving the family to Los Angeles when Odetta was six. The youngster took piano and voice lessons and by the time she entered secondary school, she was beginning to discover her immense talent as a singer. She was the star of her high school glee club and, at the age of 14, began singing at the Turnabout Theater in Hollywood. Odetta appeared to be headed for a career as a concert singer until some friends she met while studying music at Los Angeles City College introduced her to the embryonic modern folk music scene. In 1949 she began gigging in West Coast clubs as a solo act, accompanying herself on guitar. Early in her career, she purchased a wood-bodied guitar nicknamed "Baby," on which she did all of her arrangements for years. While she has never considered herself a proficient guitarist, she did in time develop a unique sound that was eventually canonized in the folk music world as "the Odetta strum."

### Unique Performance Style

Within five years, Odetta had built up a considerable reputation for herself on the West Coast. By the mid- to late 1950s, the singer was touring the United States and Canada; by 1961, she had played Carnegie Hall and appeared twice at the renowned Newport Folk Festival. Odetta was unquestionably one of the brightest stars of the folk music renaissance of the early 1960s, which also saw the first of many world tours for her. Reaching much of mainstream America through the medium of television as well, Odetta received acclaim for her appearance on a musical special with musician Harry Belafonte and stole the show from an impressive roster of singers in the 1963 program *Dinner With the President*. She also performed as an actress in several films and television programs, most notably *The Autobiogra-*

*phy of Miss Jane Pittman* and the movie version of American novelist William Faulkner's *Sanctuary.*

Odetta's unique and amalgamated style ensured her popularity beyond the 1950s and 1960s. In the *New York Times* Jon Peeples described the singer's performance in Merkin Concert Hall's 1989 Voices of Change series: "She strung together blues and spirituals, many of them unfamiliar. Over the steady rhythm of her guitar and her tapping foot, she sent her voice to its clear heights and its nasal depths, bringing out the field holler roots of her music." The musician has noted that her choice of material at a particular concert depends largely on her perception of the audience, and she prefers solo performances since they allow her the freedom to sing what she feels like singing.

### Guitar Adds Dramatic Effect

Odetta's vocals along with her self-acquired knowledge of the guitar combine to create a dramatic effect. "I'll play the same few chords," she pointed out to Robert Yelin in *Frets Magazine,* "but by varying my strumming, by harmonizing notes within a chord and picking some other notes—that way I'll achieve the sounds of fullness. I love the opposite forces I can create by singing a smooth melody line and hearing my rhythm playing churning away beneath it. I love those dramatics in music."

Often shunning the strict tenets of folk purists, Odetta explained her reason for employing numerous techniques in her performances, as quoted by Yelin: "If a song is important enough for me to sing, I'll find a way to accompany myself on guitar. I would make up chords to fit the singing—I'm not a purist in any way, shape, or form. If I felt I needed to sing a song so badly, and I couldn't play accompaniment for it, I would sing it a capella."

### Commanding Presence on Stage

One of Odetta's most notable traits is her limitless curiosity about music. In addition to demonstrating a scholarly tenacity in researching traditional forms—usually at the Library of Congress in Washington, D.C.—she has always been willing to try new styles. Accordingly, she has performed with such partners as musicians Count Basie and Bob Dylan and writer Langston Hughes and in various genres, including blues and gospel. Odetta's versatility is demonstrated in her versions of the spirituals "Hold On" and "Ain't No Grave Can Hold Me Down," her a capella arrangement of "God's a-goin' to Cut You Down," her heartrending rendition of "All the Pretty Little Horses," which evokes the injustice of plantation life in the American South, and her performance of the prison song "Been in the Pen."

Whether standing in front of a symphony orchestra or alone with her guitar, Odetta is a commanding presence on stage. Her fans claim that the best of her recordings—most of which are out of print—fall far short of capturing the impact of her live performances. In the liner notes to *Odetta Sings the Blues,* critic Adam Barnes described her as "a large and significant voice that can swell with majesty, phrase delicately, dipping deep into the bottomless well of song."

## Selected discography

*My Eyes Have Seen,* 1959.
*Sometimes I Feel Like Crying ,* RCA, 1962.
*Odetta at Town Hall,* 1962.
*Odetta,* 1963.
*Odetta Sings Folk Songs,* RCA, 1963.
*One Grain of Sand,* 1963.
*Odetta at the Gate of Horn,* Tradition.
*Odetta Sings Dylan,* 1965.
*Ballad for Americans,* 1965.
*Odetta in Japan,* 1965.

*Odetta*, 1967.
*Best of Odetta*, 1967.
*Odetta at Carnegie Hall*, 1967.
*Odetta Sings the Blues*, Riverside, 1968.
*The Essential Odetta*, Vanguard, 1973.
*Christmas Spirituals*, Alcazar.
*Movin' It On*, Rose Quartz, 1987.
*Best of Odetta*, 1991.
*Odetta and the Blues*, Fantasy Original Blues Classics, 1992.

## Sources

*Frets*, April 1981.
*High Fidelity*, November 1983.
*Jet*, October 9, 1980.
*New York Times*, September 17, 1989.
*Stereo Review*, March 1988.
*Variety*, November 6, 1985.

Other sources include album liner notes to *Odetta Sings the Blues*.

—*Joan Goldsworthy*

# Christopher Parkening

**Guitarist**

**C**hristopher Parkening is a renowned classical guitarist who has displayed dual facets of development in his career. Initially, Parkening concerned himself with the mastery of his instrument; he was a pupil of maestro Andres Segovia, who, according to *High Fidelity,* considered Parkening a brilliant guitarist, "one touched by the finger of God." Parkening's technical skill enabled him to perform in the most prestigious concert halls throughout the world while he was quite young. Even his critics acknowledged his status "as the only American classical guitarist to ever appeal to the general public in any significant way," as reported by Larry Snitzler in *Guitar Player.* But Parkening credits a spiritual renewal with the inspiration for an additional, religious aspect of his career.

Commenting on his early retirement from the concert circuit, Parkening stated to Terry Mattingly in *Christianity Today,* "I had played enough concerts to make enough money to buy the things I wanted to live 'the good life.' My dreams had all come true. . . . But I felt empty. The music I was making didn't mean anything to me." The world-class artist, hoping to integrate his religious beliefs into his music, was inspired to perform both secular and sacred compositions after reading a quotation from Bach, which Parkening often recalls when interviewed: "The aim and final reason of all music is none else but the glory of God."

### Made Formal Debut at Age 15

Parkening was born in Los Angeles in 1947. Taught the art of practicing by his father, who was a musician as well as a real estate man, Parkening studied guitar from childhood. He made his formal debut at the age of 15 in a concert sponsored by the Young Musicians Foundation. After listening to a tape of the Parkening concert, Andres Segovia invited young Christopher to join his first American master classes at the University of California, where the young guitarist would later spend his freshman year of college. Parkening transferred to the University of Southern California his second year and was asked to teach guitar. The university eventually created a guitar department, which Parkening headed beginning in 1971.

The year 1968, though, was a pivotal one for Parkening. At age 20 he began his first series of concert appearances throughout the United States and Canada. The handsome musician also released the albums *Guitar in the Classical Style* and *Guitar in the Spanish Style* for EMI/Angel Records. Critical and commercial successes, the two albums were heralded as "extraordinarily beautiful" by reviewer Shirley Fleming in *High Fidelity.*

Throughout young adulthood, Parkening continued to

win awards and attract attention with the release of the albums *Romanza, Parkening Plays Bach,* and an anthology of highlights from his earlier discs, *The Christopher Parkening Album.* The 1976 *Parkening and the Guitar* received a Grammy nomination for best classical recording, and Parkening's popular appeal merited him a citation in a *Playboy* article that read, "There's no more exciting classical guitarist than this slim, serious, twenty-four-year-old."

Despite his success, the demands of a rigorous concert circuit coupled with the need to transcribe ever more material to broaden the guitar's limited repertoire overwhelmed the exhausted Parkening. At age 32, he decided to retreat to a large ranch in Montana with his wife, Barbara. In retirement, he pursued his love for fly-fishing full time while teaching a master class once a year at Montana State University in Bozeman.

### Found a Higher Reason to Play Guitar

But the musical hiatus that had shocked his fellow performers ended when Parkening responded to a neighbor's suggestion that the guitarist attend a church service. In the church that morning, Parkening experienced a spiritual renewal, which he described to Mattingly as a realization that he could "glorify the Lord" better with his guitar than his fly-fishing rod. He related to Larry Snitzler that dissatisfaction with his life brought him to discover another aim. "It was at that point that I became a Christian and decided to play the guitar again, but for a different purpose. Instead of just playing to make the money and for the self-acclaim, I

really, truly, in my heart, want to play the guitar again to try to glorify the Lord in some small way."

The 38-year-old artist returned to the realm of classical guitar in 1984 with the recording *Simple Gifts,* a collection of sacred music. Responding to "the breathtaking standard of technical perfection and sensitivity that has become [Parkening's] trademark," a reviewer in *High Fidelity* commented on the addition of a religious aspect to Parkening's work: "Parkening's playing reflects not only a love of the great tradition that informed it, but also the religious inspiration that occasioned the creation of so many classical masterpieces." His first recording with an orchestra, *A Bach Celebration for Guitar and Orchestra,* was also made in 1984 to honor the composer whose tricentennial commemoration followed the next year.

During the 1984-1985 season, Parkening began a successful collaboration with opera soprano Kathleen Battle. After performing in concert together, the two issued a recording titled *The Pleasures of Their Company,* which earned a Grammy nomination for best classical recording in 1987. A reviewer in *High Fidelity* called Parkening's accompaniment "the jewel in the crown," offering "such extraordinary pleasures that one hopes further collaboration will follow."

### A Selective Repertoire

Though most reviewers agree that Parkening plays superbly and find little to criticize in his work, some question his selective repertoire, noting his exclusion of contemporary music and his construction of "suites" from pieces that are personal favorites. These critics complain that "his repertoire is always chosen from a rather narrow band of pieces that are usually very lyrical, conventional in harmony, and structurally predictable," as summarized by Larry Snitzler in *Guitar Player.* When Snitzler asked Parkening to respond to such criticism, the musician maintained, "I've got to be true to what I believe in and what's in my heart. I don't desire to be phony, in terms of the music I'm playing. So, for that reason, if someone doesn't like the fact that I'm not playing avant-garde music, for example, I'm sorry that I'm disappointing them. But I still won't play something that I dislike just to please people, per se."

Parkening remarked in 1987 that he hopes to "mine the riches of centuries of sacred classical music and to bring this music to the stage and recording studio," as quoted by Mattingly. In addition, Parkening would like to transcribe or commission transcription of works written for other instruments and for voice. He has continued recording, releasing an album with David Brandon in 1991 titled *Virtuoso Duets,* and he has plans to cut a set of Spanish albums.

Commenting to Mattingly about the problems of reconciling the secular and sacred aspects of his work, Parkening stated, "You're always walking the thin line between music that pleases the purists, yet is music you want to play. . . . I want to play hymns and other forms of religious music, yet I don't want to play gospel music. I want to play music that is 'classy' enough for the concert stage. I am part of the classical music tradition. I must use the gift I believe God has given me."

## Selected discography

*Guitar in the Classic Style,* EMI/Angel, 1968.
*Guitar in the Spanish Style,* EMI/Angel, 1968.
*Romanza,* EMI/Angel, 1969.
*Parkening Plays Bach,* EMI/Angel, 1972.
*The Christopher Parkening Album,* EMI/Angel, 1973.
*Parkening & the Guitar,* EMI/Angel, 1976.

*A Bach Celebration for Guitar and Orchestra,* EMI/Angel, 1984.
*Simple Gifts,* EMI/Angel, 1984.
(With Kathleen Battle) *The Pleasures of Their Company,* EMI/Angel, 1986.
*Guitar Recital,* EMI/Angel.
*Sacred Music for Guitar,* EMI/Angel.
(With David Brandon) *Virtuoso Duets,* EMI/Angel, 1991.

## Sources

*Billboard,* January 5, 1986.
*Christianity Today,* May 15, 1987.
*Guitar Player,* February 1988; January 1991.
*High Fidelity,* January 1969; February 1973; July 1987.
*International Musician,* March 1974.
*Keynote,* November 1986.
*New York Times,* February 17, 1974.
*Playboy,* September 1972.
*Stereo Review,* May 1974.

—Marjorie Burgess

# Maceo Parker

## Saxophonist

"Lord knows—just ask [singer] James Brown—there's only one Maceo," declared Gene Santoro in *Down Beat,* about Brown's peerless saxophone sideman, Maceo Parker. Though more than 70 musicians have worked with Brown, Parker is the funky player Brown chose to hail before each set with the fabled command, "Maceo, blow your horn." The musician's enduring relationship with Brown has produced some classic pop songs, including "Cold Sweat," "Lickin' Stick," "Poppa's Got a Brand New Bag," and "Popcorn." Though his renowned riffs with the James Brown Revue are the staple samplings used by many rap artists, solo recognition eluded Parker until he was 48 years old and his album *Roots Revisited* went to the Number One spot on *Billboard*'s jazz charts in the early 1990s.

"You know, you can take a tape or a record to some very private spots; your room, your house, your car," Parker observed to Cynthia Rose in her biography of James Brown, *Living in America.* "And there you are with that music and your own private thoughts. Then next week there's the same performer that you had in the bedroom, performing live the same music you heard in those very inner places. . . . That's where I think there is a magic about bein' who we are. The percentage of bein' that person—I don't know if it's greater or smaller or what percentage it is—but it's *there.* You know what I'm sayin'? That's what they callin' up when they tape-loop me or James [Brown]."

### Hired by James Brown

Raised in Kinston, North Carolina, Maceo was born to a family of musicians. His parents performed gospel music in church, but his uncle, who headed a local band called the Blue Notes, was his musical mentor. With his brothers Melvin and Kellis, Parker formed the Junior Blue Notes in grade school. Melvin played drums, Kellis played trombone, and Maceo played the saxophone. After they entered the sixth grade, the boys' uncle allowed them to perform during intermission at his band's nightclub engagements. Accomplished on the bandstand when they entered the Agricultural and Technical College of North Carolina, Melvin and Maceo kept up their musical commitments while attending school.

In 1962 James Brown heard Melvin perform in a band called Apex at the El Morocco Club in Greenville, North Carolina. Brown had just finished his own show at the Coliseum when he asked Melvin to become his drummer. Declining because he was still in school, Melvin was given an open invitation to join Brown whenever he was available. That same night at another club, Maceo

## For the Record. . .

Raised in Kinston, NC. *Education:* Attended Agricultural and Technical College of North Carolina (now North Carolina Agricultural and Technical State University).

Saxophonist. Began playing tenor saxophone as a child with local group Blue Notes; formed Junior Blue Notes in elementary school; performed in regional nightclubs in the sixth grade; played in the Disciples, 1962; joined James Brown Revue as a baritone and tenor saxophonist, 1964 (one source says 1965); formed group Maceo & All the King's Men, 1970-73; rejoined Brown as alto saxophonist, 1973—. Has recorded albums as a leader.

**Addresses:** *Record company*—Verve Records, 825 Eighth Ave., New York, NY 10019.

was performing in a group called the Disciples; both brothers would approach Brown a year and a half later.

In 1964 Melvin brought Maceo along when he went backstage to tell James Brown he was ready for a job. "I really wanted Melvin," Brown revealed in his autobiography, *James Brown, the Godfather of Soul,* "but I figured I had to hire Maceo, too, if I wanted to get his brother." Brown needed a baritone sax player for his James Brown Revue but hired Maceo, who played tenor. "I didn't know what I had got!" the singer related to Rose. While his brother would soon leave the band, Maceo remained, alternating between tenor and baritone sax with St. Clair Pinckney and eventually keeping the tenor spot.

### Joined the Funk Movement

Throughout the 1970s Parker ventured out on his own, but failed to find the success he had with Brown in popularizing a brand of rhythm and blues known as funk—a term from the African-American lexicon that originally had vulgar connotations. "I do remember," Maceo confided to Rose, "havin' to get that term 'funk' OK'd by my parents . . . to them, it was just not a gentleman's word. See, when I got out of college, it was just a way to play: funky as opposed to straight. Just a form, a style of music. *James* made it a craze." Indeed, from 1970 to 1973 Parker's bands—which included Maceo and the Macks, Maceo & All the King's Men, and Fred Wesley and the JBs—were not able to generate much interest without frontliner James Brown.

In 1973 Parker rejoined Brown and switched to alto sax,

another of his signature instruments. In the mid-1970s he experimented in the electro-funk genre with Bootsy's Rubber Band and George Clinton's Parliament and Funkadelic bands, but all paths led back to Brown for the next 20 years. It wasn't until Brown's six-year prison term in Aiken, South Carolina, in the early 1990s that Parker found his course altered. With the JBs—tenor saxophonist Fred Wesley and trombonist Alfred "Pee Wee" Ellis—Parker put together two phenomenally successful recordings.

### First Number One Album in 1990

"He's no bebopper, reborn or otherwise," noted Santoro about Parker's performance on his Number One jazz album, *Roots Revisited.* "His roots are the church and the blues . . . his sound is a joyful, cutting ribbon of light and heat burnished by grit and soul. His riff-based attack is melodic, unraveling and reweaving themes rather than running chords, and primarily rhythmic, relying on finely-shaped nuances of timing and displacement to communicate—kinda like his longtime boss' vocals, amazingly enough." "Jazz purists tend to regard [Parker's] sort of high decibel rhythm-and-blues as something less than desirable, but it should surprise no one that jazz has not eluded Parker's ears," another critic commented in *Stereo Review.* "Mind you, *Roots Revisited* . . . retains all the nasty ingredients that make us snap our fingers and twist our bodies, but it dishes up funk with a generous sprinkling of individual jazz expression."

Along with the album *For All the King's Men*—which lured rap enthusiasts with the song "Let Him Out," a dynamic plea for Brown's release from prison—*Roots Revisited* affords "a pretty good picture of the insides of Maceo's talented head," declared Santoro in *Down Beat.* Artists as varied as Bootsy Collins, Limbomaniacs, and Deee-Lite deliver the indisputable evocations of Parker, which led Bill Milkowski to conclude in *Down Beat* that in the music world of the 1990s, "Everything's coming up Maceo."

## Selected discography

*For All the King's Men,* 4th & Broadway.
*Roots Revisited,* Verve, 1990.
*Pee Wee, Fred, & Maceo,* Gramavision, 1990.
*Mo' Roots,* Verve, 1991.

### With James Brown; on Polydor Records except where noted

*Sex Machine.*
*James Brown's Funky People.*

*The Best of James Brown.*
*Doin' It to Death.*
*Ain't That a Groove.*
*In the Jungle Groove,* 1986.
*Solid Gold: 30 Golden Hits.*
*The CD of JB: Sex Machine & Other Soul Classics.*
*The CD of JB II,* 1988.
*Gravity,* reissue, Scotti Bros., 1991.


## Sources

### Books

Brown, James, with Bruce Tucker, *James Brown, the Godfather of Soul,* Macmillan, 1986.
Rose, Cynthia, *Living in America,* Serpent's Tail, 1990.

### Periodicals

*Down Beat,* September 1990; October 1990; March 1991.
*People,* January 14, 1991.
*Stereo Review,* March 1991.

—Marjorie Burgess

# Gram Parsons

**Singer, songwriter, guitarist**

**G**ram Parsons made only a brief appearance on the American music scene, but his influence was enormous both during his career and after his tragic early death. Parsons was one of the first artists to introduce country vocal harmonies and country and bluegrass instrumentation to rock and roll. His work as a solo artist and with important folk-rock groups like the Byrds and the Flying Burrito Brothers effectively bridged a gap between bluegrass, country, and rock. Parsons completed only two solo albums before his death, and his achievements are often judged more by their effect on other artists—both country and rock—than on their own merit. In *Country Music U.S.A.*, Bill C. Malone wrote: "Although Parsons' final resting place is obscure, his contributions to . . . music are much more strongly marked. His influence is still heard in the music of many young musicians, both unknown and professional."

Despite his family's wealth, Parsons did not have an easy life. He was born in Winter Haven, Florida, and given the name Cecil Ingram Connors. Brought up primarily in Waycross, Georgia, he began playing guitar in his early teens. Parsons's father, a packing-plant owner, sang country music as a sideline under the name "Coon Dog" Connors. Like most youths growing up in the 1950s, however, Parsons gravitated toward rock and roll, especially the music of Elvis Presley. When Parsons was 13, his father fatally shot himself in the head. Soon thereafter his mother—an alcoholic who also died young—married a New Orleans businessman named Robert Parsons. Thus the teenage boy was adopted and given the name Gram Parsons.

### Briefly Attended Harvard

Family life in both the Connors and Parsons households was full of upheaval and emotional turmoil. Gram attended expensive preparatory schools, but rebelled constantly, running away at 14 and drifting to New York City's Greenwich Village at 16. In the early 1960s Parsons's musical interests turned from rock to folk and country. He briefly played with a band called the Shilohs. He was persuaded to play country music during a brief stay at Harvard University, where some of the other students encouraged him to embrace his rural origins. The friendships Parsons forged at Harvard led to the formation of his first important group, the International Submarine Band.

After only four months at Harvard, Parsons dropped out and moved with his band to New York City. There the group played a unique form of rock—unique in that it included the pedal steel guitar work of J. D. Maness and a playlist of modern country songs. The Interna-

Born Cecil Ingram Connors (named changed to Gram Parsons after adoption, c. 1960), November 5, 1946, in Winter Haven, FL; died September 19, 1973, in Joshua Tree, CA; cause of death attributed to excessive drug use; buried in New Orleans, LA; son of "Coon Dog" Connors (a packing-plant owner and part-time singer); was married; children: Polly (mother's name, Nancy). *Education:* Attended Harvard University, c. 1965.

Singer, songwriter, guitarist, c. 1960-73. Folksinger in New York City, and with band the Shilohs, c. 1962; played mandolin with blugrass group the Hillmen; formed the International Submarine Band, c. 1966; member of the Byrds, c. 1966-68; with Chris Hillman, formed the Flying Burrito Brothers, 1968; solo artist, 1971-73.

tional Submarine Band cut one album—1966's *Safe at Home*—for a small label before it dissolved in 1967. *Country Music U.S.A.*'s Malone noted that the recording—now a very rare collector's item—was "well in advance of similar experiments made by the Nitty Gritty Dirt Band and other rock-oriented musicians."

In 1968 Parsons joined the Byrds, a well-known folk-rock band, through the efforts of Byrd Chris Hillman. There Parsons and Hillman—another rocker who loved old-time country music and bluegrass—moved the Byrds in the direction of country. A 1969 Byrds album, *Sweetheart of the Rodeo,* clearly displayed the influence of Parsons and Hillman; it contains pedal steel guitar, bluegrass riffs, and even a truck-driving song, but its best known cut is Parsons's beautiful "Hickory Wind." Their long hair and hippy clothes notwithstanding, the Byrds were invited to perform "Hickory Wind" at the revered Grand Ole Opry, *the* institution of country music.

### Left Byrds After Only Three Months

After only three months with the Byrds, Parsons quit the band in 1968, refusing to accompany them on a tour of South Africa due to his opposition to that country's racist government. With Hillman, Parsons drifted to California and found work at country bars on the coast. There, with the addition of steel guitarist Sneaky Pete Kleinow, they formed the Flying Burrito Brothers. According to Malone, the Flying Burrito Brothers—led by Parsons in a white cowboy suit emblazoned with marijuana leaves— "vividly illustrated the fusion of country music and youth-culture motifs." With Parsons as a

member the band cut two albums, *The Gilded Palace of Sin* and *Burrito DeLuxe.*

Malone also noted that the Flying Burrito Brothers "were strongly rock-flavored, but they also borrowed songs from the Louvin Brothers, George Jones, Merle Haggard, and other hard-core country singers. Burrito instrumentation was similarly mixed, the steel-guitar stylings of Sneaky Pete gave the group a distinctive honky-tonk flavor. The Burrito Brothers' most compelling songs were those written by Parsons and Hillman, especially the frequently performed 'Sin City' and 'Wheels,' and they were rendered by these two singers in a sweet, clear duet harmony reminiscent of the Everly Brothers." In his book *Who's Who in New Country Music,* Andrew Vaughan noted that the Burrito Brothers offered "a new kind of country music, certainly more Hank Williams than Jim Reeves. And if hip rock stars could like country music then maybe it wasn't parents' music after all." In the time-honored country tradition—and, it seems, from personal experience—Parsons, backed by the Brothers, could also sing the blues. Recalled author Pamela Des Barres in *Rolling Stone,* "Gram could hurt through his voice better than anybody I've ever heard. He hurt so damn good, he made a pitiful broken heart feel beautiful and profound."

While recuperating from a motorcycle accident in early 1970, Parsons met and befriended Mick Jagger and Keith Richards of the Rolling Stones, whose work he would significantly influence. He left the Flying Burrito Brothers in the spring of 1970 to pursue a solo career, still determined to bring country music to rock audiences; alone, he recorded two albums: the debut *GP,* and the posthumously released *Grievous Angel.* Both works feature background vocals by country giant Emmylou Harris, who was singing folk in an obscure Washington, D.C. bar before she met Parsons.

"Working with Gram was a wonderful experience," Harris told Andrew Vaughan. "He was wildly misunderstood, too country for the rockers and too weird for the Nashville establishment. But he had a vision and a love for those old Louvins harmonies that was intense and powerful." As her own star rose in Nashville, Harris never missed an opportunity to praise Parsons for daring to work within his country roots. "I had no fire in me until Gram died," she said in *Who's Who in New Country Music.* "But afterwards I felt strongly that I had to continue his work. It was hard going solo but my attitude was always, 'How would Gram do this?' and somehow my sound evolved."

### Died at 26

By 1971 Parsons—with the help of a hefty trust fund—was indulging in a jet-set lifestyle, taking drugs, and hopping from one continent to another. While staying at a desert retreat near the Joshua Tree National Monument in California, Parsons died, on September 19, 1973. He was 26. According to *The Rolling Stone Encyclopedia of Rock & Roll,* traces of morphine, cocaine, amphetamine, and alcohol were found in his blood, though the autopsy report was inconclusive as to the actual cause of death. Then, in a bizarre twist, a few days after his death, while Parsons's body was on its way to burial in New Orleans, his remains were commandeered by his manager Phil Kaufman, taken back to Joshua Tree, and set on fire. *The Rolling Stone Encyclopedia* reported that Parsons had made it clear that he would like to be cremated when he died.

Parsons's body finally came to rest in a modestly marked plot in New Orleans. Like Hank Williams, who also died young, Parsons has wielded greater power from the grave than he did while alive. His influence can be heard distinctly on the Rolling Stones releases *Sticky Fingers* and *Exile on Main Street.* In a *Rolling Stone* review of *Hickory Wind,* a biography of Parsons, Keith Richards is quoted as having said in the book, "[Gram] kind of redefined the possibilities of country music for me, personally. If he had lived, he probably would have redefined if for everybody." Parsons gave Emmylou Harris the courage to pursue traditional country balladry at a time when slick pop arrangements were in vogue. And his spirit lives on today in California-based country-rock bands like the Desert Rose Band, a group powered by his former colleagues Chris Hillman and J. D. Maness.

"There was a time when country became very boring," Harris told Vaughan. "Those were very frustrating times for those of us playing a rootsy acoustic style. . . . It was the old-time sound . . . that first drew me to country music. And when I worked with Gram Parsons it was that feel that inspired us." That "feel" has energized a whole new generation of country performers, many of whom owe a huge debt to the artistic direction initiated by the late Gram Parsons.

## Selected discography

### With the Byrds

*Sweetheart of the Rodeo,* Columbia, 1968.

### With the Flying Burrito Brothers

*The Gilded Palace of Sin,* A&M, 1969.
*Burrito Deluxe,* A&M, 1970.

### Solo Albums

*GP,* Warner Bros., 1972.
*Grievous Angel,* Warner Bros., 1973.
*Sleepless Nights,* A&M, 1976.
*Gram Parsons—The Early Years, Volume 1,* Sierra/Briar Records, 1979.

Also recorded *Safe at Home,* 1967, with the International Submarine Band.

## Sources

### Books

Brown, Charles T., *Music U.S.A.: America's Country and Western Tradition,* Prentice-Hall, 1986.
Des Barres, Pamela, *I'm With the Band: Confessions of a Groupie,* Jove, 1987.
Fong-Torres, Ben, *Hickory Wind: The Life and Times of Gram Parsons,* Pocket Books, 1991.
*The Illustrated Encyclopedia of Country Music,* Harmony, 1977.
Malone, Bill C., *Country Music U.S.A.,* University of Texas Press, 1985.
*The Rolling Stone Encyclopedia of Rock & Roll,* edited by Jon Pareles and Patricia Romanowski, Rolling Stone Press/Summit Books, 1983.
Shestack, Melvin, *The Country Music Encyclopedia,* Crowell, 1974.
Vaughan, Andrew, *Who's Who in New Country Music,* St. Martin's, 1989.

### Periodicals

*Rolling Stone,* October 3, 1991.

—Anne Janette Johnson

# Sandi Patti

## Singer

Sandi Patti has been called "The Voice" of contemporary Christian music. Gifted with a tremendous vocal talent that lends itself to a wide range of expression, Patti has enjoyed a diverse musical career. From ballads to pop to distinctive renditions of traditional gospel music, Patti bridges the gap between the secular and Christian worlds and ministers to her wide audience in a unique way.

Born July 12, 1956, Patti made her singing debut at the tender age of two while singing "Jesus Loves Me" in church. Her vocal gift, apparent even then, increased dramatically over the years, and she soon performed regularly at small gospel churches around the country with her two younger brothers in the family singing group, the Ron Patty Family. As a young adult, she studied voice at San Diego State University before transferring to Anderson College in Indiana to major in music. While at Anderson, Patti earned money as a backup singer doing jingles for Juicy Fruit gum and met her future husband, John Helvering. It was Helvering who proved instrumental in encouraging Patti to perform and made arrangements for her to record a custom album entitled *For My Friends*. Her name was misspelled "Patti" on the album, and she has used that version of her name professionally since. After hearing the album, a recording executive offered her a contract in 1979. There was no stopping "The Voice" then.

*Sandi's Song,* Patti's first contractual release, appeared in 1979 and was followed by a number of personal appearances which spread the word of her music ministry nationwide. In 1980, Patti and her husband put together a small tour, quickly realizing that music was becoming far more than a part-time occupation. When she was asked to sing backup for the Bill Gaither Trio, Patti became convinced that her future lay in the music field. Her 1982 album *Lift Up the Lord,* a tightly produced and distinctly contemporary-sounding Christian album, won two Dove awards and featured such outstanding songs as the lively title track and "How Majestic Is Your Name," balanced against such balladic powerhouses as "They Could Not." Her 1983 album *Sandi Patti Live: More Than Wonderful,* certified gold in 1985, garnered additional Dove awards and a Grammy for best gospel performance. Subsequent albums have been nominated for musical awards each year, and Patti was named *Billboard*'s Inspirational Artist of the Year for four years in a row.

Patti's first major solo tour occurred in 1984 with concerts in the one hundred largest cities in the United States. The tour corresponded with the release of the *Songs From the Heart* album and drew more than half a million fans, confirming once again her position as the leading figure in popular Christian music. Her 1986 album *Morning Like This* earned her another Grammy, as did her duet with Deniece Williams on the song "They Say." As a whole, *Morning Like This* offers a striking musical balance: the title track embraces the mystery and joyful declaration of Easter morning, while the single "Love in Any Language" reaches well beyond the varying sects in Christendom; hand-clapping, foot-stomping favorites such as "Hosanna" and "Let There Be Praise" complement the inspirational moments of songs like "In the Name of the Lord."

Striving to keep pace with changes in musical tastes while not disappointing fans who had begun to equate her with operatic high C's and ringing, emotional crescendos, Patti blazed new trails with her 1988 album, *Make His Praise Glorious.* Still present here are hallmark ballads such as "In Heaven's Eyes" and powerhouse hits like "No Other Name," but the popular "Love Will Be Our Home" contains rocklike guitar licks—something fans might not have expected. Other departures are evident in the catchy "Come Let Us Worship," which found favor with fans of electronic percussion, and "Someone Up There Loves Me," featuring heavy brass aimed at jazz buffs.

Patti's broad appeal as a performer is not hard to understand. Her tremendous vocal talent bridges the gap between her Christian audience and the secular world. ABC-TV included her inspirational recording of "The Star Spangled Banner" during its Liberty Weekend Celebration, and NBC-TV invited her to participate in the network's *Christmas in Washington* special with former U.S. president Ronald Reagan. She has also performed on numerous daily television programs, including *The Tonight Show, The Today Show,* and *Good Morning America,* on specials such as the Grammy Awards show and the CBS special *We the People,* at the 1988 Republican National Convention, and at the opening ceremonies of the 1988 presidential inauguration. In addition, after four years of planning, Patti released *Sandi Patti and the Friendship Company* in 1989, a children's album that is destined to become a classic.

Despite national exposure as a performer, Patti remains refreshingly sincere and unchanged. Her dedication remains with the Lord and to her husband and four children. The music, in all its excitement, remains a ministry. As she noted in *People:* "I don't tell people 'You have to believe this,' but rather, 'Hey, the things that Jesus taught and continues to teach flat out work, and this is where I've been and learned and maybe it fits where you're at right now.' Music is a powerful tool. We should use it to help shape positive values." Perhaps what makes Sandi Patti's work so accessible and successful is her sincerity. Husband John agrees. "She talks to the audience about hating piano lessons when she was little, about our courtship, about [our daughter] Anna being sick, as well as about the Lord's message," he explained in *People.* Most critics agree that Patti's ability to cross musical boundaries and spread the Christian word to a wide and varied audience will insure her longevity in the field.

## Selected discography

*Sandi's Song,* Benson, 1979.
*Love Overflowing,* Benson, 1981.
*Lift Up the Lord,* Benson, 1982.
*Sandi Patti Live: More Than Wonderful,* Impact, 1983.
*The Gift Goes On,* Word Records, 1983.
*Songs From the Heart,* Impact, 1984.
*Hymns Just for You,* Helvering Productions, 1985.
*Morning Like This,* A&M, 1986.
*Make His Praise Glorious,* A&M, 1988.
*Sandi Patti and the Friendship Company,* A&M, 1989.
*The Finest Moments,* A&M, 1989.
*Another Time, Another Place,* Word Records, 1990.

## Sources

*Contemporary Christian Music,* April, 1988.
*People,* December 2, 1985.

Additional information supplied by the Helvering Agency.

—*Meg Mac Donald*

# Bernadette Peters

**Actress, singer**

With her dancing talent, flexible voice, and Kewpie-doll looks, singer and actress Bernadette Peters has become a premier performer of the musical stage. Groomed for show business from an early age, she took the theater world by storm when barely 20 years old, playing a small-town chorus girl who dances her way to stardom in a spoof of 1930s musicals titled *Dames at Sea.* Adept at mimicking the performing styles and stars of past show business eras, Peters has often been cast in nostalgia vehicles, captivating audiences as man-hungry Hildy in the wartime musical *On the Town* and as silent film comedienne Mabel Normand in *Mack and Mabel.* Even when the shows she appears in flop, her portrayals are frequently hailed as "adorable."

Adapting her talents to television, motion pictures, nightclub entertaining, and solo recording, Peters has since demonstrated that beyond her flare for the camp and the cute lies a performer of great versatility and depth; "[She] is perhaps," remarked Peter Reilly in *Stereo Review,* "the finest singing actress since [Barbra] Streisand." Critiquing the entertainer's first solo album, a mix of old and new songs titled *Bernadette Peters,* the reviewer found "no camp here . . . no coy inflections, and . . . no attempt to imitate" and noted "how sensationally *good* Peters can be when she's expressing no point of view at all, just the emotion of the moment."

### A "Versatile and Affecting" Actress

Further commending Peters's varied talents, *Newsweek*'s Jack Boll described her Tony Award-winning performance as an unlucky-in-love English hat designer in *Song and Dance:* "Her 20 songs become 20 scenes and 20 moods, creating a real character out of materials that might have seemed all too banal in other hands." "Every emotion is clear and true," concluded the critic. "[Peters] is now the most versatile and affecting actress in the American musical theater."

Born Bernadette Lazzara, Peters was the youngest child of an Italian-American truck driver and his wife Marguerite, who had an ardent interest in the world of show business. By age three Bernadette was studying tap dancing and singing, and by five she was a regular performer on television's *Horn and Hardart Children's Hour.* Her surname was changed to Peters when she was very young to discourage ethnic typecasting, and she soon began appearing in local stage shows, landing her first major role at age 13 as Baby June in a road company production of *Gypsy.* She continued her show business training while a student at Quitano's School for Young Professionals in New York City, rushing home each day to catch the 4:30 movie on television. "I got to see all the great old pictures," she recalled to Reilly. "I developed a real love for Ruby Keeler and Rita Hayworth and Marty Martin, just the way they'd *stand* or look at people or dance. I have a photographic mind, and I remember exactly how *they* were sometimes when I sing."

### Received Tony Award Nominations

Fortunately for Peters—and unlike many child performers—her own career desires meshed with her mother's unbridled ambitions for her. After her 1966 graduation

from high school, she appeared in a few disappointing off-Broadway productions, until a minor role in Broadway's *George M!* brought her acclaim. Next, the saucer-eyed, warble-voiced Peters was fittingly cast as Ruby in *Dames at Sea,* and her witty portrayal earned her a Drama Desk Award. Capturing the outrageous spirit of old Busby Berkeley musicals, Peters's gift for imitation determined her success for the next few years. Though they earned mixed reviews, a 1971 revival of *On the Town* and 1974's *Mack and Mabel* brought the actress Tony Award nominations. In her quest for challenging stage roles, Peters also performed in less typical productions that showcased her versatility, including *Tartuffe* and a musical version of *La Strada.*

Looking to Hollywood in the early 1970s, Peters hoped to expand her opportunities for important parts. Her stage success, however, had little effect on the roles she obtained, which were usually limited to secondary characters in films like *W. C. Fields and Me, Vigilante Force,* and *The Jerk.* But the musical *Pennies From Heaven* found the entertainer in a starring role as a Depression-era school teacher-turned-prostitute who escapes the harsh realities of her existence by imagining herself in production numbers and songs of the day. A box office failure, the motion picture nonetheless won Peters a Golden Globe Award for best actress.

Peters's forays into television were a bit more successful, featuring variety guest spots and play performances. In 1976 she even costarred in the comedy series *All's Fair,* playing a liberal photographer in love with a conservative newspaperman. While it received positive reviews, the show failed to attract viewers and was canceled at the end of its first season.

### Made a Comeback on the Stage

After a nearly decade-long absence, Peters returned to the New York stage in 1982 in the unlikely role of a frumpy South Dakota housewife in *Sally and Marsha.* Critics found her performance accomplished and mature and felt Peters exhibited a new sincerity and directness that was evident in her next project, the unconventional Stephen Sondheim musical *Sunday in the Park With George.* Playing the model and mistress of pointillist painter George Seurat, Peters received rave reviews and won a third Tony Award nomination.

In the early 1980s the entertainer became a solo recording artist, delivering an eclectic mix of popular songs ranging from tunes by Fats Waller to Elvis Presley to Marvin Hamlisch. In the *New York Daily News* Bill Carlton declared that Peters "has perfect pipes for pop, a very supple, wide-ranging pitch that often surprises the listener with sudden delightful twists and leaps." And a *People* reviewer observed, "She has carved out quite a cozy and entertaining niche for herself as a pop music archivist." Peters pointed out to Reilly that she doesn't "sing old songs just because they're old." "I'm an actress. I have to find a reason to say those words," she explained. "They have to be 'I' songs with a hook, something that relates to the heart."

Cast in another Stephen Sondheim musical in 1987, Peters played the Witch in the acclaimed *Into the Woods,* featuring characters from such popular fairy tales as *Cinderella* and *Jack and the Beanstalk.* "As the Witch," remarked Jack Kroll in *Time,* "Bernadette Peters does wonders with the trickiest . . . part." In addition to a nine-city musical tour with composer Peter Allen in the late 1980s, Peters also appeared in several motion pictures, including starring roles in two 1989 films, *Slaves of New York* and *Pink Cadillac,* and a part in 1991's *Impromptu.* Though reviewers from both *Time* and *Newsweek* found little to praise in *Slaves of New York* and *Pink Cadillac,* both magazines pointed out the actress's irresistible charm, one of the main reasons for Peters's continued success both on and off the stage.

## Selected discography

(With others) *Dames at Sea* (original cast recording), Columbia.

(With others) *Mack and Mabel* (original cast recording), ABC.
*Bernadette Peters,* MCA, 1980.
*Now Playing,* MCA, 1981.
(With others) *Sunday in the Park With George: Original Broadway Cast Recording,* RCA, 1984.
(With others) *A Collector's Sondheim,* RCA, 1985.
*The Songs From Song and Dance,* RCA, 1986.

## Sources

*Esquire,* January 1982.
*High Fidelity,* November 1984.
*Horizon,* January/February, 1988.
*Los Angeles Times,* July 12, 1989.
*Maclean's,* April 10, 1989; June 5, 1989.
*New Republic,* April 10, 1989.
*Newsweek,* September 30, 1985; November 16, 1987; March 20, 1989; June 12, 1989.
*New York Daily News,* September 7, 1981.
*People,* June 2, 1980; October 19, 1981; March 29, 1982; April 10, 1989; April 24, 1989; June 12, 1989; April 29, 1991.
*Rolling Stone,* April 18, 1991.
*Stereo Review,* August 1980; December 1981.
*Time,* November 16, 1987; March 20, 1989; June 5, 1989.

—*Nancy Pear*

# John Prine

## Singer, songwriter

The folk songs of singer-songwriter John Prine "have the natural grace and universality one hears only from a born story teller," asserted Don Heckman in the *New York Times*. Prine, a former mail carrier from Chicago, burst onto the national folk scene in the early 1970s performing original melodies and lyrics that poetically sketched the lives of grass-roots, working-class Americans. His 1971 debut album *John Prine* was widely praised by critics, and he has since recorded several albums that have secured his reputation as a distinctly gifted storytelling songwriter. In addition, his compositions have been recorded by numerous other artists, including Bob Dylan, Kris Kristofferson, John Denver, Joan Baez, Carly Simon, and Bette Midler. According to Ed McCormack in *Rolling Stone,* Prine's songs are "wholly and unmistakably in the American grain, jukebox songs, barroom songs, blue neon light songs, liquor store songs, hobo songs . . . songs like early-American primitive paintings, bittersweet and filled with humor and gothic irony."

Prine was raised in a working-class family with strong country roots. He grew up in Maywood, Illinois, a blue-collar suburb of Chicago, where his father worked in the steel mills. Prine's family had moved to Chicago from Muhlenberg County in western Kentucky, deep in the heart of stripmining coal country, where his grandfather played guitar with such country artists as Ike Everly and Merle Travis. Prine learned the guitar at the age of fourteen from his grandfather and his older brother and soon was composing his own melodies and lyrics, many which displayed his country heritage. While growing up, Prine spent his summers in Kentucky, and his classic song "Paradise" evokes his family's hometown. He told *Time:* "Until I was 15 I didn't know that the word paradise meant anything other than the town in Kentucky where all my relatives came from."

### Performing Began as a Sideline

Prine did not originally set out to make a career of performing and songwriting. After graduating from high school and serving in the army, he worked as a mail carrier in Chicago. As a break from the drudgeries of his postal job, he began performing his songs—many conceived during his delivery route—in the coffee houses of Chicago's Old Town district. Prine was heard by singer-songwriters Kris Kristofferson and Paul Anka, who were immediately impressed and felt Prine deserved national exposure. Both helped the young singer obtain bookings in folkclubs in New York City and Los Angeles and led him towards his first recording contract with Atlantic Records.

When his debut album, *John Prine,* was released in

1971, Prine was hailed by critics as a major new folk talent. The American idiom of his lyrics and his rough-edged vocal stylings brought comparisons to 1960s folk-giant Bob Dylan, yet critics singled out the impact of Prine's lyrical portraits of ordinary people. A contributor to *Time* wrote: "His leisurely, deceptively genial songs deal with the disillusioned fringe of Middle America, hauntingly evoking the world of fluorescent-lit truck stops, overladen knickknack shelves, gravel-dusty Army posts and lost loves. In a plangent baritone . . . he squeezes poetry out of the anguished longing of empty lives."

### Developed Loyal Folk Following

Prine went on to release four other albums with Atlantic and, although never breaking through with a large chart-topping record, maintained a dedicated cult following. According to Irwin Stambler and Grelun Landon in *The Encyclopedia of Folk, Country, and Western Music,* Prine's Atlantic recordings "represent some of the high points of American folk music in the 1970s." Included in this group are some of Prine's better-known songs such as "Hello in There," "Paradise," "Sam Stone," "Yes I Guess They Oughta Name a Drink After You," and "Grandpa Was a Carpenter." These first recordings, according to John Rockwell in the *New York Times,* portrayed "a songwriter of real wit and originality." During the early 1970s, Prine toured heavily as a performer, playing at music festivals, concerts, and folkclubs across the United States. Reviewing Prine in a New York City performance in 1973, a *Village Voice* reviewer described him as "a completely relaxed, friendly, unshow-biz performer. . . . Simple, even pure, in the kind of thing he does."

In 1978, Prine switched over to Asylum Records, and *Bruised Orange*—his first record with the label—received wide acclaim. Cited by *Time* as one of the ten best albums of 1978, *Bruised Orange* contained the songs "If You Don't Want My Love," "Fish and Whistle," and "Sabu Visits the Twin Cities Alone." The latter, according to Rockwell, is "ostensibly about a circus performer toiling on a tour to support a film, but clearly a self-image full of amused mockery and controlled grotesquerie." The entire album, Rockwell continued, amply displays Prine's gift "to marry the unpretentious basics of folk musical styles and poetic imagery with an almost bizarrely exaggerated imagination."

The following year, Prine's *Pink Cadillac* was released and, according to Robert Palmer in the *New York Times,* represented "Prine's masterpiece to date." Displaying a stronger rock and roll sound than Prine's previous albums, *Pink Cadillac* was co-produced by Prine and veteran Memphis record-maker Jerry Phillips in a way to preserve the sense of live musicians recording together. The album featured five new Prine songs, including "Saigon" and "Down by the Side of the Road," and also the contributions of rockabilly singer Billy Lee Riley. Palmer claimed *Pink Cadillac* "courts a kind of greatness that's extremely rare in contemporary popular music."

### Maintained Reputation as Lyrical Storyteller

Since 1980, Prine has recorded with Los Angeles-based Oh Boy Records, of which he is also president. Prine has released four albums with Oh Boy, including 1986's well-received *German Afternoons,* and in 1988 was part of a successful tour which paired him with folk-country singer Nanci Griffith. His 1989 double-album, *John Prine Live,* gives "a virtual career retrospective" of his work from the 1970s through 1980s, a contributor to *Wilson Library Bulletin* wrote. The albums are a "vivid representation of the ample skills" Prine brings to his live performances, and showcase his "extraordinary storytelling songs."

After a four-year hiatus from recording, Prine returned to the studio, this time with Howie Epstein of Tom Petty's Heartbreakers as producer. The resulting album, *The Missing Years,* was released in 1992 on the Oh Boy label and garnered sensational reviews. Featuring background vocals by such noted singers as Bonnie Raitt, Bruce Springsteen, and Tom Petty, the songs on *The Missing Years* bear Prine's trademark observations on human nature. Many of the tunes grapple with the universal feelings of passion, frustration, disappointment and regret. On the more capricious side, though, the title track traces the so-called "missing years" in the life of Jesus Christ, speculating from a 1960s point of view on how he might have spent his adolescence.

Commenting on Prine's overall contribution to the folk

genre, *Rolling Stone* contributor David Wild declared: "He was, and is, a songwriter's songwriter, widely admired for his ability to intermingle gracefully the humorous and the heartbreaking." "If this record hadn't done well, I probably would have quit," Prine told Gil Asakawa in *Pulse!* "Now, I can't stop."

## Selected discography

*John Prine*, Atlantic, 1971.
*Diamonds in the Rough*, Atlantic, 1972.
*Sweet Revenge*, Atlantic, 1973.
*Common Sense*, Atlantic, 1975.
*Prime Prine: The Best of John Prine*, Atlantic, 1976.
*Bruised Orange*, Asylum, 1978.
*Pink Cadillac*, Asylum, 1979.
*Storm Windows*, Asylum, 1980.
*Aimless Love*, Oh Boy, 1984.
*German Afternoons*, Oh Boy, 1986.
*John Prine Live*, Oh Boy, 1988.
(Collaborator) Nitty Gritty Dirt Band, *Will the Circle Be Unbroken, Volume Two*, Universal, 1989.
*The Missing Years*, Oh Boy, 1991.

## Sources

### Books

Baggelaar, Kristin, and Donald Milton, *Folk Music: More Than a Song,* Crowell, 1976.
Stambler, Irwin, and Grelun Landon, *The Encyclopedia of Folk, Country, and Western Music,* 2nd edition, St. Martin's, 1983.

### Periodicals

*Audio,* August 1989.
*Entertainment Weekly,* November 22, 1991.
*New York Times,* November 5, 1971; June 18, 1972; February 27, 1973; April 20, 1975; December 17, 1975; May 28, 1978; July 13, 1978; September 23, 1979.
*Pulse!,* February 1992.
*Rolling Stone,* October 12, 1972; January 23, 1992; February 20, 1992.
*Stereo Review,* April 1991.
*Time,* July 24, 1972.
*Village Voice,* December 20, 1973; April 21, 1975.
*Wilson Library Bulletin,* January 1989.

—*Michael E. Mueller*

# The Red Hot Chili Peppers

**Rock band**

The Red Hot Chili Peppers emerged in the mid-1980s as one of the trailblazing bands in the world of alternative rock and spearheaded the wave of groups that fused hard rock and thrash with 1970s funk. Though this heady musical brew earned them a loyal underground following, the band didn't begin to reach mass audiences until videos from their 1989 album *Mother's Milk* began to appear regularly on MTV. The Peppers' hard-edged style wasn't the only thing standing between them and mainstream success, however; the tumultuous offstage lives of the band members generated a great deal of controversy as well.

The band's frenetic tempos, churning guitar chords, and onstage mania—they quickly became notorious for appearing at performances wearing nothing but tubesocks over their genitals—owe a great deal to the punk movement of the late seventies and early eighties. On the other hand, the slapping bass and funky drums that grace much of their material come out of the band's devotion to funk and soul, especially the various projects of George Clinton, the father of what became

## For the Record. . .

Band formed c. 1983; members include **Anthony Kiedis** (born c. 1963 in Michigan), vocals; **Flea** (born Michael Balzary c. 1962 in Melbourne, Australia), bass; **Hillel Slovak** (born c. 1963, died of a heroin overdose in 1988), guitar; **Jack Sherman,** guitar; **Jack Irons,** drums; **John Frusciante** (born c. 1970 in Los Angeles), guitar; **Chad Smith** (born c. 1963 in Detroit, Michigan), drums.

Performed in Los Angeles area in 1983. Signed by EMI, released first album in 1984. Balzary and Kiedis acted in motion pictures. Signed by Warner Bros. in 1989.

**Addresses:** *Record company*—Warner Bros. Records Inc., 3300 Warner Blvd., Burbank, CA 91505-9090.

known as "P. Funk." Clinton's bands, most notably Parliament and Funkadelic, fused psychedelic rock and dance music in the early seventies and exercised a huge influence on the next generation of rock musicians. According to guitarist John Frusciante, "The truest, heaviest metal is on early Funkadelic records." Clinton's style no doubt influenced the band's self-description as a "hardcore, bone-crunching, mayhem, psychedelic sex-funk band from heaven."

### Formed in L.A., Gained Cult Following

The band that would become the Red Hot Chili Peppers began in the early 1980s. Singer Anthony Kiedis and bassist Michael Balzary, who calls himself Flea, were classmates at Hollywood's Fairfax High School. Kiedis, a child of divorced parents, had moved from his mother's home in Michigan to live with his father, actor Blackie Dammett, in Los Angeles. Kiedis did some film acting in his teens, playing Sylvester Stallone's son in the 1978 movie *F.I.S.T.* Flea was born in Melbourne, Australia, and arrived in the United States in 1967, moving to L.A. in 1972. He was a trumpet prodigy in his childhood, but grew up to play bass for the punk band Fear. "I only had one bass lesson," he told *Guitar Player's* Joe Gore. "The teacher gave me an Eagles song . . . but I just wasn't into it, so I decided to figure things out on my own." Flea added that he played in a band with the Peppers' first two guitarists, Jack Sherman and Hillel Slovak. "Actually," he confided, "it was Hillel who taught me how to play bass."

The Peppers' earliest incarnation appeared at a Hollywood club in 1984. Kiedis and Flea joined up with

Slovak and drummer Jack Irons for an impromptu jam. The quartet called itself Tony Flow and the Miraculously Majestic Masters of Mayhem; when asked to return for a second performance, they adopted the name The Red Hot Chili Peppers, which Kiedis claims to have seen on "a psychedelic bush in the Hollywood Hills that had band names on it."

The band's debut for EMI, 1984's *The Red Hot Chili Peppers,* broadened the band's cult appeal. The record, according to *Interview's* Dimitri Ehrlich, "established the Peppers as prophets of a type of music whose time was about to come: not rock that you could dance to, but rock that you must dance to." In addition to rave-ups like "True Men Don't Kill Coyotes" and "Mommy Where's Daddy," the LP featured the first in a series of distinctive cover versions of classic songs, a funk-rap rendition of Hank Williams's country standard "Why Don't You Love Me." Neither Slovak nor Irons played on the first album, but Slovak returned for their 1985 follow-up *Freaky Styley,* produced by none other than the band's idol George Clinton. *Freaky* continued in the vein of the first album, featuring a cover of funk master Sly Stone's "If You Want Me to Stay" and emphasizing the band's lewd side a bit more with such numbers as "Sex Rap" and "Catholic School Girls Rule." In fact, the group's crowing about sex would get louder with each record, just as their onstage exhibitionism and aggressiveness with female fans would cause band members trouble.

Irons took over drum duties on the Peppers' next effort, 1987's *The Uplift Mofo Party Plan.* Though it yielded no hits, this record featured a number of solid funky originals and a rap version of folkrocker Bob Dylan's sixties hit "Subterranean Homesick Blues." The album also contained the group's most directly sexual—some would say very sexist—song so far, "Party on Your Pussy," the title of which did not appear on the record sleeve. The Red Hot Chili Peppers remained a cult band, and reviews like the following from *Stereo Review* didn't help: "I want to like an album as aggressively bad as 'The Uplift Mofo Party Plan.' But I just can't. The Red Hot Chili Peppers do everything in their power to chafe, outrage, and sicken, cranking out with truly dizzying energy a goulash of electrified funk, chest-thumping rap, and vaguely suggestive nonsense lyrics." The reviewer concluded that this was "an album that recreates the sensation of being seventeen and drunk on cheap wine." Whether the Peppers would consider this a negative sensation was unclear. The group released *The Abbey Road E.P.,* a mini-collection of earlier favorites, in 1988. The cover parodied the classic Abbey Road album by The Beatles, only the Peppers appeared dressed only in their tube socks. This record, too, failed to generate major sales.

## Guitarist's Death Changed Band's Course

In 1988 tragedy struck the band: Slovak died of a heroin overdose. Up until this point the band had been cavalier about its drug use, but Slovak's death changed everything. For a time it looked as if the band would fall apart completely. Irons was devastated by the loss of Slovak; he left and eventually joined the band Eleven. Kiedis and Flea decided to carry on. At first they recruited former Funkadelic guitarist Blackbyrd McKnight and drummer D. H. Peligro from the San Francisco punk band Dead Kennedys, but the chemistry didn't work. Finally Frusciante, a guitar player in his late teens influenced equally by funk and hard rock, left his band Thelonius Monster to play with the Peppers. The group auditioned a number of drummers, settling finally on Detroit native Chad Smith, whom Kiedis described in *Interview* as "a molten core of sheer power."

The new Red Hot Chili Peppers released the album *Mother's Milk* in 1989. The original songs were a mix of more serious tunes like "Knock Me Down," inspired by Slovak's death, and "Johnny Kick a Hole in the Sky," which continued the band's use of Native American themes, as well as straight-out sex songs like "Stone Cold Bush" and "Sexy Mexican Maid." The band broke through commercially, however, with its cover of funk and soul legend Stevie Wonder's "Higher Ground." The video began to appear regularly on MTV, and suddenly the band had the national visibility it had sought all along. The band scored again with the videos for "Knock Me Down" and "Taste the Pain," and *Mother's Milk* quickly reached half a million sales. *Guitar Player* remarked, "The current edition of Red Hot Chili Peppers may be the most intense yet."

In 1990 the band moved into a Hollywood Hills mansion to begin recording its next album. Its contract with EMI had run out, and Warner Bros. signed them. Producer Rick Rubin suggested the move to the mansion, and though the band claimed that the house had a few ghosts, they had no complaints. Flea had married and his wife Loesha and daughter Clara shared the mansion's festive atmosphere. The band wasn't free of controversy, however. Kiedis was convicted of exposing himself at a performance in 1989 and had to pay a substantial fine. In March, during an MTV broadcast, Flea and Smith grabbed a female fan and spanked her. They narrowly escaped prison sentences for battery, disorderly conduct, and solicitation to commit an unnatural act. Slovak's death had affected the band members' behavior in some ways, however; they swore off hard drugs and began to talk a lot about spiritual values in their music. "It's a matter of unity," Flea told *Guitar Player*, "of four guys listening to each other and playing together." According to Frusciante, "What this band is about is helping your brothers."

This new sense of unity found its way into the Peppers' 1991 release, *Blood Sugar Sex Magik*, which was written, recorded, and produced in their mansion. As Flea disclosed in a Warner Bros. press package, "The whole house was really just a big, warm, beautiful, peaceful place. Not for one minute did we feel any negative energy. Even living together, which could really create tension, turned out perfectly." The album catapulted them as close to mainstream as they have ever been, hitting music stores at the same time the Peppers kicked off an extensive United States tour. Suddenly, it was impossible to tune into alternative and even some classic rock radio stations without hearing the funky new hit "Give it Away" playing at least several times a day. With generally enthusiastic critical reaction and no less than passionate endorsement from fans—veteran and newly initiated—*Blood Sugar Sex Magik* has secured the Peppers' place in music's big time.

# Selected discography

The Red Hot Chili Peppers (contains "True Men Don't Kill Coyotes," "Mommy Where's Daddy," and "Why Don't You Love Me"), EMI, 1984.
Freaky Styley (contains "If You Want Me to Stay," "Sex Rap," and "Catholic School Girls Rule"), EMI, 1985.
The Uplift Mofo Party Plan (contains "Party on Your Pussy" and "Subterranean Homesick Blues"), EMI, 1987.
The Abbey Road E.P., EMI, 1988.
Mother's Milk (contains "Knock Me Down," "Johnny Kick a Hole in the Sky," "Stone Cold Bush," "Sexy Mexican Maid," "Higher Ground," and "Taste the Pain"), EMI, 1989.
Taste the Pain, EMI, 1989.
Blood Sugar Sex Magik (contains "Give It Away" and "Blood Sugar Sex Magik"), Warner Bros., 1991.

# Sources

Guitar Player, December 1989; April 1990.
Interview, August 1991.
People, April 16, 1990.
Rolling Stone, May 17, 1990.

*Spin*, October 1991.
*Stereo Review*, February 1988.

Additional information obtained from a Warner Bros. press release on *Blood Sugar Sex Magik*, 1991.

*—Simon Glickman*

# Django Reinhardt

**Jazz guitarist, composer**

The first European musical virtuoso to influence American jazz was Django Reinhardt, a French-speaking Belgian gypsy who had only two working fingers on his left hand. He is regarded as the jazz guitar's most dazzling soloist, most exciting improvisor, and most important innovator. Despite the fire injury at age 18 that crippled his fretting hand and challenged his very will to live, this extravagant, romantic, and illiterate genius went on to hasten the acceptance of the guitar as a popular solo instrument and to inspire musicians as varied as Yehudi Menuhin, Julian Bream, Les Paul, Barney Kessel, Chet Atkins, Joe Pass, and Carlos Santana.

Not only did Reinhardt become France's most famous jazz performer, but during World War II he also assumed the status of national hero by refusing large sums of money to perform for the Nazi occupiers. After the war, expecting to reap some of his reputation's benefits, he eagerly went to the United States to tour with the Duke Ellington Orchestra. Disappointed by his reception in America, he returned to France and spent

the remaining seven years of his life playing and recording with a variety of combos, fishing, playing billiards, and painting. He died unexpectedly of a stroke at the age of 43.

Born Jean Baptiste Reinhardt on January 23, 1910, this musical prodigy began his uncommon life in a gypsy *roulotte* (or caravan, a horse-drawn wagon) in the Belgian town of Liverchies, near the French border. A gypsy of the Manouche band, he is said to have possessed the gypsy's wandering impulse throughout his life, joining passing caravans while on tour, going off with various questionable "cousins" for meals or drinks instead of making gigs, and never really feeling comfortable unless he lived and traveled in a wagon. According to Rich Kienzle in *Great Guitarists,* Reinhardt most likely inherited his musical talent from his "probable father, Jean Ve'es," who was a comic and violinist. At the age of ten, Django (a gypsy dialect name meaning John, alternatively spelled "Jiango," or "Djengo," as on his gravestone) was given a banjo-guitar, which he practiced obsessively, becoming good enough by age 13 to perform as a sideman in low-level Parisian dance halls. Thereafter he was also playing violin and banjo, and within a few years he had recorded with a singer named Chabel.

### Sustained Serious Injuries in Caravan Fire

Reinhardt reportedly first heard American-style jazz in 1925 or 1926, and soon he had garnered such local attention that he was playing with the accordionist-bandleader Maurice Alexander in the Belleville section of Paris. In his 1961 biography *Django Reinhardt,* author Charles Delaunay indicated that by 1928 Reinhardt had been signed by English bandleader Jack Hylton to appear in London with his orchestra. Before he could meet that obligation, however, a disastrous fire struck the caravan in which he and his wife were living, leaving him seriously injured and threatening an end to his musical career.

Most of the accounts of this terrible accident follow Delaunay's description, but some sources differ in their description of Reinhardt's resulting physical impairments. Was it his left or right leg that a doctor wanted to amputate? Or was it his left arm below the elbow? Were his "two middle fingers seared together," as George Hoefer related in *Down Beat,* or is Art Wrightman's account, as told to *Down Beat* interviewer Dennis Hensley, more accurate? "His leg mended well enough for him to walk without a limp," Wrightman was quoted as saying, "but his left hand was extremely mutilated. His ring finger and pinky were permanently hooked, his skin was scarred, and his hand muscles were distorted." In any case, Reinhardt spent the next two years in relentless and courageous self-conducted therapy, and he taught himself a compensatory technique that allowed him once again to play the guitar. As Wrightman related: "Eventually, he was able to play certain ninth chords by hooking his little finger against the solo E string, but even that was rare. He was strictly a two-fingered player."

### Returned to European Jazz Circuit with Famed Quintet

With his brother Joseph, Reinhardt was playing again by 1930 in front of the cafes and in the courtyards of Paris, passing the hat for money. The pair then toured the south of France, encountering artist Emile Savitry, who introduced Reinhardt to recordings by Louis Armstrong, Duke Ellington, Joe Venuti, and American guitar player Eddie Lang. Back in Paris in late 1931, he met Stephane Grappelli, then a pianist with alto saxophonist Andre Ekyan's band. In the same year, the University Jazz Club was established in Paris, sponsored by Hugues Panassie, one of Europe's first jazz critics. Within a year this became the Hot Club of France. Between 1934 and 1939 the club would become world famous for presenting the Quintet of the Hot Club of France, the unique jazz group formed around Grappelli, playing the violin with elegance, and rough-hewn guitarist Reinhardt.

The mid-1930s saw the phenomenal growth of the quintet's quality and renown—and also of Reinhardt's individual artistry as both player and songwriter. During these pre-World War II years, the unlikely string quintet recorded swinging renditions of American pop and jazz standards like "Dinah," "Tiger Rag," "Lady Be Good," "Stardust," "St. Louis Blues," and dozens of others well known to traditional jazz and swing aficionados. But Reinhardt also showed creative genius and sensitivity to his mixed European roots in original compositions, some in collaboration with Grappelli, such as "Djangology," "Minor Swing," "Bricktop," "Swing 39," and the international hit "Nuages." In the latter years of the quintet's existence, he continued to compose in earnest while also recording often with several other European bands and visiting with American artists such as Benny Carter, Coleman Hawkins, Rex Stewart, Barney Bigard, and Billy Taylor. As in the United States, the years just before World War II in Europe produced a great flowering of happily popular jazz in the four-beat, swinging mode. For his efforts with this sizzling Quintet of the Hot Club of France, Django Reinhardt quickly became famous as the world's greatest jazz guitarist.

With Grappelli electing to live in England during the war, Reinhardt kept the quintet going in Vichy, France, by adapting it to available musicians. In addition to recording with a modified quintet, Reinhardt put together a number of big bands with French musicians, and in November of 1945, he recorded four sides with Django Reinhardt and His American Swing Band, made up of so-called American GIs newly arrived in liberated Paris. At about the same time, rampant and unsubstantiated rumors of Reinhardt's death gained such currency abroad that *Down Beat* actually printed an erroneous announcement that he had died. Delaunay and other writers have furnished anecdotal information about Reinhardt's adventures in occupied France during the early 1940s, including a bungled escape attempt to Switzerland that briefly put him into German custody and another attempt to flee during which he was turned back by the Swiss immigration officials because he was neither a Negro nor a Jew.

Reinhardt first enjoyed his postwar freedom and international fame in 1946 when Duke Ellington invited him to tour the United States with his orchestra. The tour was only mildly successful, the guitarist was less than thrilled, and the American jazz critics were scarcely impressed. Within two weeks of the tour's end, Reinhardt returned home disappointed with America, despite learning some bebop, trying out the electrically amplified guitar, and listening to Frank Sinatra.

From 1947 until 1953, Reinhardt led a somewhat reclusive life, performing irregularly, touring his cherished south of France only seldom, but recording plentifully with a revived Hot Club quintet. With three different clarinetists, and occasionally with Grappelli, these recordings were devoted predominantly to his original French-flavored songs (like "Babik," "Crepuscule," "Feerie,

Artillerie Lourde"), as well as his symphony from the war years, *Manoir de mes Reves*. In the first two months of 1949, he and Grappelli recorded 68 numbers in Rome—a session which, because of the modern Italian rhythm section and the soloists' brilliance, "made this far more than a trip down Memory Lane preserving prewar swing," according to Kienzle.

He continued experimenting in the bop style and with the amplified guitar (much to the discouragement of his older devotees), jammed with Dizzie Gillespie in February of 1953, and made his last commercial recording on April 8, 1953, with a progressive group consisting of vibes ("Fats" Lallemand), piano (Martial Solal), bass

---

*"If Django had wanted to stay in the United States and learn the language, I'm convinced he would have altered the course of the music itself."*
*—Barney Kessel*

---

(Pierre Michelot), and drums (Pierre Lemarchand). After returning from a strenuous Swiss tour in mid-May, he complained of headaches and numbness in his arms. Refusing to see a doctor, he collapsed from a severe stroke and died in a Fontainebleau hospital the next day.

### Achieved Legendary Status as Jazz Guitar Innovator

Reinhardt's innovations in guitar virtuosity included devices (some now common) like double-string picking, octave melodic voicing, flamenco-like "rumbling," and fiercely percussive chordal attacks. His trademark, however, is still not so common: bursts of extended melodic runs, astoundingly executed with just two fretting fingers. American guitarist Charlie Byrd, who played with Reinhardt in Paris while serving with the U.S. Army in 1945, described this facility for "scintillating passages of single notes," concluding in *Down Beat* that "it would take years of concentrated study" to imitate. In the same article, Barney Kessel, who was equally influenced by Reinhardt, cites the "intensity and emotion, the real *fire*" of his playing. "He was one of the real originals," Kessel proclaimed, adding, "If Django had wanted to stay in the United States and learn the language, I'm convinced he would have altered the course of the music itself."

---

What seems to astonish jazz fans and critics about Reinhardt's playing is its inventive range—a lyrical blend of European romanticism, classical regularity, gypsy nonchalance, and the forcefulness of jazz. Reinhardt's ear was infallible, according to virtually every musician who played with him. He is said to have been able to detect mistakes or intonation problems in individual instruments performing a symphony. His intuitive feeling for the guitar was unconstrained, and his technique was unsurpassed. Nobody playing the acoustic jazz guitar in the 1930s and 1940s could match his "biting attack and unremitting drive" and "the utterly fearless manner in which he positively leaps into his up-tempo solos," noted Stan Britt in *The Jazz Guitarists*. Reinhardt is credited as the only modern jazz guitarist—in any mode, at any tempo—to have produced improvisational figures of such constantly breathtaking inventiveness.

The variety and contradictions in Reinhardt's playing style complement the fluctuations in his personal life and behavior. He was notoriously unreliable, missing gigs or showing up hours late just because he happened to meet some old friends. At the same time, he is said to have been extremely sensitive, capable of being reduced to tears by the beauty of a piece of music or someone's playing. Perhaps it is true that he gradually tired of the impositions placed on him by his celebrity, as claimed by his longtime friend, critic Andre Hodeir. In his book *Toward Jazz*, Hodeir related that Reinhardt, "only a few weeks before his death, muttered: 'The guitar bores me.'"

Despite his premature death, Reinhardt succeeded in joining the ranks of the few indisputable giants of jazz: Armstrong, Ellington, Charlie Parker, and Art Tatum. Like them, he was a natural musician who overcame substantial obstacles to become a household name in the realm of musical artistry.

# Selected discography

*Django '35-'39*, GNP Crescendo Records, 1973.

*Django Reinhardt and Stephane Grappelli* (recorded in 1953), Vogue, 1990.
*The Quintet of the Hot Club of France* (recorded 1947-49), GNP Crescendo Records, 1991.
*Nuages* (recorded 1947-49), Vogue, 1991.
*Django Reinhardt & Le Quintet du Hot Club de France* (recorded 1934-37), EPM, 1991.
*Djangology*, RCA.
*Django Reinhardt* (three volumes), Everest Records, Archive of Jazz and Folk.
*First Recordings*, GNP Crescendo Records.
*Paris 1945*, Columbia.
*Parisian Swing*, GNP Crescendo Records.
*Django and His American Friends* (French), EMI Odeon CLP.
*Django: The Later Years*, La Roulette.

# Sources

### Books

Britt, Stan, *The Jazz Guitarists*, Blandford Press, 1984.
Collier, Graham, *Jazz*, Cambridge, 1975.
Delaunay, Charles, *Django Reinhardt*, Cassell, 1961.
Hodeir, Andre, *Toward Jazz*, Grove Press, 1962.
Kienzle, Rich, *Great Guitarists*, Facts on File, 1985.
Lyons, Leonard, and Don Perlo, *Jazz Portraits: The Lives and Music of the Jazz Masters*, Morrow, 1989.
Summerfield, Maurice J., *The Jazz Guitar: Its Evolution and Its Players*, Ashley Mark, 1978.
Zwerin, M., *La Tristesse de Saint Louis: Swing Under the Nazis*, [London], 1985.

### Periodicals

*Down Beat*, July 14, 1966; February 26, 1976.
*Jazz Journal*, Volume 24, Number 6, 1971.
*Newsweek*, November 18, 1946; May 25, 1953; August 21, 1972.
*New Yorker*, February 14, 1977.
*New York Times*, May 18, 1953.
*Saturday Review*, June 27, 1953.

—Peter W. Ferran

# The Replacements

**Rock and roll band**

The Replacements' combination of songcraft and rock and roll energy made them one of the most admired alternative bands of the 1980s. Though the 'Mats, as they are also known, started out as a scruffy Midwestern punk-pop outfit, they soon matured into a formidable presence on rock's cutting edge. Singer-songwriter Paul Westerberg's passionate lyrics and powerful tunes, combined with the band's onstage intensity and humor, attracted the praise of critics and the devotion of a diverse group of fans. Yet by the end of the 1980s, the Replacements faced growing doubts about their coherence as a band; the group's future seemed as unpredictable as their legendary live shows. Their 1990 album *All Shook Down,* though a smash with critics, did little to settle the matter.

The punk rock wave of the late seventies and early eighties, which began with American bands like the Ramones and such British groups as the Sex Pistols and the Clash, invigorated independent rock and roll on both sides of the Atlantic. As with any revival, certain cities played prominent roles in the new music scene.

## For the Record. . .

Band formed c. 1980 in Minneapolis, MN; members include **Paul Westerberg** (born c. 1961), guitar and vocals; **Tommy Stinson** (born c. 1967), bass and vocals; **Bob Stinson,** lead guitar and vocals (left band 1987); **Chris Mars,** drums; and **Slim Dunlap** (joined, 1987), lead guitar and vocals.

Performed in Minneapolis area in 1980-81, recorded first LP in 1981. Signed by Sire Records 1986. Single "I'll Be You" reached *Billboard* Top 100 Singles Chart.

**Addresses:** *Record company*—Sire Records, 75 Rockefeller Plaza, 20th Floor, New York, NY 10019-6979.

In England, for example, Manchester and Liverpool fostered a score of important postpunk bands. Among the towns with substantial music scenes in the United States were Athens, Georgia, which produced R.E.M., the B-52's, and others; Akron, Ohio, home of Chrissie Hynde of the Pretenders as well as Devo; and Minneapolis, Minnesota, which brought together Husker Du, Prince and the Revolution, and the Replacements. The excitement of the Minneapolis scene in the early 1980s fueled the success of Westerberg and his band. The Replacements began as a teenaged garage band featuring Westerberg, bassist Tommy Stinson, who was then 12 years old, Tommy's brother Bob on guitar, and drummer Chris Mars.

The band began opening for other punk bands and released its first record *Sorry Ma, Forgot to Take Out the Trash* for the Twin/Tone label in 1981. *Rolling Stone*'s Steve Pond called this debut effort and the 'Mats' 1982 EP *Stink* "fast and hard and mean, close to hardcore but a little too smart and sentimental." These early recordings were very much in the punk spirit, with slamming drums, basic guitar, and song titles like "I Hate Music" and "Gimme Noise." The band became notorious, however, as one of underground rock's most wildly unpredictable live acts. Group members were often drunk and peppered their sloppy renditions of original songs with campy cover versions of old country songs, heavy metal anthems, and TV themes. The country feel made its way into their 1983 LP, *Hootenanny.* While the band's overindulgence seemed to provide some inspiration and fun to their shows, it also led to serious problems. Bob Stinson's drinking in particular affected his performances, and Westerberg too had come to rely on alcohol. "I've been waking up for years looking in the mirror and thinking, 'I've got to put the bottle down,'" he recalled in a 1990 interview with *Musician*'s Bill Flanagan. "One day I looked in the mirror and said, 'If I was the bottle I'd put *me* down.'"

## The Band's Importance to Rock Became Clear

In 1984 the 'Mats released *Let it Be,* their most critically acclaimed independent album. Less of a punk record but still energetic and witty, the record made clear the Replacements' importance to the independent rock world. Steve Simmels of *Stereo Review* referred to *Let it Be* as "monumental." Westerberg noted in a 1989 *Rolling Stone* interview, "We had a big dose of attitude in the early days, and it's kinda hard to put attitude down on tape. But we tried for, like, three records. And kinda gave up the ghost on *Let it Be,* and let a little bit of music happen, too. And that was the right mixture." The mixture includes intense rockers like "We're Coming Out" and the furious "Seen Your Video," tongue-in-cheek tunes like "Tommy Gets His Tonsils Out" and a cover of "Black Diamond" by seventies rock idols Kiss, and such surprisingly tender songs as "Androgynous," a piano-and-vocal turn by Westerberg which shows the influence of sixties avant-rockers The Velvet Underground. *Let it Be* persuaded Sire Records to sign the Replacements. Twin/Tone's last 'Mats release was the 1984 live cassette *The Shit Hits the Fans,* which was actually a bootleg recording confiscated from a fan. The show immortalized on the tape was a raucous performance in Oklahoma that featured cover versions of Led Zeppelin tunes and R.E.M.'s "Radio Free Europe."

Longtime 'Mats fans worried that a contract with a major label would soften the band's sound, but their 1985 release *Tim* calmed most of those fears. Simmels referred to the album as "a flat-out stunner. It is the most passionately felt piece of music to have emanated from an American garage since . . . *Let it Be.*" High *Fidelity* called *Tim* "the richest, most complex record these American underdogs have made." And if the "mature songs" *High Fidelity* found on this effort suggested too much growing up, the band's video for the blistering single "Bastards of Young" was refreshingly adolescent: nothing but footage of a speaker in a teenager's room, throbbing to the song's relentless beat until the end, when a sneakered foot kicked it over. The video summed up much of the appeal of the band's attitude; their refusal to play the image-obsessed game of rock video looked like a genuine act of rebellion in the mid-eighties.

In the meantime, however, Bob Stinson's drinking and behavior were so out of control that the band decided to kick him out. They recorded their next LP, *Pleased to Meet Me,* as a trio. Though it didn't create as powerful an impression as *Tim,* it further showcased Westerberg's songwriting. The band toured in 1987 to support the album with new guitarist Slim Dunlap. As Ira Robbins noted in *Rolling Stone,* "Set lists rather than inebriated whimsy guided the band's performances." The band also contributed its version of "Cruella DeVille," from the film *101 Dalmatians,* to *Stay Awake,* the 1988 A&M compilation of songs from Walt Disney movies.

## Maturity and Uncertainty

The band's increased seriousness may have motivated Sire's decision to give a sincere promotional push to the group's 1989 album *Don't Tell a Soul.* The video for the single "I'll Be You," a song that suggests Westerberg's weariness of the punk rebel's role, appeared frequently on MTV and reached *Billboard's* Top 100 Singles chart. Though reviews of the album were mixed, the 'Mats had reached a new level of visibility on the rock scene, appearing on the covers of magazines as well as on TV screens. *People's* David Hiltbrand wrote that *"Don't Tell a Soul* is not as strong an album as its predecessor, *Pleased to Meet Me.* But for fans of the Replacements and of the rock and roll spirit, it's a treat." Robbins labeled *Don't Tell a Soul* "an audacious album that reclaims its valued independence by confounding audience expectations." Chuck Eddy of *High Fidelity* disagreed, calling the record "nondescript," and lacking in musical force and lyrical wit. Tommy Stinson remarked in a *Newsweek* interview, "We're gettin' older and our music is gettin' older. And our f—— ideas are gettin' older." This new "maturity" was bound to alienate some listeners, but the band and the label hoped to open the Replacements to a wider audience. Unfortunately, *Don't Tell a Soul* only sold around 300,000 copies.

The next album, *All Shook Down,* was originally intended as a Paul Westerberg solo album. Released in 1990, it featured a number of acoustic songs as well as musicians from outside the band. Rumors circulated through the music world that the band was about to break up, even as this new album garnered enthusiastic reviews and considerable prestige. Chris Mundy's review in *Rolling Stone* called *All Shook Down* "the record the Replacements should have made" to impress the critics who lined up to praise *Don't Tell a Soul.* Despite the quieter tone of the record, Mundy noted, "songs are now presented with a hushed urgency that demands immediate attention." Even with this and similar accolades, the band's future was as uncertain

as ever. Westerberg did a number of interviews in the unique position of promoting a band that might break up at any moment. Jeffrey Ressner reported in *Rolling Stone* that "the Replacements stand as a band on the verge. It could be the verge of success or it could be the verge of failure. More than anything else these days, it seems that the Replacements are teetering on the verge of a nervous breakdown."

Westerberg's uncertainty about the band's destination and his newfound "maturity" hadn't changed his views about singing and songwriting. Lauded by *Spin* as "the soul of rock 'n' roll," he remarked in an interview with the magazine, "To me, the soul of rock 'n' roll is mistakes. Mistakes and making mistakes work for you. . . . The people who shy away from change and mistakes and play it safe have no business playing rock 'n' roll."

# Selected discography

*Sorry Ma, Forgot to Take Out the Trash* (contains "I Hate Music"), Twin/Tone, 1981.
*Stink* (contains "Gimme Noise"), Twin/Tone, 1982.
*Hootenanny,* Twin/Tone, 1983.
*Let it Be* (contains "We're Coming Out," "Seen Your Video," "Tommy Gets His Tonsils Out," "Black Diamond," and "Androgynous"), Twin/Tone, 1984.
*The Shit Hits the Fans* (contains "Radio Free Europe"), Twin/Tone, 1984 (cassette only).
*Tim* (contains "Bastards of Young"), Sire, 1985.
*Please to Meet Me,* Sire, 1987.
*Don't Tell a Soul* (contains "I'll Be You"), Sire, 1989.
*All Shook Down,* Sire, 1990.

Contributors of "Cruella DeVille" to *Stay Awake,* A&M, 1988.

# Sources

*High Fidelity,* March 1986; May 1989.
*Musician,* December 1990.
*Newsweek,* June 19, 1989.
*People,* February 27, 1989.
*Rolling Stone,* February 9, 1989; June 1, 1989; December 14, 1989; October 4, 1990; October 18, 1990.
*Spin,* August 1991.
*Stereo Review,* February 1986.

—Simon Glickman

# Lee Ritenour

**Guitarist, songwriter**

Lee Ritenour "is a chopmeister from way back," penned Bill Milkowski in *Down Beat,* describing the versatile studio musician, producer, arranger, composer, and guitarist. "They don't call him Captain Fingers for nothing." An ace studio player in Los Angeles, Ritenour has provided guitar back-up for such artists as Sergio Mendes, Herbie Hancock, Peggy Lee, Carly Simon, Pink Floyd, Stevie Wonder, and Cher. His original fusing of Latin music, jazz, soul, and rock has produced albums that have crossed over several music charts regularly since Ritenour began his solo career in 1976. An innovator who brought state-of-the-art technology to the fusion movement, Captain Fingers is one of electric jazz's finest guitarists.

Ritenour was born January 11, 1952, in Los Angeles. Musically precocious, he began playing the guitar when he was five years old. At eight, his interest in the instrument went beyond the ordinary. "I'd study hit records and listen to the licks the studio guitarists were playing," Ritenour recalled to Robert Palmer in *Rolling Stone.* "'I can play that,' I'd say. What I didn't realize then—and a lot of young guitarists don't realize—is that the hard part is *inventing* the licks." His parents supported Lee, often finding him new and better instructors; at the age of 12, Ritenour was under the tutelage of Duke Miller, future head of the guitar department at the University of Southern California and purported at the time to be the finest guitar teacher in Los Angeles.

## Played in Studio Sessions at Age 18

As an adolescent, Ritenour played in his first group, the Esquires, a precursor of a series of teenage bands. He was only 15 years old when John Phillips, leader of the rock and roll group the Mamas and the Papas, heard one of his bands and then hired Ritenour to play in a studio session. Talented enough to be hired by studios at the age of 18, Ritenour instead made the choice to continue his education. He entered the University of Southern California, where he studied classical guitar with another musician first in his field, Christopher Parkening. Ritenour remained at the university for two and a half years, until he got the opportunity to play with Brazilian pop-jazz musician Sergio Mendes.

Touring with Mendes was Ritenour's introduction to Latin music and to prestigious musicians, including jazz pianist and producer Dave Grusin. Highly recommended on the studio circuit by Grusin and others, Ritenour was working 15 to 20 sessions a week in a lucrative business during the early seventies. "When I started working studio dates," Ritenour recounted to Palmer, "they asked me to sound like all the other guitar players. But I had some sort of spunk in me that made

## For the Record. . .

Born January 11, 1952 (one source says November 1, 1952), in Los Angeles, CA. *Education:* Attended University of Southern California.

Studio musician, electric guitarist, composer, arranger, and producer. Taught classical guitar at University of Southern California; toured with Sergio Mendes; provided back-up for major musicians, including Cher, Steely Dan, and Olivia Newton-John; made solo recording debut with album *First Course*, 1976. Played guitar with bands Friendship, late 1970s, and Fourplay, beginning in 1991.

**Addresses:** *Record company*—Rhino Records, 2225 Colorado Ave., Santa Monica, CA 90404.

me want to go beyond that. There's a lot of session players who always sound just like everyone else; it's real hard for a studio musician to find an identity. But I started reaching for mine, and eventually I found it.

### Nicknamed Captain Fingers

Three thousand sessions later, having backed such stars as George Benson, Steely Dan, Olivia Newton-John, and the Bee Gees, Ritenour earned the nickname Captain Fingers. His noteworthy output was profitable, but Ritenour grew fidgety. "I've always liked to keep moving," he admitted in *Down Beat*. "That's the most important thing for me. That's what keeps me fresh." In 1976 he made his solo debut with the album *First Cause* and experimented with group work. The make-up of his band Friendship—formed in the late 1970s—was transitory, but the guitarist continued working with highly successful studio session artists. "Ritenour is an especially distinctive musician," wrote Palmer in 1980, reviewing a Friendship performance. "He has one of the cleanest tones you'll ever hear from an electric guitar."

A commercial success, Ritenour has toured and recorded as a leader and a sideman beginning in the early 1970s. He moves easily back and forth between rock and jazz, incorporating his love for the Brazilian music he discovered while on tour with Sergio Mendes in 1974. Ritenour helped define the West Coast fusion sound with the 1977 release *Captain Fingers,* on which he introduced the guitar synthesizer. A pioneer in the use of synthaxes, computers, and controllers, he extolled music technology in *Down Beat:* "It's unbeliev-

able what's happening in the music world with the innovations in equipment. It's revolutionary, and there's a lot of great music being made on these devices."

### Released Successful Crossover Albums

In 1981 Ritenour's album titled *Rit* put him in the pop music spotlight and crossed over seven different music charts, including rhythm and blues, disco, adult contemporary, and jazz. And *Festival,* his highly successful 1988 LP, took the Number One position on seven music charts. The album, which featured outstanding Brazilian artists Joao Bosco and Caetano Veloso as well as various New York studio musicians, prompted David Hiltbrand in *People* to cite Ritenour as "the first among equals, smoothing and fusing." Phyl Garland in *Stereo Review* stated that "Ritenour's ever-impeccable technique applied to this superior material" makes the album "one of his best recorded efforts."

"I think there's a certain maturity level among some musicians that, maybe they feel the limitations of the contemporary thing a little bit," Ritenour mused to James Jones IV in a 1990 *Down Beat* interview, after the release of his straightlaced jazz album, *Stolen Moments.* "Maybe we need a breath of fresh air, a little bit of a break." Critics were caught off guard by the record, which lacks the technology and Brazilian influence prevalent on his previous albums. "Mouths are dropping" wrote Jones, but *Stereo Review* affirmed Ritenour's purpose: "This is real jazz, performed in a high style that knows no time frame." *Stolen Moments* reflects Ritenour's departure from the cloning process he sees beginning in fusion—the tendency of record labels to consistently market a repetitive type of album. Jim Ferguson in *Guitar Player* commended the musician for his originality: "Much more than a derivative rehashing of old styles, the album sparkles with the freshness of a player eager to try out new ideas in a freer setting."

Further extending his talents in the music industry, Ritenour joined keyboardist Bob James, drummer Harvey Mason, and Bassist Nathan East to form the pop-jazz group Fourplay in 1991. Their self-titled, debut album contains songs that *Entertainment Weekly* contributor Josef Woodward called "perfectly hummable" and "perfectly polished." Ever willing to take on new projects, Ritenour reflected in *Down Beat,* "There's really so much to learn aside from learning your instrument. . . . You really never stop learning, not if you're gonna last and have a good career."

## Selected discography

First Course, Epic, 1976.
Guitar Player, MCA Coral, 1976.
Gentle Thought, JVC, 1977.
Captain Fingers, Epic, 1977.
The Captain's Journey, Elektra, 1978.
(With Friendship) Friendship, Elektra, 1978.
Feel the Night, Elektra, 1979.
Rit (includes "Is It You"), Elektra, 1981.
Rit/2, Elektra, 1982.
Banded Together, Elektra, 1984.
Best of Lee Ritenour, Epic.
Portrait, GRP.
Color Rit, GRP.
Stolen Moments, GRP.
(With Fourplay) Fourplay, Warner Bros., 1991
(With Raul Julia) The Monkey People, Rhino, 1992.

### With Dave Grusin

Harlequin, GRP, 1985.

Festival, GRP, 1989.
Rio, Elektra/Musician.
On the Line, Elektra/Musician.
Earth Run, GRP.

## Sources

Down Beat, February 1982; March 1987; March 1988; May 1989; February 1990; May, 1990.
Entertainment Weekly, December 6, 1991.
Guitar Player, August 1990; September 1990.
People, November 21, 1988.
Rolling Stone, May 29, 1980; July 10, 1980.
Stereo Review, March 1989; July 1990.

—Marjorie Burgess

# Sonny Rollins

**Saxophonist, composer**

"**R**ollins played with a vivacity and amplitude so far beyond the ken of most musicians," wrote Gary Giddins in the *Village Voice* about tenor saxophonist Sonny Rollins's 1988 Town Hall concert, "that it might shame many into another line of work." Revered as a jazz master whose improvisational work has made him one of the most influential musicians in the genre, Rollins is a complex performer. He has remained popular over four decades, despite periodically dropping out of the jazz scene, and is often considered one of the greatest saxophonists in the music industry.

Rollins was born Theodore Walter Rollins on September 7, 1930, in New York City. "The year was 1930, but I had to put my age up when it came time to get working papers, so some of the books say 1929," Rollins explained to Bob Blumenthal in *Rolling Stone*. Located in Harlem, his family's first apartment was within walking distance of such popular jazz hangouts as the Savoy Ballroom and the Cotton Club. The young Rollins dreamed of visiting both night spots, but contented himself at the Apollo Theater. "I went down there at least once a week and caught practically everybody— Lionel Hampton, Fletcher Henderson, Duke Ellington, Count Basie," Rollins recounted to Blumenthal.

At home, Rollins's parents expected him to study piano like his sister, but the eight-year-old rebelled. He preferred the baseball field, where he acquired the nickname "Newk" because he idolized Brooklyn Dodgers pitcher Don Newcombe. Two years passed before Rollins, struck by the sight of a saxophone in its case, discovered his instrument. He began taking lessons on an alto while spending his time listening to Louis Jordan records.

### Jammed With Miles Davis

In the early 1940s, Rollins's family moved to a new neighborhood further uptown, which was home to numerous well-known musicians. Proximity to the post-World War II Harlem jazz world made introductions easy for Rollins and, entranced by the music of Charlie Parker and Coleman Hawkins, he bought his first tenor sax in 1946. In 1948 when he was 18 years old, Rollins began recording on the tenor sax with trombonist J. J. Johnson and vocalist Babs Gonzales. He soon made contact with pianists Bud Powell and Thelonious Monk, and trumpeter Miles Davis; in 1951 Davis asked Rollins to join his band.

Critical and popular acclaim came easily while Rollins jammed with Davis during the early 1950s, but the saxophonist's personal life was overshadowed by his addiction to heroin. Charlie Parker, his mentor at the time, urged Rollins to get away from drugs, which were prevalent among jazzmen. Rollins recalled to Blumenthal, "Charlie Parker told me I could be a great musician if I didn't mess around, and that stayed on my mind." In 1954 Rollins finally gave up his habit at a federal drug facility in Lexington, Kentucky. Parker, himself an addict, died without knowing about Rollins's recovery.

While continuing his work with Davis, Rollins joined the Clifford Brown-Max Roach quintet in 1955. Rollins's career soared with the group, which is considered one of the outstanding combos in the history of jazz. Landmark albums, including *Saxophone Colossus* and *Worktime,* appeared in 1956 and secured Rollins's standing as a premier saxophonist. *New Leader* contributor Bruce Cook had nothing but praise for Rollins's sound, which he felt "accelerated, if it did not start, the very healthy shift away from the 'cool school' of the West Coast that had come to dominate jazz." In 1957 Rollins left Roach and Davis to lead his own group after Clifford Brown and pianist Richie Powell were killed in an automobile accident.

### Embarked on Self-Exploratory Sabbaticals

Rollins subsequently entered an intensely productive period, during which he defined his own style as a leader by omitting the customary piano player. Forming trios with only tenor sax, bass, and drums, Rollins made three more landmark albums: *Way Out West* with Ray Brown and Shelley Manne and *A Night at the Village Vanguard* with Wilbur Ware and Elvin Jones appeared in 1957, and *Freedom Suite* with Oscar Pettiford and Roach followed in 1958.

Rollins quit performing in 1959 in order to practice his sax alone on a walkway over New York City's Williamsburg bridge. His "woodshedding" in Manhattan meant to other musicians that Rollins was taking time to turn inward in a solitary exploration of his craft. Writer Ralph Burton even penned a short story in 1961 entitled "Metronome," which was inspired by Rollins's romantic vigil. Rollins, however, called this and future exits from the music business "sabbaticals," explaining to Blumenthal, "I've always been about getting my own self together."

In 1961 Rollins reappeared on the jazz scene and was labeled by the *New Yorker* "the most influential practitioner on his instrument to come along since Lester Young and Coleman Hawkins." The hero of the hardbop school, Rollins experimented, making several albums with a young Jim Hall and using a piano anew, but his composing for the soundtrack to the 1966 film *Alfie* was his major success of the decade. In 1968 Rollins took another sabbatical—this time to India—after becoming disillusioned by a growing preoccupation with finances rather than quality in the recording industry.

### Incorporated the Sounds of Fusion

The appointment of his wife, Lucille, as his manager in the 1970s initiated Rollins's return to jazz at a time when less emphasis was on the player than on the instrument. In *New Leader* Bruce Cook described Rollins's sound as "an increasingly coarser and rougher tone," influenced by the variety possible with fusion. He applauded the saxophonist's push "further in a new direction" and increased use of electronics and rock, demonstrated in the 1978 album *Don't Stop the Carnival* and in the recordings of the 1980s. The artist, awarded a Guggenheim fellowship in 1972, told Blumenthal, "You have to change as you hear different sounds. . . . I like to think of myself as relating to all these things, not just as some guy who made great records in the Fifties."

In a *Down Beat* interview at the close of the 1980s, Gene Kalbacher designated Rollins "the world's greatest living improvisor," paying tribute to the musician's ability to take a tune like "There's No Business Like Show Business" and tenderize the unlikely song into a jazz vehicle. In 1986, *G-Man*—a compilation of the music Rollins mixed for Robert Mugge's movie *Saxo-*

phone Colossus—and *The Solo Album* won Rollins further praise, and the nearly 60-year-old saxophonist expressed to Kalbacher that he was ready for more risks.

Though critics' reactions to Rollins's albums of the late 1980s and early 1990s were mixed, the musician continues to stun fans with his live performances. *People* contributor David Grogan watched Rollins "nearly blow" Branford Marsalis off the Carnegie Hall stage at a live concert. And when Grogan reviewed the album *Falling in Love With Jazz,* he concluded, "No one is better than Rollins when it comes to transforming a familiar melody into an occasion for utter astonishment."

## Selected discography

*Sonny Rollins, Vol. 1,* Blue Note, 1956.
*More From the Vanguard,* Blue Note, 1957.
*Bass and Trio,* Verve, 1958.
*Tenor Titan,* Verve, 1958.
*What's New,* 1962.
*The Bridge,* RCA, 1962.
*Sonny Meets Hawk,* 1963.
*East Broadway Rundown,* Impulse, 1966.
(With Herbie Hancock and Coleman Hawkins) *All the Things You Are* (recorded 1963-64), Bluebird, 1990.
*The Way I Feel,* Milestone, 1976.
*Don't Ask,* Milestone, 1979.
*Love at First Sight,* Milestone, 1980.
*No Problem,* Milestone, 1981.
*Reel Life,* Milestone, 1982.
*Sunny Days, Starry Nights,* Milestone, 1984.
(With Horace Silver and Thelonious Monk) *Sonny Rollins, Vol. 2* (recorded mid-1950s), Blue Note, 1985.
*The Solo Album,* Milestone, 1985.
*Concerto for Saxophone and Orchestra,* 1986.
*On Impulse* (recorded 1965), reissue, MCA/Impulse, 1986.
*Alternate Takes* (recorded 1957), Contemporary, 1986.
*G-Man* (recorded 1986-87), Milestone, 1987.
*Plus Four* (recorded 1956), reissue, Fantasy/OJC, 1987.
*A Night at the Village Vanguard,* Blue Note, 1987.
*Next Album* (recorded 1972), Fantasy/OJC, 1988.
*Dancing in the Dark* (recorded 1987), Milestone, 1988.
*The Best of Sonny Rollins,* Blue Note, 1989.
*Quintet* (recorded 1957), Zeta, 1989.
*Don't Stop the Carnival* (recorded 1978) Milestone, 1989.
*East Broadway Rundown,* MCA, 1990.
*Falling in Love With Jazz,* Milestone, 1990.
*Here's to the People,* Milestone, 1991.

*Nucleus* (recorded 1975), Fantasy/OJC, 1991.
*On the Outside,* Bluebird, 1991.
(With Wynton Kelly, Doug Watkins, and Philly Joe Jones) *Newk's Time* (recorded 1958), Blue Note.
*Easy Living,* Milestone.
*The Essential Sonny Rollins on Riverside,* Riverside.
*Plays for Bird,* Fantasy/OJC.
*& the Contemporary Leaders,* Fantasy/OJC.
*Cutting Edge,* Fantasy/OJC.
*Live in Paris, 1963,* Magnetic.
*Scandinavian Concerts, 1965,* Magnetic.
*With Modern Jazz Quintet* (recorded 1951 and 1953), Fantasy/OJC.
*Vintage Sessions* (recorded 1951, 1953, and 1954), Prestige.
*Moving Out* (recorded 1954), Fantasy/OJC.
*Worktime* (recorded 1955), Fantasy/OJC.
*Tenor Madness* (recorded 1956), Fantasy/OJC.
*The Sound of Sonny* (recorded 1957), Fantasy/OJC.
*Tour de Force* (recorded 1957), Fantasy/OJC.
*Freedom Suite* (recorded 1958), Fantasy/OJC.
*Horn Culture* (recorded 1973), Fantasy/OJC.
(With Tommy Flanagan, Doug Watkins, and Max Roach) *Saxophone Colossus,* Fantasy/OJC.
*Sonny Boy,* Fantasy/OJC.
(With Ray Brown and Shelley Manne) *Way Out West,* Fantasy/OJC.
*Sonny Rollins Plays,* Fresh Sound.
*Taking Care of Business* (recorded 1956), Prestige.
*Great Moments With . . . ,* MCA.
*There Will Never Be Another You,* Impulse.
*Pure Gold,* RCA.
*Green Dolphin Street,* Quintessence.

## Sources

*Down Beat,* November 16, 1978; January 25, 1979; July 1988; June 1990; October 1990; July 1991.
*Harper's,* November 1962.
*High Fidelity,* April 1989.
*New Leader,* November 6, 1978.
*New Republic,* April 1, 1978.
*Newsweek,* December 4, 1961.
*New Yorker,* November 18, 1961; April 1, 1972.
*People,* April 30, 1990.
*Rolling Stone,* November 16, 1978; July 12, 1979; December 13, 1990.
*Saturday Review,* October 30, 1965.
*Stereo Review,* October 1990.

—*Marjorie Burgess*

# Roomful of Blues

**Blues band**

**S**ome people may look at Roomful of Blues, a nine-piece, stomping, swinging, low-down, bluesy big band, as just a nostalgia trip back to the 1940s. Then again, someone who knows better would say they're "the hottest white blues band I've ever heard." At least that's what Count Basie told *Down Beat* after Roomful opened for his orchestra at the Newport Jazz Festival. Since forming in 1967 the band has averaged well over 200 gigs per year, released eight albums (two of which were Grammy nominees), and backed up stellar artists like Big Joe Turner, Eddie Cleanhead Vinson, and Earl King.

During the psychedelic craze of the late 1960's, a Westerly, Rhode Island, youth named Duke Robillard was tucked away in his attic practicing guitar licks and digging blues based music. In 1967, fresh out of high school, Robillard formed a basic Chicago-style blues ensemble (guitar, bass, drum, piano and harp) with 16-year-old Al Copley and Fran Christina. The lineup soon dissolved, however, and Robillard moved to Providence to form the band Black Cat. That's when he heard a Buddy Johnson LP, *Rock 'N' Roll,* and decided

## For the Record...

Band formed in 1967 in Westerly, RI, by **Duke Robillard** (guitar and vocals); original members included **Fran Christina** (drums) and **Al Copley** (keyboards); dissolved in 1967; reformed in 1970 with the addition of **Doug James** (baritone sax), **Rich Lataille** (alto sax), and **Greg Piccolo** (tenor sax and vocals); **Preston Hubbard** (bass) joined band during the 1970s; **Ronnie Earl** (guitar) replaced Robillard and **Jimmy Wimpfheimer** (bass) replaced Hubbard, both in 1980; **Bob Enos** (trumpet), joined band in 1980; later additions to the band include **Porky Cohen** (trombone; retired, 1988), **Tony K** (guitar), **Ron Levy** (keyboards), **Rory McLeod** (bass), **Danny Motta** (trumpet), **Sugar Ray Norica** (vocals and harmonica), and **John Rossi** (drums). Current lineup includes Enos, James, Lataille, Norica, Piccolo, Rossi, **Junior Brantley** (piano and vocals), **Larry Peduzzi** (bass), **Carl Querfurth** (trombone), and **Chris Vachon** (guitar).

**Awards:** Grammy nominations for *Eddie Cleanhead Vinson and Roomful of Blues*, 1983, and for *Big Joe Turner with Roomful of Blues*, 1984.

**Addresses:** *Manager*—Bob Bell, 209 Lennox, Providence, RI 02907.

to switch gears. "Discovering big city, horn-based R & B completely changed my life," he told Frank Joseph in *Guitar Player,* "to me, it was something I could do realistically. I could make it work." Robillard figured he could pull off a Louis Jordan tune a lot easier than one by Muddy Waters.

Robillard moved back to Westerly and reformed Roomful of Blues with Rich Lataille, Doug James, and Greg Piccolo as the horn section in 1970. Piccolo described the transition to the *Detroit News:* "When I first joined, they had a sound between Chicago blues and a more horn-based sound. We were always changing, doing a different period of rhythm and blues. . . . We've been influenced by jazz, R & B, Chicago blues, New Orleans-style blues, Kansas City-style blues, classic blues. . . . If I was going to put a label on us, though, I'd say we are good dance music."

## Big Band Sound

The addition of horns was an excellent complement to the T-Bone Walker-Oscar Moore guitar sound that Robillard was now playing. He also turned the band on to the fashions of the era and soon they were dressing like the old jazzers. "We developed this sort of novelty image and sparked a fad in New England where people

would come to jitterbug to us," Robillard told *Guitar Player.* "And the fact that it's great music helped us along."

Roomful was developing a strong following on the East Coast when record producer and songwriter Doc Pomus secured them a record contract with Island Records in 1977. Their first album, *Roomful of Blues,* was released in 1978 and sounded as authentic as any original big band. The group headed south for a tour, including a stop in New Orleans that proved influential on their follow-up LP the next year, *Let's Have a Party.* Roomful recreated classic tunes authentically and added the spicy flavorings of the Crescent City.

## Personnel Changes

Some of the members' insistence on exclusively reproducing old songs led to the departure of Robillard and Hubbard shortly thereafter. Robillard moved on to Robert Gordon's group and then to the Legendary Blues Band before forming his own Pleasure Kings, which is currently playing original swing, rock, blues, rockabilly and R & B tunes. Hubbard joined the Fabulous Thunderbirds.

For Roomful's 1980 album, *Hot Little Mama,* guitarist Ronnie Earl, bassist Jimmy Wimpfheimer and trumpeter Bob Enos were recruited. Earl added a sharper guitar tone to the band with his Fender Stratocaster (as opposed to Robillard's mellower arch top sound), but the group retained their big band flavor nonetheless. Without Robillard though, the band was without their main vocalist. The problem was solved, however, according to Larry Birnbaum in *Down Beat:* "Roomful alleviates its chronic vocal shortcomings by platooning . . . singers, but the band's forte is still its precise and passionate ensemble playing."

## Earned Grammy Nominations

Piccolo handled vocal chores on 1984's *Dressed Up To Get Messed Up* in an effort to keep the band going. "We're almost an extinct animal," he told *Down Beat,* "there aren't too many real bands around." In 1983 Eddie Cleanhead Vinson recognized the band's potential and used them for his MUSE recording, which earned a Grammy nomination that year. "We just went in and did it with no planning at all," continued Piccolo. A year later another veteran bluesman, Big Joe Turner, followed Vinson's suit by recording yet another Grammy nominee with Roomful. Hubbard returned for the album, on which Turner "was really putting out," as Piccolo described to *Down Beat.* "He passed out at the end of the session."

1986 was a busy year for Roomful as they recorded *Glazed* with legendary New Orleans songwriter/guitarist Earl King, who produced some of his finest work to date with the band. Roomful also released a rousing live set, *Live at Lupo's*, which featured them in their most natural setting. "In live performance, even more so than on wax, Roomful captures the spirit of golden-age [R & B] with a fidelity seldom matched by modern reunions of first-generation players," wrote Larry Birnbaum in his (4.5 out of 5 stars) review in *Down Beat*.

Guitarist Ronnie Earl left to form his own band, the Broadcasters, and trombonist Porky Cohen, a veteran of Benny Goodman, Tommy Dorsey, and Artie Shaw units, retired in early 1988 at the age of 63. Unfortunately for their fans, Roomful has not been under contract since *Glazed* but has continued playing dates across the United States and in 1991 backed up Pat Benatar on her *True Love* album.

## Selected discography

*Roomful of Blues: The First Album*, Island, 1978; reissued, Varrick, 1988.

*Let's Have a Party*, Antilles, 1979.
*Hot Little Mama*, Blue Flame, 1980; reissued, Varrick, 1985.
*Dressed Up to Get Messed Up*, Varrick, 1984.
*Eddie Cleanhead Vinson and Roomful of Blues*, MUSE, 1983.
*Big Joe Turner with Roomful of Blues*, MUSE, 1984.
*Earl King with Roomful of Blues—Glazed*, Blacktop, 1986.
*Live at Lupo's Heartbreak Hotel*, Varrick, 1987.

Also served as backup band for Pat Benatar on *True Love*, Chrysalis, 1991.

## Sources

*Detroit News*, May 4, 1988; February 9, 1990.
*Down Beat*, March 1984; May 1987; November 1987; March, 1991.
*Guitar Player*, September 1984; April 1985; September 1988.
*Guitar World*, March 1989.
*Rolling Stone*, March 9, 1978; May 18, 1978.
*Stereo Review*, September 1991.

—*Calen D. Stone*

# John Scofield

## Jazz guitarist

"I have a couple of bags. The funk bag, the slow melodic bag, the jazz bag, the blues bag. . . . I think everybody has about three or four tunes in them—Beethoven included. And you just keep writing them over and over again, trying to get them right," jazz guitarist and composer John Scofield told Bill Milkowski in *Down Beat*. Tagged "post-modern" because his music blends together a variety of disparate influences, Scofield appeals both to the connoisseur and the ordinary jazz enthusiast: he won *Down Beat*'s International Critics Poll in 1986 and ranked third on the magazine's Reader's Poll the same year. Scofield's so-called jazz-rock fusion style combines the best of fusion, bebop, and the influences of legendary jazz trumpeter and composer Miles Davis. "Sco's distinctive sound and approach," praised Jim Ferguson in *Guitar Player,* "coupled with his expert talents as a composer, place him at the vanguard of contemporary jazz guitarists."

Born in Ohio on December 26, 1951, Scofield grew up in the suburb of Wilton, Connecticut. Although his parents had no special musical talents, young Scofield displayed an interest in the field at an early age. Having received his first guitar at the age of eleven, he is said to have stopped doing his homework for an entire year to concentrate on his music. His parents were concerned about his future but eventually yielded to his desire to pursue a career as a jazz guitarist. As Scofield revealed to Sam Freedman in *Down Beat,* he was enthralled by the time he was fifteen with the prospect of becoming a professional musician: "There was something at first about the image of New York being this great, cosmopolitan place, and jazz being the sound of New York, but all that romanticism got replaced really early by just a love for the music—abstractly, not connecting the music with any culture or groove. It was just the sound, the sound."

### An Unlikely Jazzman

"The music of my people—who knows what that is?" replied Scofield to Howard Mandel in *Down Beat* when questioned about his unlikely jazz origins. "The Connecticut Sound's not a big part of my thing." Throughout his career, Scofield has had to answer for a less than traditional musical background. Defending his early instruction, he explained to Mandel, "I learned from records and the radio and the few live bands and musicians I met. . . . And that's the background of everybody I know, whether they're from the ghetto or wherever. They learned from the media, and the few good musicians they'd meet."

In the early 1970s Scofield spent three years taking

classes at the Berklee School of Music in Boston. While frequenting some jazz clubs in the area, he met a highly respected local guitarist, Mick Goodrick, who became his mentor. When Goodrick, who often worked as a sideman, withdrew from a show at Carnegie Hall reuniting Gerry Mulligan and Chet Baker in 1974, he recommended Scofield to replace him. After the concert, which was recorded on two albums, Scofield was asked to join the Billy Cobham/George Duke fusion band. Though he played with the band for two years, Scofield was uncomfortable as the guitar hero of the fusion movement. "Billy's band was really hot when I got the call," he told Milkowski, "so all of the sudden I started getting national exposure. And all this time, ironically, I was trying to learn how to play bebop." Scofield left the band in 1977 to perform on the sideman circuit with distinguished jazz artists Charles Mingus and Jay McShann, among others.

The next year Scofield joined Gary Burton and then formed a band with drummer Adam Nussbaum and bassist Steve Swallow, each of whom played bebop in the mode of Jim Hall. In the era that followed, the group's albums *Bar Talk, Shinola,* and *Out Like A Light* debuted to critical success, but they lacked popular acceptance in the United States. Around the same time, Scofield also played in the Dave Liebman quintet. But he found his largest audience in Europe in the early 1980s.

## Big Break with Miles Davis Band

Scofield recorded *Solar,* a duet of standard bop with John Abercrombie, in 1982. The limited success of the album fueled Scofield's doubts about the breadth of his marketability: "It is possible to play this music for audiences that are not incredibly sophisticated. But let's face it, it's a connoisseur's music," he told Freedman. After resigning himself to a limited popular appeal, Scofield soon found himself in an advantageous position: he was asked to join the legendary Miles Davis band.

"My public persona expanded 100%," Scofield told Ferguson in *Guitar Player,* summarizing his work from 1983-1985 with Davis's band. "I can't remember the first time I ever heard of Miles," he related to Milkowski. "It seems I've been listening to him ever since I could think." The aspiring artist was also interested in joining the ranks of such noted musicians as John McLaughlin, Ron Carter, Keith Jarrett, Herbie Hancock, and Chick Corea—all of whom worked with Davis's band at some point in their careers. With *You're Under Arrest* and *Star People* under Davis, Scofield made contributions to the group as performer and co-composer, but the album *Decoy* established Scofield as an electric guitarist of unparalleled distinction. "Scofield grabs Most Valuable Player honors on that album," commented Milkowski in *Down Beat.*

## Gained Solo Success

Feeling he should leave Davis's band while audiences still remembered the success of *Decoy,* the 35-year-old guitarist began to do solo work and concentrate on his own group in 1986. That same year, Scofield won top honors in *Down Beat*'s International Critics Poll and third place in the magazine's Readers Poll. His 1985 release *Still Warm,* featuring a new group composed of drummer Omar Hakim, bassist Daryl Jones, and keyboardist Don Grolnick, presented a more muscular, rhythmic sound than his work with the Davis Band. With the album *Blue Matter* in 1986, Scofield led one of his most successful partnerships, uniting drummer Dennis Chambers and bassist Gary Grainger. The group recorded several additional albums together, including the live from Japan release *Pick Hits.*

Throughout his career, critics have lauded Scofield's play and compositions. "One quality that has always come out in his playing, no matter what context— fusion, bop, Miles, or his post-Miles solo career—is an authentic feeling for the blues," wrote Milkowski. "And he's evolving a distinctive voice as a composer as well." Critic Mandel concurred: "His band may be an ensemble of several years' accomplishment, a trio he called together, or a spur-of-the-moment collaboration. Scofield's music is by turns piercing, lyrical, reckless, thoughtful—depending on his mood, the response of his colleagues and audience. When he's hot—and he has a true professional's consistency—he shoots off steely, far-from-predictable lines with natural, funky rhythm. . . . Scofield can rock a house with altered Tin Pan melodies, post-bop harmonies, and what-the-hell spirit."

Critics frequently question Scofield's tendency to abandon a musical group or style at the height of its success. When questioned by Mandel about the contradiction of moving from fusion to blues to other interests, Scofield admitted a need for novelty, concluding, "I don't know if I'm going to do anything new in my life but I would like to . . . because all the stuff that I admire is new and different."

## Selected discography

*Live*, Enja/Inner City, 1977.
*Rough House*, Enja/Inner City, 1978.
*Shinola*, Enja, 1982.
*Still Warm*, Gramavision, 1985.
*Blue Matter*, Gramavision, 1986.
*Loud Jazz*, Gramavision, 1987.
*Pick Hits*, Gramavision, 1987.
*Flat Out*, Gramavision, 1989.
*Slo Sco*, Gramavision, 1990.
*Time on My Hands*, Blue Note, 1990.
*Meant to Be*, Blue Note, 1991.
*Grace Under Pressure*, Blue Note, 1992.
*Who's Who*, Arista/Novus.
*Bar Talk*, Arista/Novus.

*Out Like a Light*, Enja.
*Electric Outlet*, Gramavision.

**Other**

(With John Abercrombie) *Solar*, Palo Alto, 1982.
(With Miles Davis) *Decoy*, Columbia, 1984.
(With Ray Anderson) *Blues Bred in the Bone*, Gramavision.
(With Paul Bley) *The Paul Bley Group*, Soul Note.
(With Gary Burton) *Times Like These*, GRP.
(With Billy Cobham) *Funky Thide of Sings*, Atlantic.
(With Cobham) *Life and Times*, Atlantic.
(With Cobham/Duke Band) *Live on Tour in Europe*, Atlantic.
(With Davis) *Star People*, Columbia.
(With Davis) *You're Under Arrest*, Columbia.
(With Davis) *Siesta*, Warner Bros.
(With Marc Johnson) *Bass Desires*, ECM.
(With Johnson) *Second Sight*, ECM.
(With Dave Liebman) *If They Only Knew*, Impulse.
(With Jay McShann) *Big Apple Bash*, Atlantic.
(With McShann) *Last of the Blue Devils*, Atlantic.
(With Charles Mingus) *3 or 4 Shades of Blues*, Atlantic.
(With Missing Links) *Missing Links*, MCA.
(With Don Pullen and George Adams) *Live at Montmartre*, Timeless.
(With Bennie Wallace) *Twilight Time*, Blue Note.
(With Wallace) *Sweeping Through the City*, Enja.
(With Wallace) *Bordertown*, Blue Note.

## Sources

Down Beat, September 1982; January 1987; March 1989; August 1989; December 1989.
Guitar Player, September 1984; June 1987; July 1988; January 1992.

—Marjorie Burgess

# Russell Simmons

**Record company executive, producer, music promoter**

**T**he explosive entry of rap music onto the national music scene in the late 1980s was greatly due to the efforts and vision of rap record producer and artist manager Russell Simmons. Co-owner and founder of the rap label Def Jam Records and head of Rush Artist Management—producer of top-selling rap acts Run-DMC, Public Enemy, and L. L. Cool J, among others—Simmons took "rap music, an often misunderstood expression of inner-city youth, and . . . established it as one of the most influential forms of Black music," explained Nelson George in *Essence.* Often deemed by the media as the "impresario" and "mogul" of rap, Simmons began as a fledgling promoter of a new breed of street music, and today, as chairman of New York City's RUSH Communications, is at the helm of a multimillion-dollar entertainment company—complete with its own film and television division—that is the largest black-owned music business in the United States.

Some have described Simmons as the "Berry Gordy of his time," referring to the man who brought the polished, crossover, black Motown sound to mainstream America in the 1960s, yet Simmons's approach is fundamentally different. According to Maura Sheehy in *Manhattan, Inc.,* "Like Gordy, Simmons is building a large, diverse organization into a black entertainment company, only Simmons's motivating impulse is to make his characters as 'black' as possible," where Gordy sought to attract white listeners with his relatively colorless "Motown Sound." Also commenting on comparisons between Simmons and Gordy, *Black Enterprise* contended that Simmons is far more aggressive than Gordy. In all, Simmons runs a total of eight record labels, is developing a slew of feature films, and is creating several television programs for cable service Home Box Office and syndicated release.

### The Rapper Next Door

Simmons is insistent on presenting rap images that are true to the tough urban streets from which rap arose; as a result, his groups don such recognizable street garb as black leather clothes, expensive high-top sneakers, and gold chains. He explained his objectives to Stephen Holden in the *New York Times:* "In black America, your neighbor is much more likely to be someone like L. L. Cool J or Oran 'Juice' Jones than Bill Cosby. . . . A lot of the black stars being developed by record companies have images that are so untouchable that kids just don't relate to them. Our acts are people with strong, colorful images that urban kids already know, because they live next door to them."

Simmons was born in Hollis and grew up in a middle-

## For the Record. . .

**B**orn c. 1957; raised in Queens, NY; father's name, Daniel Simmons (a public-school attendance supervisor). *Education:* Attended City College of New York.

Co-founder, and owner of Def Jam Records, 1985—; owner of Rush Artist Management; chairman of RUSH Communications. Production associate for rap films *Krush Groove,* 1985, and *Tougher Than Leather,* 1988. Director of music videos.

**Addresses:** *Home*—New York, NY. *Office*—Def Jam Records, 652 Broadway, New York, NY 10012.

class neighborhood, both in the New York City borough of Queens, and as a youth was himself involved with a street gang. It was in the mid-1970s, while enrolled at the Harlem branch of the City College of New York—studying sociology—that Simmons became aware of rap music and its appeal to young inner-city blacks; he saw rappers as they would converge in parks and on street corners, and then take turns singing rap songs to gathering crowds.

*Manhattan, Inc.*'s Sheehy depicted the exchange between rappers and their audience in those beginning days of rap: "Rappers, called MCs (emcees) then, told stories and boasted—about street life, tenements, violence, and drugs; about their male prowess, their talents; about 'sucker MCs'; and about women. Their raps romanticized the dangerous, exciting characters of the street, sanctified its lessons into wisdom, made poverty and powerlessness into strength by making rappers superhuman, indomitable. The audience followed, finding their power in dancing and dressing styles of the moment; in mimicking the swaggering, tougher-than-leather attitude; and by worshiping their street 'poets.'"

### Spotted Huge Untapped Market

Simmons saw in rap enthusiasts a vast audience untapped by the recording industry. He left his college studies and began tirelessly promoting local rap artists, producing recordings on shoestring budgets, and conducting "rap nights" at dance clubs in Queens and Harlem. In 1984 he joined fellow aspiring rap producer Rick Rubin to form Def Jam Records; Def Jam caught the attention of CBS Records, which agreed to distribute the label. Within three years Def Jam albums like the Beastie Boys' *Licensed to Ill,* L. L. Cool J.'s *Bigger and Deffer,* and Run-DMC's *Raising Hell* dominated the black music charts.

Throughout, Simmons has been the manager of all Def Jam acts and has emphasized authenticity with each group. "Our artists are people you can relate to," he told Fayette Hickox in *Interview.* "Michael Jackson is great for what he is—but you don't know anybody like that. The closest Run-DMC comes to a costume is a black leather outfit. . . . It's important to look like your audience. If it's real, don't change it." Some critics, however, find the "authenticity" of rappers disturbing. "It is the look of many rap artists—hard, belligerent, unassimilated, one they share with their core audience—that puts many folks on edge," noted George in *Essence.* The group Public Enemy, which represents itself with a logo of a black teen in the scope of a police gun, is representative, as Simmons told George, of how many black teenagers feel—like "targets that are looked down upon." Simmons added: "Rush Management identifies with them. That's why we don't have one group that doesn't look like its audience."

### Rap an Expression of Attitudes

The lyrics and antics of some male rap artists have also infuriated women's groups, who find woman-hating messages in many of their songs and stage acts; public officials have even brought charges of lewdness against rappers in concert. Simmons distances himself from censoring the content of his rap groups' songs, telling George that "rap is an expression of the attitudes of the performers and their audience." He does, however, ultimately uphold rappers as positive role models for many black youths.

As an example of the affirmative position rappers can take, Simmons commented to Holden that the members of Run-DMC, which include Simmons's younger brother, Joseph, "are more than musicians. . . . They're from a particular community, and have succeeded on their own terms without any compromise. . . . If you take a look at the pop cultural landscape or the black political landscape now, there aren't a lot of heroes. If you're a 15-year-old black male in high school and look around, you wonder what you can do with your life. How do you better yourself? Run-DMC has opened up a whole new avenue of ambition. You can grow up to be like Run-DMC. It's possible."

## Sources

### Books

George, Nelson, *The Death of Rhythm and Blues,* Pantheon, 1988.

## Periodicals

*Black Enterprise,* December 1991.
*Essence,* March 1988.
*Interview,* September 1987; September 1991.
*Jet,* May 28, 1990.
*Manhattan, Inc.,* February 1990.
*New York Times,* August, 1987; February 20, 1991.

—*Michael E. Mueller*

# Isaac Stern

**Violinist**

Isaac Stern has triumphed not only as one of the premiere violin virtuosos of the twentieth century, but also as a leading political force in the world of music. Stern's trademarks as a violinist, according to *The International Cyclopedia of Music and Musicians,* are "a beautiful, incandescent tone" and a playing style that "is notable for its intensity and power." An active concert and recording artist throughout his career, Stern has received numerous Grammy Awards and was designated by CBS Masterworks Records in 1984 as its first "artist laureate." But Stern is equally well known for his tireless efforts on behalf of musical causes. He has been a leading recruiter of new musical talent, an ambassador bringing his artistry to countries around the world, and the driving force behind saving New York City's venerable Carnegie Hall from the wrecker's ball in the early 1960s. In 1975 Stern received the first-ever Albert Schweitzer Award, bestowed for "a life's work dedicated to music and devoted to humanity."

Born in the Soviet Ukraine in 1920, the son of music-loving parents, Stern was brought to the United States as an infant and was raised in San Francisco. He began playing the piano when he was six years old and took up the violin two years later. As a teenager he studied at the San Francisco Conservatory of Music and became a student of violinist Naoum Blinder. Stern also studied chamber music with musicians of the San Francisco Symphony Orchestra and, at the age of 15, made his concert debut with the orchestra, performing the Bach Double Concerto with Blinder. Stern's early music teachers provided guidance, yet allowed him to develop largely on his own—a crucial ingredient to his becoming a musician among musicians. "I studied with Blinder until I was seventeen, and after that I never studied with anyone—I was responsible for my own mistakes," Stern told Simon Collins in *Strad.* "It is a process of intellectual and personal involvement with music as an idea and a way of life, *not* as a profession or career, but a rapport with people who think and feel and care about something—you have to find your own way of thinking, feeling and caring."

### Glory at Carnegie Hall

Stern made his New York City debut in 1937 at the age of 17, by which time he was heralded as a musician of great promise. He then returned to California and undertook an arduous apprenticeship, studying fervently and performing concerts whenever possible. His debut at Carnegie Hall five years later demonstrated the development of his talents. Hailed as "one of the world's master fiddle players," by one New York critic, Stern's

Carnegie Hall success launched a career over the course of which he would become one of the violin's foremost maestros.

With his accompanist, Alexander Zakin, Stern was a frequent concert performer during the 1940s and in 1945 began what would become a prolific recording tenure with CBS Records. By the 1950s he was widely held as one of the great violinists of his time and began performing extensively overseas, including a 1956 tour of the Soviet Union—the first American musician allowed to do so. In addition to his solo pursuits, Stern was a member of the highly regarded Istomin-Rose-Stern Trio from 1962 to 1983. The violinist's career, which has spanned seven decades, has been marked by remarkable breadth; he has performed nearly every major work for the violin—both classical and contemporary—and has played with practically every major orchestra in the world, under most of the leading conductors.

## Impeccable Musicianship

Many critics feel that Stern's foremost quality as a violinist is his musicianship—the way in which his understanding of composition results in a particularly masterful and balanced interpretation. Wrote Margaret Campbell in *The Great Violinists,* "Stern can relate his own phrasing and style to the orchestral requirements, and . . . is aware of the structure of the music and instinctively feels the harmonies underlying every phrase." Similarly, critic Peter G. Davis praised Stern's "stylistic flexibility" in the *New York Times Magazine.* According to Davis, he "invariably seems to perceive all music from the inside with an instinctual sense of what is right in terms of tone, gesture and expression—a treasurable gift." And of Stern's colleagues, violinist Itzhak Perlman told Annalyn Swan in *Newsweek* that Stern, "unlike many violinists, . . . never gets lost in mannerisms. He plays like a musician instead of like a virtuoso." Stern confirmed these testimonials when he commented to Swan on his feelings about the continuity of performer and composition: "No line, no phrase . . . lives alone. Everything is coming from somewhere and going somewhere else. There is a natural rise and fall, like with the human voice. You must never lose the direction of the music."

Stern's role as musical activist came to the fore in 1960 when he successfully led a drive to preserve Carnegie Hall, the historic New York City performance venue. The landmark threatened with demolition, Stern formed and led the Committee to Save Carnegie Hall, which, through fundraisers, awareness campaigns, and meetings with government officials, was able to amass the financial and public support necessary to save the hall. Stern went on to serve for over two decades as president of Carnegie Hall, an advantageous position from which to conduct another sideline: developing new musical talent. Among Stern's protegees have been violinists Perlman, Pinchas Zukerman, Miriam Fried, Shlomo Mintz, Gergiu Luca, and cellist Yo-Yo Ma. Stern remarked to *New York Times Magazine* contributor Stephen E. Rubin of his role as a powerbroker in the music world: "I didn't make power; I was granted power, as any person who is successful in public life is granted it. What do you do? Just sit back and say, 'Look at me now?' You have to give some of it back. You can't just *take* all the time; it's simply not right."

## Ties With Israel

Throughout his career Stern has also been active as a musical ambassador. In addition to his groundbreaking Soviet Union trip, he visited mainland China in 1979 by invitation from the Communist government. Stern toured the musically isolated country giving lectures, conducting master classes, and searching for new talent. His trip became the basis for the 1980 documentary film *From Mao to Mozart: Isaac Stern in China,* which won an Academy Award for best short subject. Stern's greatest foreign ties, however, are with Israel. Christopher Porterfield wrote in *Time* that Stern "serves as a sort of patriarch of Israeli musical life." In 1964 Stern became chairman of the American-Israel Cultural Foundation, which subsidizes Israeli musicians, and in 1973 he founded the Jerusalem Music Academy, where Israeli musicians play and study with some of the world's leading performers. Not surprisingly, Stern has been a frequent performer in Israel throughout his career.

During a February, 1991, concert in Jerusalem, while the Persian Gulf War ravaged the Middle East, Stern's performance was interrupted by air-raid sirens warning of an Iraqi Scud-missile attack. The 800-member audience put on gas masks and the orchestra left the stage; Stern, however, returned moments later without his mask and played a Bach piece to settle the crowd. "I was so moved, looking out over that sea of masks. It was surreal," Stern told *People.* "The gas mask is temporary, but the music I was playing will go on. That's the only reason one does this." Echoing this response, Boris Schwarz wrote in *Great Masters of the Violin:* "Stern's distinctive playing style reflects his vibrant personality—a total involvement in music and intense communication with his audience. He uses his virtuoso command of the instrument only in the service of music, never for technical display." Schwarz went on to report that Stern lives by the motto "To use the violin to make music, never to use music just to play the violin," and concluded that "he never plays 'down' to his audience, nor does he have to: those who come to listen to Stern expect the best music interpreted in the best style."

# Selected discography

Bach, Johann Sebastian: *Concerto for Violin and String Orchestra, S. 1041, A Minor,* CBS Masterworks, 1967.
Bach and Antonio Vivaldi: *Concerto in D Minor for 2 Violins and String Orchestra; Concerto in C Minor for Oboe, Violin, and Orchestra* (Bach); *Concerto in A Minor for 2 Violins and Orchestra* (Vivaldi), CBS Masterworks, 1982.
Bach: *Sonatas of J. S. Bach and Sons,* CBS Masterworks, 1983.
Bach: *Trio Sonatas,* CBS Masterworks, 1983.
Barber, Samuel: *Concerto for Violin and Orchestra,* Columbia, 1965.
Bartok, Bela, *Concerto for Violin,* CBS Masterworks, 1962.
Bartok: *Concerto for Violin and Orchestra; Rhapsody No. 1; Rhapsody No. 2,* CBS Masterworks, 1962.

Bartok and Alban Berg: *Two Rhapsodies for Violin and Orchestra* (Bartok); *Concerto for Violin and Orchestra* (Berg), CBS Masterworks, 1962.
Bartok: *Sonata No. 1 for Violin and Piano,* Odyssey, 1978.
Beethoven, Ludwig van: *The Complete Piano Trios,* CBS Masterworks, 1960.
Beethoven: *Trio for Piano, Violin, and Cello, No. 6 in B-Flat Major,* Columbia, 1966.
Beethoven: *Concerto for Violin and Orchestra, Op. 61, D Major; Concerto for Violin and Orchestra, Op. 26, G minor,* CBS Masterworks, 1967.
Beethoven: *Sonata No. 7 in C Minor for Violin and Piano,* Odyssey, 1979.
Beethoven and Kreutzer: *Sonata No. 9 in A Major for Violin and Piano* (Beethoven); *Sonata No. 5 in F Major for Violin and Piano* (Kreutzer), CBS Masterworks, 1984.
Beethoven: *The Complete Sonatas for Violin and Piano,* CBS Masterworks, 1985.
Berg, Alban: *Kammerkonzert—For Piano and Violin with 13 Wind Instruments; Concert for Violin and Orchestra; To the Memory of an Angel,* CBS Masterworks, 1986.
Bernstein, Leonard: *Serenade for Violin Solo, Strings, and Percussion,* Odyssey, 1978.
Bloch, Ernest: *Baal Shem—Three Pictures of Chassidic Life; Sonata No. 1 for Violin and Piano,* Columbia, 1965.
Bock, Jerry: *Fiddler on the Roof* (selections), Liberty, 1971.
Brahms, Johannes: *The Trios for Piano, Violin, and Cello,* CBS Masterworks, 1967.
Brahms: *Brahms Violin Concerto,* Columbia, 1972.
Brahms: *Isaac Stern Plays Brahms,* Columbia, 1973.
Brahms: *Double Concerto in A Minor for Violin and Cello,* Odyssey, 1977.
Brahms: *Double Concerto, Op. 102; Piano Quartet,* CBS Masterworks, 1988.
Bruch, Max: *Concerto No. 1 in G Minor for Violin and Orchestra,* Columbia, 1967.
*The Classic Melodies of Japan,* CBS Masterworks, 1978.
*The Concert of the Century,* Columbia, 1976.
Copland, Aaron: *Copland Performs and Conducts Copland,* Columbia, 1974.
Debussy, Claude: *Sonata in G Minor for Violin and Piano,* Columbia, 1960.
Dutilleux, Henri, and Sir Peter Maxwell Davies: *L'arbre des songes; concerto pour violon et orchestre* (Dutilleux); *Concerto for Violin and Orchestra* (Davies), CBS Masterworks, 1987.
Dvorak, Antonin: *Concerto in A Minor for Violin and Orchestra; Romance,* Columbia, 1966.
Frank, Cesar: *Sonata in A Major for Violin and Piano,* Odyssey, 1979.
*The Great Violin Concertos,* CBS Masterworks, 1986.
*Greatest Hits: The Violin,* Columbia, 1972.
Haydn, Joseph: *"London" Trio No. 2 in G Minor; "London" Trio No. 3 in G Major; Divertissement No. 2 in G Major; Divertissement No. 6 in D Major; "London" Trio No. 4 in G Major,* CBS Masterworks, 1982.

Hindemith, Paul: *Concerto for Violin and Orchestra*, Columbia, 1965.

Hindemith: *Sonata for Violin and Piano*, Odyssey, 1979.

*Isaac Stern Plays Saint-Saens, Chausson, Faure*, Columbia, 1976.

*Isaac Stern 60th Anniversary Celebration*, CBS Masterworks, 1981.

Lalo, Edouard Victor Antoine: *Symphonie espagnole*, Columbia, 1976.

Mendelssohn, Felix, and Pyotr Ilich Tchaikovsky: *Concerto in E Minor for Violin and Orchestra* (Mendelssohn); *Concerto in D Major for Violin and Orchestra* (Tchaikovsky), CBS Great Performances, 1981.

Mendelssohn: *Trio No. 1 in D Minor; Trio No. 2 in C Minor*, CBS Masterworks, 1981.

Mozart, Wolfgang Amadeus: *Concerto No. 1 in B-Flat Major for Violin and Orchestra; Concerto No. 5 in A Major for Violin and Orchestra (Turkish)*, Columbia, 1964.

Mozart: *Concerto No. 3 in G Major for Violin and Orchestra; Sinfonia Concertante in E-Flat Major for Violin, Viola, and Orchestra*, CBS Masterworks, 1968.

Mozart: *The Mozart Flute Quartets*, CBS Masterworks, 1971.

Mozart: *Sinfonia concertante in E Flat, K. 364, for Violin, Viola, and Orchestra*, Columbia, 1972.

Mozart: *Concerto in C Major for Two Violins and Orchestra*, Columbia, 1974.

Mozart: *Divertimento in E-Flat Major for String Trio*, Columbia, 1975.

Mozart: *Concerto No. 4 in D Major for Violin and Orchestra, Concerto No. 2 in D Major for Violin and Orchestra*, Columbia, 1978.

Mozart: *Concerto No. 4 for Violin and Orchestra in D Major; Concerto No. 5 for Violin and Orchestra in A Major (Turkish)*, Columbia, 1978.

Mozart: *Concerto in G; Concerto in D; Andante in C*, RCA Red Seal, 1979.

Mozart: *Sonata No. 26 in B-Flat Major for Violin and Piano*, Odyssey, 1979.

Penderecki, Krzysztof: *Violin Concerto*, Columbia, 1979.

Pleyel, Ignaz Joseph: *Sinfonie Concertante in B-Flat Major*, Columbia, 1974.

Prokofiev, Sergey Sergeyevich: *Concerto No. 1 in D Major for Violin and Orchestra; Concerto No. 2 in G Minor for Violin and Orchestra*, Columbia, 1964.

Prokofiev: *Sonata in F Minor for Violin and Piano; Sonata in D Major for Violin and Piano*, Odyssey, 1979.

Rochberg, George: *Violin Concerto*, Columbia, 1979.

*Romance: Favorite Melodies for the Quiet Hours*, Columbia, 1972.

Schubert, Franz: *Trio in E-Flat Major for Piano, Violin, and Cello*, Columbia, 1970.

Shostakovich, Dmitri: *Trio No. 2 for Violin, Cello, and Piano; Sonata for Cello and Piano*, CBS Masterworks, 1988.

Sibelius, Jean: *Concerto in D Minor for Violin and Orchestra; Karelia Suite*, Columbia, 1970.

Stamitz, Karl: *Sinfonia Concertante in D Major*, Columbia, 1972.

Stravinsky, Igor: *Concerto in D Major for Violin and Orchestra; Symphony in Three Movements*, Columbia, 1962.

Tchaikovsky: *Concerto in D Major for Violin and Orchestra; Meditation*, Columbia, 1979.

Viotti, Giovanni Battista: *Concerto No. 22 in A Minor for Violin and Orchestra*, Odyssey, 1979.

Vivaldi: *The Four Seasons*, Columbia, 1978.

Vivaldi: *Concerto in D Minor; Concerto in C Minor*, Columbia, 1978.

Vivaldi, Bach, and Mozart: *Le quattro stagioni* (Vivaldi); *Konzert fuer 2 Violinen und Streicher d-moll; Konzert fuer 4 Violinen, Streicher und Cembalo h-moll* (Bach); *Sinfonia concertante fuer Violine, Viola und Orchester Es-dur* (Mozart), Deutsche Grammophon, 1983.

Wieniawski, Henri: *Concerto No. 2 in D Minor for Violin and Orchestra*, Odyssey, 1979.

## Sources

### Books

Campbell, Margaret, *The Great Violinists*, Doubleday, 1980.

*The International Cyclopedia of Music and Musicians*, 10th edition, edited by Oscar Thompson, Dodd, Mead, 1975.

Schwarz, Boris, *Great Masters of the Violin: From Corelli and Vivaldi to Stern, Zukerman, and Perlman*, Simon & Schuster, 1983.

### Periodicals

*Newsweek*, November 17, 1980.

*New York Times Magazine*, October 14, 1979.

*People*, March 11, 1991.

*Strad*, August 1977; November 1985.

*Time*, July 7, 1980.

*U.S. News & World Report*, August 13, 1990.

### Other

*From Mao to Mozart: Isaac Stern in China* (documentary film), 1980.

*Isaac Stern, Itzhak Perlman, Pinchas Zukerman* (video), Paramount Home Video, 1988.

*Jerusalem* (video), 1986.

—*Michael E. Mueller*

# Ray
# Stevens

**Singer, songwriter**

**R**ay Stevens has carved a niche for himself as country's reigning musical clown. The burgeoning popularity of the Nashville Network and live country television shows has proven a boon for the zany comedian-songwriter who broke into the business in 1962 with "Ahab the Arab." Stevens's silly songs capitalize on national scandals and fads and they usually leave the audience laughing at both the lyrics and their antic delivery. According to an *Associated Press* wire report, Stevens doesn't mind being pigeonholed as a comedian. "I enjoy doing these nutty songs," he said. "I'm one of the few doing them."

*Akron Beacon Journal* correspondent Mark Faris noted: "To say there is anything beautiful about Stevens' music would seem to be stretching matters a mite. But it does have a couple of things going for it. For one, it usually manages to hit timely—if not exactly pressing—topics. . . . For another, Stevens' vocal sound effects . . . are just bizarre enough for folks to want another listen or two to make sure their ears aren't deceiving them." Stevens's wider talents, however, are not completely masked by his jocularity. *Chicago Tribune* contributor Jack Hurst praised the singer as "a superior musician whose work most often shows his prodigious skills in only the most oblique ways."

Stevens was born Ray Ragsdale in Clarkdale, Georgia, in 1939. He grew up listening to rhythm and blues and early rock and roll on the radio, but his own musical training was decidedly more rigorous. By his teens he was an accomplished piano player, and he attended Georgia State University as a student of classical piano and music theory.

While he was in college Stevens became interested in recording music and decided to become a singer. "When I first started recording," Stevens recounted in the *Chicago Tribune,* "I did a lot of straight love songs and couldn't get arrested. So I started writing these off-the-wall songs, and people liked them, and I got airplay, made enough money to put gas in my car." Stevens, in fact, began earning a considerable amount of money, especially after he hit the Top Ten with "Ahab the Arab."

A quintessentially silly song, "Ahab the Arab" describes the adventures of a hapless bedouin and his camel, Clyde. Stevens's irreverent classic includes camel grunts and double entendres and is sung with just a hint of a Southern accent. The song put Stevens on the pop music map and paved the way for other equally loony hits, including "Guitarzan," "The Streak," and "Would Jesus Wear a Rolex on His TV Show?"

Both "The Streak" and "Would Jesus Wear a Rolex"

Born Ray Ragsdale, January 24, 1939, in Clarkdale, GA. *Education:* Georgia State University, B.A., c. 1960.

Singer, songwriter, and producer, 1960—; plays guitar, banjo, and piano. Recorded first novelty song, "Jeremiah Peabody's Polyunsaturated Quick Dissolving Fast Acting Green and Purple Pills," 1961; released first pop hit, "Ahab the Arab," 1962. Has made recordings with numerous labels, including Judd, Mercury, Monument, Barnaby, Janus, Warner Bros., and MCA.

**Selected awards:** Grammy Awards, 1970, for "Everything Is Beautiful" and 1976, for instrumental version of "Misty."

**Addresses:** *Office*—Ray Stevens Music, 1707 Grand Ave., Nashville, TN 37212. *Agent*—Williams Artists Management, 816 North LaCienega Blvd., Los Angeles, CA 90069.

Again, Margaret," about a redneck obscene phone caller.

Stevens's comedy translates particularly well to music video, where he can add ridiculous costumes and facial gestures to his vocal work. He has profited tremendously from appearances on the Nashville Network and such syndicated programs as *Hee Haw;* for a number of years he has won industry awards as best musical comic in Nashville. Also performing some two hundred live shows each year throughout the United States, Stevens maintains a touring pace commensurate with that of chart-topping, serious country stars.

Few other artists have risen to challenge Stevens as the funniest country singer, and he likes it that way. "I still have in the back of my mind that one day, if I feel it's right, I'll put out another serious record," Stevens declared in the *Chicago Tribune* in 1988. "But I think I can raise my visibility doing what I'm doing now. The public wants an entertainer to be easy to identify, and I figured that's what people expect of Ray Stevens, so I said, 'Okay, I'll do that for a while and see what happens.' And it's turning out pretty well."

went gold within weeks of being released. Both songs hit the airwaves in timely fashion: "The Streak" coincided with the beginning of a fad of running nude in public that became popular in 1970, and "Would Jesus Wear a Rolex" was released at the very moment when television evangelist Jim Bakker was driven from his ministry by scandal. "It's invaluable when you've got the media hyping what you are singing about," Stevens commented, according to an *Associated Press* wire report. "To be funny, you have to be relevant."

Stevens was indeed relevant, but he was also lucky: his compositions were actually recorded *before* their topics became fodder for the media. The songs were ready and waiting for events to catch up to them, and Stevens—who wears a Rolex watch himself—was tickled pink with the timing. "When you've got a hot news topic, you increase your sales tremendously," he remarked, as quoted by the *Associated Press.*

For a time in the 1970s, Stevens considered a career in straight country music. In 1970 he released the song "Everything Is Beautiful," an optimistic, sing-along work that won him a Grammy Award. And he earned a second Grammy in 1976 for his bluegrass rendition of "Misty," which highlighted his instrumental prowess. Stevens's pure country work can be heard on such albums as *Turn Your Radio On* and *Nashville.*

The impulse to lunacy, however, eventually became Stevens's trademark. He remains best known for his outlandish tunes, which include "Mama's in the Sky with Elvis," "Bridget the Midget," "Shriner's Convention," "The Mississippi Squirrel Revival," and "It's Me

## Selected discography

### Singles

"Sergeant Preston of the Yukon," 1959.
"Jeremiah Peabody's Polyunsaturated Quick Dissolving Fast Acting Pleasant Tasting Green and Purple Pills," 1961.
"Ahab the Arab," 1962.
"Guitarzan," 1969.
"The Streak," 1970.
"Everything Is Beautiful," 1970.
"Would Jesus Wear a Rolex on His TV Show?," 1987.

### LPs

*Nashville,* Barnaby, 1973.
*I Have Returned,* MCA, 1985.
*Collector's Series,* RCA, 1986.
*Surely You Joust,* MCA, 1986.
*Crackin' Up!,* MCA, 1987.
*The Best of Ray Stevens,* Mercury, 1987.
*Greatest Hits,* MCA, 1987.
*Greatest Hits, Vol. 2,* MCA, 1987.
*I Never Made a Record I Didn't Like,* MCA, 1988.
*Beside Myself,* MCA, 1989.
*Everything Is Beautiful & Other Hits,* RCA, 1990.
*All Time Greatest Comic Hits,* Curb/CEMA, 1990.
*Lend Me Your Ears,* Capitol Nashville, 1990.
*#1 With a Bullet,* Capitol Nashville, 1991.

Also recorded *Turn Your Radio On,* 1971, *Both Sides of Ray*

*Stevens*, Crown, *Shriner's Convention*, RCA, and *He Thinks He's Ray Stevens*, MCA.

# Sources

### Books

*The Illustrated Encyclopedia of Country Music,* Harmony, 1977.

### Periodicals

*Akron Beacon Journal,* July 20, 1987; July 28, 1989; July 31, 1989.
*Associated Press* (wire report), May 29, 1987.
*Chicago Tribune,* August 17, 1988.
*People,* October 10, 1983; August 10, 1987; September 21, 1987.
*Stereo Review,* July 1980; November 1982; May 1985; February 1987.
*Variety,* February 6, 1985.

*—Anne Janette Johnson*

# They Might Be Giants

**Pop-rock duo**

Even in the alternative rock world, which allows for more diversity and eccentricity than mainstream music, They Might Be Giants seem an unlikely success story: absurd, surrealistic lyrics sung over bright melodies played on accordion, guitar, boom box, and a variety of sampled instruments. Yet only a few years after their first independent release, this New York pop duo became a major force on the alternative scene. Their knack for deadpan silliness wrapped in a catchy musical package won over college audiences, and their wildly inventive videos caught the attention of MTV viewers.

The two musician-songwriters who make up They Might Be Giants, John Linnell and John Flansburgh, first met in elementary school in Lincoln, Massachusetts. They became good friends in high school, even writing some songs together, but only began playing seriously years later. Linnell, singer, accordionist, and keyboardist for the Giants, studied music for a year after high school, but elected to leave his studies to play keyboards for a Rhode Island rock band called the Mundanes. Guitarist Flansburgh attended several colleges before dropping out of the university scene entirely; he taught himself to play guitar while working in a parking lot booth. In 1981, the two Johns moved into the same Brooklyn, New York, apartment building on the same day, marking the beginning of their musical partnership. Rather than form a traditional rock band, however, the two started using a drum machine and tape recorder to round out the songs. "At first we taped because we couldn't afford a live drummer," Linnell told Steve Dougherty of *People*. Flansburgh finished the thought: "Now we do it because we can use strange rhythms and not worry about the drummer's head exploding." The song "Rhythm Section Want Ad," which appeared on their first LP, seems to suggest that potential bandmates didn't share the duo's vision: "Do you sing like Olive Oyl on purpose/You guys must be into the Eurythmics."

Taking their name from a little-known movie starring George C. Scott, the pair began playing in the SoHo area of New York. Linnell played organ, while Flansburgh operated a drum tape in addition to playing guitar. Soon, They Might Be Giants were playing regularly in East Village clubs. Though they generated no record company interest in this period, they came up with an ingenious new way to share recorded material with a large audience: They put new songs on a telephone answering machine, changing the tapes regularly and leaving space at the end for listeners' comments. Thus "Dial-a-Song" was born. By 1988, the Giants' phone-machine song repertoire featured more than three hundred tunes. The gimmick worked well, and the band was soon receiving over one hundred calls a day.

## For the Record. . .

**B**and members are: **John Linnell** (vocals, keyboards, accordion), born c. 1959 in Lincoln, MA, son of a psychiatrist and an artist, attended University of Massachusetts, played in rock bands and worked as a bicycle messenger, founded They Might Be Giants in 1984; **John Flansburgh** (guitar, vocals, drum programming), born c. 1960 in Lincoln, MA, son of an architect and a Boston tour organizer, earned B.F.A. in printmaking from Pratt Institute, Brooklyn, NY, worked as parking lot attendant and as people counter at Grand Central Station, New York, NY.

Pop-rock recording and performing duo. Pair began collaborating in 1981; began playing under current name in 1984; recorded first independent album in 1987; signed with Elektra Records in 1989; released first major-label album and toured Pacific region in 1990.

**Awards:** Rated best new act in *Q* magazine readers' poll, 1990; awarded British Silver Record for selling 100,000 copies of *Flood*, 1990.

**Addresses:** *Record company*—Elektra Records, 75 Rockefeller Plaza, New York, NY 10019. *Other*—TMBG Information, P.O. Box 110553, Williamsburg Station, Brooklyn, NY 11211.

### Called Ultimate MTV Band

Linnell and Flansburgh decided to put out their own record, and released *They Might Be Giants* in 1987 on the small New Jersey label Bar/None, which was founded by Hoboken record store owner Tom Prendergast and his partner Glenn Morrow. The album contained 20 songs, and the Giants filmed two inexpensive videos for the songs "Don't Let's Start" and "Put Your Hand Inside the Puppet Head." MTV representatives saw the videos and decided that, in executive Rick Krim's words, "the Giants were the ultimate MTV band. They're very visual and very entertaining." By early 1988 the video for "Don't Let's Start," which features Linnell and Flansburgh with a variety of bizarre props, was playing regularly on the music video channel. As a result the record, which had been selling 1,000 copies a month, began selling 50,000 copies a month. Suddenly record companies expressed interest in the band. 1988 also saw the release of two They Might Be Giants EPs, *Don't Let's Start* and *(She Was a) Hotel Detective*. Both recordings mixed songs from the first album with unreleased material. *High Fidelity* called the EPs "chock full o' fun."

By mid-1988 They Might Be Giants finished their second album, *Lincoln*. Bar/None joined Enigma Records, and the album sold even better than the Giants' debut. The first video, "Ana Ng," became one of the most popular alternative clips on MTV when it appeared. Though the second clip, "They'll Need a Crane," was less successful, the record sold impressively, even knocking the popular group U2 out of first place on the college radio singles chart. The LP also featured "Purple Toupee," a weird parody of sixties nostalgia, and "Shoehorn with Teeth," whose chorus proclaims that "people should get beat up for stating their beliefs." *Lincoln* earned the band some very positive reviews: Michael Small, reviewing the album in *People,* referred to the Giants as "probably the most inventive rock and roll duo on earth. *Lincoln . . .* includes more of the weird, catchy and wonderful music that has earned this band an ever-expanding cult following." Steve Simels of *Stereo Review* called the album "a clever, quirky, often brilliantly arranged and produced piece of postmodern art." *Rolling Stone's* Ira Robbins wrote that "the Giants' unique blend of the Beatles, [*Alice in Wonderland* author] Lewis Carroll, [British songwriter] Elvis Costello, and [jazz bandleader and novelty musician-composer] Spike Jones begins with finely crafted melodies . . . but invariably adds lyrics that wander into topsy-turvy land." Shortly after releasing *Lincoln,* the band put out another Bar/None EP, *They'll Need a Crane.* In January of 1989, They Might Be Giants signed a record deal with Elektra.

### Torrent of Success, Not Praise, for *Flood*

Their first major-label album, *Flood,* released in 1990, garnered mixed reviews. Small praised its "torrent of catchy tunes and surprising lyrics in a range of styles, including reggae, country, swing, folk rock and even Monty Python-style parodies of show tunes and TV jingles." David Browne's review in *Rolling Stone,* however, remarked that "this is music with one sole purpose: to attract attention to its own cleverness." *New York's* Elizabeth Wurtzel was similarly disappointed: "The Giants have failed to make an album that will matter to more than the select few who are in on the joke. Linnell and Flansburgh seem to be afraid that if they make another album with emotional depth [like *Lincoln*], instead of being clever spinmeisters with attitude, they might become the cranky, bloated rock stars that their music implicitly mocks."

Even so, the Giants once again made waves on MTV with their videos for the album's first two singles, "Birdhouse in Your Soul" and a dance-oriented version of the fifties song "Istanbul (Not Constantinople)." Produced by the band with the exception of four tracks produced by studio veterans Clive Langer and Alan Winstanley, and featuring a variety of guest musicians, the album had a more polished feel than the duo's earlier records. Even so, the distinctive TMBG songwriting style shone through on tunes like "Particle Man" and "We Want a Rock," which features the refrain "Everybody wants prosthetic foreheads on their real heads." Although the songs on *Flood* retained the satirical and often nonsensical vision of the Giants, the album also showed the band's more serious side, particularly on "Your Racist Friend," which contains the lines "I know politics bores you/But I feel like a hypocrite talking to you/You and your racist friend."

The British pop music magazine *Q* voted They Might Be Giants the best new act of 1990. The award, based on a poll of the magazine's readers, reflected the band's popularity in the United Kingdom, where *Flood's* excellent sales earned the Giants a British Silver Record. Late in 1990 the band embarked on an extended tour that included performances in Hawaii, New Zealand, Australia, and Japan. The Giants' manager, Jamie Kitman, told *The Might Be Times* that at the time of the duo's Japanese concerts, "Screaming mobs of teenage girls were chasing them through the streets. It was like something out of [the Beatles film] 'A Hard Day's Night.'" Following the tour, Flansburgh and Linnell set about writing songs for their next LP, which the band anticipated releasing in 1992.

Given their escalating popularity, the band's name began to sound less and less like a clever joke. The challenge would be to stay true to their unconventional instincts while appealing to a mass audience. As Linnell remarked in *Rolling Stone,* "The most desirable thing is to be completely explicit about what you're doing and still have it be something that can't be encapsulated."

## Selected discography

*They Might Be Giants* (includes "Don't Let's Start" and "Put Your Hand Inside the Puppet Head"), Bar/None, 1987.
*Don't Let's Start,* Bar/None, 1988.
*(She Was a) Hotel Detective,* Bar/None, 1988.
*Lincoln* (includes "Ana Ng," "They'll Need a Crane," "Purple Toupee," and "Shoehorn with Teeth"), Bar/None-Enigma, 1988.
*They'll Need a Crane,* Bar/None-Enigma, 1988.
*Flood* (includes "Birdhouse in Your Soul," "Istanbul [Not Constantinople]," "Particle Man," and "We Want a Rock"), Elektra, 1990.
*Istanbul (Not Constantinople),* Elektra, 1990.
*Apollo 18,* Elektra, 1992.

## Sources

*High Fidelity,* October 1988.
*The Might Be Times,* December 18, 1990.
*The Nation,* February 27, 1988.
*New York,* February 6, 1989.
*People,* June 20, 1988; January 30, 1989; February 12, 1990.
*Rolling Stone,* January 12, 1989; February 22, 1990.
*Seventeen,* April 1989.
*Stereo Review,* March 1989.

—*Simon Glickman*

# Richard Thompson

**Singer, songwriter, guitarist**

Richard Thompson has made a career of confounding musical categories and forcing critics to strain their vocabularies to describe his music. He has been likened to a "sixteenth-century Jeff Beck" and "a Delta bluesman from Lebanon," by Steve Simels and Louis Meredith of *Stereo Review;* and he has been called "a card-carrying guitar hero" and "a songwriter whose roots draw equal nourishment from Scottish folk reels and American rockabilly" by Jon Young and Mark Rowland of *Musician.*

Other influences that can be traced in Thompson's composing and playing are the free jazz of John Coltrane, the electric guitar explorations of Jimi Hendrix, the modal drone of Celtic bagpipes and fiddles, New Orleans rock and roll, the country ballads of Hank Williams, traditional jazz, and Arab folk music. His lyrics reflect what Steve Pond of *Rolling Stone* called his blackly humorous, oblique yet emotionally charged sensibility," drawing on the imagery of English folk songs to tell stories that can be grim or whimsical. Thompson told Rowland in *Musician:* "I like to think that everything is based on or comes back to traditional music. . . . [But] it's the hybrids that excite—where African music meets European in New Orleans and it's jazz, or hillbilly music meets the blues in Memphis and it's rock 'n' roll. Cross-fertilization is the exciting stuff of music."

## Began Career with Fairport Convention

Thompson began his musical career at the age of eighteen, when he co-founded the seminal folk-rock band Fairport Convention. The British blues revival of the 1960s was in full swing and, as Thompson told Terri Gross of National Public Radio's "Fresh Air," "I was slightly repulsed by the blues revival. . . . There were suddenly thousands of British kids playing what were really inferior versions of Howling Wolf and B.B. King and Otis Rush. . . . So I sort of went the other way, really. I think the blues revival and the popularity of soul music in Britain in the sixties really drove Fairport to traditional music."

The Fairport Convention sound, as heard on the two albums widely considered to be their definitive work, *Unhalfbricking* and *Liege and Lief,* was based on traditional ballads and dance tunes like "Matty Groves" and "The Lark in the Morning," as well as original songs in a traditional vein. But the songs were played with rock energy and instrumentation: electric bass, drums, electric fiddles and mandolins, and Thompson's dense, skirling guitar lines. Fairport's influence can be heard in British and Irish bands as diverse as Jethro Tull, U2, and the Pogues.

### Formed Duo with Wife

Thompson left Fairport Convention in 1972 to record a solo album, *Henry the Human Fly.* Linda Peters was hired to sing backup vocals, and a short time later she and Thompson were married and began recording and performing as a duo. Their first album, *I Want to See the Bright Lights Tonight,* was praised by Kurt Loder of *Rolling Stone,* who wrote: "One of those LPs with not a single track that's less than luminous, it captures the Thompsons at the top of their artistic form: rooted in Celtic folk, reveling in the possibilities of rock and pop and radiant in the spiritual obsessions that characterize so much of their best work."

The Thompsons' career as a duo lasted eight years, culminating in *Shoot Out the Lights,* considered by many to be their finest work. Sam Sutherland, in *High Fidelity,* called it "a riveting array of uptempo rock, lambent ballads, and puckish folk dances . . . addressing the turmoil of collapsed emotional commitments." *Stereo Review* named it an "album of the year," and *Rolling Stone* ranked it ninth among the hundred best albums of the decade: "Richard's lyrics are crystal-clear portraits of dissolving relationships . . . and riveting tales of death and violence. . . . The poignancy of English folk music is evident in songs like Linda's heartbreaking 'Walking on a Wire' and Richard's caustic 'Back Street Slide.' The latter, the album's hardest rocker, modifies an Anglo-Irish folk melody with an odd-metered, almost Zeppelinesque riff pinched from a tune the guitarist had heard on Algerian radio." *Rolling Stone* also praised the record for Richard's "most inspired and unrestrained guitar playing since the glory days of Fairport Convention."

### Pursued Solo Career

During the recording of *Shoot Out the Lights* and the stormy tour that followed, the Thompsons' marriage was disintegrating. Some have seen the album as a reflection of the turmoil in their relationship, but Richard has insisted that he doesn't write autobiographical songs. He told Terri Gross: "I've never really enjoyed that thing where you write about your own life. . . . It's interesting to use . . . other characters as a way of expanding what you're able to write about. . . . Obviously if you're writing for a man's voice and a woman's voice, you have to write some songs from a woman's point of view, so it almost looks as though you're writing a kind of soap opera." And he told Bill Flanagan, author of *Written in My Soul:* "When you're on stage or singing on a record, you're wearing another hat. . . . You're assuming some kind of role. This doesn't mean you're not sincere about what you sing . . . but it's not necessarily the truth as lived by you in your life."

Thompson's subsequent recordings have also met with enthusiastic reviews, but only modest sales. His eclectic approach does not fit neatly into any radio format, and on the release of *Rumour and Sigh,* Hank Bordowitz of *CD Review* noted that Thompson "is a living definition of 'cult artist. . . .' He does so many things so well and—here's the rub—with such a surfeit of intelligence and wit that he's bound to leave the average pop fan bewildered. . . . *Rumour and Sigh* will do little to change this—even though the disc is one of the most devastating and varied efforts since *Shoot Out the Lights.*" Simels, reviewing Thompson's previous album, *Amnesia,* in *Stereo Review* observed that Thompson "does not mince words or melodies. . . . He lays bare his heart, soul, brain, and guts. Maybe that's why this magnificent artist has never sold many records: His music is dangerously strong."

## Selected discography

### With Fairport Convention

*Fairport Convention,* Cotillion/Atlantic, 1968.
*Fairport Convention* (U.K. title: *What We Did on Our Holiday*), A & M, 1970.
*Unhalfbricking,* A & M, 1970.
*Liege and Lief,* A & M, 1971.
*Full House,* A & M, 1972.

*Angel Delight,* A & M, 1972.
*The History of Fairport Convention,* Island, 1972.
*The Fairport Chronicles,* A & M, 1975.
*House Full,* Hannibal, 1977.

## With Linda Thompson

*I Want to See the Bright Lights Tonight,* Island, 1974.
*Hokey Pokey,* Island, 1976.
*Pour Down Like Silver,* Island, 1976.
*Live (More or Less),* Island, 1977.
*First Light,* Chrysalis, 1978.
*Sunnyvista,* Chrysalis, 1980.
*Shoot Out the Lights,* Hannibal, 1982.

## Solo Albums

*Henry the Human Fly,* Reprise, 1972.
*Richard Thompson,* Island, 1976.
*Strict Tempo!,* Island, 1981.
*Hand of Kindness,* Hannibal, 1983.
*Across a Crowded Room,* Polydor, 1986.
*Daring Adventures,* Polydor, 1986.
*Amnesia,* Capitol, 1988.
*Rumour and Sigh,* Capitol, 1991.

## On Video

*Across a Crowded Room,* Sony, 1986.

# Sources

## Books

Flanagan, Bill, *Written in My Soul,* Contemporary Books, 1987.
*The Rolling Stone Encyclopedia of Rock & Roll,* edited by Jon Pareles, Rolling Stone Press, 1983.

## Periodicals

*CD Review,* August 1991.
*Detroit Free Press,* July 31, 1991.
*Down Beat,* February 1985; March 1987.
*High Fidelity,* September 1983; December 1983; May 1985; March 1987.
*Musician,* December 1988; January 1990; June 1991.
*New York,* November 1983.
*Rolling Stone,* March 29, 1984; March 28, 1985; May 9, 1985; September 25, 1986; August 27, 1987; November 16, 1989; July 11, 1991; August 22, 1991.
*Spin,* August 1991.
*Stereo Review,* October 1983; May 1985; April 1986; January 1989.

## Other

"Fresh Air," National Public Radio, June 28, 1991.

—Tim Connor

# Mel Tillis

**Singer, songwriter**

**M**el Tillis is an enduring favorite on the country music scene, a singer and comedian who has turned a speech impediment into an entertainment asset. Tillis has been performing since the late 1950s and has recorded music in a wide variety of country styles. For many years he wrote all of his own material and provided songs for a number of other singers as well. In addition, he has his own live television show, featuring a popular mix of music and comedy. In her book *Behind Closed Doors: Talking with the Legends of Country Music,* Alanna Nash labeled Tillis "one of country music's most versatile and underrated talents . . . a genuine article, someone who cares about the music and its evolution."

Tillis was born in the tiny Florida hamlet of Pahokee in 1932, one in a family of four children. When he was only three he contracted malaria, and the disease—along with emotional difficulties brought on by his father's neglect—left him with a stutter that often rendered him unable to voice even the simplest words. The Tillises were very poor, and when Mel was seven his father deserted the family for five years to work on a dredge boat in the Caribbean.

Growing up in a small town, Tillis was rarely mocked for his stutter. Instead, his classmates and teachers accepted him and encouraged him to explore his talents. In high school he played drums in the band and was a star player on the football team. He also discovered that he did not stammer when he was singing. At 16 he made his performance debut in a talent show in Pahokee, and he decided that he wanted to be a musician. Even before he graduated from high school he was writing songs, and after a stint in the Air Force—where he experienced discrimination because of his stutter—he travelled to Nashville to try his luck in the music industry.

Tillis felt the same prejudice from executives in Nashville as he had in the Air Force. Most of them scoffed at the idea of a shy, stuttering Florida boy who wanted to be a country star. Tillis did have talent, however, and he was soon able to sell his songs to other artists. In 1956 his composition, "I'm Tired," became a hit for Webb Pierce and enabled Tillis to secure salaried employment with Cedarwood Publishing Company, which would later come under Tillis's ownership.

After penning a few more hits for other performers, Tillis finally earned a recording contract of his own from Columbia Records in 1958. His first release, "The Violet and the Rose," became a Top 30 country hit. During the 1960s Tillis rose to stardom gradually, releasing such popular songs as "Wine," "Who's Julie?," and "These Lonely Hands of Mine." He also continued to write for other entertainers, giving Bobby Bare a huge hit with

"Detroit City" and penning the Kenny Rogers classic "Ruby, Don't Take Your Love to Town."

The 1960s and 1970s proved to be challenging decades for the country music industry. The popularity of rock and roll eroded country's fan support, and a number of country artists struggled to survive the competition. One performer who flourished through this trying time was Mel Tillis. Between 1968 and 1978 he released more than 30 Number One country singles, including "The Arms of a Fool," "Commercial Affection," "Heaven Everyday," "In the Middle of the Night," and "Southern Rain." His guest appearances on *Hee Haw* and *The Glen Campbell Goodtime Hour* confirmed that he could clown as well as sing, and soon he was touring the country with an enormous band and an elaborate stage show. At one point his touring band contained 17 pieces, including four fiddles.

The highlight of Tillis's career came in 1976, when he was named Entertainer of the Year by the Country Music Association. The award came at a time when producers were pushing for a mainstream, country-pop sound that would appeal to middle-of-the-road audiences. Tillis bought into the country-pop concept for a brief period, at one point cutting a duet album with Nancy Sinatra.

In his autobiography, though, Tillis expressed some reservations about recording crossover songs. As excerpted in the *New York Times Book Review*, the singer stated: "I'd like to ask why—without it sounding like sour grapes, which it's not, since my career is pretty well set, thank the Lord—the Country Music Association, of which I'm a long-standing member, is hell bent on inviting the whole pop and rock performing world into the country music business?" In the early 1980s the singer returned to his roots in uptown honky-tonk with several well-received MCA recordings. Tillis has never been married to one style, however. He is equally at home with Texas swing numbers, pure country ballads, and honky-tonk. In *Stereo Review*, Nash labeled him "one of country music's real vocal masters."

Tillis's comedic talents have helped him draw an audience outside the borders of country music. He has appeared in films and onstage in Las Vegas, as well as on the Grand Ole Opry, and he is in great demand as a live performer. Since his hectic schedule of appearances leaves him little time to write music, the singer is inclined to record other writers' material.

Commenting on his speech impediment, Tillis told Alanna Nash that he became a performer *because* he stuttered. "Most of the people in the country business came from, well, not *tragic* backgrounds," he said. "Some of 'em did, like Hank Williams, you know. But I think that if there's a large family, you may feel like . . . you didn't get as much attention as the other kids did, and maybe that's right. I think the stutter made me work harder to become an entertainer. I would have done anything."

# Selected discography

*Walk on By*, Columbia, 1961.
*The Violet and the Rose*, Columbia, 1962.
*Wine*, Ric, 1967.
*Heart Over Mind*, Columbia, 1970.
*After All This Time*, MCA, 1983.
*The Best of Mel Tillis*, MCA.
*Big 'n' Country*, MCA.
*California Road*, RCA, 1985.
*Greatest Hits of Mel Tillis*, MCA.
*I Believe in You*, MCA.
*I Believe in You/Heart Healer*, MCA.
*M-M-Mel Live*, MCA.
*M-M-Mel Live/Are You Sincere*, MCA.
*The Very Best of Mel Tillis*, MCA.
*California Road*, RCA, 1985.
*Brand New Mister Me*, Polydor, 1988.
*American Originals*, Columbia, 1990.
*Greatest Hits*, Curb/CEMA, 1991.

# Sources

## Books

Brown, Charles T., *Music U.S.A.: America's Country and Western Tradition,* Prentice-Hall, 1986.

*The Illustrated Encyclopedia of Country Music,* Harmony, 1977.

Nash, Alanna, *Behind Closed Doors: Talking With the Legends of Country Music,* Knopf, 1988.

Shestack, Melvin, *The Country Music Encyclopedia,* Crowell, 1974.

Stambler, Irwin, and Grelun Landon, *The Encyclopedia of Folk, Country, and Western Music,* St. Martin's, 1969.

## Periodicals

*Country Music,* May/June 1990.

*High Fidelity,* February 1981.

*New York Times Book Review,* May 19, 1985.

*People,* March 16, 1981; December 14, 1981; June 28, 1982; September 19, 1983; November 14, 1983; September 21, 1987; May 27, 1991.

*Stereo Review,* September 1982; July 1983.

*—Anne Janette Johnson*

# Travis Tritt

---

**Singer, songwriter, guitarist**

---

As one of his songs says, Travis Tritt has put some "drive" into country music. Tritt's hard-rocking, rowdy style has observers labeling him the latest addition to the "outlaw" tradition—the arm of country music that has a rock and roll flare. Bearded and clad in blue jeans, the talented performer appears to have stepped on the stage fresh from a day with a construction crew; his music proudly extols the joys, sorrows, and values of the blue-collar lifestyle.

Since signing with Warner Bros. Records—and securing management from the legendary Ken Kragen—Tritt has left the bar and dance hall scene behind and is performing at major venues throughout the United States. His particular brand of country music, while exhibiting similarities to the style of country greats Merle Haggard and George Jones, definitely ignites rock and roll sparks. "There have been times when I have turned on the radio and have heard one slow, draggy ballad after another," Tritt commented in the *Gary Post-Tribune*. "I get inspired by certain things that are a little bit up-tempo and have a little bit of drive to them."

Though he had not yet reached the age of 30 when he attained country fame, Tritt's dedication to music stretched back almost a decade. He was born and raised near Marietta, Georgia, the son of a farmer who supplemented the family income by working variously as a bread truck driver, automobile mechanic, and school bus driver. The Tritt family's life was not easy, and Travis harbored few high expectations for his own future.

### Emulated the "Outlaws"

At the age of eight Tritt got his first guitar and taught himself to play. His idols included the Southern rock bands Lynrd Skynrd, the Allman Brothers, and the Charlie Daniels Band, as well as the "outlaws," which included Waylon Jennings, Johnny Cash, and Willie Nelson. Tritt—who went on to become an opening act for Daniels—once said that the older rocker taught him many valuable lessons.

Tritt married at the age of 18 and seemed destined to stay in Marietta. His wife discouraged him from following a career in music, so he took a post-high-school job with a company that distributed heating and air-conditioning equipment. Both the job and the marriage were short-lived, however, and Tritt found himself drawn back to music when a friend of his—another small-time Georgia musician—sold a song in Nashville. Tritt accompanied his friend to Tennessee to see the song recorded and quit his day job shortly thereafter.

Many lean years followed; Tritt and his band played for

minimal wages in American Legion halls and at small county fairs, nearly starving between jobs. The singer recalled to an *Associated Press* wire reporter that he "would go to the grocery store once a week and buy canned vienna sausage, a head of lettuce, a jar of mayonnaise, a loaf of bread and two or three cans of soup. This was breakfast, lunch and dinner for the entire week." In the country music business, Tritt added, "you almost have to have as much patience as you do talent."

## Music Deals With Everyday Life

Tritt's patience and talent eventually caught the attention of the executives at Warner Bros. Records, which recorded and released his first single, "Country Club." The song was a hit, and Warner signed Tritt to cut an album. The label also suggested that Tritt hire a new manager, one with more influence in the business. Tritt chose Ken Kragen, the former manager of such musical superstars as Lionel Richie, the Smothers Brothers, and Olivia Newton-John. Kragen had narrowed his client list to one star—singer Kenny Rogers—and was rumored to be in semi-retirement. Nevertheless, Tritt approached him, and—to everyone's surprise—Kragen agreed to manage the young country rocker.

Kragen worked wonders for his new client, securing a line of credit for Tritt and personally calling large radio stations to urge them to play "Country Club." Kragen also featured Tritt in a Kenny Rogers television special, giving the newcomer a national network television audience for the first time. As "Country Club" climbed the

charts, Tritt embarked on several national tours and was soon performing nearly 280 shows a year.

Tritt's success continued into the 1990s, when his debut album, *Country Club,* went gold and yielded the Top Ten hit "Put Some Drive in Your Country." Premiering at the Grand Ole Opry in 1991, he was named best new male vocalist of the year by *Billboard* magazine, and a growing legion of fans began comparing him to mega-star Hank Williams, Jr. According to the *Associated Press,* Tritt is extremely gratified that he has become a top-draw entertainer who can perform the kind of music he prefers—hard-core country rock. "I think we've struck a nerve with a part of middle America that really is looking for honesty in music. . . . The music deals with real situations, real people, everyday, ordinary life. You don't have to be a poetry major or literature student to understand country music."

## Avoided the "Sophomore Jinx"

Tritt's success with *Country Club* led to another hit album, *It's All About to Change,* which was released in 1991. "People have told me about the importance of a second album and of avoiding the sophomore jinx," the singer remarked, according to a Warner Bros. press release. "When we finished this album, we felt it was even stronger than the first one. So if that second album is about solidifying your career, it gives another meaning to the phrase, 'it's all about to change.'" In the opinion of *Country Music* contributor Bob Allen, who thought that Tritt's single "Country Club" was a "hokey and artless . . . novelty item," *It's All About to Change* is an "exciting, gutsy, irreverent" record. The critic continued, "it's great to see a young, unreconstructed, long-haired rebel like Travis Tritt coming on strong."

On both of his albums, Tritt celebrates the blue-collar South without embarrassment or apology. The music and lyrics, in fact, have a genuine ring to them; the artist is the son of working class parents and has not forgotten the hard times he endured on his way to the top. Even though he prefers the up-tempo tunes, his gravelly baritone is particularly effective on such ballads as the moving "Drift off to Dream," which became a hit in 1991. Tritt summed up his philosophy in the *Gary Post-Tribune:* "My music is geared toward the working man and I write from my personal experiences. If I haven't lived it, I can't write it. And even if I do fail, at least I'll always know that I gave it my best shot." The musician concluded, "I've always looked at life as paying off the best when you take the largest risks."

## Selected discography

*Country Club,* Warner Bros., 1990.
*It's All About to Change,* Warner Bros., 1991.

**Other**

*It's All About to Change* (video), 1991.

## Sources

*Akron Beacon Journal,* January 21, 1990.
*Associated Press* (wire report), June 29, 1990.
*Country Music,* July/August 1990; September/October 1990;
   September/October 1991.
*Gary Post-Tribune,* April 5, 1991.
*Stereo Review,* August 1990.

Information for this profile was obtained from a Warner Bros.
press release, May 1991.

—*Anne Janette Johnson*

# McCoy Tyner

"**N**ot Bill Evans, not Herbie Hancock, not Ahmad Jamal nor Cecil Taylor—with all due respect to each of those greats, no pianist since Bud Powell has had as widespread an influence as McCoy Tyner," wrote Kevin Whitehead in *Down Beat,* summing up the legacy of the pianist who revolutionized jazz improvisation with African rhythms, modes and pentatonic scales, and quartal and quintal harmonies. McCoy Alfred Tyner, once a member of the legendary John Coltrane Quartet, learned his lessons well under the tutelage of Coltrane. "What made [Coltrane's approach] such a vital force and also truly part of the lineage of the music . . . was this firm foundation . . . very simple, but yet complex at the same time," Tyner, an acclaimed soloist and group leader for several decades, told David Wild in *Down Beat.* "Which kind of reminds me of life in itself. Being made up of simple elements but yet very complex in many ways."

Born in Philadelphia, Pennsylvania, on December 11, 1938, Tyner was raised in a jazz-oriented environment. Tyner's mother as well as the neighbors around the corner—budding jazz stars Bud and Richie Powell— played piano. Tyner grew up interested in the sound produced by different pianists, and after beginning formal piano studies at age 13, he held jam sessions with his friends at his mother's beauty salon. As an adolescent, Tyner received musical training and introductions to various jazzmen while playing in local blues bands and rhythm and blues groups. It was during the summer of 1955 that he met the legendary saxophonist John Coltrane. "I used to go to John's house and sit on the porch and talk about music—about a lot of things that he eventually began to get into," Tyner related to Wild. "So I think theoretically I was sort of involved in his way of thinking quite early . . . we coincided."

At the age of 18, Tyner had an opportunity to tour with saxophonist Sonny Rollins and Richie Powell, both well-known jazz performers, but he refused. Since he had just graduated from high school and met his future wife, he was not ready to leave Philadelphia.

A few years later, though, in 1959, Tyner joined Benny Golson on a tour of San Francisco and then moved to New York City to become part of the Benny Golson-Art Farmer Jazztet. Bebop was on the decline during Tyner's six-month stint with the group, and he waited for a call from John Coltrane. (Coltrane and Tyner had made a verbal commitment to work with each other after Coltrane left the Miles Davis band.) Tyner was 21 years old in June of 1960, when Coltrane asked him to become part of the John Coltrane Quartet, which tabloids later dubbed the "Classic Quartet." Composed of tenor and soprano saxophonist Coltrane, bassist Jimmy Garrison, drummer Elvin Jones, and pianist Tyner, the John Coltrane

Quartet stayed together until December of 1965. Tyner recounted to Wild, "It was a tremendous learning experience for me and it reached the point where it was actually a *jubilant* experience, being on stage with them."

## Music Influenced by Sociopolitical Movement

With the civil rights movement and the rise of black consciousness in the United States during the 1960s, African roots and culture became a source of creative inspiration for black writers, artists, and musicians, including Tyner. Experimenting with structural alternatives, Tyner won international acclaim for his adaptations of scales, tonalities, and African rhythms, which changed jazz piano improvisation. "The 'classic' Coltrane Quartet of Trane, Tyner, bassist Jimmy Garrison, and drummer Elvin Jones nearly exhausted the horizons of modal playing and exploded the jazz world into the avant garde," noted John Diliberto in *Down Beat*. "Its instrumentation was the common saxophone-plus-rhythm, but the exceptional interplay of its members . . . created something special within the familiar framework," observed Wild. "[The group's] evolving stylistic approach exerted a dominant influence on the development of music. And Tyner's experiments with modes and chord voicing taught a generation of pianists how to create in the increasingly free idiom of Coltrane."

Tyner eventually found that the subtleties of piano could not compete in Coltrane's experiments with volume—in which the sounds of horns and drums were intensified—and left the group in the mid-1960s to begin his solo career. Although he had recorded on his own during his tenure with Coltrane, Tyner's late sixties LPs were largely unsuccessful, until the release of the album *Sahara* on the Milestone label.

Tyner subsequently embarked on a productive recording career with Milestone that lasted throughout the late 1970s. Doug Clark remarked in *Down Beat* in 1978 that "McCoy Tyner no longer stands in the shadow of John Coltrane. On the edge of 40, McCoy has come into his own as a jazz giant." Tyner was even invited by former President Jimmy Carter to join saxophonist Sonny Rollins and bassist Ron Carter for a performance at the White House in June of 1978. That same year, Milestone Records launched Tyner, Rollins, Carter, and drummer Al Foster on an American tour.

## A Virtuoso With the Milestone Jazzstars

Billed as the Milestone Jazzstars, the group performed in symphony concert halls and civic auditoriums to standing ovations. "In short," maintained Clark, "McCoy is free to do nearly anything he wants to, and he does. He plays with virtuosity: his hands are equal partners, and he utilizes the entire keyboard with stunning effectiveness. In terms of 20th century piano music, McCoy has taken up where [Hungarian composer Bela] Bartok left off." At the close of the 1970s, a *Down Beat* critic named Tyner "one of the most brilliant pianists and commanding leaders in modern music" for his "extraordinary forcefulness and prowess" demonstrated on the album *The Greeting*.

By the mid-1980s Tyner had published a volume of transcriptions, *Inception to Now*, and recorded more than two dozen Milestone albums. Jazz was at a low ebb when the pianist, hoping to reach a wider audience, released the recording *Looking Out*, featuring guitarist Carlos Santana. Diliberto dubbed the blend of pop, rock and roll, and jazz on the album "uncomfortable," but acknowledged Tyner as "more than just a pianist or composer. He is an entire concept of music whose force remains undiminished."

## Entered His "Classic Phase"

Forming a quintet with saxophonist Gary Bartz and violinist John Blake, Tyner bounded back, and at the close of the eighties, he put together another successful collaboration called the McCoy Tyner Trio, which included bassist Avery Sharpe and drummer Louis Hayes. In 1989, the pianist recorded *Revelations*, his second solo album since the 1972 Coltrane tribute *Echoes of a Friend*. A compilation of standards, the album also demonstrated that Tyner had entered his "classic phase," noted Whitehead. "He's turning more and more to the standard repertory . . . letting more vintage mannerisms into his playing."

In 1990, *Stereo Review* proclaimed Tyner's LP *Things Ain't What They Used to Be,* featuring tenor saxophonist George Adams and guitarist John Scofield, his "finest album in years, perhaps his best ever. . . . Indeed, things ain't what they used to be—they're better." Finding the pianist "a more peaceable player the last decade or so," Frank-John Hadley wrote in *Down Beat* that the "interpretations of several more jazz warhorses and the occasional original" in the album "loom collectively as testimony of [Tyner's] great facility and emotional largess. Tyner and Steinway go it alone . . . within a personalized language informed by the blues, gospel, and Harlem stride."

A prolific recording artist and coveted performer, Tyner has earned his place at the pinnacle of jazz. According to Hadley, the pianist once made the statement, "After awhile [the acoustic piano] becomes an extension of yourself, and you and your instrument become one." Tyner continues to play and compose in the tradition of John Coltrane, who felt jazz was one means of coming closer to God. *People* contributor David Grogan numbered McCoy Tyner among the jazz musicians "brave enough to continue [Coltrane's] quest."

# Selected discography

*Inception,* Impulse, 1962, reissue, Fantasy, 1988.
*The Real McCoy,* Blue Note, 1967.
*Sahara,* Milestone, 1972.
*Song for My Lady,* Milestone, 1972, reissue, Fantasy, 1988.
*Echoes of a Friend,* Milestone, 1972, reissue, Fantasy, 1991.
*Song of the New World,* Milestone, 1973, reissue, Fantasy, 1991.
*Supertrio,* Milestone, 1977, reissue, 1989.
*Four Times Four,* Milestone, 1980.
*Reunited,* Blackhawk, 1982.
*Tender Moments* (recorded 1968), Blue Note, 1985.
*Just Feelin',* Palo Alto, 1985.
*Time for Tyner: McCoy Tyner Trio* (recorded 1968), Blue Note, 1987.
*Double Trios,* Denon, 1987.
*Nights of Ballads and Blues,* MCA/Impulse, 1988.
*Revelations,* Blue Note, 1989.
*McCoy Tyner Plays Ellington* (recorded 1964), MCA, 1990.
*Bon Voyage* (recorded 1987), Timeless, 1990.
*Enlightenment* (recorded 1973), Milestone, 1990.

*Things Ain't What They Used to Be,* Blue Note, 1990.
*Remembering John,* Enja, 1991.
*Today and Tomorrow,* GRP/Impulse, 1991.
*44th Street Suite,* Red Baron, 1991.
*New York Reunion,* Chesky, 1991.
*Soliloquy,* Blue Note, 1992.
*Fly With the Wind* (recorded 1976), Milestone.
*Dimensions,* Elektra/Musician.
*The Greeting,* Milestone.
*Atlantis,* Milestone.
*Expansions,* Blue Note.
*Looking Out,* Columbia.
*Blues for Coltrane,* Impulse.

## With John Coltrane

*A Love Supreme* (recorded 1964), MCA/Impulse, reissue, 1986.
*John Coltrane & Johnny Hartman* (recorded 1963), MCA/Impulse, reissue, 1986.
*Impressions* (recorded 1961-63), MCA/Impulse, reissue, 1987.
*Crescent* (recorded 1964), MCA/Impulse, reissue, 1987.
*Live at the Village Vanguard* (recorded 1961), MCA/Impulse, reissue, 1990.
*Meditations* (recorded 1965), MCA, 1990.
*The Gentle Side of John Coltrane* (recorded 1961-65), GRP/Impulse, reissue, 1991.
*Coltrane Live at Birdland* (recorded 1963), MCA/Impulse.
*Selflessness* (recorded 1963-65), MCA/Impulse.
*Coltrane's Sound* (recorded 1960), Atlantic.
*John Coltrane Quartet Plays* (recorded 1965), MCA/Impulse.
*Om,* MCA/Impulse.

## With others

*New York Reunion,* Chesky, 1991.
*Blue Bossa,* LRC, 1991.
*In Concert,* Milestone.

# Sources

*Audio,* February 1989.
*Billboard,* April 7, 1990.
*Down Beat,* November 16, 1978; July 12, 1979; February 1984; March 1988; April 1989; July 1989; November 1989; August 1991; November 1991.
*Guitar Player,* August 1990.
*High Fidelity,* August 1988; April 1989.
*People,* January 9, 1989; December 23, 1991.
*Stereo Review,* November 1990.
*Variety,* July 4, 1990.

—Marjorie Burgess

# The Velvet Underground

**Rock band**

The Velvet Underground spent the early part of their career as the musical component of Pop artist and impresario Andy Warhol's 1960s multi-media "happenings." In the following decades, however, the influence of the Velvets' sometimes druggy, sometimes aggressive sound would permeate virtually every "alternative" corner of popular music, laying the seeds for punk rock and opening up new possibilities for lyricists and musicians alike. During their time together, though, the members of the Velvet Underground had to contend with hostile critics, unappreciative crowds, indifferent record companies, and playing quite literally in the shadow of Warhol's extravaganzas.

The Velvets were founded in New York by Lou Reed and Sterling Morrison, who met at Syracuse University in the early sixties. Reed was in a rock and roll band, much to the disappointment of his parents, who had wanted him to be a classical pianist. At 15 he recorded his first record—the single "So Blue"—with his band, the Shades. His penchant for irreverence surfaced frequently at Syracuse; Reed was ejected from the

Members included **John Cale** (born December 5, 1940, in Crynant, Wales; bass, viola, guitar, and vocals; left group in 1967, was replaced on base by **Doug Yule,** 1968), **Sterling Morrison** (born Holmes Sterling Morrison, Jr., August 29, 1942, in East Meadow, NY; guitar and vocals), **Nico** (born Christa Paffgen, [most sources say] March 15, 1943, in Budapest, Hungary [one source says Cologne, Germany]; left group in 1966; died in 1988; vocals), **Lou Reed** (born Louis Firbank, March 2, 1942 [one source says 1944], in Freeport, NY [one sources says Brooklyn, NY]; vocals, guitar, and piano; left group in 1970), and **Moe Tucker** (born Maureen Tucker, c. 1945, in New Jersey; drums and vocals).

Group formed in 1965; played gigs in New York City; appeared in Pop artist Andy Warhol's film *The Velvet Underground and Nico: A Symphony of Sound,* 1966; toured with Warhol's multi-media show The Exploding Plastic Inevitable; signed with MGM/Verve and released first album, *The Velvet Underground & Nico,* 1966; left MGM and signed with Atlantic, released final studio album, *Loaded,* and disbanded, 1970.

campus ROTC program for holding a gun to the head of his commanding officer. He also developed his literary streak there, falling in with troubled poet Delmore Schwartz, whose promising career would be destroyed by pills and alcohol. Schwartz exercised a huge influence on Reed, whose lyrics would reflect a fondness for the well-wrought image and an avant-gardist's eye for the bizarre. Sterling Morrison, who also admired Schwartz, played with Reed in bands called Moses and his Brothers, Pasha and the Prophets, and L.A. and the El Dorados.

### Primitive Beginnings

Reed hooked up with a small record company called Pickwick, which paid him nominal sums for songs that would be attributed to non-existent acts. "There were four of us literally locked in a room writing songs," Reed recalled in the book *Up-Tight.* High on marijuana or racing on speed, Reed and his colleagues wrote dozens of songs per day; when the company decided to release one of his singles, it needed a group to perform it. Thus Reed's absurdist dance number "The Ostrich," which featured "Sneaky Pete" on its flip side, was credited to a recording sensation called the Primitives. The company then enlisted a group of musicians—

Morrison, his friend Tony Conrad, and a Welsh music student named John Cale—to tour with Reed as the Primitives. The band had its moment of small-scale fame, but the record was not a hit.

Reed's musical instincts were a complex mix; he was inspired by the feel of rhythm and blues, but found the experimentalism of avant-garde jazz artists like saxophonist Ornette Coleman equally fascinating. His interest in underground literature and modern poetry encouraged him to explore dark themes in his compositions; while writing throwaway tunes for Pickwick, he also composed songs like "Heroin," which would become a Velvets classic. Reed and Cale found themselves unexpectedly compatible as songwriters and musicians. Cale's classical background and musical experimentalism—he once helped perform composer John Cage's "Vexations," which consists of an 80-second piece of music repeated 840 times by a relay team of pianists—found liberation and sympathy in Reed's artistic sensibility. Reed moved into Cale's apartment. He recalled in *Up-Tight* that he met Sterling Morrison again on the subway. Soon the three joined underground art-scene denizen and drummer Angus MacLise to form the earliest incarnation of the then-unnamed Velvet Underground, with Reed and Morrison on guitars and Cale on bass and viola. Reed's deal with Pickwick had folded, so the former would-be commercial pop stars decided to play music to please themselves.

It was 1965 and underground cinema—influenced by surrealism and other experimentalist trends in art—was flourishing in New York City. Angus MacLise had ties to several filmmakers, including Piero Heliczer. Heliczer organized a multi-media event that included film, dance, slides, lights, and music by Reed, Cale, Morrison and MacLise. Suddenly the band had an avenue apart from the Manhattan club scene, which at that time was dominated by rhythm and blues acts.

They provided music—live and taped—for several other film shows and recorded a demo in July of 1965 that included the songs "Venus in Furs" and "Heroin." Reed and company sent the demo to a number of music industry people, including British promoter Miles Copeland. Cale traveled to England several times to help drum up interest in the band, and the quartet was about ready to move to London when they met Andy Warhol. Before that fateful encounter, however, they survived by playing to small but appreciative crowds. Still, it seemed unlikely that they would achieve real success in the United States and they still had no name. Then Morrison's friend Conrad found a paperback book on the street and showed it to his colleagues. The book, *The Velvet Underground,* billed itself as "a documentary on the sexual corruption of our age." It told a lurid tale of sadomasochism and other sexual adventures in New York City. The band had a name at last.

### Enter Tucker and Warhol

The Velvet Underground gathered instant notoriety when one of Heliczer's films of the band appeared on a CBS television feature on underground cinema. The Velvets received a call from journalist and aspiring entrepreneur Al Aronowitz as a result of this exposure. After seeing one of their performances at a Heliczer "happening," Aronowitz offered the band a spot opening at New Jersey's Summit High School for the Myddle Class, a group he was managing. MacLise refused to begin and finish playing at another band's command—even for the extravagant sum of $75—and when his fellow musicians pressed him to take the offer, he left the band. In need of a new drummer, Reed enlisted Maureen "Moe" Tucker, the sister of an old friend of his and Morrison's. Tucker worked as a computer operator by day and had quit her previous band when their guitarist was shot onstage. The other Velvets initially told her she wasn't a full-fledged member because, she remembered in *Up-Tight,* "John was adamant about not wanting any girls in the band."

The Summit performance shocked and confused the audience, but Aronowitz saw potential. Deciding that the Velvets needed practice, he arranged a regular performance at Greenwich Village's Cafe Bizarre. The band made very little money and did not endear themselves to the patrons or the management, but the gig afforded them a chance to earn their "chops" and try out new material. Tucker—by then a full-time member—played tambourine because the Cafe didn't want drums. In the midst of their dissatisfaction with the place, the Velvet Underground met Andy Warhol. Soon the Cafe Bizarre's management told them that if they played the "Black Angel's Death Song" again they'd be fired; the Velvets responded with an especially heartfelt version of the song and got the axe.

Warhol and a group of hangers-on spent New Year's Eve, 1965, at the apartment that Reed and Morrison were then sharing. Soon after, Warhol's headquarters—The Factory—became a second home for the Velvets as well as the scene of much brainstorming and networking. The Pop impresario wanted to include the Velvets in his upcoming discotheque experiment, but also wanted them to play with a young European chanteuse named Nico. A model, actress, and singer, Nico had appeared in famed Italian film director Federico Fellini's film *La Dolce Vita;* Warhol felt that her deep, frosty vocals and startling beauty would nicely complement the Velvets' sound. The band resisted, not wanting to be anyone's backing group, but Warhol persuaded them to let her sing some of their songs and even got them to change their name to the Velvet Underground and Nico. The band members had swallowed their pride, knowing that Warhol's influence in the art world provided a genuine chance for widespread recognition.

In January of 1966 Warhol shot a film of the new lineup entitled *The Velvet Underground and Nico: A Symphony of Sound.* Police broke up the shooting because of complaints about noise, but the film prevailed, later providing a backdrop for Velvets live shows. Warhol wanted to project movies onto the members of the band

> *"My prime ambition was to knock the door down on what rock & roll songs were about."*
> —Lou Reed

as they played and surround them with light shows and dancers. The first such multi-media event took place at the Cinematheque; it became known as "Andy Warhol, UpTight," and soon went on the road. After a shaky start, the show hit its stride at the University of Michigan Film Festival in Ann Arbor. "Ann Arbor went crazy," Warhol said in *Up-Tight.*

### The Exploding Plastic Inevitable, and Other Gigs

After the tour Warhol and his associates—including filmmaker Paul Morrissey—looked for a nightclub where the Velvets could play on a regular basis and "become famous." Through some friends they found a club called The Dom. Pressed for a name for the new "happening," Morrissey culled the words "Exploding Plastic Inevitable" from the liner notes to a record by folk-rock superstar Bob Dylan. The new show was instantly successful. Warhol, as the visionary behind the event, was featured prominently in numerous press reviews, but the Velvets got their share of attention. Rock critic Richard Goldstein, in a review quoted in *Up-Tight,* called their sound "a savage series of atonal thrusts and electronic feedback. . . . [It] seems to be the product of a secret marriage between Bob Dylan and the Marquis de Sade."

Warhol and Morrissey decided to bring the Velvets and Nico into the studio to record an album; Reed, allegedly jealous of Nico, left her at first with nothing to sing. The project took only a few days to record, with Warhol acting nominally as producer. What he actually did in the studio remains unclear—Morrissey told Malanga in *Up-Tight* that Warhol showed up "once or twice"—but there is no doubt that he provided the motivation and initial funds for the album. Reed told *Rolling Stone*'s David Fricke that Warhol mainly assisted by "keeping people away from us." MGM/Verve agreed to release the record, largely on the strength of Warhol's connections. Warhol also lent his artistic talents to the record by designing its cover, which would become one of the most famous in rock history: plain white with an enormous banana, the "peel" of which could be pulled away. The only words that appeared on the front were Warhol's signature.

The record, simply titled *The Velvet Underground & Nico,* featured 11 songs, almost all of which have became classics. Nico crooned "Femme Fatale" and a few other tunes well suited to her oddly dispassionate, chilly voice. As Morrison told the authors of *Up-Tight,* the singer-star came by her "haunting" vocal style naturally: "Nico was just really depressed." Reed delivered "I'm Waiting for My Man," "Venus in Furs," "Heroin," and several others in his trademark deadpan style. The content of many of the lyrics—notably focusing on drug addiction, sadomasochism, and transvestism—severely limited the album's chance at commercial success. Reed's take on drug use and fringe life lacked the clear moral "lessons" and tidy value judgments that would have made the music more accessible. The band's sound stretched from crystalline pop to raw, percussive rock that verged on the atonal. "We're musical primitives," Cale told Goldstein in an interview reprinted in *Up-Tight. Rolling Stone*'s Fricke, reviewing the re-mastered editions of the Velvet Underground albums released by Polydor in 1985, called the first LP "a powerful summation of art and fear."

The Velvets continued performing with The Exploding Plastic Inevitable—or E.P.I.—though tensions mounted between Nico and the rest of the group. They wore sunglasses onstage to protect their eyes from the harsh lights, and Tucker began playing garbage cans and other non-traditional drums. Soon they were booked to play several dates in Los Angeles; their show with Frank Zappa's psychedelic art-rock ensemble the Mothers of Invention left listeners alternately impressed and bemused. The two bands did not get along, however, and the Los Angeles Sheriff's Department closed down their joint performances on the third day. After the L.A. dates, San Francisco music promoter Bill Graham persuaded the E.P.I. to play at his Fillmore theater with the Mothers and then-unknown psychedelic rock band the Jefferson Airplane. But, the Velvets held the entire San Francisco scene in contempt and fought bitterly with Graham. Their preoccupation with grungy reality, addiction, and sexual power relations and their discomfiting sound and "uptight" attitude clashed violently with the flower-power atmosphere of the mid-1960s California rock scene.

## Exit Nico and Warhol

Nico left the group in 1967, partly because her solo performance schedule at the Dom clashed with the Velvets' tour plans. Reed fired Warhol as the band's manager, reportedly prompting him to ask Reed if he wanted to play museums for the rest of his life. Reed's answer was to find a new manager, Steve Sesnick. The Velvets recorded their second album—the uncompromising *White Light/White Heat*—for Verve over a few days in September of 1967. This sophomore effort features the loudest, most abrasive music the Velvets ever produced: feedback-drenched lead guitars, churning rhythms, fuzz, and pure noise surrounding tunes about transvestites, getting high, and even a bizarre Reed-penned short story called "The Gift," recited by Cale over a chugging rhythm track.

Perhaps the epitome of *White Light/White Heat*'s irreverence and experimentation is the 17-minute jam "Sister Ray," a grinding anthem to decadence. "The only way to go through something is to go right into the middle," Reed remarked about the record in *Up-Tight.* "The only way to do it is to not kid around." He added that "Sister Ray," a spontaneous studio jam inspired by avant-garde jazz, exercised a huge influence on subsequent rock: "I mean, if 'Sister Ray' is not an example of heavy metal, then nothing is." *Billboard*'s reviewer predicted good "underground" sales and commented on the group's "intriguing lyrics." Despite expectations, the label did not support the album and it failed to sell. In September of 1968 Cale left the Velvet Underground to pursue a solo career. Tensions between Cale and Reed had escalated and the latter had called a meeting of the band to announce Cale's departure. Morrison and Tucker felt they had to side with Reed or risk dissolution of the band, but the episode inspired ill will on all fronts. Bassist Doug Yule, a Boston native, joined the band for its next tour dates and went into the studio with the Velvets to record their third LP, *The Velvet Underground,* which MGM released directly—rather than on its subsidiary, Verve—in March of 1969. This record included some of the band's loveliest melodies, in particular "Pale Blue Eyes," "Jesus" and "Candy Says" as well as upbeat songs like "What Goes On" and "Beginning To See the Light." Reviewers responded favorably: *Cashbox* wrote that "the group creates an evocative, sensuous sound, and the LP could pick up considerable sales." Some critics —writing much later, after the release of the Polydor reissues—saw the album's strengths even more clearly. *Rolling Stone's* Fricke referred to the record as "gently expansive" compared to the sonic assault of *White Light*. *High Fidelity's* Michael Hill called the third LP "their most consistent and accessible effort." Yet MGM did not distribute the album adequately to generate real sales despite Sesnick's attempts to aggressively promote it.

The Velvets recorded tracks for a fourth MGM LP, but the label dropped them and the album was never released. These songs would not be available except on bootleg recordings and overpriced, poorly mastered imports until their release as *VU* in 1985. The band toured extensively in 1969 and a live album of this period—released in 1974 by Mercury as *1969 The Velvet Underground Live*—showcases the Reed-Morrison-Tucker-Yule lineup at the height of its power. Despite the ferocity of their touring schedule, the Velvet Underground had no money and no label at the end of 1969. In early 1970 Sesnick closed negotiations for a contract with Atlantic Records. In June the band played a famous series of gigs at a Manhattan club called Max's Kansas City. A live album of those shows, which features Yule's brother Billy substituting for a pregnant Tucker, was released on Atlantic in 1972— remixed from a fan's cassette recording.

The Velvet Underground recorded one more studio album, 1970's *Loaded,* but Reed quit the band before it was mixed. Featuring studio versions of Reed classics "Rock and Roll" and the much-covered "Sweet Jane," as well as "New Age," "Oh Sweet Nuthin'," and several other tuneful rockers, *Loaded* served as the Velvets' swan song. Yule sang lead on a couple of songs and played lead guitar, keyboards, and some drums as well as bass. The album—over which fans have long been divided—featured the guitar-driven, gospel- and blues-tinged quality that would dominate mainstream rock in the first half of the 1970s.

### Posthumous Fame

It quickly became evident to the remaining Velvets that without Reed the band could not last. He went on to a tempestuous and often highly acclaimed solo career; Tucker got married and moved to Florida to raise her family, periodically putting out low-budget solo records; Morrison became a university English professor, and Yule established a furniture-crafting business in New Hampshire, playing music occasionally. By the mid-1970s, however, it became apparent that the Velvets had been a stunning catalyst to the development of alternative rock. The influence of the Velvet

Underground's sound and imagery was amply evident at the birth of the glam-rock and punk movements of the seventies. By the post-punk explosion of the 1980s, rock and roll bands across the spectrum—from country-rock to rap—displayed the mark of the first "uptight" band. Hugely successful groups like R.E.M. covered Velvets tunes and sang the late group's praises. The 1985 re-release of the Velvets' early and unreleased material secured their posthumous fame. It has become a rock and roll truism that only a thousand people heard the first Velvet Underground LP, but they all formed bands.

Nico and Warhol died in 1988. Reed and Cale joined forces for a "song cycle" about Warhol, *Songs for Drella,* which they performed to critical raves and released as an album in 1990. The work recounts much of the Velvets' early history and even re-ignites some of the embers Reed and Cale left smoldering more than two decades earlier. "All the promise we showed in those two albums, we never delivered on it," Cale reflected in *Up-Tight* in 1983. Many of the Velvets' admirers share this same sense of a mission uncompleted. Reviewing Moe Tucker's 1992 album *I Spent a Week There the Other Night*—which features guest performances by Reed, Cale, and Morrison, and even one track that boasts all four—Kurt Loder asked in *Esquire,* "Why doesn't the Velvet Underground just reunite, make an album of its own, and instantly become the most meaningful band on the planet?" Should such a reunion occur, it would no doubt afford the Velvets the recognition they never got as a young band. Still, the Velvet Underground consistently emphasized in its material the obstacles to such happy resolutions. "My prime ambition," recalled Reed in a 1986 *Rolling Stone* interview, "was to knock the door down on what rock & roll songs were about." As the 1990s wore on, it seemed, the world was knocking the Velvets' door down.

## Selected discography

The Velvet Underground & Nico (includes "Femme Fatale," "I'm Waiting for My Man," "Venus in Furs," and "Heroin"), MGM/ Verve, 1966, reissued, Polydor, 1985.

White Light/White Heat (includes "The Gift" and "Sister Ray"), MGM/Verve, 1967, reissued, Polydor, 1985.

The Velvet Underground (includes "Pale Blue Eyes," "Jesus," "Candy Says," "What Goes On," and "Beginning To See the Light"), MGM, 1969, reissued, Polydor, 1985.

Loaded (includes "Sweet Jane," "Rock and Roll," "New Age," and "Oh! Sweet Nuthin'"), Atlantic, 1970.

The Velvet Underground Live at Max's Kansas City, Atlantic, 1972.

1969 The Velvet Underground Live, Mercury, 1974.

*VU,* Polydor, 1985.
*Another View,* Polydor, 1986.
(John Cale and Lou Reed) *Songs for Drella,* Sire, 1990.
(Moe Tucker, featuring former members of the Velvet Underground) *I Spent a Week There the Other Night,* New Rose, 1992.

## Sources

### Books

Bockris, Victor, and Gerard Malanga, *Up-Tight: The Velvet Underground Story,* Omnibus, 1983.

### Periodicals

*Atlantic,* April 1990.
*Billboard,* February 24, 1968.
*Cashbox,* June 28, 1969.
*Esquire,* February 1992.
*High Fidelity,* May 1985.
*Interview,* October 1989.
*Nation,* February 27, 1989.
*New York,* November 25, 1985.
*Rolling Stone,* November 22, 1984; March 14, 1985; September 25, 1986; May 4, 1989; January 11, 1990.
*Stereo Review,* May 1985.

Further information for this profile was obtained from liner notes to Polydor reissues of Velvet Underground LPs, written by Kurt Loder, December 1984.

—*Simon Glickman*

# The Village People

**Disco group**

"The music was fun, the garb was outrageous, and that's all that mattered to the heartland partisans of these six hip hunks," said *Entertainment Weekly* contributor Jess Cagle of the late-1970s phenomenon that was the Village People, a group that was on tour as late as 1991. Largely members of the gay community of New York City's Greenwich Village, the half-dozen-strong ensemble dominated the disco era with outfits and campy song lyrics that found their genesis in caricatures of macho heroes.

A well-orchestrated stage act helped the Village People edge out the Bee Gees as *Billboard's* disco group of the year in 1978. The group earned three platinum albums that produced the monster hits "Y.M.C.A.," "San Francisco," "Macho Man," "In the Navy," and "Go West" over the course of the late 1970s. "So much happens so quickly and [the] kick-drum pounds so relentlessly, that the show becomes a loud blur of hilarity, too patently absurd to be erotic," wrote Ken Emerson, appraising the act's appeal in a 1978 *Rolling*

## For the Record. . .

**M**embers include **Alex Briley** (the GI), **David Hodo** (the construction worker), **Glenn Hughes** (the biker), **Jeff Olson** (the cowboy; replaced **Randy Jones**), **Felipe Rose** (the Indian chief), **Ray Simpson** (the cop; replaced **Victor Willis** as lead singer, 1979; replaced at one point by **Miles Jay,** beginning in 1982).

Group based on album cover concept of record produced by Jacques Morali, 1977; took legitimate shape in 1978; debut album, *Village People,* 1978, produced international hit singles, "Macho Man," "Y.M.C.A.," "San Francisco," "In the Navy," "Go West"; group performed in the film *Can't Stop the Music,* 1980; released "new romantic" new wave album *Renaissance,* 1981; songs featured in films; released single "Sex on the Phone," 1985; performed in Dallas and Austin, Texas, 1989; toured the U.S. and abroad, 1991.

**Awards:** Six gold and four platinum records, and three platinum albums; voted disco group of the year by *Billboard* International Disco Forum, 1978.

**Addresses:** *Agent*—c/o Talent Consultants International Ltd., 200 West 57th St., Ste. 910, New York, NY 10019.

*Stone* article. "You can't help but dance, you can't help but laugh."

The disco music fad was brief, but heady for the original members of the Village People. Victor Willis, David Hodo, Felipe Rose, Alex Briley, Randy Jones, and Glenn Hughes reeled when record sales slumped in the early 1980s. "It felt like we'd been group-loved by the world, then all of a sudden group-rejected," disclosed Hodo to *Entertainment Weekly*'s Cagle. Ray Simpson and Jeff Olson eventually replaced Willis and Jones, respectively, and the group struggled through bad times in the following years, only occasionally employed as singers and dancers. But disco music was revived as "trash disco" on the Southern club circuit by the end of the decade and crowds were again spelling out the letters "Y.M.C.A." with their arms as they danced to the old favorite. The early 1990s saw a general revival of seventies music and fashion and the Village People, capitalizing on nostalgia, went back on the road; warmly greeted in the U.S and abroad, the boys were indeed back.

### Group Masterminded by Jacques Morali

The Village People were a concept born in the mind of producer Jacques Morali in the late 1970s. A native of France, Morali studied music for ten years at the Paris Conservatory. He weathered a hodge-podge of musical experiences before becoming house composer at Paris's Crazy Horse Saloon in 1975. His first hit on the music market was a conversion of Arriba Rosa's song "Brazil" into a disco number. With money he borrowed to go to the States in 1976, Morali hired studio musicians to perform the song under the name the Ritchie Family. When Morali wanted to make a follow-up recording, the record companies he approached balked at his inability to deliver a bona fide group for promotional tours and live appearances. Since the Ritchie Family was just a creation based on the name of Morali's collaborator, arranger Ritchie Rome, Morali needed to find live performers to make up the group. Not surprisingly, personnel problems ensued almost from the start. Morali fired the first set of Ritchie Family singers—all women—and replaced them with three ex-showgirls who made their debut at the wedding of Princess Caroline of Monaco.

While working out details with the Ritchie Family in 1977, Morali—who regularly patronized American discotheques—went to a New York gay bar called the Anvil. That night he noticed dancer Felipe Rose dressed as an Indian, complete with bells on his feet. Morali spotted Rose, clad again in Indian garb, a week later at a West Village disco called 12 West. Rose happened to be dancing near one man dressed as a cowboy and another wearing a construction hat. "And after that I say to myself," Morali told *Rolling Stone*'s Emerson, "'You know, this is fantastic'—to see the cowboy, the Indian, the construction worker with other men around. And also, I think in myself that the gay people have no group, nobody to personalize the gay people, you know? And I say to Felipe, 'One of these days I'm going to employ you.'"

### Appeal Transcended Gay Market

That same week, Morali began production of a disco record with masculine stereotypes in mind, but no set group of performers. "I never thought that straight audiences were going to catch on to it," Morali divulged to Emerson. "I wanted to do something only for the gay market." Working with lyricists Phil Hurtt and Peter Whitehead, Morali composed "Fire Island" and "San Francisco." Actor and singer Victor Willis, who had appeared in the Broadway shows *The River Niger* and *The Wiz*, was enlisted to sing lead vocals on the tunes, joined by Alex Briley in the chorus. Morali photographed models clothed in leather, hard hat, and cowboy attire to pose on the record jacket and entitled the album *Village People.*

After sales of *Village People* reached over 200,00 on the disco circuit, Morali advertised in New York City's *Village Voice* and show business papers for attractive gay singers and dancers with mustaches. "Why should you hire a group and spend all the money on them until you have a hit record first? You cannot ask the performers to leave their jobs and take the chance that the record will be a commercial success," Morali asserted to Steven Gaines in *New York* magazine. After a lackluster initial performance on the television show *Soul Train,* Morali regrouped, recruiting Hodo, Jones, and Hughes to join Willis, Rose, and Briley. Attired as a construction worker, cowboy, biker, cop, Indian chief, and GI, the Village People recorded the hit single "Macho Man" and graced the cover of the album from which it sprang—*Macho Men.* Willis and company provided the professionalism necessary to make Morali's elaborate stage routines successful. "The album was an immediate success in the discos, but everyone agrees it is the act, which the Village People have been taking across the country for six months now, that has made the record an across-the-board smash," explained *Rolling Stone* contributor Emerson in 1978.

### Struggled Until Disco and 1970s Revivals

Some gays recognized the Village People as a parody, but others, along with most of their straight audience, didn't think too hard about the group's image and simply relished their productions. By the late 1970s, Village People album sales totaled 18 million around the globe. In 1978 Morali sold his rights to the group to Bill Aucoin, manager of the rock group Kiss, for one million dollars. But, unable to maintain its huge momentum, the disco craze began to dwindle the next year. This coincided with the replacement of Victor Willis by Ray Simpson (brother of singing-songwriting duo Ashford and Simpson's Valerie Simpson) as lead singer. By 1980, hamstrung by the box office failure of their movie, *Can't Stop the Music,* the Village People found themselves in an abrupt downward spiral. A year later, the release of the album *Renaissance*—an attempt at a "new romantic," new wave musical rebirth—was met by little success. In 1985 the group released the single "Sex on the Phone" to modest acclaim, but the real savior of the Village People was the disco revival of the decade's end.

"Trash disco—in which modern youths recall bell-bottoms, platform shoes and polyester, and pine for the golden years of not so long ago by dancing on lighted dance floors to such faded luminaries as Donna Summer, the Bee Gees, Parliament/Funkadelic, and the Gap Band—thrives in Dallas, Houston, and Austin," reported *Texas Monthly*'s Joe Nick Patoski, citing appearances by the Village People in Dallas and Austin as the big events of the 1989 trash-disco season. By 1991, when a full-blown seventies fever gripped the hip across the U.S., the Village People were on tour in 75 cities across America and abroad. Costumed as of old, but celebrating with some new music, the Village People delighted audiences with their evocations of nostalgic imagery. "Everybody loves cowboys and Indians and anything American," Hodo told *Entertainment Weekly*'s Cagle, relating how the group has always, "pushed a button universally." Pushing that button remains the Village People's impetus for musical and pop-culture glory.

## Selected discography

*Village People* (includes "Fire Island" and "San Francisco"), Casablanca, 1977.
*Macho Men* (includes "Macho Man"), Casablanca, 1978.
*Cruisin'*, Casablanca, 1979.
*Go West,* Casablanca, 1979.
*Renaissance*, RCA, 1981.
*Fox in the Box* (not released in the U.S).
*Greatest Hits*, Rhino, 1988.

## Sources

### Books

*The Rolling Stone Encyclopedia of Rock & Roll,* edited by Jon Pareles and Patricia Romanowski, Rolling Stone Press/Summit Books, 1983.

### Periodicals

*Entertainment Weekly,* July 19, 1991.
*New York,* September 25, 1978.
*Rolling Stone,* October 5, 1978.
*Texas Monthly,* November 1989.

—*Marjorie Burgess*

# Fats Waller

**Keyboards player, songwriter, bandleader, singer**

**W**hile best remembered for his comic songwriting and musical performances, show business legend Fats Waller was a gifted jazz musician whose greatest contribution to music lay in his brilliant stride piano compositions. Introduced to this particular piano idiom by Harlem stride master James P. Johnson, Waller was a wizard at this successor to ragtime, in which the left hand carries the beat and the right delivers the melody. His dynamic, creative keyboard style extended to the organ and the celesta; he was, in fact, the first significant jazz organist, his swing on the pipe organ unsurpassed. But because "white America preferred its jazzmen to be Falstaffs rather than . . . Hamlets," suggested Jack Kroll in *Newsweek*, "Waller . . . was granted a certain measure of success because he agreed to emphasize his real gift for comedy and buffoonery, letting the jazz fall where it might."

Becoming an international star performing popular songs and satiric tunes like "Ain't Misbehavin'," "Honeysuckle Rose," and "Your Feet's Too Big," the 300-pound Waller cultivated an exuberant stage persona that audiences heartily embraced. With wagging head and joking asides, he slyly poked fun at the feeble songs he was frequently asked to perform; "He would disembowel Tin Pan Alley's more inane creations vocally and on the keyboard," observed *National Review* contributor Ralph De Toledano, "but even in his lightest moments, he was always the virtuoso, always the master of ragtime *cum* jazz." Said Kevin Whitehead in *Down Beat*, "He always found something of value in the rubbish. Fats had the double curse of being able to sing anything, and always being asked to prove it. But Waller's verbal comedy was too lively for someone just going through the motions, and he enjoyed subverting weak material . . . making it sublimely ridiculous."

The son of an Abyssinian Baptist minister, Thomas Wright Waller was raised in New York City's Harlem. At the age of six he began to play the reed organ; by ten he was performing in school concerts and before his father's congregation. The senior Waller considered jazz "the devil's music" and encouraged his son to become a classical pianist; but by the time young Thomas had reached his teens he had met James P. Johnson, and his father's battle was lost. Abandoning high school to become a movie theater organist, Waller studied jazz piano with Johnson. Soon word of the young man's artistry began to spread. By the early 1920s Waller—his girth quickly earning him the nickname "Fats"—was one of Harlem's most prominent keyboards players, delighting patrons in cabarets and nightclubs accompanying blues singers like Bessie Smith and Alberta Hunter, or performing piano and organ solos. In 1922 Waller cut his first player-piano roll, "Got to Cool My Doggies Now." That year he also

Born Thomas Wright Waller, May 21, 1904, in New York, NY; died of pneumonia near Kansas City, MO, December 15, 1943; son of Edward Martin (a Baptist minister) and Adeline (Lockett) Waller; married second wife, Anita Priscilla Rutherford, 1926; children: (first marriage) Thomas Wright, Jr., (second marriage) Maurice, Ronald. *Education:* Studied with stride pianists Willie Smith and James P. Johnson; studied classical piano with Leopold Godowsky and composition with Carl Bohm at the Juilliard School.

Began playing the harmonium at age six, was playing the organ at father's Harlem church by ten; began professional career at 15 as organist at Lincoln Theater, New York City; played in New York city cabarets and nightclubs as accompanist and solo performer, early 1920s; cut first player-piano rolls and records, 1922; radio debut, 1923, headlined radio show *Fats Waller's Rhythm Club*; composer and performer of popular and show tunes; worked as sideman and frontman for various jazz combos; formed ensemble Fats Waller and His Rhythm, 1934; toured and recorded with own big band. Appeared in motion pictures *Hooray for Love!*, 1935, *King of Burlesque*, 1935, and *Stormy Weather*, 1943.

made his solo recording debut, "Muscle Shoals Blues/ Birmingham Blues," for Okeh Records.

A prolific songwriter, Waller sold his first tune, "Squeeze Me," in 1923; by the late twenties his compositions were being performed and recorded by the most popular entertainers of the day, most notably Fletcher Henderson and Cab Calloway. In 1928 Waller and lyricist Andy Razaf wrote much of the music for the all-black Broadway musical *Keep Shufflin'*. Later Waller-Razaf collaborations included the stage show *Connie's Hot Chocolates*, which featured the enduring hit song "Ain't Misbehavin.'" Frequently pressed for money, the free-living Waller sometimes sold the rights to a song for taxi fare or the price of a meal, though he would later regret it; playing fast and loose with traditional business practices, he sometimes obtained cash advances for songs he never finished or sold the same piece to more than one publisher. He took his keyboards compositions more seriously, however, recording an important series of stride piano pieces—"Handful of Keys," "Smashing Thirds," "Numb Fumblin'," "Valentine Stomp," "Viper's Drag," "Alligator Crawl," and "Clothes Line Ballot"—between 1929 and 1934. Waller also recorded on occasion as a sideman in jazz combos like Morris's Hot Babes and McKinney's Cotton Pickers, as well as heading his own small ensembles. His Fats Waller's

Buddies was one of the earliest recorded interracial groups.

In 1934 Waller assembled a sextet called Fats Waller and His Rhythm that consisted of Eugene "Honey Bear" Sedric on reeds, Al Casey on guitar, Charles Turner on bass, Yank Porter or Harry Dial on drums, and Herman Autrey (sometimes replaced by Bill Coleman or John "Bugs" Hamilton) on trumpet. Featuring Waller's humorous vocal interpretations and masterful stride playing, the group recorded scores of songs for the Victor label over the next few years, producing the hits "I'm Gonna Sit Right Down and Write Myself a Letter," "Lulu's Back in Town," and "Your Feet's Too Big." Many of the tunes the performer skewered were his own; yet "his comedy wasn't merely verbal," wrote *Down Beat's* Whitehead. "[Waller] conveyed sly humor with rolling piano triplets, bright rips up the keyboard's top octaves, and amply buoyant rhythm." With a popularity that rivaled famed trumpet player Louis Armstrong's, Waller performed regularly on radio and toured throughout the U.S. and abroad before record crowds. Visiting Europe in 1938, he even played jazz on the organ in Paris's Notre Dame Cathedral.

Waller died of pneumonia at the age of 39, his health ruined by his heavy work schedule and passion for food, drink, and revelry. While a number of pianists kept his stride style alive, most of his nearly 500 songs almost faded into obscurity—until 1978 and the Broadway musical "Ain't Misbehavin'." A revue of some thirty-odd songs Waller wrote or made famous—performed by a cast of five headed by the sassy Nell Carter—the show was a smash hit that toured the country, was performed on television, and eventually immortalized on vinyl. Director Richard Maltby, Jr., hoped that the success of "Ain't Misbehavin'" would spur a revival of Waller's music, bringing more lost songs and records to light. "Waller was a national resource," Maltby rhapsodized in *Time*. "He grabbed an armful of life in an exhilarating way, and I want people everywhere to feel that exalting spirit."

## Selected compositions

(With Harry Brooks; lyrics by Andy Razaf) "Ain't Misbehavin,'" 1929.
(With Razaf; lyrics by Razaf) "Honeysuckle Rose."
(With Alex Hill) "I'm Crazy 'Bout My Baby (and My Baby's Crazy 'Bout Me)," 1931.
(With Brooks, lyrics by Razaf) "What Did I Do To Be So Black and Blue," 1929.

**For the stage**

*Keep Shufflin'*, 1928.
(Nightclub revue) *Load of Coal.*
*Connie's Hot Chocolates*, 1929.
*Early to Bed*, 1943.

**Jazz pieces for organ and piano**

"Handful of Keys."
"Valentine Stomp."
"Jitterbug Waltz."

Also composed classical piano suite "London Sketches."

# Selected discography

Waller recorded prolifically from 1922 until his death in 1943, principally for Victor, beginning in 1926. Posthumous compilations of his recordings include:

*The Complete Fats Waller*, Volume 1: *1934-35* (reissue), Volume 2: *1935* (reissue), Volume 3: *1935-36* (reissue), Volume 4, Bluebird, 1987.
*Fine Arabian Stuff,* Muse.
*Waller in London* (recorded 1922-39), Swing.
*The Joint Is Jumpin'* (recorded 1929-43), Bluebird, 1987.
*The Last Years: Fats Waller and His Rhythm, 1940-43,* Bluebird.
*The Legendary Fats Waller* (recorded 1929-38), RCA.
*Fats Waller Live at the Yacht Club* (recorded 1938), Giants of Jazz.

*Fats Waller Live,* Volume 2 (recorded 1938, 1940), Giants of Jazz.
*Twenty Golden Pieces of Fats Waller,* Bulldog.
*Piano Solos: 1929-41,* Bluebird.
*Parlor Piano Solos,* Volume I: *Piano Rolls, 1923-24,* Volume 2: *1924-31,* Volume 3, Biograph.
*Classic Jazz From Rare Piano Rolls* (recorded 1923-27), Biograph, 1989.

# Sources

### Books

Feather, Leonard, *The New Edition of the Encyclopedia of Jazz,* Horizon Press, 1960.
*The New Grove Dictionary of Jazz,* edited by Barry Kernfeld, Macmillan, 1988.
*The Penguin Encyclopedia of Popular Music,* edited by Donald Clarke, Viking, 1989.

### Periodicals

*Down Beat,* November 2, 1978; March 1988; April 1990.
*National Review,* October 1, 1982.
*Newsweek,* May 22, 1978.
*New Yorker,* September 5, 1988.
*Stereo Review,* September 1988.
*Time,* February 27, 1978; June 5, 1978.

*—Nancy Pear*

# Keith Whitley

**Singer, songwriter**

When country singer Keith Whitley died in 1989, most critics agreed that the genre had lost one of its most promising young stars. After singing bluegrass with groups for many years, he became a solo artist in 1984. Whitley waited until his second album, *L.A. to Miami,* for his first chart hit, "Miami, My Amy," and then took a few more years to follow up with the album *Don't Close Your Eyes.* The title track and "I'm No Stranger to the Rain" became even bigger smashes, and Whitley became extremely popular with country fans and critics, evoking comparisons to greats like Lefty Frizzell and Merle Haggard. Another of Whitley's albums, *I Wonder Do You Think of Me,* was released posthumously in late 1989.

Whitley was born in Kentucky during the mid-1950s. He became involved professionally in country music while still a very young man; he first came to the attention of fans as a singer with Ralph Stanley's Clinch Mountain Boys and was frequently paired for duets with another vocalist who went on to achieve solo country fame, Ricky Skaggs. Hazel Smith recalled seeing Whitley and Skaggs perform at a concert in Camp Spring, North Carolina in *Country Music:* "It was awesome. I'll never forget the look on [Stanley's] face. . . . He knew that he'd come across a duo that was out of this world."

### Joined J.D. Crowe and the New South

After Skaggs left the Clinch Mountain Boys, Whitley followed suit. By the early 1970s he was lead vocalist for J.D. Crowe and the New South; Smith saw Whitley perform with this bluegrass band as well, and declared that when he sang his version of country classic "Window Up Above," "cold chills ran from the nape of my neck to the tip of my spine." Whitley also made recordings with the New South, including what Bob Allen of *Country Music* hailed as "a couple of amazing albums" that "showcased his striking vocal talents": 1981's *My Home Ain't In the Hall of Fame* and the following year's *Somewhere Between.*

Perhaps these two efforts brought Whitley to the attention of RCA's executives in Nashville as solo material. At any rate, he signed a contract with the company, and because industry insiders had already heard some of his excellent work with both Stanley and Crowe, "all of Nashville rolled out the red carpet," as Allen put it. Whitley himself recalled for Allen: "I rode into town in a blaze of glory, so to speak. The day I cut my first session at RCA, everybody who is anybody in the industry was there. I mean, it was like a major star coming in to record."

### Debut LP Met Indifferent Response

The result of all of this expectation was Whitley's debut album, *A Hard Act to Follow.* Unfortunately, the songs from it received little airplay. Apparently, as Whitley explained to Allen, even the country radio stations "said it was too country for them." Smith felt that the problem was that Whitley had not yet found his own style on *Hard Act,* and further noted her reactions to it: "I was disillusioned. Oh, the music was there all right. If you liked Keith Whitley singing one line like George Jones and the next line like Lefty Frizzell, the music was there. It was awesome, but it wasn't [Whitley]."

Whitley's next album, *L.A. to Miami,* was a little more "countripolitan," in Allen's phrasing. "It did get Keith on country radio," he reported further, "but it also alienated many of his longtime supporters." After watching other performers such as Randy Travis and George Strait score big hits with some of the same songs he had recorded on the album, Whitley finally had his own chart-climber off *L.A. to Miami* with "Miami, My Amy."

Whitley went on tour in support of the album, and his live performances were extremely well-received by his audiences. He confessed to Allen: "I'd have all these people come out and see me in concert, and they'd say, 'Man, I can't believe how much better you are live!'" At around the same time, following a divorce from his first wife, he began dating Grand Ole Opry singer Lorrie Morgan; Whitley married her in November of 1986.

### Scored Solo Success in 1988

Whitley had already recorded a follow-up album to *L.A.*
*to Miami* when he realized he was not satisfied with its style; RCA allowed him to begin work on another album. The result was 1988's *Don't Close Your Eyes,* which Alanna Nash of *Stereo Review* lauded as "a winner from start to finish." The album also caused her to proclaim Whitley as "one of the most promising of country music's neo-honky-tonkers."

In addition to the hit title track and the follow-up smash "I'm No Stranger to the Rain"—which Smith declared Whitley sang "with the conviction of a man who was wet from [a] rain storm that was always there"—other noteworthy songs from *Don't Close Your Eyes* include "I Never Go Around Mirrors" and "Flying Colors"; the latter song was compared to the humorous work of country singer John Anderson. Nevertheless, most country music critics agreed that the singer had finally found his own style. Allen assessed that *Don't Close Your Eyes* marked "the first time since his early 1980's albums with J.D. Crowe" that Whitley's "subtle and unmistakable powers as a singer come through on vinyl."

### Tragic Death Ended Nascent Career

Whitley had been an alcoholic from the beginning of his career, long before he had reached the legal drinking age. He had unsuccessfully tried treatment and therapy, and had even claimed to have conquered the disease, but this was not so. Whitley was not a social drinker, rather he consumed liquor when he was alone, making it difficult for those around him to detect his drinking. Indeed, though relatives saw Whitley and claim that he was sober as late as two hours before his death, he was found dead in his home near Nashville on May 9, 1989, with a large quantity—nearly five times Tennessee's legal limit for driving—of alcohol in his bloodstream; traces of Valium and cocaine were also found.

Whitley's influence on the country music genre did not, however, end with his death. When he died, he had just completed work on his fourth solo album, *I Wonder Do You Think of Me.* Ralph Novak of *People* asserted that "this final album . . . compounds the sadness [of Whitley's death] by demonstrating how he had matured as a singer." Allen concurred, calling *I Wonder Do You Think of Me* "a great album—easily the best Whitley made in his all too brief career and lifetime." Songs from the disc include the hit "It Ain't Nothin'," "I'm Over You," "Between an Old Memory and Me," and the ironic "Tennessee Courage," about turning to alcohol to solve personal problems. Whitley also made an impact on the genre by encouraging the singing career of his wife Lorrie

Morgan and bringing her to the attention of RCA. She has gone on to have her own hits since Whitley's death.

## Selected discography

**With J.D. Crowe and the New South**

*My Home Ain't In the Hall of Fame,* 1981.
*Somewhere Between,* 1982.

**Solo**

*A Hard Act to Follow,* RCA, 1984.
*L.A. to Miami* (includes "Miami, My Amy," "On the Other Hand," and "Nobody in His Right Mind"), RCA, 1986.
*Don't Close Your Eyes* (includes "Don't Close Your Eyes," "I'm No Stranger to the Rain," "Flying Colors," "It's All Coming Back to Me Now," "Honky-Tonk Heart," and "I Never Go Around Mirrors"), RCA, 1988.
*I Wonder Do You Think of Me* (includes "Brother Jukebox," "Tennessee Courage," "It Ain't Nothin'," "Between an Old Memory and Me," and "I'm Over You"), RCA, 1989.
*Kentucky Bluebird,* RCA, 1991.

Also recorded albums with the Clinch Mountain Boys and duet albums with Ricky Skaggs.

## Sources

*Country Music,* July/August 1988; September/October 1988; September/October 1989; November/December 1989; January/February 1990.
*People,* October 2, 1989; May 7, 1990.
*Stereo Review,* March 1989.

—*Elizabeth Wenning*

# "Weird Al" Yankovic

**Singer, rock parodist, accordionist**

"**W**eird Al" Yankovic's method is simple: Take the title of a popular song, change it slightly to make it sound ridiculous, write funny lyrics to go with the new title, and make an equally funny video to go with the resulting song. Yankovic has used these means for over a decade to establish himself as pop music's premier parodist.

Yankovic told Lynn Van Matre of the *Chicago Tribune* that the "warped outlook" that characterizes his work is the result of the accordion lessons he took as a child; it was the accordion that helped Yankovic take his first step toward stardom. In 1979 Yankovic was an architecture student who also worked at his college radio station. At the station one day, he took his accordion into the men's room and recorded "My Bologna," a parody of the flash-in-the-pan pop group the Knack's "My Sharona." He sent the song to Dr. Demento, host of a nationally syndicated radio show featuring offbeat, obscure, and humorous recordings. "My Bologna" was a hit with Dr. Demento's nutty audience, and Capitol Records offered Yankovic a contract to issue the song as a single. He followed it with a parody of Queen's "Another One Bites the Dust" entitled "Another One Rides the Bus," which became the most requested song in the first decade of Dr. Demento's show and led to a recording contract with Rock 'n' Roll Records.

Yankovic's first album, *Weird Al Yankovic,* was released in 1983 and featured a mix of his Dr. Demento hits and new parodies. One of the new songs was "Ricky," which put lyrics about Ricky and Lucy Ricardo, of the long-running 1950s television series *I Love Lucy,* to the tune of Toni Basil's hit pop tune "Mickey." The result was a single that made *Billboard's* Top 100 and a video that gave Yankovic his first exposure on cable network MTV. He was quoted by Gary Graff of the *Detroit Free Press* as saying, "Ricky Ricardo has always been one of my major role models. I always wanted to grow up to be a Puerto Rican band leader."

### Rode Michael Jackson's Coattails

But Yankovic has come to be associated more with superstar Michael Jackson than with Ricky Ricardo. Yankovic's biggest hit came in 1984 when "Eat It," his parody of Jackson's "Beat It," made the Top 20. The video of the song was also hugely popular, imitating the sets and dance routines of Jackson's video, but making food the subject matter. In 1988 Yankovic did another send-up of Jackson, entitling his album *Even Worse* in response to Jackson's album *Bad,* and parodying the title song from Jackson's album with the single and video "Fat." In the video Yankovic wore prosthetic makeup that took three hours to put on and transformed

B orn Alfred Matthew Yankovic, October 23, 1959. *Education:* California Polytechnic State University, B.S. in architecture, 1979.

Began writing and recording parodies of rock songs in high school; received first widespread attention on the syndicated *Dr. Demento Radio Show* with "My Bologna," 1979; produced hit single and video of "Eat It," 1984; hosted "Al TV" on MTV, 1988; co-wrote and starred in feature film *UHF,* Orion, 1989.

**Awards:** Grammy Award nomination for best comedy recording, for *Dare to Be Stupid,* 1986.

**Addresses:** *Home*—Los Angeles, CA. *Office*—c/o Scotti Bros., 2214 Pico Blvd., Santa Monica, CA 90405.

him into a grotesquely overweight facsimile of Jackson, complete with black leather, jheri curls, and buckles aplenty. Of course, in order to make these parodies, Yankovic had to obtain Jackson's permission to use the melodies of his hit songs. Yankovic told the *Chicago Tribune*'s Van Matre that Jackson "has a good sense of humor. He really seems to appreciate the things I do."

Evidently plenty of other songwriters and performers have had a sense of humor over the years as well. Yankovic has written parody lyrics and made videos of Madonna's "Like a Virgin" ("Like a Surgeon"), the Police's "King of Pain" ("King of Suede"), Cindy Lauper's "Girls Just Want to Have Fun" ("Girls Just Want to Have Lunch"), and Greg Kihn's "Jeopardy" ("I Lost on Jeopardy"), among others. The popularity of his videos afforded "Weird Al" the opportunity to branch out a bit, which led to a 1985 television special on the cable service Showtime entitled *Weird Al Yankovic: The Compleat Al.* In 1988 he hosted a semi-regular show on MTV called "Al TV," which featured his favorite music videos along with sales pitches for "Weird Al" paraphernalia.

### Lampooned American Popular Culture

Performing parodies has brought Yankovic success, but his considerable abilities go beyond writing new lyrics to other people's tunes. His albums have always included original compositions that feature satirical lyrics about some of the tackier aspects of American life. "Mr. Popeil," "I'm Stuck in the Closet with Vanna White," and "Velvet Elvis" have all poked fun at staples of American popular culture; the title track of his 1985

album, *Dare to Be Stupid,* reflected clueless Americans in general. Describing both his parodies and original songs, Yankovic told Van Matre, "Most of my songs are about food or television or other important aspects of the American pop culture." Once, when asked if he had considered giving up his spoofs to concentrate on performing original songs, Yankovic told the *Detroit Free Press*'s Graff, "I think there'd be a big public backlash if I did. The public is used to me doing parodies. When we do an original, they'll come up and say, 'That's great, Al, but what's it a parody of?'"

### Brought Trademark Weirdness to *UHF*

His reputation as a parodist enabled Yankovic to expand his range with the 1989 feature film *UHF,* a parody of television that he co-wrote and starred in. Yankovic played a man who inherits a television station with chronically low ratings and transforms it by replacing reruns of old sitcoms with game shows like *Wheel of Fish* and *Name That Stain.* Describing the movie to Patrick Goldstein of the *Los Angeles Times,* Yankovic called it "a cross between [the Frank Capra classic] *It's a Wonderful Life,* [Prince's movie] *Purple Rain,* and *The Texas Chainsaw Massacre.*"

In both his original compositions and his parodies, on video and in the movies, Yankovic has been constant in poking fun at familiar aspects of popular culture in America. Yankovic told Graff that his continued success with this brand of humor has run contrary to conventional wisdom: "Just doing the kind of material I do, people tag me as a one-hit wonder, a novelty artist." A decade of success, though, has demonstrated Yankovic's unique ability to consistently use to his greatest advantage the popular culture he so hilariously lampoons.

## Selected discography

### Singles

"My Bologna," Capitol, 1979.
"Another One Rides the Bus," Rock 'n' Roll/CBS, 1983.
"I Love Rocky Road," Rock 'n' Roll/CBS, 1983
"Ricky," Rock 'n' Roll/CBS, 1983.
"Eat It," Rock 'n' Roll/CBS, 1984.
"I Lost on Jeopardy," Rock 'n' Roll/CBS, 1984.
"King of Suede," Rock 'n' Roll/CBS, 1984
"Dare to Be Stupid," Rock 'n' Roll/CBS, 1985.
"Like a Surgeon," Rock 'n' Roll/CBS, 1985.
"Fat," Rock 'n' Roll/CBS, 1988.

**LPs; originally on Rock 'n' Roll/CBS, reissued on Scotti Bros.**

*Weird Al Yankovic*, 1983.
*Weird Al Yankovic in 3-D*, 1984.
*Dare to Be Stupid*, 1985.
*Even Worse*, 1988.

**Videos**

"Ricky," 1983.
"Eat It," 1984.
"I Lost on Jeopardy," 1984.
"Dare to Be Stupid," 1985.
"Like a Surgeon," 1985.
"Fat," 1988.

Also produced and edited record *Babalu Music* (clips from the *I Love Lucy* TV series), Sony, and accompanying video, CBS Video, 1991.

## Sources

### Books

*Contemporary Newsmakers 1985*, Gale, 1986.

### Periodicals

*Chicago Tribune*, May 8, 1988; July 21, 1989.
*Detroit Free Press*, April 16, 1984; August 7, 1985.
*Los Angeles Times*, April 17, 1988.
*People*, June 6, 1988.

—Lloyd Hemingway

# Faron Young

## Singer, guitarist

On any given Saturday night, the Grand Ole Opry may be hosted by the lean and silver-haired Faron Young, an Opry regular since 1952. Young's strong, virile voice and his ability to range from traditional country to middle-of-the-road pop numbers made him one of the biggest country stars of the 1950s and 1960s. For almost two decades he regularly placed songs on the country charts, and, having been boosted in his own career by other stars, he helped guarantee the success of some promising young performers.

Young continues to pursue an active schedule of touring and appearing on the Opry. Much of his show consists of the dozens of hits he produced between 1952 and 1971, including "Go Back You Fool" and "Live Fast, Love Hard, and Die Young." In *Country Music U.S.A.,* Bill C. Malone referred to Young as an artist "who flirted with the country-pop idiom, yet never really strayed very far from the mainstream." "Young seems never to have consciously sought pop acceptance," Malone continued, "and has always shown a fondness for twin fiddle accompaniment; nevertheless, his big voice, precise articulation, and pop phrasing made him a likely candidate for country-pop stardom."

Born in Shreveport, Louisiana, in 1932, Faron was still a baby when his father purchased a small farm outside of town; Young grew up there amidst a herd of dairy cows. He was still in grade school when he got his first guitar, and he more or less taught himself how to play it by experimenting with chords and melody. By high school he could sing all the latest country hits he heard on the radio, providing his own guitar accompaniment.

Young formed his first band while attending Fair Park High School in Shreveport. The group kept busy playing at school functions and at country fairs in the area, and before long young Faron had amassed some local popularity. Nevertheless, he decided to continue his education after high school, spending part of 1950 at Centenary College in Louisiana. The lure of the music business was strong, however, and he soon left college, signing a contract at KWKH radio in Shreveport.

KWKH was a well-known station with a strong signal and offered Saturday night competition for the Grand Ole Opry with its own show, *Louisiana Hayride.* Young joined the *Hayride* cast and quickly became a favorite. His budding career was helped immensely when he sparked the interest of Webb Pierce, then a major country star. Pierce invited Young to be a featured vocalist on his tours, and the young singer was soon traveling across the entire South, performing at fairs and in concert halls.

Capitol Records signed Young in 1951, and he produced two hit singles, "Tattle Tale Tears" and "Have I

Waited Too Long." Though still in his teens, he seemed to be an entertainer blessed with all the qualities stardom requires: he had a dark, handsome face, an easy way with an audience, and a fine baritone voice. The same year he turned 20 he was made a regular cast member of the Grand Ole Opry.

Even the Korean War could not slow the advance of Young's career. He was drafted in the fall of 1952, but as soon as he had completed basic training, he won an Army talent show on ABC-TV and was placed in an entertainment unit. Young served his tour of duty singing for troops stationed all over the world, and he also starred on the Army's radio recruiting show. While still in the service, he wrote and recorded "Goin' Steady," a song that made the Top Ten in 1953. An unusual number for Young, "Goin' Steady" was an up-tempo tune aimed at the teen market; it remains a staple of early rockabilly anthologies.

After his discharge from the Army, Young returned to the Opry and was given a royal welcome. Between 1954 and 1964—a time when the country music industry was striving valiantly to survive the onslaught of rock and roll—Young was a certified headliner, turning out hit after hit. His best-known works from the period include "Live Fast, Love Hard and Die Young," "It's a Great Life," "Sweet Dreams," "Country Girl," "The Yellow Bandana," and "You'll Drive Me Back (Into Her Arms Again)."

One of Young's Number One hits during the period was "Hello, Walls," a song written by Willie Nelson. Nelson was a newcomer on the Nashville scene when Young chose to record his song, and the single was instrumental in boosting both men's careers. Young also helped singer Roger Miller get his foot in the door in Nashville. Miller—who had a wealth of musical experience—was working as a bellhop at the Andrew Jackson Hotel in Nashville in the late 1950s. Young hired him as a percussionist and got not only a drummer, but a songwriter as well.

In the 1960s—a time when record producers took desperate measures to move country music toward middle-of-the-road acceptance—Young was willing to experiment with a country-pop sound and did some Frank Sinatra-like crooning. Still, the core of his fans remained the country stalwarts, and the singer was more than willing to drift back in the direction of pure country. Throughout the 1960s and 1970s he maintained a dizzying touring schedule and was always in demand at county fair shows.

Though Young's once jet-black hair has been silver for some time, he remains a country favorite. In addition to his work as a performer, he has widely diversified business interests, including part ownership of Nashville's trade paper, *Music City News.* Affectionately known as "The Sheriff"—after a part he once played in a low-budget movie—Young has been a Nashville staple for some 40 years and has said that retirement is simply out of the question.

## Selected discography

### On Capitol Records

*Sweethearts or Strangers.*
*This Is Faron Young.*
*Talk About Hits.*
*The Best of Faron Young.*
*Fan Club Favorites.*
*All Time Great Hits.*
*Hello, Walls.*
*Memory Lane.*

### On Mercury Records

*This Is Faron.*
*Faron Young Aims at the West.*
*Songs for Country Folks.*
*Dance Favorites.*
*Songs of Mountains and Valleys.*
*Faron Young's Greatest Hits.*
*Faron Young Sings the Best of Jim Reeves.*
*I'd Just Be Fool Enough.*
*Best of Faron Young, Volume 2.*

**Other**

(With others) *Hillbilly Music . . . Thank God! Volume 1,* Bug/Capitol, 1989.
*All Time Greatest Hits,* Curb/CEMA, 1990.
*Country Spotlight,* Dominion, 1991.

# Sources

**Books**

*The Illustrated Encyclopedia of Country Music,* Harmony, 1977.
Malone, Bill C., *Country Music U.S.A.,* revised edition, University of Texas Press, 1985.

Shestack, Melvin, *The Country Music Encyclopedia,* Crowell, 1974.
Stambler, Irwin, and Grelun Landon, *The Encyclopedia of Folk, Country, and Western Music,* St. Martin's, 1969.

**Periodicals**

*Country Music,* May/June 1985; September/October 1985; July/August 1986; March/April 1987; January/February 1989; July/August 1989; September/October 1990.
*Newsweek,* March 20, 1989.
*Rolling Stone,* April 20, 1989.

—*Anne Janette Johnson*

# Subject Index

Volume numbers appear in **bold.**

Boyd, Liona **7**
Bronfman, Yefim **6**
Canadian Brass **4**
Chang, Sarah **7**
Clayderman, Richard **1**
Copland, Aaron **2**
Davis, Chip **4**
Fiedler, Arthur **6**
Galway, James **3**
Gingold, Josef **6**
Harrell, Lynn **3**
Horowitz, Vladimir **1**
Jarrett, Keith **1**
Kissin, Evgeny **6**
Kronos Quartet **5**
Ma, Yo-Yo **2**
Marsalis, Wynton **6**
Midori **7**
Ott, David **2**
Parkening, Christopher **7**
Perlman, Itzhak **2**
Phillips, Harvey **3**
Rampal, Jean-Pierre **6**
Salerno-Sonnenberg, Nadja **3**
Schickele, Peter **5**
Segovia, Andres **6**
Stern, Isaac **7**
Takemitsu, Toru **6**
von Karajan, Herbert **1**
Wilson, Ransom **5**
Yamashita, Kazuhito **4**
Zukerman, Pinchas **4**

## Composers
Anka, Paul **2**
Atkins, Chet **5**
Bacharach, Burt **1**
Bernstein, Leonard **2**
Clarke, Stanley **3**
Coleman, Ornette **5**
Cooder, Ry **2**
Cooney, Rory **6**
Copland, Aaron **2**
Davis, Chip **4**
Davis, Miles **1**
de Grassi, Alex **6**
Ellington, Duke **2**
Enya **6**
Gillespie, Dizzy **6**
Glass, Philip **1**
Grusin, Dave **7**
Guaraldi, Vince **3**
Hamlisch, Marvin **1**
Handy, W. C. **7**
Hartke, Stephen **5**
Hunter, Alberta **7**
Jarre, Jean-Michel **2**
Jarrett, Keith **1**
Jones, Quincy **2**
Jordan, Stanley **1**
Kitaro **1**
Lloyd Webber, Andrew **6**
Mancini, Henry **1**
Masekela, Hugh **7**
Metheny, Pat **2**
Monk, Meredith **1**
Monk, Thelonious **6**
Morton, Jelly Roll **7**
Nascimento, Milton **6**
Newman, Randy **4**
Ott, David **2**
Parker, Charlie **5**
Reinhardt, Django **7**
Ritenour, Lee **7**
Rollins, Sonny **7**
Satriani, Joe **4**
Schickele, Peter **5**
Shorter, Wayne **5**
Solal, Martial **4**

Story, Liz **2**
Summers, Andy **3**
Sun Ra **5**
Takemitsu, Toru **6**
Talbot, John Michael **6**
Tyner, McCoy **7**
Washington, Grover Jr. **5**
Zimmerman, Udo **5**

## Conductors
Bacharach, Burt **1**
Bernstein, Leonard **2**
Copland, Aaron **2**
Domingo, Placido **1**
Fiedler, Arthur **6**
Jarrett, Keith **1**
Mancini, Henry **1**
Marriner, Neville **7**
Rampal, Jean-Pierre **6**
Schickele, Peter **5**
von Karajan, Herbert **1**
Zukerman, Pinchas **4**

## Contemporary Dance Music
Abdul, Paula **3**
B-52s **4**
The Bee Gees **3**
Brown, Bobby **4**
Brown, James **2**
Cherry, Neneh **4**
Clinton, George **7**
De La Soul **7**
Depeche Mode **5**
Eurythmics **6**
Expose **4**
Fox, Samantha **3**
Hammer, M.C. **5**
Harry, Deborah **4**
Ice-T **7**
Idol, Billy **3**
Jackson, Janet **3**
Jackson, Michael **1**
James, Rick **2**
Madonna **4**
Pet Shop Boys **5**
Prince **1**
Queen Latifah **6**
Salt-N-Pepa **6**
Simmons, Russell **7**
Technotronic **5**
The Village People **7**
Was (Not Was) **6**
Young M.C. **4**

## Cornet
Handy, W. C. **7**

## Country
Acuff, Roy **2**
Alabama **1**
Anderson, John **5**
Asleep at the Wheel **5**
Atkins, Chet **5**
Auldridge, Mike **4**
Black, Clint **5**
Buffett, Jimmy **4**
Campbell, Glen **2**
Carpenter, Mary-Chapin **6**
The Carter Family **3**
Cash, Johnny **1**
Cash, June Carter **6**
Cash, Rosanne **2**
Clark, Roy **1**
Cline, Patsy **5**
Coe, David Allan **4**
Cooder, Ry **2**
Cowboy Junkies **4**
Crowe, J. D. **5**
Daniels, Charlie **6**

Denver, John **1**
Desert Rose Band **4**
Dickens, Little Jimmy **7**
Dylan, Bob **3**
Flatt, Lester **3**
Ford, Tennessee Ernie **3**
Gayle, Crystal **1**
Gill, Vince **7**
Gilley, Mickey **7**
Griffith, Nanci **3**
Haggard, Merle **2**
Hall, Tom T. **4**
Harris, Emmylou **4**
Hartford, John **1**
Hay, George D. **3**
Healey, Jeff **4**
Highway 101 **4**
Jackson, Alan **7**
Jennings, Waylon **4**
Jones, George **4**
the Judds **2**
Kentucky Headhunters **5**
Kristofferson, Kris **4**
Lang, K. D. **4**
Lee, Brenda **5**
Little Feat **4**
Loveless, Patty **5**
Lovett, Lyle **5**
Lynn, Loretta **2**
Lynne, Shelby **5**
Mandrell, Barbara **4**
Mattea, Kathy **5**
Miller, Roger **4**
Milsap, Ronnie **2**
Monroe, Bill **1**
Murray, Anne **4**
Nelson, Willie **1**
The Nitty Gritty Dirt Band **6**
The Oak Ridge Boys **7**
O'Connor, Mark **1**
Oslin, K. T. **3**
Owens, Buck **2**
Parsons, Gram **7**
Parton, Dolly **2**
Pearl, Minnie **3**
Pride, Charley **4**
Rabbitt, Eddie **5**
Raitt, Bonnie **3**
Rich, Charlie **3**
Rodgers, Jimmie **3**
Rogers, Kenny **1**
Scruggs, Earl **3**
Skaggs, Ricky **5**
Stevens, Ray **7**
Strait, George **5**
Tillis, Mel **7**
Tritt, Travis **7**
Tubb, Ernest **4**
Tucker, Tanya **3**
Twitty, Conway **6**
Van Shelton, Ricky **5**
Watson, Doc **2**
Wells, Kitty **6**
Whitley, Keith **7**
Williams, Don **4**
Williams, Hank, Jr. **1**
Williams, Hank, Sr. **4**
Wills, Bob **6**
Wynette, Tammy **2**
Yoakam, Dwight **1**
Young, Faron **7**

## Dobro
Auldridge, Mike **4**
 Also see the Country Gentlemen
 Also see the Seldom Scene
Burch, Curtis
 See New Grass Revival
Knopfler, Mark **3**

## Drums
See **Percussion**

## Dulcimer
Ritchie, Jean **4**

## Fiddle
See **Violin**

## Film Scores
Anka, Paul **2**
Bacharach, Burt **1**
Bernstein, Leonard **2**
Cafferty, John
  See the Beaver Brown Band
Copland, Aaron **2**
Ellington, Duke **2**
Ferguson, Maynard **7**
Grusin, Dave **7**
Guaraldi, Vince **3**
Hamlisch, Marvin **1**
Harrison, George **2**
Hedges, Michael **3**
Jones, Quincy **2**
Knopfler, Mark **3**
Lennon, John
  See the Beatles
Mancini, Henry **1**
McCartney, Paul
  See the Beatles
Metheny, Pat **2**
Nascimento, Milton **6**
Richie, Lionel **2**
Robertson, Robbie **2**
Rollins, Sonny **7**
Sager, Carole Bayer **5**
Schickele, Peter **5**
Taj Mahal **6**
Waits, Tom **1**
Williams, Paul **5**
Young, Neil **2**

## Flute
Galway, James **3**
Rampal, Jean-Pierre **6**
Wilson, Ransom **5**

## Folk/Traditional
Baez, Joan **1**
Blades, Ruben **2**
Bragg, Billy **7**
The Carter Family **3**
Chapin, Harry **6**
Chapman, Tracy **4**
The Chieftains **7**
Childs, Toni **2**
Cohen, Leonard **3**
Collins, Judy **4**
Crosby, David **3**
de Lucia, Paco **1**
Dr. John **7**
Dylan, Bob **3**
Elliot, Cass **5**
Enya **6**
Estefan, Gloria **2**
Galway, James **3**
Griffith, Nanci **3**
Guthrie, Arlo **6**
Guthrie, Woodie **2**
Harding, John Wesley **6**
Hartford, John **1**
Iglesias, Julio **2**
Indigo Girls **3**
Kuti, Fela **7**
Ladysmith Black Mambazo **1**
Lavin, Christine **6**
Leadbelly **6**
Lightfoot, Gordon **3**
Los Lobos **2**

Masekela, Hugh **7**
McLean, Don **7**
Mitchell, Joni **2**
Morrison, Van **3**
Nascimento, Milton **6**
N'Dour, Youssou **6**
Near, Holly **1**
Ochs, Phil **7**
O'Connor, Sinead **3**
Odetta **7**
Parsons, Gram **7**
Paxton, Tom **5**
Peter, Paul & Mary **4**
The Pogues **6**
Prine, John **7**
Redpath, Jean **1**
Ritchie, Jean, **4**
Rodgers, Jimmie **3**
Santana, Carlos **1**
Seeger, Pete **4**
Simon, Paul **1**
Snow, Pheobe **4**
Sweet Honey in the Rock **1**
Taj Mahal **6**
Thompson, Richard **7**
Vega, Suzanne **3**
Watson, Doc **2**

## French Horn
Ohanian, David
  See Canadian Brass

## Funk
Brown, James **2**
Clinton, George **7**
Fishbone **7**
Jackson, Janet **3**
Parker, Maceo **7**
Prince **1**
The Red Hot Chili Peppers **7**

## Fusion
Anderson, Ray **7**
Beck, Jeff **4**
Clarke, Stanley **3**
Coleman, Ornette **5**
Corea, Chick **6**
Davis, Miles **1**
Fishbone **7**
Jarreau, Al **1**
Metheny, Pat **2**
O'Connor, Mark **1**
Reid, Vernon **2**
Ritenour, Lee **7**
Shorter, Wayne **5**
Summers, Andy **3**
Washington, Grover, Jr. **5**

## Gospel
Brown, James **2**
The Carter Family **3**
Charles, Ray **1**
Cleveland, James **1**
Cooke, Sam **1**
Ford, Tennessee Ernie **3**
Franklin, Aretha **2**
Houston, Cissy **6**
Knight, Gladys **1**
Little Richard **1**
The Oak Ridge Boys **7**
Presley, Elvis **1**
Redding, Otis **5**
Take 6 **6**
Watson, Doc **2**
Williams, Deniece **1**
Womack, Bobby **5**

## Guitar
Ackerman, Will **3**
Allman, Duane
  See the Allman Brothers
Atkins, Chet **5**
Baxter, Jeff
  See the Doobie Brothers
Beck, Jeff **4**
Belew, Adrian **5**
Berry, Chuck **1**
Betts, Dicky
  See the Allman Brothers
Boyd, Liona **7**
Buck, Peter
  See R.E.M.
Buckingham, Lindsey
  See Fleetwood Mac
Campbell, Glen **2**
Clapton, Eric **1**
Clark, Roy **1**
Collins, Albert **4**
Cooder, Ry **2**
Daniels, Charlie **6**
de Grassi, Alex **6**
de Lucia, Paco **1**
Dickens, Little Jimmy **7**
Diddley, Bo **3**
Earl, Ronnie **5**
    Also see Roomful of Blues
The Edge
  See U2
Flatt, Lester **3**
Frampton, Peter **3**
Frehley, Ace
  See Kiss
Garcia, Jerry **4**
George, Lowell
  See Little Feat
Gibbons, Billy
  See ZZ Top
Gilmour, David
  See Pink Floyd
Gill, Vince **7**
Green, Peter
  See Fleetwood Mac
Guy, Buddy **4**
Haley, Bill **6**
Harrison, George **2**
Healey, Jeff **4**
Hedges, Michael **3**
Hendrix, Jimi **2**
Hillman, Chris
  See Desert Rose Band
Holly, Buddy **1**
Hooker, John Lee **1**
Howlin' Wolf **6**
Jardine, Al
  See the Beach Boys
Johnson, Robert **6**
Jones, Brian
  See the Rolling Stones
Jordan, Stanley **1**
Kantner, Paul
  See Jefferson Airplane
King, Albert **2**
King, B. B. **1**
Knopfler, Mark **3**
Leadbelly **6**
Lindley, David **2**
Marr, Johnny
  See the Smiths
May, Brian
  See Queen
Metheny, Pat **2**
Montgomery, Wes **3**
Nugent, Ted **2**
Owens, Buck **2**
Page, Jimmy **4**
    Also see Led Zeppelin

Sager, Carole Bayer **5**

**New Age**
Ackerman, Will **3**
Davis, Chip **4**
de Grassi, Alex **6**
Enya **6**
Hedges, Michael **3**
Jarre, Jean-Michel **2**
Kitaro **1**
Kronos Quartet **5**
Story, Liz **2**
Summers, Andy **3**

**Opera**
Battle, Kathleen **6**
Cotrubas, Ileana **1**
Domingo, Placido **1**
Norman, Jessye **7**
Pavarotti, Luciano **1**
Price, Leontyne **6**
Sills, Beverly **5**
Te Kanawa, Kiri **2**
von Karajan, Herbert **1**
Zimmerman, Udo **5**

**Percussion**
Bonham, John
  See Led Zeppelin
Collins, Phil **2**
  Also see Genesis
DeJohnette, Jack **7**
Densmore, John
  See the Doors
Dunbar, Aynsley
  See Jefferson Starship
  See Whitesnake
Fleetwood, Mick
  See Fleetwood Mac
Hart, Mickey
  See the Grateful Dead
Henley, Don **3**
Jones, Kenny
  See The Who
Jones, Spike **5**
Kreutzman, Bill
  See the Grateful Dead
Mason, Nick
  See Pink Floyd
Moon, Keith
  See The Who
N'Dour, Youssou **6**
Palmer, Carl
  See Emerson, Lake & Palmer/Powell
Powell, Cozy
  See Emerson, Lake & Palmer/Powell
Sheila E. **3**
Starr, Ringo
  See the Beatles
Watts, Charlie
  See the Rolling Stones

**Piano**
Arrau, Claudio **1**
Bacharach, Burt **1**
Basie, Count **2**
Bronfman, Yefim **6**
Bush, Kate **4**
Charles, Ray **1**
Clayderman, Richard **1**
Cleveland, James **1**
Cole, Nat King **3**
Collins, Judy **4**
Collins, Phil **2**
  Also see Genesis
Connick, Harry, Jr. **4**
DeJohnette, Jack **7**
Domino, Fats **2**
Dr. John **7**

Ellington, Duke **2**
Feinstein, Michael **6**
Flack, Roberta **5**
Frey, Glenn **3**
Glass, Philip **1**
Grusin, Dave **7**
Guaraldi, Vince **3**
Hamlisch, Marvin **1**
Horn, Shirley **7**
Hornsby, Bruce **3**
Horowitz, Vladimir **1**
Jackson, Joe **4**
Jarrett, Keith **1**
Joel, Billy **2**
John, Elton **3**
Kissin, Evgeny **6**
Lewis, Jerry Lee **2**
Little Richard **1**
Manilow, Barry **2**
McDonald, Michael
  See the Doobie Brothers
McVie, Christine
  See Fleetwood Mac
Milsap, Ronnie **2**
Monk, Thelonious **6**
Morton, Jelly Roll **7**
Newman, Randy **4**
Professor Longhair **6**
Rich, Charlie **3**
Roberts, Marcus **6**
Russell, Mark **6**
Schickele, Peter **5**
Sedaka, Neil **4**
Solal, Martial **4**
Story, Liz **2**
Tyner, McCoy **7**
Waits, Tom **1**
Waller, Fats **7**
Winwood, Steve **2**
Wonder, Stevie **2**
Wright, Rick
  See Pink Floyd

**Piccolo**
Galway, James **3**

**Pop**
Abdul, Paula **3**
Adams, Bryan **2**
Aerosmith **3**
Armatrading, Joan **4**
Astley, Rick **5**
Atkins, Chet **5**
Avalon, Frankie **5**
B-52s **4**
Bacharach, Burt **1**
Bailey, Pearl **5**
Basia **5**
The Beach Boys **1**
The Beatles **2**
The Beaver Brown Band **3**
The Bee Gees **3**
Bennett, Tony **2**
Benton, Brook **7**
Blood, Sweat and Tears **7**
The BoDeans **3**
Bolton, Michael **4**
Bowie, David **1**
Bragg, Billy **7**
Branigan, Laura **2**
Brickell, Edie **3**
Brown, Bobby **4**
Browne, Jackson **3**
Buffett, Jimmy **4**
Campbell, Glen **2**
Carey, Mariah **6**
Carnes, Kim **4**
Chapin, Harry **6**
Chapman, Tracy **4**

Charles, Ray **1**
Checker, Chubby **7**
Cher **1**
Cherry, Neneh **4**
Chicago **3**
Clapton, Eric **1**
Clayderman, Richard **1**
The Coasters **5**
Cocker, Joe **4**
Cole, Natalie **1**
Cole, Nat King **3**
Collins, Judy **4**
Collins, Phil **2**
Connick, Harry, Jr. **4**
Cooke, Sam **1**
Costello, Elvis **2**
Crenshaw, Marshall **5**
Croce, Jim **3**
Crosby, David **3**
Daltrey, Roger **3**
  Also see The Who
D'Arby, Terence Trent **3**
Darin, Bobby **4**
Davies, Ray **5**
Davis, Sammy, Jr. **4**
Dayne, Taylor **4**
Denver, John **1**
Depeche Mode **5**
Diamond, Neil **1**
Dion **4**
The Doobie Brothers **3**
The Doors **4**
Duran Duran **4**
Dylan, Bob **3**
The Eagles **3**
Easton, Sheena **2**
Electric Light Orchestra **7**
Elliot, Cass **5**
Estefan, Gloria **2**
Eurythmics **6**
The Everly Brothers **2**
Exposé **4**
Fabian **5**
Ferguson, Maynard **7**
Ferry, Bryan **1**
Fiedler, Arthur **6**
Fitzgerald, Ella **1**
Flack, Roberta **5**
Fleetwood Mac **5**
Fogelberg, Dan **4**
Fox, Samantha **3**
Frampton, Peter **3**
Franklin, Aretha **2**
Frey, Glenn **3**
  Also see the Eagles
Garfunkel, Art **4**
Gaye, Marvin **4**
Gayle, Crystal **1**
Genesis **4**
Gibson, Debbie **1**
Gift, Roland **3**
Goodman, Benny **4**
Gordy, Berry, Jr. **6**
Grant, Amy **7**
Grebenshikov, Boris **3**
Guthrie, Arlo **6**
Hall & Oates **6**
Hammer, M.C. **5**
Harding, John Wesley **6**
Harrison, George **2**
  Also see the Beatles
Harry, Deborah **4**
Healey, Jeff **4**
Henley, Don **3**
  Also see the Eagles
Herman's Hermits **5**
Holland-Dozier-Holland **5**
Hornsby, Bruce **3**
Ian, Janis **5**

Dion **4**
Domino, Fats **2**
The Everly Brothers **2**
Haley, Bill **6**
Holly, Buddy **1**
James, Etta **6**
Lewis, Jerry Lee **2**
Little Richard **1**
Nelson, Rick **2**
Orbison, Roy **2**
Paul, Les **2**
Phillips, Sam **5**
Presley, Elvis **1**
Professor Longhair **6**
Sedaka, Neil **4**
Spector, Phil **4**
Twitty, Conway **6**
Wilson, Jackie **3**

**Saxophone**
Carter, Benny **3**
Clemons, Clarence **7**
Coleman, Ornette **5**
Coltrane, John **4**
Kirk, Rahsaan Roland **6**
Parker, Charlie **5**
Parker, Maceo **7**
Rollins, Sonny **7**
Sanborn, David **1**
Shorter, Wayne **5**
Washington, Grover, Jr. **5**

**Songwriters**
Acuff, Roy **2**
Adams, Bryan **2**
Anderson, John **5**
Anka, Paul **2**
Armatrading, Joan **4**
Atkins, Chet **5**
Bacharach, Burt **1**
Baez, Joan **1**
Balin, Marty
    See Jefferson Airplane
Barrett, (Roger) Syd
    See Pink Floyd
Basie, Count **2**
Becker, Walter
    See Steely Dan
Belew, Adrian **5**
Benton, Brook **7**
Berry, Chuck **1**
Black, Clint **5**
Blades, Ruben **2**
Bono
    See U2
Bragg, Billy **7**
Brickell, Edie **3**
Brown, Bobby **4**
Brown, James **2**
Browne, Jackson **3**
Buck, Peter **5**
    See R.E.M.
Buck, Robert
    See 10,000 Maniacs
Buckingham, Lindsey
    See Fleetwood Mac
Buffett, Jimmy **4**
Bush, Kate **4**
Calloway, Cab **6**
Carpenter, Mary-Chapin **6**
Cash, Johnny **1**
Cash, Rosanne **2**
Cetera, Peter
    See Chicago
Chapin, Harry **6**
Chapman, Tracy **4**
Charles, Ray **1**
Childs, Toni **2**
Clapton, Eric **1**

Cleveland, James **1**
Clinton, George **7**
Cohen, Leonard **3**
Cole, Nat King **3**
Collins, Albert **4**
Collins, Judy **4**
Collins, Phil **2**
Cooder, Ry **2**
Cooke, Sam **1**
Costello, Elvis **2**
Crenshaw, Marshall **5**
Croce, Jim **3**
Crofts, Dash
    See Seals & Crofts
Crosby, David **3**
Crowe, J. D. **5**
Daniels, Charlie **6**
Davies, Ray **5**
Denver, John **1**
Diamond, Neil **1**
Diddley, Bo **3**
Difford, Chris
    See Squeeze
Dion **4**
Domino, Fats **2**
Dozier, Lamont
    See Holland-Dozier-Holland
Dylan, Bob **3**
The Edge
    See U2
Ellington, Duke **2**
Emerson, Keith
    See Emerson, Lake & Palmer/Powell
Etheridge, Melissa **4**
Everly, Don
    See the Everly Brothers
Everly, Phil
    See the Everly Brothers
Fagen, Don
    See Steely Dan
Ferry, Bryan **1**
Flack, Roberta **5**
Flatt, Lester **3**
Fogelberg, Dan **4**
Fogerty, John **2**
Frampton, Peter **3**
Frey, Glenn **3**
    Also see the Eagles
Gabriel, Peter **2**
Garcia, Jerry **4**
Gaye, Marvin **4**
George, Lowell
    See Little Feat
Gibb, Barry
    See the Bee Gees
Gibb, Maurice
    See the Bee Gees
Gibb, Robin
    See the Bee Gees
Gibbons, Billy
    See ZZ Top
Gibson, Debbie **1**
Gift, Roland **3**
Gill, Vince **7**
Gilley, Mickey **7**
Gilmour, David
    See Pink Floyd
Goodman, Benny **4**
Gordy, Berry, Jr. **6**
Grant, Amy **7**
Griffith, Nanci **3**
Guthrie, Arlo **6**
Guthrie, Woodie **2**
Guy, Buddy **4**
Haggard, Merle **2**
Hall, Daryl
    See Hall & Oates
Hall, Tom T. **4**
Hamlisch, Marvin **1**

Hammer, M.C. **5**
Harding, John Wesley **6**
Harley, Bill **7**
Harris, Emmylou **4**
Harrison, George **2**
    Also see the Beatles
Harry, Deborah **4**
Hartford, John **1**
Healey, Jeff **4**
Hedges, Michael **3**
Hendrix, Jimi **2**
Henley, Don **3**
    Also see the Eagles
Hidalgo, David
    See Los Lobos
Hillman, Chris **4**
Holland, Brian
    See Holland-Dozier-Holland
Holland, Eddie
    See Holland-Dozier-Holland
Holly, Buddy **1**
Hornsby, Bruce **3**
Hutchence, Michael
    See INXS
Ian, Janis **5**
Ice-T **7**
Idol, Billy **3**
Isaak, Chris **6**
Jackson, Alan **7**
Jackson, Joe **4**
Jackson, Michael **1**
Jagger, Mick **7**
    Also see the Rolling Stones
James, Rick **2**
Jarreau, Al **1**
Jennings, Waylon **4**
Jett, Joan **3**
Joel, Billy **2**
Johansen, David **7**
John, Elton **3**
Jones, Brian
    See the Rolling Stones
Jones, George **4**
Jones, Mick
    See the Clash
Jones, Quincy **2**
Jones, Rickie Lee **4**
Joplin, Janis **3**
Judd, Naomi
    See the Judds
Kane, Big Daddy **7**
Kantner, Paul
    See Jefferson Airplane
King, Albert **2**
King, B. B. **1**
King, Ben E. **7**
King, Carole **6**
Knopfler, Mark **3**
Kravitz, Lenny **5**
Kristofferson, Kris **4**
Lake, Greg
    See Emerson, Lake & Palmer/Powell
Lang, K. D. **4**
Lavin, Christine **6**
Lehrer, Tom **7**
Lennon, John
    See the Beatles
Lennon, Julian **2**
Lightfoot, Gordon **3**
Little Richard **1**
Llanas, Sammy
    See the BoDeans
L.L. Cool J **5**
Loggins, Kenny **3**
Loveless, Patty **5**
Lovett, Lyle **5**
Lowe, Nick **6**
Lynn, Loretta **2**
Lynne, Jeff **5**

See Canadian Brass
Severinsen, Doc **1**

**Tuba**
Daellenbach, Charles
   See Canadian Brass
Phillips, Harvey **3**

**Vibraphone**
Hampton, Lionel **6**

**Viola**
Dutt, Hank
   See Kronos Quartet
Jones, Michael
   See Kronos Quartet
Killian, Tim

See Kronos Quartet
Zukerman, Pinchas **4**

**Violin**
Acuff, Roy **2**
Anderson, Laurie **1**
Bush, Sam
   See New Grass Revival
Chang, Sarah **7**
Coleman, Ornette **5**
Daniels, Charlie **6**
Gingold, Josef **6**
Gray, Ella
   See Kronos Quartet
Harrington, David
   See Kronos Quartet
Hartford, John **1**

Hidalgo, David
   See Los Lobos
Lewis, Roy
   See Kronos Quartet
Marriner, Neville **7**
Midori **7**
O'Connor, Mark **1**
Perlman, Itzhak **2**
Salerno-Sonnenberg, Nadja **3**
Shallenberger, James
   See Kronos Quartet
Sherba, John
   See Kronos Quartet
Skaggs, Ricky **5**
Stern, Isaac **7**
Wills, Bob **6**
Zukerman, Pinchas **4**

# Musicians Index

Volume numbers appear in **bold**.

The Doobie Brothers **3**
The Doors **4**
Douglas, Jerry
　See the Country Gentlemen
Dowd, Christopher
　See Fishbone
Dozier, Lamont
　See Holland-Dozier-Holland
Dr. Dre
　See N.W.A.
Dr. John **7**
Drew, Dennis
　See 10,000 Maniacs
Dryden, Spencer
　See Jefferson Airplane
Duffey, John
　See the Country Gentlemen
　See the Seldom Scene
Dunbar, Aynsley
　See Jefferson Starship
　See Whitesnake
Duncan, Steve
　See Desert Rose Band
Dunlap, Slim
　See the Replacements
Dunn, Holly **7**
Duran Duran **4**
Dutt, Hank
　See Kronos Quartet
Dylan, Bob **3**
E., Sheila
　See Sheila E.
The Eagles **3**
　Also see Frey, Glenn
　Also see Henley, Don
　Also see Walsh, Joe
Earl, Ronnie **5**
　Also see Roomful of Blues
Easton, Sheena **2**
Eazy-E
　See N.W.A.
Eckstine, Billy **1**
The Edge
　See U2
Edwards, Dennis
　See the Temptations
Edwards, Mike
　See Electric Light Orchestra
Eldridge, Ben
　See the Seldom Scene
Electric Light Orchestra **7**
Elias, Manny
　See Tears for Fears
Ellington, Duke **2**
Elliot, Cass **5**
Elliot, Joe
　See Def Leppard
ELO
　See Electric Light Orchestra
Ely, John
　See Asleep at the Wheel
Emerson, Bill
　See the Country Gentlemen
Emerson, Keith
　See Emerson, Lake & Palmer/Powell
Emerson, Lake & Palmer/Powell **5**
Enos, Bob
　See Roomful of Blues
Entwistle, John
　See The Who
Enya **6**
Estefan, Gloria **2**
Estrada, Roy
　See Little Feat
Etheridge, Melissa **4**
Eurythmics **6**
Evans, Dave
　See U2
Evans, Mark

　See AC/DC
The Everly Brothers **2**
Everly, Don
　See the Everly Brothers
Everly, Phil
　See the Everly Brothers
Everman, Jason
　See Soundgarden
Exposé **4**
Fabian **5**
The Fabulous Thunderbirds **1**
Fadden, Jimmie
　See the Nitty Gritty Dirt Band
Fagan, Don
　See Steely Dan
Faith No More **7**
Falconer, Earl
　See UB40
Fallon, David
　See the Chieftains
Farrell, Perry
　See Jane's Addiction
Farriss, Andrew
　See INXS
Farriss, Jon
　See INXS
Farriss, Tim
　See INXS
Fay, Martin
　See the Chieftains
Fearnley, James
　See the Pogues
Feinstein, Michael **6**
Fela
　See Kuti, Fela
Felder, Don
　See the Eagles
Ferguson, Keith
　See the Fabulous Thunderbirds
Ferguson, Maynard **7**
Ferry, Bryan **1**
Fiedler, Arthur **6**
Fielder, Jim
　See Blood, Sweat and Tears
Finer, Jem
　See the Pogues
Fishbone **7**
Fisher, Jerry
　See Blood, Sweat and Tears
Fisher, John "Norwood"
　See Fishbone
Fisher, Phillip "Fish"
　See Fishbone
Fisher, Roger
　See Heart
Fitzgerald, Ella **1**
Flack, Roberta **5**
Flansburgh, John
　See They Might Be Giants
Flatt, Lester **3**
Flavor Flav
　See Public Enemy
Flea
　See the Red Hot Chili Peppers
Fleck, Bela
　See New Grass Revival
Fleetwood Mac **5**
Fleetwood, Mick
　See Fleetwood Mac
Fletcher, Andy
　See Depeche Mode
Flynn, Pat
　See New Grass Revival
Fogelberg, Dan **4**
Fogerty, John **2**
Ford, Mark
　See the Black Crowes
Ford, Tennessee Ernie **3**
Fossen, Steve

　See Heart
Fountain, Pete **7**
Fox, Oz
　See Stryper
Fox, Samantha **3**
Frampton, Peter **3**
Francis, Mike
　See Asleep at the Wheel
Franklin, Aretha **2**
Franklin, Larry
　See Asleep at the Wheel
Franklin, Melvin
　See the Temptations
Frantz, Chris
　See Talking Heads
Frehley, Ace
　See Kiss
Freiberg, David
　See Jefferson Starship
Frey, Glenn **3**
　Also see the Eagles
Frusciante, John
　See the Red Hot Chili Peppers
Gabriel, Peter **2**
　Also see Genesis
Gahan, Dave
　See Depeche Mode
Gaines, Timothy
　See Stryper
Gale, Melvyn
　See Electric Light Orchestra
Gallup, Simon
　See The Cure
Galway, James **3**
Garcia, Jerry **4**
　Also see the Grateful Dead
Gardner, Carl
　See the Coasters
Garfunkel, Art **4**
Garland, Judy **6**
Gaskill, Jerry
　See King's X
Gaudreau, Jimmy
　See the Country Gentlemen
Gaye, Marvin **4**
Gayle, Crystal **1**
Genesis **4**
　Also see Collins, Phil
　Also see Gabriel, Peter
Gentry, Teddy
　See Alabama
George, Lowell
　See Little Feat
Gibb, Barry
　See the Bee Gees
Gibb, Maurice
　See the Bee Gees
Gibb, Robin
　See the Bee Gees
Gibbons, Billy
　See ZZ Top
Gibson, Debbie **1**
Gibson, Wilf
　See Electric Light Orchestra
Gift, Roland **3**
Gill, Vince **7**
Gillespie, Dizzy **6**
Gilley, Mickey **7**
Gilmour, David
　See Pink Floyd
Gingold, Josef **6**
Gioia
　See Exposé
Glass, Philip **1**
Glover, Corey
　See Living Colour
Godchaux, Donna
　See the Grateful Dead
Godchaux, Keith

See the Grateful Dead
Golden, William Lee
  See the Oak Ridge Boys
Goodman, Benny **4**
Gordy, Berry, Jr. **6**
Gore, Martin
  See Depeche Mode
Gorman, Steve
  See the Black Crowes
Gould, Billy
  See Faith No More
Gradney, Ken
  See Little Feat
Gramolini, Gary
  See the Beaver Brown Band
Grant, Amy **7**
Grant, Lloyd
  See Metallica
The Grateful Dead **5**
Gray, Ella
  See Kronos Quartet
Gray, Tom
  See the Country Gentlemen
  See the Seldom Scene
Gray, Walter
  See Kronos Quartet
Grebenshikov, Boris **3**
Green, Karl Anthony
  See Herman's Hermits
Green, Peter
  See Fleetwood Mac
Green, Susaye
  See the Supremes
Green, Willie
  See the Neville Brothers
Greenspoon, Jimmy
  See Three Dog Night
Griffin, Bob
  See the BoDeans
Griffith, Nanci **3**
Groucutt, Kelly
  See Electric Light Orchestra
Grusin, Dave **7**
Guaraldi, Vince **3**
Guns n' Roses **2**
Gunther, Cornell
  See the Coasters
Gustafson, Steve
  See 10,000 Maniacs
Guthrie, Arlo **6**
Guthrie, Woodie **2**
Guy, Billy
  See the Coasters
Guy, Buddy **4**
Hackett, Steve
  See Genesis
Haggard, Merle **2**
Haley, Bill **6**
Hall & Oates **6**
Hall, Daryl
  See Hall & Oates
Hall, Tom T. **4**
Hall, Tony
  See the Neville Brothers
Hamilton, Tom
  See Aerosmith
Hamlisch, Marvin **1**
Hammer, M.C. **5**
Hammett, Kirk
  See Metallica
Hammond, John **6**
Hampson, Sharon
  See Sharon, Lois & Bram
Hampton, Lionel **6**
Handy, W. C. **7**
Hanna, Jeff
  See the Nitty Gritty Dirt Band
Harding, John Wesley **6**
Harley, Bill **7**

Harrell, Lynn **3**
Harrington, David
  See Kronos Quartet
Harris, Damon Otis
  See the Temptations
Harris, Emmylou **4**
Harris, Evelyn
  See Sweet Honey in the Rock
Harrison, George **2**
  Also see The Beatles
Harrison, Jerry
  See Talking Heads
Harry, Deborah **4**
Hart, Mickey
  See the Grateful Dead
Hartford, John **1**
Hartke, Stephen **5**
Hartman, Bob
  See Petra
Hartman, John
  See the Doobie Brothers
Hassan, Norman
  See UB40
Hay, George D. **3**
Haynes, Warren
  See the Allman Brothers
Hayward, Richard
  See Little Feat
Headon, Topper
  See the Clash
Healey, Jeff **4**
Heart **1**
Hedges, Michael **3**
Helm, Levon
  See the Nitty Gritty Dirt Band
Hendrix, Jimi **2**
Henley, Don **3**
  Also see the Eagles
Herman's Hermits **5**
Herndon, Mark
  See Alabama
Hetfield, James
  See Metallica
Hewson, Paul
  See U2
Hidalgo, David
  See Los Lobos
Highway 101 **4**
Hill, Dusty
  See ZZ Top
Hillman, Chris
  See Desert Rose Band
Hirt, Al **5**
Hodo, David
  See the Village People
Hoffman, Guy
  See the BoDeans
Holiday, Billie **6**
Holland, Brian
  See Holland-Dozier-Holland
Holland-Dozier-Holland **5**
Holland, Eddie
  See Holland-Dozier-Holland
Holland, Julian "Jools"
  See Squeeze
Holly, Buddy **1**
Hooker, John Lee **1**
Hopwood, Keith
  See Herman's Hermits
Horn, Shirley **7**
Hornsby, Bruce **3**
Horowitz, Vladimir **1**
Hossack, Michael
  See the Doobie Brothers
Houston, Cissy **6**
Howlin' Wolf **6**
Hubbard, Preston
  See the Fabulous Thunderbirds
  See Roomful of Blues

Hughes, Glenn
  See the Village People
Hughes, Leon
  See the Coasters
Hunt, Darryl
  See the Pogues
Hunter, Alberta **7**
Hunter, Shepherd "Ben"
  See Soundgarden
Hutchence, Michael
  See INXS
Hutton, Danny
  See Three Dog Night
Hyman, Jerry
  See Blood, Sweat and Tears
Ian, Janis **5**
Ibbotson, Jimmy
  See the Nitty Gritty Dirt Band
Ice Cube
  See N.W.A.
Ice-T **7**
Idol, Billy **3**
Iglesias, Julio **2**
Indigo Girls **3**
INXS **2**
Irons, Jack
  See the Red Hot Chili Peppers
Isaak, Chris **6**
The Jackson 5
  See the Jacksons
Jackson, Alan **7**
Jackson, Freddie **3**
Jackson, Jackie
  See the Jacksons
Jackson, Janet **3**
Jackson, Jermaine
  See the Jacksons
Jackson, Joe **4**
Jackson, Karen
  See the Supremes
Jackson, Marlon
  See the Jacksons
Jackson, Michael **1**
  Also see the Jacksons
Jackson, Randy
  See the Jacksons
Jackson, Tito
  See the Jacksons
The Jacksons **7**
Jagger, Mick **7**
  Also see the Rolling Stones
Jam Master Jay
  See Run-D.M.C.
James, Cheryl
  See Salt-N-Pepa
James, Doug
  See Roomful of Blues
James, Etta **6**
James, Rick **2**
Jane's Addiction **6**
Jardine, Al
  See the Beach Boys
Jarre, Jean-Michel **2**
Jarreau, Al **1**
Jarrett, Keith **1**
Jay, Miles
  See the Village People
Jeanrenaud, Joan Dutcher
  See Kronos Quartet
Jefferson Airplane **5**
Jefferson Starship
  See Jefferson Airplane
Jennings, Waylon **4**
Jessie, Young
  See the Coasters
Jett, Joan **3**
Joel, Billy **2**
Johansen, David **7**
Johanson, Jai Johanny

See the Allman Brothers
John, Elton **3**
Johnson, Brian
See AC/DC
Johnson, Courtney
See New Grass Revival
Johnson, Daryl
See the Neville Brothers
Johnson, Robert **6**
Johnson, Shirley Childres
See Sweet Honey in the Rock
Johnston, Bruce
See the Beach Boys
Johnston, Tom
See the Doobie Brothers
Jones, Brian
See the Rolling Stones
Jones, Davy
See the Monkees
Jones, George **4**
Jones, John Paul
See Led Zeppelin
Jones, Kendall
See Fishbone
Jones, Kenny
See the Who
Jones, Michael
See Kronos Quartet
Jones, Mick
See the Clash
Jones, Quincy **2**
Jones, Rickie Lee **4**
Jones, Spike **5**
Jones, Steve
See the Sex Pistols
Jones, Will "Dub"
See the Coasters
Joplin, Janis **3**
Jordan, Stanley **1**
Jorgensor, John
See Desert Rose Band
Joyce, Mike
See the Smiths
Judds **2**
Jurado, Jeanette
See Exposé
Kahlil, Aisha
See Sweet Honey in the Rock
Kakoulli, Harry
See Squeeze
Kalligan, Dick
See Blood, Sweat and Tears
Kaminski, Mik
See Electric Light Orchestra
Kanawa, Kiri Te
See Te Kanawa, Kiri
Kane, Big Daddy **7**
Kanter, Paul
See Jefferson Airplane
Karajan, Herbert von
See von Karajan, Herbert
Kath, Terry
See Chicago
Katz, Steve
See Blood, Sweat and Tears
Kaukonen, Jorma
See Jefferson Airplane
Keane, Sean
See the Chieftains
Kendricks, Eddie
See the Temptations
Kentucky Headhunters **5**
Kibble, Mark
See Take 6
Kibby, Walter
See Fishbone
Kid 'n Play **5**
Kiedis, Anthony
See the Red Hot Chili Peppers

Killian, Tim
See Kronos Quartet
King, Albert **2**
King, B. B. **1**
King, Ben E. **7**
King, Carole **6**
King's X **7**
Kirk, Rahsaan Roland **6**
Kirwan, Danny
See Fleetwood Mac
Kiss **5**
Kissin, Evgeny **6**
Kitaro **1**
Knight, Gladys **1**
Knight, Jon
See New Kids on the Block
Knight, Jordan
See New Kids on the Block
Knopfler, Mark **3**
Knudsen, Keith
See the Doobie Brothers
Konto, Skip
See Three Dog Night
Kooper, Al
See Blood, Sweat and Tears
Kramer, Joey
See Aerosmith
Kravitz, Lenny **5**
Kreutzman, Bill
See the Grateful Dead
Krieger, Robert
See the Doors
Kristofferson, Kris **4**
Kronos Quartet **5**
Kulick, Bruce
See Kiss
Kunkel, Bruce
See the Nitty Gritty Dirt Band
Kuti, Fela **7**
Ladysmith Black Mambazo **1**
Lake, Greg
See Emerson, Lake & Palmer/Powell
Lamm, Robert
See Chicago
Lang, K. D. **4**
Lataille, Rich
See Roomful of Blues
Laurence, Lynda
See the Supremes
Lavin, Christine **6**
Lavis, Gilson
See Squeeze
Lawry, John
See Petra
Lawson, Doyle
See the Country Gentlemen
Leadbelly **6**
Leadon, Bernie
See the Eagles
See the Nitty Gritty Dirt Band
Leavell, Chuck
See the Allman Brothers
LeBon, Simon
See Duran Duran
Leckenby, Derek "Lek"
See Herman's Hermits
Ledbetter, Huddie
See Leadbelly
Led Zeppelin **1**
Also see Plant, Robert
Lee, Brenda **5**
Lee, Tommy
See Mötley Crüe
Leese, Howard
See Heart
Lehrer, Tom **7**
Lennon, John
See the Beatles
Lennon, Julian **2**

Lennox, Annie
See Eurythmics
Leonard, Glenn
See the Temptations
Lesh, Phil
See the Grateful Dead
Levene, Keith
See the Clash
Levy, Ron
See Roomful of Blues
Lewis, Jerry Lee **2**
Lewis, Otis
See the Fabulous Thunderbirds
Lewis, Roy
See Kronos Quartet
Lightfoot, Gordon **3**
Lilienstein, Lois
See Sharon, Lois & Bram
Lindley, David **2**
Linnell, John
See They Might Be Giants
Lipsius, Fred
See Blood, Sweat and Tears
Little Feat **4**
Little, Keith
See the Country Gentlemen
Little Richard **1**
Living Colour **7**
Llanas, Sammy
See the BoDeans
L.L. Cool J. **5**
Lloyd Webber, Andrew **6**
Loggins, Kenny **3**
Los Lobos **2**
Loughnane, Lee
See Chicago
Love, Mike
See the Beach Boys
Loveless, Patty **5**
Lovett, Lyle **5**
Lowe, Chris
See Pet Shop Boys
Lowe, Nick **6**
Lozano, Conrad
See Los Lobos
Lucia, Paco de
See de Lucia, Paco
Lupo, Pat
See the Beaver Brown Band
Lynn, Loretta **2**
Lynne, Jeff **5**
Also see Electric Light Orchestra
Lynne, Shelby **5**
Ma, Yo-Yo **2**
MacGowan, Shane
See the Pogues
Madonna **4**
Malone, Tom
See Blood, Sweat and Tears
Mancini, Henry **1**
Mandrell, Barbara **4**
Maness, J. D.
See Desert Rose Band
Manilow, Barry **2**
Manzarek, Ray
See the Doors
Marini, Lou, Jr.
See Blood, Sweat and Tears
Marley, Bob **3**
Marley, Ziggy **3**
Marr, Johnny
See the Smiths
Marriner, Neville
Mars, Chris
See the Replacements
Mars, Mick
See Mötley Crüe
Marsalis, Wynton **6**
Martin, Barbara

Patti, Sandi **7**
Patton, Mike
  See Faith No More
Paul, Les **2**
Pavarotti, Luciano **1**
Paxton, Tom **5**
Payne, Bill
  See Little Feat
Payne, Scherrie
  See the Supremes
Pearl, Minnie **3**
Pedersen, Herb
  See Desert Rose Band
Peduzzi, Larry
  See Roomful of Blues
Pendergrass, Teddy **3**
Pengilly, Kirk
  See INXS
Penn, Michael **4**
Perez, Louie
  See Los Lobos
Perkins, Steve
  See Jane's Addiction
Perlman, Itzhak **2**
Perry, Joe
  See Aerosmith
Pet Shop Boys **5**
Peter, Paul & Mary **4**
Peters, Bernadette **7**
Petra **3**
Phelps, Doug
  See Kentucky Headhunters
Phelps, Ricky Lee
  See Kentucky Headhunters
Philips, Anthony
  See Genesis
Phillips, Chynna
  See Wilson Phillips
Phillips, Harvey **3**
Phillips, Sam **5**
Phungula, Inos
  See Ladysmith Black Mambazo
Piccolo, Greg
  See Roomful of Blues
Pierson, Kate
  See B-52s
Pilatus, Rob
  See Milli Vanilli
Pink Floyd **2**
Pinnick, Doug
  See King's X
Plant, Robert **2**
  Also see Led Zeppelin
The Pogues **6**
Poindexter, Buster
  See Johansen, David
Pop, Iggy **1**
Porter, Tiran
  See the Doobie Brothers
Posdnuos
  See De La Soul
Potts, Sean
  See the Chieftains
Powell, Cozy
  See Emerson, Lake & Palmer/Powell
Presley, Elvis **1**
Price, Leontyne **6**
Price, Louis
  See the Temptations
Price, Rick
  See Electric Light Orchestra
Pride, Charley **4**
The Primettes
  See the Supremes
Prine, John **7**
Prince **1**
Professor Longhair **6**
Public Enemy **4**
Queen **6**

Queen Latifah **6**
Querfurth, Carl
  See Roomful of Blues
Rabbitt, Eddie **5**
Raitt, Bonnie **3**
Rampal, Jean-Pierre **6**
Ranken, Andrew
  See the Pogues
Ray, Amy
  See Indigo Girls
Reagon, Bernice Johnson
  See Sweet Honey in the Rock
The Red Hot Chili Peppers **7**
Redding, Otis **5**
Redpath, Jean **1**
Reed, Lou **1**
  Also see the Velvet Underground
Reeves, Martha **4**
Reid, Christopher
  See Kid 'n Play
Reid, Vernon **2**
  Also see Living Colour
Reinhardt, Django **7**
R.E.M. **5**
Ren, M.C.
  See N.W.A.
The Replacements **7**
Rhodes, Nick
  See Duran Duran
Rich, Charlie **3**
Richards, Keith
  See the Rolling Stones
Richie, Lionel **2**
Ritchie, Jean **4**
Ritenour, Lee **7**
Roberts, Marcus **6**
Robertson, Robbie **2**
Robillard, Duke **2**
  Also see Roomful of Blues
Robinson, Chris
  See the Black Crowes
Robinson, Rich
  See the Black Crowes
Robinson, Smokey **1**
Rodgers, Jimmie **3**
Rogers, Kenny **1**
The Rolling Stones **3**
Rollins, Sonny **7**
Romm, Ronald
  See Canadian Brass
Ronstadt, Linda **2**
Roomful of Blues **7**
Roper, De De
  See Salt-N-Pepa
Rosas, Cesar
  See Los Lobos
Rose, Axl
  See Guns n' Roses
Rosenthal, Phil
  See the Seldom Scene
Ross, Diana **1**
Rossi, John
  See Roomful of Blues
Roth, David Lee **1**
Rotten, Johnny
  See the Sex Pistols
Rourke, Andy
  See the Smiths
Rudd, Phillip
  See AC/DC
Ruffin, David **6**
  Also see the Temptations
Run-D.M.C. **4**
Russell, Mark **6**
Rutherford, Mike
  See Genesis
Ryland, Jack
  See Three Dog Night
Sade **2**

Sager, Carole Bayer
St. John, Mark
  See Kiss
Salerno-Sonnenberg, Nadja **3**
Saliers, Emily
  See Indigo Girls
Salt-N-Pepa **6**
Sanborn, David **1**
Sanders, Steve
  See the Oak Ridge Boys
Sanger, David
  See Asleep at the Wheel
Santana, Carlos **1**
Satriani, Joe **4**
Savage, Rick
  See Def Leppard
Schermie, Joe
  See Three Dog Night
Schickele, Peter **5**
Schlitt, John
  See Petra
Schmit, Timothy B.
  See the Eagles
Schneider, Fred III
  See B-52s
Schuur, Diane **6**
Scofield, John **7**
Scott, Bon (Ronald Belford)
  See AC/DC
Scruggs, Earl **3**
Seals & Crofts **3**
Seals, Jim
  See Seals & Crofts
Sears, Pete
  See Jefferson Starship
Sedaka, Neil **4**
Seeger, Pete **4**
Segovia, Andres **6**
The Seldom Scene **4**
Seraphine, Daniel
  See Chicago
Severinsen, Doc **1**
The Sex Pistols **5**
Shabalala, Ben
  See Ladysmith Black Mambazo
Shabalala, Headman
  See Ladysmith Black Mambazo
Shabalala, Jockey
  See Ladysmith Black Mambazo
Shabalala, Joseph
  See Ladysmith Black Mambazo
Shallenberger, James
  See Kronos Quartet
Sharon, Lois & Bram **6**
Sheila E. **3**
Sherba, John
  See Kronos Quartet
Sherman, Jack
  See the Red Hot Chili Peppers
Shocked, Michelle **4**
Shogren, Dave
  See the Doobie Brothers
Shorter, Wayne **5**
Siberry, Jane **6**
Sills, Beverly **5**
Silva, Kenny Jo
  See the Beaver Brown Band
Simmons, Gene
  See Kiss
Simmons, Joe "Run"
  See Run-D.M.C.
Simmons, Patrick
  See the Doobie Brothers
Simmons, Russell **7**
Simon, Carly **4**
Simon, Paul **1**
Simonon, Paul
  See the Clash
Simpson, Ray